Microsoft Power BI Data Analyst Certification Guide

A comprehensive guide to becoming a confident and certified Power BI professional

Orrin Edenfield

Edward Corcoran

BIRMINGHAM—MUMBAI

Microsoft Power BI Data Analyst Certification Guide

Copyright © 2022 Packt Publishing

All rights reserved. No part of this book may be reproduced, stored in a retrieval system, or transmitted in any form or by any means, without the prior written permission of the publisher, except in the case of brief quotations embedded in critical articles or reviews.

Every effort has been made in the preparation of this book to ensure the accuracy of the information presented. However, the information contained in this book is sold without warranty, either express or implied. Neither the authors, nor Packt Publishing or its dealers and distributors, will be held liable for any damages caused or alleged to have been caused directly or indirectly by this book.

Packt Publishing has endeavored to provide trademark information about all of the companies and products mentioned in this book by the appropriate use of capitals. However, Packt Publishing cannot guarantee the accuracy of this information.

Publishing Product Manager: Heramb Bhavsar
Senior Editor: David Sugarman
Content Development Editor: Joseph Sunil
Technical Editor: Devanshi Ayare
Copy Editor: Safis Editing
Project Coordinator: Aparna Ravikumar Nair
Proofreader: Safis Editing
Indexer: Pratik Shirodkar
Production Designer: Sinhayna Bais
Marketing Coordinator: Priyanka Mhatre

First published: June 2022

Production reference: 4120822

Published by Packt Publishing Ltd.
Livery Place
35 Livery Street
Birmingham
B3 2PB, UK.

ISBN 978-1-80323-856-2

www.packt.com

Contributors

About the authors

Orrin Edenfield has 20 years of experience in designing and implementing data and analytics solutions. Orrin contributes to Microsoft certification exams as well as architecture best practices and blueprints, helping to solve BI problems using Power BI and more. As a cloud solution architect, Orrin helps customers solve technical obstacles and helps develop Azure platforms.

Edward Corcoran has spent 20 years working in data warehousing and business intelligence. As a cloud solution architect, Ed helps customers use Microsoft data and analytics services to solve technical obstacles and helps develop customer implementation projects to ensure easy adoption. Ed also collaborates with product engineering to aid with the development of Microsoft products and Azure platforms.

About the reviewers

Udit Kumar Chatterjee is an experienced data analytics and data science professional with a demonstrated history of working in statistical data analysis, insights mining, and business analytics. He has worked across various sectors, including manufacturing, market research, retail, and accounting, and with reputed and big-4 firms. He is an MCT (Microsoft Certified Trainer) and a 13-times Microsoft Certified Professional, including holding the PL-300 certification and the MCSE (Microsoft Certified Solutions Expert) certification. He likes to empower and educate people in the field of data by actively contributing to various community platforms and LinkedIn.

I wish to thank my beloved parents for inspiring and encouraging me to achieve more on both the personal and professional fronts.

Joseph Gnanaprakasam is a data architect, husband, and father living in Virginia. He has over a decade of experience in building data engineering and business intelligence solutions. Recently, he has started sharing his musings on data at joegnan.com. He is an avid photographer and enjoys traveling.

Table of Contents

Preface

Part 1 – Preparing the Data

1
Overview of Power BI and the PL-300 Exam

A brief overview of Power BI	4	PL-300 Analyzing Data with Microsoft Power BI	8
Power BI for business intelligence	4		
Power BI as a solution	6	Microsoft tests	8
Why get certified?	7	Timelines	10
		Strategies to get a passing grade	10
		Summary	11
		Questions	11

2
Connecting to Data Sources

Technical requirements	14	Power BI dataflows	20
Identifying data sources	14	Query performance tuning	22
Local data sources, files, and databases	15	Reducing the data size	22
Cloud and SaaS data sources	15	DirectQuery optimization	23
Connecting to data sources	16	Composite model optimization	24
On-premises data gateway	16	Advanced options (what-if parameters, Power Query parameters, PBIDS files, and XMLA endpoints)	26
Exploring query types	18		
Power BI datasets	20		

What-if parameters	26	XMLA endpoints	31
Power Query parameters	28	**Summary**	**32**
PBIDS files	29	**Questions**	**33**

3
Profiling the Data

Technical requirements	**36**	Column distribution	41
Identifying data anomalies	**36**	Column profile	42
Interrogating column properties	38	**Summary**	**45**
Examining data structures	39	**Questions**	**46**
Interrogating data statistics	**41**		

4
Cleansing, Transforming, and Shaping Data

Technical requirements	**48**	Combine files	58
Accessing Power Query in Power BI	**48**	**Enriching data with AI**	**59**
		Language detection	60
Sorting and filtering	**49**	Key phrase extraction	60
Managing columns	**51**	Sentiment analysis	60
Using column transformations	**51**	Image tagging	61
Transforming any data type columns	52	Azure ML	63
Transforming text columns	53	**Using advanced operations of Power Query**	**63**
Transforming number columns	53		
Transforming date and time columns	54	Using the Advanced Editor	63
Adding columns	54	Using the Query Dependencies tool	65
Using row transformations	**55**	R and Python scripts	65
Combining data	**56**	**Summary**	**66**
Using merge queries	56	**Questions**	**67**
Append queries	58		

Part 2 – Modeling the Data

5
Designing a Data Model

Technical requirements	72	**Define quick measures**	84
Define the tables	72	**Resolve many-to-many relationships**	86
Flatten out a parent-child hierarchy	72	**Create a common date table**	87
Star schema	73	Power BI date hierarchy tables	88
Defining relationships	76	Using your own date table	89
Cardinality	78	Date math	90
Cross-filter direction	79	Model size	90
Relationship test tips	79	Role-playing with our date table	91
Define role-playing dimensions	80	**Define the appropriate level of data granularity**	91
Date table as a role-playing dimension	80		
Configure table and column properties	81	**Design the data model to meet performance requirements**	92
The General section	81	**Summary**	93
The Formatting section	82	**Questions**	94
The Advanced section	84		

6
Using Data Model Advanced Features

Technical requirements	95	**Applying natural-language Q&A capability**	99
Using sensitivity labels	96	Using Q&A in reports and dashboards	100
Implementing row-level security	97	Q&A linguistic models	103
Setting up row-level security	97	Optimizing Q&A in data models	106
Managing row-level security	99	**Summary**	107
		Questions	107

7
Creating Measures Using DAX

Technical requirements	110	The X functions	121
Building complex measures with DAX	110	When to use calculated columns	122
		When to use measures	122
Quick measures	111	**Using basic statistical functions to enhance data**	123
Creating your own measure	112		
Measures versus calculated columns	112	Changing the default summarization	124
Default summarization	113	Binning and grouping histograms	125
Context is everything!	113		
Using CALCULATE to manipulate filters	114	**Implementing top N analysis**	128
		Ranking function	128
Simple filtering	115	Top N functions	129
The FILTER function	115	**Creating semi-additive measures**	133
The ALL function	116		
Implementing time intelligence using DAX	118	Additive measures	133
		Non-additive measures	134
Date tables	118	Semi-additive measures	134
Role-playing dimensions	119	**Summary**	134
Replacing numeric calculated columns with measures	120	**Questions**	135

8
Optimizing Model Performance

Technical requirements	138	**Optimizing measures, relationships, and visuals**	141
Optimizing data in the model	138		
Removing unnecessary rows and columns	138	Optimizing relationships	146
Splitting numeric and text column data	140	Optimizing visuals	146

Optimizing with aggregations	148	Understanding query diagnostics	151
Query diagnostics	149	Summary	152
Session diagnostics	150	Questions	152
Step diagnostics	151		

Part 3 – Visualizing the Data

9

Creating Reports

Technical requirements	158	Importing a custom visual	185
Understanding the capabilities of Power BI	159	Configuring conditional formatting	187
Adding visualization items to reports	161	Configuring small multiples	190
		Applying slicing and filtering	190
Choosing an appropriate visualization type	164	Adding an R or Python visual	193
		Adding a smart narrative visual	193
Table and matrix visualizations	165	Configuring the report page	196
Bar and column charts	168	Designing and configuring for accessibility	198
Line and area charts	170		
Pie chart, donut chart, and treemaps	171	Report accessibility checklist	200
Combination charts	174		
Card visualization	175	Configuring automatic page refresh	200
Funnel visualization	176		
Gauge chart	177	Creating a paginated report	202
Waterfall chart	178	Using Power BI datasets in Excel PivotTables	204
Scatter chart	178		
Map visuals	179		
Q&A visualization	180	Summary	206
		Questions	206
Formatting and configuring visualizations	181		
Formatting options for a visualization	182		

10
Creating Dashboards

Technical requirements	208	Optimizing dashboards	217
Introducing Power BI dashboards	208	Configuring views of a dashboard	217
Creating a dashboard	210	Optimizing the performance of a dashboard	219
Setting a dashboard theme	212	Summary	221
Using a dashboard	213	Questions	221
Pinning tiles	214		

11
Enhancing Reports

Technical requirements	224	Using drillthrough and cross-filter	242
Using bookmarks	224	Drilling down into data using interactive visuals	243
Using the selection pane	226	Exporting report data	243
Creating custom tooltips	227		
Interactions between visuals	232	Designing reports for mobile devices	245
Configuring navigation for a report	235	Summary	248
Applying sorting	237	Questions	249
Sync slicers	241		

Part 4 – Analyzing the Data

12
Exposing Insights from Data

Technical requirements	254	Summary	265
Exploring slicers and filters	254	Questions	265
The Analytics pane	261		

13
Performing Advanced Analysis

Technical requirements	268	Binning	276
Identifying outliers	268	Key influencers	278
Using anomaly detection	270	Decomposition tree visual	279
Conducting time series analysis	271	Applying AI insights	280
Grouping and binning	273	Summary	281
Grouping	273	Questions	282

Part 5 – Deploying and Maintaining Deliverables

14
Managing Workspaces

Technical requirements	286	Creating a deployment pipeline	297
Using workspaces	286	Unassigning a workspace to a deployment pipeline stage	300
Using workspace roles	286	Automating deployment pipelines	300
Workspace licensing	288		
Distributing reports and dashboards	289	Monitoring workspace usage	301
Creating a Power BI app	289	Using usage reports	301
Using deployment pipelines	296	Summary	302
		Questions	303

15
Managing Datasets

Technical requirements	306	Configuring row-level security group membership	310
Configuring a dataset scheduled refresh	306	Providing access to datasets	312
Identifying when a gateway is required	309	Summary	315
		Questions	316

Part 6 – Practice Exams

16
Practice Exams

Practice test 1	319	Practice Test 1	344
Practice Test 2	331	Practice Test 2	346
Answer keys	344		

Appendix: Practice Question Answers

Chapter 1, Overview of Power BI and the PL-300 Exam	352	Chapter 8, Optimizing Model Performance	357
Chapter 2, Connecting to Data Sources	352	Chapter 9, Creating Reports	358
Chapter 3, Profiling the Data	353	Chapter 10, Creating Dashboards	359
Chapter 4, Cleansing, Transforming, and Shaping Data	354	Chapter 11, Enhancing Reports	359
Chapter 5, Designing a Data Model	354	Chapter 12, Exposing Insights from Data	360
Chapter 6, Using Data Model Advanced Features	355	Chapter 13, Performing Advanced Analytics	361
Chapter 7, Creating Measures Using DAX	356	Chapter 14, Managing Workspaces	362
		Chapter 15, Managing Datasets	363

Index

Other Books You May Enjoy

Preface

Microsoft Power BI enables organizations to create a data-driven culture with business intelligence for all. This guide to achieving the Microsoft Power BI Data Analyst Associate certification will also help you to take control of your organization's data.

From getting started with Power BI to connecting to data sources, including files, databases, cloud services, and SaaS providers, to using Power BI's built-in tools to build data models and produce visualizations, this book will walk you through everything from setting up to preparing for the certification exam. Throughout the chapters, you'll get detailed explanations and learn how to analyze your data, prepare it for consumption by business users, and maintain an enterprise environment in a secure and efficient way.

By the end of this book, you'll be able to create and maintain robust reports and dashboards, enabling you to manage a data-driven enterprise, and be ready to take the PL-300 exam with confidence.

Who this book is for

This book is designed for data analysts and business intelligence professionals who want to become more competent in Microsoft Power BI. The content presented in this book is intended to help you pass the PL-300 exam, but there are plenty of other practical applications beyond exam preparation in the chapters too.

What this book covers

Chapter 1, *Overview of Power BI and the PL-300 Exam*, provides you with an overview of the Pl-300 exam and the value of the certification as well as Power BI.

Chapter 2, *Connecting to Data Sources*, prepares you for connecting to various data sources that can provide the raw data needed for use in downstream processes.

Chapter 3, *Profiling the Data*, helps you to understand the shape of data (columns, data types, and rows) as well as overall statistics (counts, mean, max, and min values) where appropriate. This will, in turn, allow you to understand what kind of cleansing and reshaping will be needed for this data to be valuable to the end analytics consumer.

Chapter 4, *Cleaning, Transforming, and Shaping Data*, showcases the capabilities of Power BI in being able to clean and transform data so that it can be trusted and is reliable to meet the required needs of the organization.

Chapter 5, *Designing a Data Model*, shows you how you can design data models depending on various use cases, and the various tools needed for the exam.

Chapter 6, *Using Data Model Advanced Features*, showcases the various advanced features that you can use for data models, including security and hierarchies.

Chapter 7, *Creating Measures Using DAX*, explores DAX and showcases how to use measures and columns using it.

Chapter 8, *Optimizing Model Performance*, covers the most important data model optimization methods. It is important for every Power BI solution to be optimized at every architectural layer and starting with an optimized data model is key to ensuring performance and maintainability.

Chapter 9, *Creating Reports*, starts with basic report creation and ends with advanced report capabilities, such as integration with other enterprise services.

Chapter 10, *Creating Dashboards*, walks you from creating your first dashboard to designing multiple dashboards with KPIs and tiles from paginated reports and optimizing dashboards for performance.

Chapter 11, *Enhancing Reports*, explores the capabilities that allow for tailoring reports to custom graphics, inclusive design, drillthrough reports allowing users to further explore data to gain insights, and also programmatic features that allow reports to behave similarly to applications.

Chapter 12, *Exposing Insights from Data*, covers tools and techniques in Power BI that enable users to expose insights from data. Tools such as slicers, top N analysis, statistical summaries, and quick insight tools allow users to take data from visuals in a report, complete some analysis, and draw conclusions from the reports. This is the essence of unlocking information from data.

Chapter 13, *Performing Advanced Analysis*, covers advanced analytics that are often used by data analysts or scientists that need to unlock a deeper understanding of data and the business processes behind data. This includes time series analysis, binning data, and detecting outliers. This chapter will introduce these concepts and show how users can use Power BI for these kinds of analyses.

Chapter 14, *Managing Workspaces*, explains what a workspace is, how to secure it, and how to use deployment pipelines so you can have separate development, test, and production environments. We will also cover monitoring your workspace to see who is doing what and when.

Chapter 15, *Managing Datasets*, starts by looking at refreshing datasets from both cloud-based and on-premises sources. Then, we'll move on to sharing our datasets and helping others to identify what's in them. We'll then talk about lineage, which allows you to see who is using your dataset and allows you to see what data your dataset depends on. Finally, we have a section on security. Topics covered will include Microsoft Information Protection, encryption, watermarking, and cloud app security.

Chapter 16, *Practice Exams*, covers the exam format and has various key questions, along with their answer keys, so that you can prepare yourself.

To get the most out of this book

Software/hardware covered in the book	Operating system requirements
Power BI	Windows/macOS/Linux

If you are using the digital version of this book, we advise you to type the code yourself or access the code from the book's GitHub repository (a link is available in the next section). Doing so will help you avoid any potential errors related to the copying and pasting of code.

Download the example code files

You can download the example code files for this book from GitHub at https://github.com/PacktPublishing/Microsoft-Power-BI-Data-Analyst-Certification-Guide. If there's an update to the code, it will be updated in the GitHub repository.

We also have other code bundles from our rich catalog of books and videos available at https://github.com/PacktPublishing/. Check them out!

Download the color images

We also provide a PDF file that has color images of the screenshots and diagrams used in this book. You can download it here: https://static.packt-cdn.com/downloads/9781803238562_ColorImages.pdf.

Conventions used

There are a number of text conventions used throughout this book.

`Code in text`: Indicates code words in text, database table names, folder names, filenames, file extensions, pathnames, dummy URLs, user input, and Twitter handles. Here is an example: "To help us, we're going to use the slicer visual and add the `ca_state` column to the slicer visual."

A block of code is set as follows:

```
% Product Gross Revenue =
DIVIDE(
    SUM(Sales[Gross Revenue]),
    SUM(Sales[Gross Revenue])
    )
```

Bold: Indicates a new term, an important word, or words that you see onscreen. For instance, words in menus or dialog boxes appear in **bold**. Here is an example: "Now we can easily see that **Missouri** has higher net store sales than **Iowa**."

> Tips or Important Notes
> Appear like this.

Get in touch

Feedback from our readers is always welcome.

General feedback: If you have questions about any aspect of this book, email us at customercare@packtpub.com and mention the book title in the subject of your message.

Errata: Although we have taken every care to ensure the accuracy of our content, mistakes do happen. If you have found a mistake in this book, we would be grateful if you would report this to us. Please visit www.packtpub.com/support/errata and fill in the form.

Piracy: If you come across any illegal copies of our works in any form on the internet, we would be grateful if you would provide us with the location address or website name. Please contact us at `copyright@packt.com` with a link to the material.

If you are interested in becoming an author: If there is a topic that you have expertise in and you are interested in either writing or contributing to a book, please visit `authors.packtpub.com`.

Share Your Thoughts

Once you've read *Microsoft Power BI Data Analyst Certification Guide*, we'd love to hear your thoughts! Scan the QR code below to go straight to the Amazon review page for this book and share your feedback.

`https://packt.link/r/1-803-23856-9`

Your review is important to us and the tech community and will help us make sure we're delivering excellent quality content.

Learn more on Discord

To join the Discord community for this book – where you can share feedback, ask questions to the author, and learn about new releases – follow the QR code below:

`http://packt.link/lcncdserver`

Part 1 – Preparing the Data

This section covers how you can connect to various data sources, view data, and modify, cleanse, and prepare data for use in a data visualization, report, or dashboard.

This section comprises the following chapters:

- *Chapter 1, Overview of Power BI and the PL-300 Exam*
- *Chapter 2, Connecting to Data Sources*
- *Chapter 3, Profiling the Data*
- *Chapter 4, Cleaning, Transforming, and Shaping Data*

1
Overview of Power BI and the PL-300 Exam

First off, welcome to this study guide.

There are many reasons why you may have gotten this book. You may be required by work to get certified in Power BI. You may be looking for a new job or career advancement and realize that technical certifications provide a great means to demonstrate technical mastery. You may just want to learn more about Power BI and realize that a study guide would, by necessity, provide an overview of the entire landscape of Power BI.

In this chapter, we'll be covering the following topics:

- A brief overview of Power BI
- Why get certified?
- PL-300 Analyzing Data with Power BI

A brief overview of Power BI

The **BI** in Power BI stands for **business intelligence**. Business intelligence is a field of technology that concerns itself with everything from reporting to using math to predict the future. You may have heard it referred to by some other names, such as data mining or analytics.

Whatever name it is called in your organization, the goal of business intelligence is to distill the massive volume of data gathered and generated by modern businesses into actionable intelligence.

Basing your plans on data-driven decision making will allow you a deeper understanding of not only what you are doing but *why*. Data-guessing decision making or, worse, *we've always done it this way* decision making will become anathema to your data culture.

The reason for this is that your competitors will start driving their business decisions based on data analytics. Their businesses will become more intelligent, see market opportunities and trends before you do, and respond to customer needs, wants, and desires faster than you.

Microsoft defines business intelligence this way (`https://powerbi.microsoft.com/en-us/what-is-business-intelligence/`):

Business intelligence (BI) helps organizations analyze historical and current data, so they can quickly uncover actionable insights for making strategic decisions. Business intelligence tools make this possible by processing large data sets across multiple sources and presenting findings in visual formats that are easy to understand and share.

The key to this is that business intelligence must provide a business with "actionable insights." Which customer segment should we spend our marketing dollars on? What trucks will be off the road next month for scheduled maintenance? How many hours has that pump been running since we put it into production? Who has signed up to bring cupcakes to the bake sale? These questions and many more are answered every hour of every day by businesses and governments around the world.

Power BI for business intelligence

Power BI is Microsoft's premier enterprise data visualization tool for modern businesses. Power BI is also Microsoft's reporting tool for "citizen developers." Power BI is easy enough to use that anyone with a familiarity with Microsoft Excel should be able to understand and use it. Power BI is also powerful enough that it is the primary reporting tool for some of the largest companies in the world.

Power BI allows users to create interactive reports that lead to actionable intelligence for business decision making. Although Power BI is usually thought of as a reporting tool, it's also a complete business intelligence solution. It can, and often is, the entry point for businesses that need to start making data-driven decisions. For some businesses, Power BI provides all the business intelligence they will ever need.

As you will find in this book, Power BI is a collection of services, applications, connectors, and software. These things all work together to turn your data into actionable insights by turning that data into interactive, immersive reports and dashboards. To do these things, Power BI requires data.

Data is at the heart of Power BI. But there is a huge problem in modern businesses…

Reporting challenges

Data is everywhere. One of the biggest challenges in modern businesses is trying to get an end-to-end view of what is happening now or what has happened in the past. Many businesses have data in disparate locations. Data is spread out, some of it on-premises and some in the cloud. Companies try to keep important data in large relational databases but many times, crucial information is contained in Excel spreadsheets or in a SharePoint document library.

It is often very difficult for modern business users to see a complete picture of what is happening across the entire enterprise.

Power BI provides an overall, holistic view of all data within your business, providing that single pane of glass that shows what is happening everywhere within the business. With Power BI, you can see dashboards and reports that display rich, interactive visualizations and KPIs from data that can be residing both on-premises and in the cloud.

It has been said that data is the new gold. Data is the new oil. Businesses value their data estates as much as their manufacturing equipment or supply chains. Your data is a valuable asset.

As businesses learn to use their data, they also learn the importance of having that data. But data is only useful if it can be turned into actions.

For example, Cerner is a global healthcare technology company. They track more than 80 million patient visits every year. Cerner uses Power BI to help streamline the healthcare process, providing valuable insights in seconds instead of the weeks it used to take.

It's not just used in healthcare. The world of retail is being transformed by access to real-time information. T-Mobile uses Power BI to grant front-line workers access to analytical data so they can do their jobs better. Managers and associates can see activations, scorecards, and traffic numbers as they are generated. This allows managers to immediately allocate resources where needed and associates to see whether they are meeting their goals.

Financial companies are usually at the forefront of modernization. It's not just the giants of finance that are adopting Power BI; Members 1st Credit Union is a small credit union located in rural Pennsylvania. Operating 56 small- to mid-sized branches meant that monthly reports took hundreds of employee hours to collate and analyze. By taking advantage of some of Power BI's data features, such as automated refreshes and drillthrough analysis, Members 1st was able to save more than 10,000 hours a year, which is huge for a small, rural financial institution. (Full disclosure, one of the authors banks at Members 1st.)

As you will see in upcoming chapters, not only can Power BI connect to many different data sources, but Power BI can also combine data sources. Power BI is designed from the ground up to allow a user to easily bring data from multiple sources together in one location. These connections allow you to see data from your **Enterprise Resource Planning (ERP)** system mixed with data in an Excel spreadsheet and GitHub data.

You can bring together data from hundreds of sources and mix them together to discover new facts, new correlations, and new data points about your business.

Power BI as a solution

Power BI has two main versions: **Power BI Desktop** and the **Power BI service**.

Power BI Desktop

Power BI Desktop is a visual data exploration and interactive reporting tool, providing a free-form canvas for drag-and-drop exploration of your data, an extensive library of interactive visualizations, and an authoring experience for ease of report creation for the Power BI service. It produces interactive reports and data models.

Power BI Desktop is a free, downloadable Windows desktop application optimized for the Power BI service. Although it is a Microsoft Office application, sharing much of its user interface with products such as Excel and Word, it does not require or depend on Microsoft Office.

With Power BI Desktop, you get an application that specializes in delivering interactive visualizations for data analysis. With it, you can manipulate and consolidate multiple data sources into one report, allowing you to see data from disparate sources on one pane of glass.

The Power BI service, sometimes referred to as `app.powerbi.com`, allows you to create beautiful visualizations to tell compelling data stories. It's optimized to build rich, live dashboards that turn data into business insights.

With the Power BI service, you can securely share reports, dashboards, and Power BI apps with other people in your company, or even with trusted vendors and partners. This secure sharing is one of the biggest reasons for the popularity of Power BI.

The Power BI service also allows you to see your data on the go. With the Power BI mobile app, you can securely see your reports and dashboards from anywhere in the world.

So, with all of the benefits of Power BI in mind, let's consider the certification.

Why get certified?

Probably one of the biggest reasons to get certified in Power BI, or any technology really, is to demonstrate to your employer, or a future employer, that you understand and know what it does and how it works. Employers are often looking for people with knowledge and experience. Certification can let you easily demonstrate your knowledge.

Even if you are not looking for a new job, your PL-300 certification will demonstrate your Power BI knowledge to your boss, co-workers, and everyone who sees your LinkedIn profile.

Beyond just demonstrating technical knowledge, another key benefit is that you keep current with all the changes in Power BI. The process of gaining and keeping your PL-300 certification necessitates that you learn about Power BI.

Yes, that previous sentence said *keeping* your certification. Microsoft announced that starting December 15, 2020, you will have to renew your PL-300 certification every 2 years. We'll cover this more in the next section.

PL-300 Analyzing Data with Microsoft Power BI

The PL-300 Analyzing Data with Microsoft Power BI exam is a Microsoft **role-based** exam. Starting in 2019, Microsoft announced they were moving to a role-based model of exams and certifications.

Historically, Microsoft exams were centered around a single product, such as Windows Server or Exchange. Microsoft realigned their entire learning and certification process around the idea of roles. Currently, Microsoft has organized exams into 12 different roles. PL-300 is a test for the Data Analyst Associate track.

Because Microsoft wants to keep their certifications relevant and valuable, they target the questions of the exam to the level of the test. The PL-300 exam is targeted at an intermediate level. This means, as you will see in the *Knowledge needed to pass* section, this test covers a lot of ground.

Microsoft tests

Microsoft has been testing and certifying people for decades. Over that time, the tests have evolved and become much more complex. Microsoft exams are not just multiple-choice questions. During your exam, you will be presented with different types of questions, depending on what Microsoft considers the best way to make certain you know the answer.

Microsoft does not deduct points for wrong answers. Make certain to answer every question, even if you are uncertain.

PL-300 is about 55 questions long and you are given 3 hours to take the exam. Plan on it taking 3½ hours, as there will be some prep before the test. There is also an optional survey at the end.

You will have to score 700 out of a possible 1,000 points to pass the exam.

Types of questions

Some of the types of questions you might face include the following:

- **Multiple choice** – These types will more than likely make up much of the PL-300 exam.
- **Best answer** – Perhaps my least favorite is this type of question. Much like multiple choice, but with the possibility that more than one answer will work and only one of the answers is "best."

- **Build list** – These questions present you with a scenario, then a list of steps that can be used to solve the scenario. You drag the steps from one side of the screen to the other and place them in the correct order. Usually, not all of the presented steps are part of the solution. Do not worry if you have steps left over.

- **Drag and drop** – Much like the build list type, with drag and drop you will be presented with a scenario and a series of processes or technologies. You match the process or technology to an answer by dragging it from the list to where it matches. As with the build list, Microsoft often provides more answers than needed. You may see this in the DAX section, where you will have to drag DAX commands into the appropriate place in the script.

- **Active screen** – This type of question will present you with a scenario part of a user interface. You must complete actions to achieve the desired outcome as specified by the scenario. You may see this type of question during the administration part of the exam. You may be asked to make a selection in the Power BI admin user interface.

Knowledge needed to pass

Microsoft publishes a list of topics covered by the PL-300 exam, and what percentage of the overall grade each topic will be worth. As you are going through the list, you may notice that it tracks with the layout of this book. This was intentional. If Microsoft is going to provide us with an outline, we are more than pleased to use it.

Here is the current list of exam topics and what percentage of your overall grade they are worth:

- Prepare the Data (20-25%)
- Model the Data (25-30%)
- Visualize the Data (20-25%)
- Analyze the Data (10-15%)
- Deploy and Maintain Deliverables (10-15%)

You may notice from the table of contents that this book is broken down into sections that follow these topics in this order. That was intentional.

Timelines

Microsoft has decided to make most of their role-based and specialty certifications valid for 2 years from the date of achievement. Six months before your certification expires, Microsoft will provide a link on your Certification Dashboard (`https://aka.ms/CertDashboard`) for you to take an assessment. Passing the assessment on Microsoft Learn is the only way to renew a certification. Renewing your certification will then become an annual requirement.

You will also receive an email telling you it's time to renew.

This process ensures that you, and everyone else with the PL-300 certification, is up to date with all the changes in Power BI. As Power BI can change radically within a year, this is a good thing. The fact that renewal is free is amazing.

The best part is that you can retake the renewal test as many times as you need. You must pass it before your certification expires, but you have 6 months, unlimited retakes, and access to the internet while taking the renewal.

If you do not pass your renewal assessment, then you must pay for and pass the PL-300 exam again.

Strategies to get a passing grade

So, now we know what's on the test, let's talk about how to prepare to take the test. If you search the internet, you will find many slightly different strategies for studying for and passing Microsoft certification exams:

- **Set a date** – The most important step is the first one. If you set a date, it allows you to work backward from that date to plan your studying. Some people even go as far as to purchase their test voucher for a date in the future, thus committing them to that data.

- **Buy a nice study guide** – Might I recommend this one?

- **Get hands-on** – Most of the test is centered around Power BI Desktop, a free-to-use application; no license is required. You can download Power BI Desktop from `https://powerbi.com` or, as I prefer to do, install it from the Microsoft Store. The Microsoft Store version will get the monthly updates automatically.

- **Learn the technology** – This study guide is great, but nothing is better than getting hands-on with the technology. Create reports for your work, for yourself, and for your friends.

- **Learn the vocabulary** – Knowing what things are called will help immensely with the test. Many times, you can eliminate one or two answers from a multiple-choice question just by knowing the terminology.
- **Know what to expect** (again, a nice study guide is a good idea) – Look at the table of contents for this book. Review the previous *Knowledge needed to pass* section. Make sure you have at least a passing familiarity with each subheading.

Do not stress out! Power BI is intuitive and fun. Plus, Microsoft does not put a record of failed attempts on your transcript.

Summary

In this chapter, we covered the basics of why Power BI is a great reporting tool. We also went over Microsoft certifications, what they are, why they're great, and what's on the one you will be studying for. We also reviewed the types of questions asked and the topics that will be covered in this exam.

In the next chapter, we will dive right into what will be on the exam. As with most reporting things, we start with data. Power BI is great at aggregating data from disparate sources. We will cover the connection to those sources and how to organize your data for better reporting.

Questions

1. What does the "BI" in Power BI stand for?

    A. Business information

    B. Bidirectional information

    C. Business intelligence

    D. Big industry

2. The Power BI service allows you to:

    A. Download software allowing you to explore data and create reports.

    B. Create spreadsheets that calculate values based on formulas.

    C. Author presentations using the slideshow concept.

    D. Share reports, dashboards, and apps with other users.

3. How often must Microsoft certifications be renewed?

    A. Never, they last forever.
    B. Every 6 months.
    C. Every 2 years.
    D. Every 4 years.

2
Connecting to Data Sources

In most organizations, data tends to be stored in various data stores, such as filesystems, proprietary and open source databases, or even distributed filesystems for high-performance compute platforms. Often the data has meaning and is useful while being stored in the source systems, such as a transactional database that keeps track of sales from a group of point-of-sale systems. In this example, data is stored in a relational database that is tuned to keep track of each sale. For analytics purposes, we will likely want to use this data in concert with data from a separate system that tracks the inventory of items we have for sale. The inventory will likely be a different relational database, possibly from another technology vendor. To better understand whether we are stocking too many items (or not enough) for sale, we need to create a view of the data from both sales and inventory databases.

Over the past few decades, this has been the goal of data warehousing – to allow data from all over an organization to be combined to help answer meaningful business questions with the goal of helping organizations to run more efficiently, and to help them enable further transformations to help in the competing marketplace. The data warehousing industry exists to help make this easier, but this is always an increasing challenge as new technologies for data storage and processing arise.

The end goal of data warehousing is to allow businesses to have a 360-degree view of their business, and to do that not only do data warehouses need to connect to disparate data sources but so do BI and other reporting tools. Many times, data is stored outside the enterprise data warehouse that also needs to be incorporated into the analysis. The rise of more popular **Software-as-a-Service (SaaS)** providers also means that data can live in the cloud, and it also needs to be incorporated into BI and reporting analysis in order to provide the whole picture to the business decision makers.

Microsoft Power BI provides some of the most comprehensive connectivity capabilities on the BI reporting and analytics tools on the market. This means Power BI can connect to disparate data sources for use in creating reports and dashboards.

In this chapter, we're going to cover the following topics:

- Identifying data sources
- Connecting to data sources
- Power BI datasets
- Power BI dataflows
- Query performance tuning
- Advanced options (what-if parameters, DAX parameters, PBIDS files, and XMLA endpoints)

Technical requirements

The following are the prerequisites in order to complete the work in this chapter:

- Microsoft Power BI Desktop installed on a Microsoft Windows PC.
- Access to some data to use. We're also providing synthetic data that can be used. This is available in the GitHub repository for this book here: `https://github.com/PacktPublishing/Microsoft-Power-BI-Data-Analyst-Certification-Guide/tree/main/example-data`.

Identifying data sources

In this section, we will review the various data source options that Power BI provides.

Local data sources, files, and databases

Most BI developers will work from a local Windows PC. Usually, that PC is not also running an enterprise database or functioning as a corporate file server. Power BI provides the ability to connect local data on your PC just the same as if the data is stored on a corporate file server (using network connectivity or Windows file share) or if you're running a development server on your local machine. For ad hoc and testing purposes, many users will also want to import data files, such as CSV or Excel, from their local PC as well. Power BI supports various formats and makes it easy to import local files/data.

You can also import a folder of files or a Microsoft SharePoint folder of files.

Power BI also supports connecting to databases in the most popular databases. Most enterprise organizations run their business using data stored in databases, so sourcing data from a database is a common occurrence using Power BI. Some of the most popular databases include Microsoft SQL Server, Oracle Database, and SAP.

To see a complete list of supported files and databases, be sure to review the official documentation at https://docs.microsoft.com/power-bi/connect-data/power-bi-data-sources.

Cloud and SaaS data sources

In recent years, as more organizations have seen the value and adopted the cloud to help digitally transform their business, support for common cloud databases and SaaS providers has also been very important. Power BI supports a wide range of Microsoft Azure cloud services, including Azure Synapse Analytics and Amazon Redshift.

Outside of these dedicated connectors to databases and cloud services, Power BI also includes capabilities that enable connectivity using open or standards-based solutions, such as ODBC, REST API, and OData.

To see a complete list of supported cloud and SaaS data sources, check the official documentation at https://docs.microsoft.com/power-bi/connect-data/power-bi-data-sources.

It's important for BI tools to connect to the data sources where data is stored. If an organization uses a data store that the BI tool does not support, then the data needs to be moved to a supported data store. For the exam, it is important to know some of the common data sources supported by Power BI. The wide connectivity to data has helped Power BI become one of the leading BI tools on the market today.

Connecting to data sources

You may want to include data from a variety of different sources, each of which has its own methods of connecting. We'll look at a couple of types of data sources in this section.

On-premises data gateway

Since Power BI lives as both a desktop tool and an online SaaS that provides the hosting of reports and dashboards, it is important to connect to non-online-hosted data sources as well. This is accomplished with the **on-premises data gateway** (referred to as the data gateway). The data gateway is a free download from the Microsoft Download Center that works with the online Power BI service to enable this connectivity on local resources from the cloud.

It is important to understand how the on-premises data gateway is different from other gateway software that may have been used in the past. The data gateway software runs on a local Windows computer, and it needs to have an internet connection to connect to an intermediary Azure Service Bus. This encrypted connection to **Azure Service Bus** (provided by the Power BI service) allows the data gateway to work with the Power BI service, without needing any firewall ports to be opened. This allows a cloud service to connect to the local network. Most enterprise network security teams want to maintain or consistently improve the security posture of their organization and using the on-premises data gateway architecture will help those teams meet security goals as well.

Please note that the data gateway supports different data sources in different ways. Some sources are supported and some are not; it's important to make note of the sources you intend to use and check for the needed support, either directly from the Power BI service or using the on-premises data gateway.

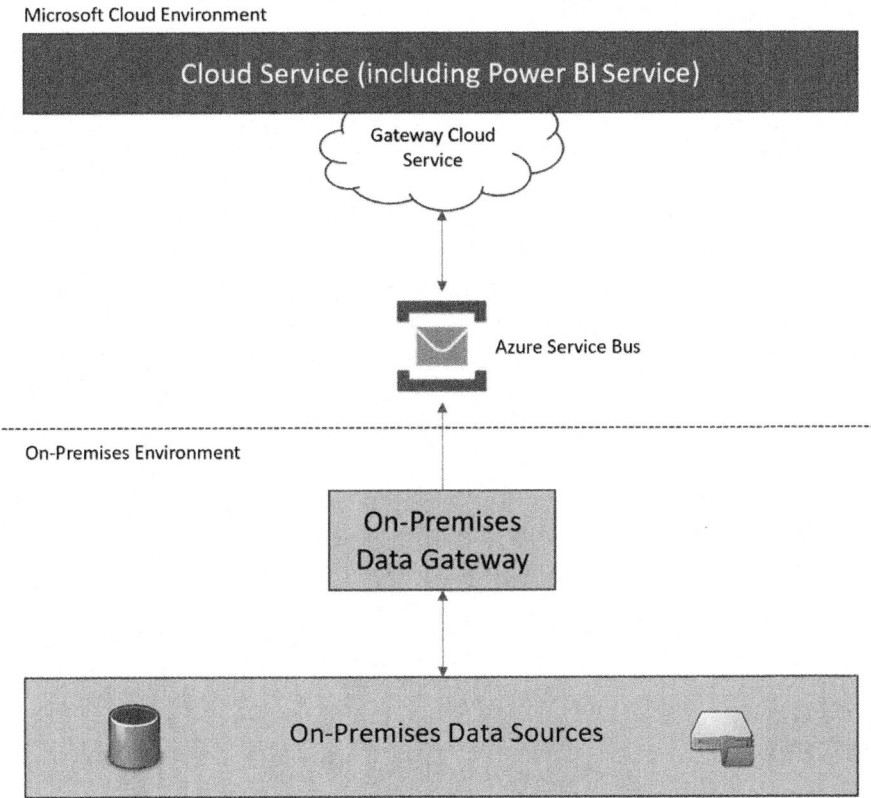

Figure 2.1 – Architecture of the on-premises data gateway

A data gateway can function in two modes: **personal mode** and **standard mode**. Standard mode is typically used in organizations on server hardware and provides DirectQuery and live connection to Analysis Services support. Standard mode, however, must run as a service on the computer and requires administrator privileges, while personal mode does not. When running in standard mode, this data gateway also works with **Azure Analysis Services**, **Azure Logic Apps**, **Power Apps**, **Power Automate**, and **Power BI dataflows**.

The data gateway is available for download from `https://powerbi.microsoft.com/gateway/`.

Anytime Power BI connects to a data source (directly or with the on-premises data gateway), it uses one of two types of queries. Next, we'll look at query types.

Exploring query types

When Power BI connects to any data source, it makes one of two types of connections or queries.

DirectQuery

The first type is called **DirectQuery**, or a live connection to the data. This means that Power BI is storing credentials and a connection string to the data source. For example, this could be the relational database storing inventory data used in a warehouse. This DirectQuery connection allows Power BI to query the inventory database and retrieve information such as the tables and views available in the source database, the schema of those tables and views, as well as records contained in the tables and views. Once a connection has been made, the data retrieved is used and displayed by Power BI. DirectQuery is useful when the underlying data has the potential to be changed quickly and the most up-to-date information is needed for use in Power BI reports and dashboards. For example, if a real-time inventory system has been implemented in the warehouse and the inventory system itself keeps an up-to-the-second record of goods for sale, then it's possible the purchasing team may also need up-to-the-second reports that allow them to make the most informed decisions when it comes to refilling stock in the warehouse.

Import Query

The second type of connection is called **Import Query**. Import will connect to a data source and store the same credentials and connection string, but it will also import the data and store that in memory in Power BI (either the Desktop authoring tool or the Power BI online service). Import is useful when all the necessary data can fit into memory, but can also dramatically speed up the performance of reports inside Power BI since the underlying data source does not need to be queried for each report/dashboard view. Import Query makes Power BI do all the work (storing the data as well as calculating fields, rendering the dynamic report visuals, and so on), while DirectQuery allows Power BI to share some of this work with the underlying data source using a pushdown query. Import Query is generally the best place to start (from a performance perspective) as Power BI can optimally store data in its own internal **VertiPaq** format when using Import Query. VertiPaq is the proprietary storage engine inside Power BI and is highly optimized for data compression as well as calculations needed to render reports. For example, if a business analyst wants to create a new report for management and the data comes from four or five different Microsoft Excel files, then it's likely that Import Query should be used. The performance of the report will be optimized since Power BI is handling the queries/calculations, storage of the data imported from Excel, and rendering of the visuals. This means no network latency and no dependency upon external data storage.

Import Query also has an additional feature that is important to note: it allows data to be refreshed. When using Power BI Desktop, this can be completed by clicking the **Refresh** button but once a report is published to the Power BI service, then it's possible to schedule a refresh at a regular or timed interval. This is useful when reports need to import data into Power BI to provide the best report performance experience, but also need to show updated data (that doesn't need to be up to the second). There are limitations on the number of times data can be refreshed by the Power BI service depending on the capacity where the report is deployed. For many organizations, there is a need for fresh data in reports and dashboards, but it doesn't need to be up to the second, so for those use cases, a daily or few-times-a-day refresh will work and make for an excellent report viewing experience.

It should be noted that DirectQuery and Import Query support different data sources in different ways. For example, when the data source is a CSV file stored on a local filesystem, it must use Import Query because there is no underlying query engine to which Power BI can send a pushdown query. CSV data will get imported into the Power BI storage engine and used for reporting. Upon clicking **Refresh**, this data will again be pulled by Power BI from the source CSV file into the Power BI storage engine. Another example would be an **Azure Synapse Analytics SQL dedicated pool** (a common cloud-based data warehouse); in this case, the creator of the Power BI report has the option to choose either DirectQuery or Import Query. Knowing the trade-offs between DirectQuery and Import Query is important in this case, as they will have an impact on both the Power BI report and the underlying data source.

	DirectQuery	**Import Query**
Data freshness	Pro	Con
Report performance	Con	Pro

Figure 2.2 – Query performance versus freshness comparison

For example, if Import Query uses Synapse Analytics SQL dedicated as a source, but those who manage the service regularly pause the SQL dedicated pool over the weekends, then it would be important to note that Power BI would not be able to do a scheduled refresh at this time. Additionally, there would be more load on the SQL dedicated pool when the Power BI refresh is running.

When a query is created in Power BI, then a definition of the data is created in the data model. This component of the Power BI data model is called a Power BI dataset. Next, we'll look at Power BI datasets in depth.

Power BI datasets

Data used in Power BI reports uses a Power BI dataset. Power BI datasets are basically a connection string and credentials that Power BI uses to connect to a data source. Every report that is created in Power BI must have a dataset associated with it. This ensures the report has data to visualize.

Power BI datasets are often created using the Power BI Desktop tool. At the time a report is published, both the report (containing visuals) and the dataset are published to the Power BI service. It is important to note that credentials are not sent to the Power BI service and must be re-entered upon publishing – this is useful to allow report developers to create reports locally using their own credentials (often with development data sources) but then change the connection string and credentials after reports are published (to production data sources).

Datasets can be used or shared among reports or can come from uploading Excel files to the Power BI service directly or come from push or streaming sources as well. For example, the Azure Stream Analytics service provides the capability of streaming data directly to a Power BI service streaming dataset for use with dashboards created on the Power BI service.

Power BI dataflows

As data needs change, Power BI continues to adapt to those needs to help organizations understand and use their data to meet continuously changing market demands. **Dataflows** are a capability in Power BI that empowers Power BI users to perform self-service data preparation, which is sometimes a necessary component of the end-to-end reporting and analytics solution.

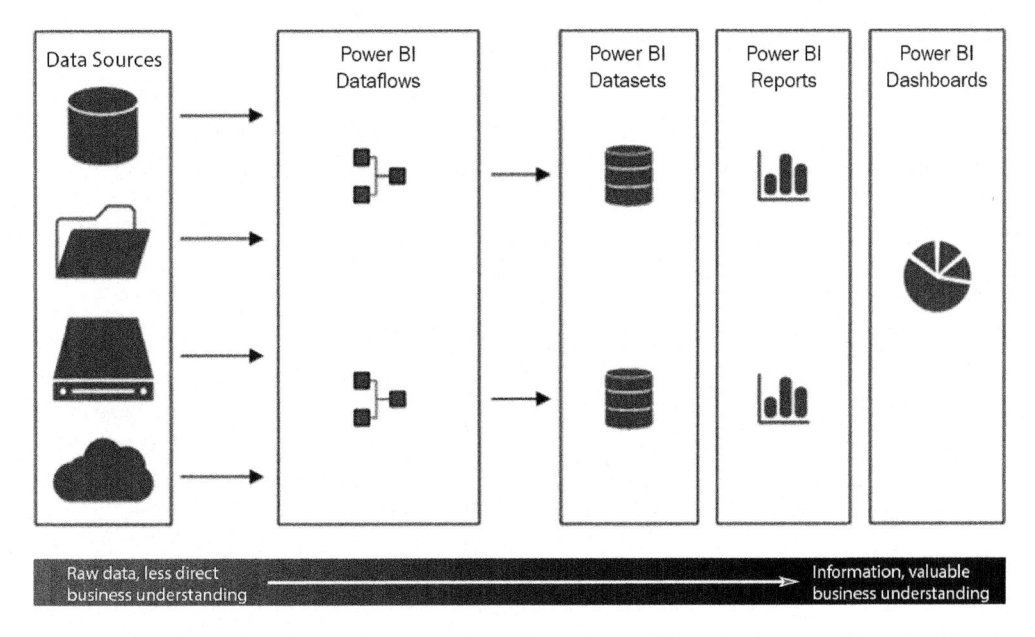

Figure 2.3 – Visual representation of how Power BI dataflows work with other Power BI assets and content

Like other data transformation tools, Power BI dataflows connect to disparate data sources and then perform a transformation on the data before it gets used as a Power BI dataset. This is useful when an organization wants to prevent report developers from needing to access the underlying data sources directly (potentially for security or performance reasons). Dataflows also enable the capability of optimizing data transformation that might always need to take place in order to make data usable in reports. For example, if database data columns always need to be renamed and joined with data in another table in order to be used by report creators, then doing it once in a dataflow might be an optimized way to do this rather than needing report creators to do this each time (and possibly different ways each time).

Dataflows also provide a place where data can uniformly be transformed and made ready for Power BI report consumption from other Power Platform or Azure services. Using the Microsoft Azure cloud backbone, services such as Microsoft Dataverse and Dynamics 365 are popular sources for use with dataflows but other cloud services also apply.

While dataflows can be used by Power BI Pro users, some features require **Premium Per User** (**PPU**) or **Premium capacity**. These are features such as DirectQuery from data sources, incremental refresh, computed and linked entities, and the enhanced compute engine.

Query performance tuning

When considering optimizing the performance of Power BI queries, there are a few places to start, and the recommendation is to look at each as a layer of performance tuning to undertake. These layers include reducing the size of the data, optimizing DirectQuery (when used), and optimizing composite models (when used).

Reducing the data size

This technique is the idea of limiting the amount of data that Power BI needs to work with to only what is needed for the report. For example, if the sales database being used as the source for the report contains sales data for 70 countries but there is only a need to report sales for 5 countries, then it makes sense to only use data for the 5 needed countries. This can be accomplished when connecting to the source database and using a WHERE clause that limits the data to only the rows for the needed countries.

While this technique works well with rows of data, it can be applied to columns also. It's not uncommon for enterprise databases to have tables that are very wide or contain many columns. Depending on the reporting use case, many columns will not be needed and can be left out of the Power BI data model. This will further reduce the data size. In this case, only the necessary columns can be selected by using the SELECT clause of a custom query when connecting to the data source. It's possible to write a custom query selecting only the rows and columns needed for the report by clicking **Advanced options** when connecting to the data source in Power BI. Keep in mind that not every data source will support limiting the data imported this way. Some sources may require some prefiltering to limit the dataset to only the needed data before connecting to it from Power BI.

Depending on the use cases, it's also possible to do precalculations or summarization outside of Power BI before the data is loaded into Power BI. In cases where preprocessing or filtering is needed, it's also a worthwhile exercise to see whether there are any calculations or pre-aggregations that can take place on the data before it gets used by Power BI. This has the possibility of greatly reducing data sizes but there may be trade-offs depending on the scenario. Depending on the situation, doing pre-aggregation may not always be possible or preferred.

For example, if the sales database contains detailed transaction-level data (think every single item and price for every single customer purchase), if the retail store had five different sales on the same day to different customers and each one of them purchased a bottle of soda, then the sales detail table might contain five rows of data to record each sale of soda to each customer on that day. The report might not need data at that granular level but instead, it might be fine to just have a sum of all the sales for that soda for that day, which would be one row of data. In this case, we could pre-aggregate this data using a view in the database or in a custom SQL query used in Power BI when we connect to the sales database. Both methods would result in fewer rows of data in Power BI while still meeting the business requirements of the report.

In review, some of the important techniques to remember for reducing data size include the following:

- Reducing to only the rows and columns of data required
- Completing precalculation and summarization prior to use in Power BI

Next, let's look at optimizing DirectQuery data sources.

DirectQuery optimization

When using DirectQuery, it's important to remember that the total performance experienced is dependent upon both Power BI and the underlying data source. Many times, Power BI reports will use a data warehouse such as Azure Synapse Analytics as the data source and for enterprise data warehouses like this, there are several considerations to keep in mind when optimizing the performance of DirectQuery. Some or all of these techniques may not always be possible, but they are often worth considering. They are listed here in the order you should consider them:

1. **Indexes** – Relational databases support the building of indexes. Indexes allow the efficient query and retrieval of data at the cost of storage to maintain the index data structure. As data storage has continually decreased in recent years, adding indexes to database tables and views often becomes advantageous to help decrease the time needed to return data with a query.

2. **Dimension-to-fact table key integrity** – When fact and dimension tables are used in a data warehouse it's important that dimension tables contain a key that provides proper data cardinality. This means that records in the dimension table can be matched (or joined) to records in the fact tables(s) without causing a Cartesian product – which is generally something to avoid for both storage and performance reasons.

3. **Materialize data and dates** – When possible, materializing calculated data and date tables in the source database can help solve performance in DirectQuery scenarios because it reduces the need to perform these calculations downstream in Power BI.

4. **Distributed tables** – For **Massively Parallel Processing** (**MPP**) data warehouses, it's often worth considering reviewing the query performance of the distributed tables stored in the data warehouse. MPP databases store data and query over multiple compute nodes in a cluster, and database tables are typically organized in such a way that the storage of data on compute nodes is distributed in a manner that makes joins efficient and performant for queries. It is possible that distributed tables in the MPP database aren't set up for efficient queries and it would be beneficial to consider how the tables are distributed by changing query patterns or changing the distributed table setup.

Next, let's look at optimizing composite models.

Composite model optimization

When something is composite, it is made up of more than one thing. **Composite models** in Power BI mean that a single data model contains data from multiple sources, and these can be both Import and DirectQuery. Note that composite models can't be used for every data source type, and they introduce complexity to the data model that needs to be managed. If possible, consider *not* using composite models, for the sake of reducing complexity and security. Since data from imported datasets can be used to cross-filter data in DirectQuery datasets, queries that push down to the DirectQuery datasets could contain sensitive information, and since relational databases usually log all queries that are processed, that means it's possible sensitive information that was imported will now end up in the query logs of the relational database used in the DirectQuery dataset.

In general, as stated previously, it's best to start with Import Query for data models and then only consider DirectQuery if there are very large volumes of data or there is a need for up-to-the-second reporting of a supported data source. Switching to a composite model allows the following:

- Using DirectQuery with multiple DirectQuery-supported data sources
- Using DirectQuery with additional data imported into the model
- Boosting the performance of a DirectQuery data model by importing selected tables into storage and optimizing the query operations

In order to optimize a composite model, there are two main areas to consider: table storage and the use of aggregations.

Table storage

When a composite model is enabled, each table can be configured in one of three different modes:

- **DirectQuery** – This mode functions like DirectQuery always has: no data is stored in the Power BI model and data is always queried back to the underlying data source when needed by Power BI. This is best used when data needs to be the most up to date from the source or when data volumes are very large and unable to be imported. It's common that large fact tables will be best set to DirectQuery mode.

- **Import** – This mode functions like Import always has: data is copied into the in-memory storage in the Power BI data model. It's sometimes possible for dimension tables to be set to Import mode to help increase performance when grouping and filtering. When data is stored in memory in the model, we'll see the highest performance in Power BI.

- **Dual** – This mode allows tables to behave like both Import and DirectQuery. This is useful when it's possible that a cross-filter query or slice of data in a visual will generate a query that pushes down to the same DirectQuery source for both tables. Since Dual allows data to be stored in memory in the data model, it's possible this will aid performance.

Aggregations

Composite models support storing DirectQuery tables as Import tables. They also add the ability for data to be aggregated when it is stored in the data model. Storing aggregated data in memory in the Power BI data model will increase query performance over very large DirectQuery datasets. The rule of thumb for aggregation tables is that the underlying source table should be no less than 10x larger. For example, if the underlying data warehouse table contains 5 million records, then the aggregation table should contain no more than 500,000 records. If it contains more than 500,000 records, then it's likely the trade-off for creating and managing the aggregation table will not be worth the minimal performance gain compared to using the existing DirectQuery table. However, if the aggregation table results in 500,000 or fewer records, then it will likely show great performance gains and will be worth the creation and management of the aggregation table.

Advanced options (what-if parameters, Power Query parameters, PBIDS files, and XMLA endpoints)

Power BI provides many advanced capacities. From tools for creating what-if analysis to dynamic DAX code, to storing data sources and structures for ease of use to serving advanced connections, to a myriad of data consumers using **XML for Analysis** (**XMLA**), including other non-Power BI tools, this portion of the chapter will dive deeper into these advanced capabilities.

What-if parameters

Power BI parameters allow for advanced analysis using multiple values for different scenarios. This capability is like **What-If Analysis** in Microsoft Excel. It allows for the creation of measures that calculate percentage value increases of existing numeric values. What-if parameters make it easy to see and use multiple percentage increases/decreases by automatically creating a slicer and a table with generated values. By creating a measure using the generated values of the what-if parameter, you can simulate changes to numeric data in a data model. For example, in our sales data, we can have aggregated total monthly sales. By using the what-if parameters capability, we can generate data used in a sales target of 100% to 200% and see the corresponding impact of that increase across the total monthly sales.

To use the what-if parameters, we can use the following steps:

1. Click the **New Parameter** button on the **Modeling** toolbar in Power BI Desktop.
2. Provide a name for the parameter. We'll use `Sales Increase`.
3. Select a data type. For this example, we'll select **Fixed decimal number**.
4. For **Minimum** and **Maximum**, select **1.00** and **2.00**, respectively – to represent 100% and 200%.
5. Set the **Increment** value to the granularity desired in the slicer. If you want the slicer to move at 10% increments, then set this value to **0.10**.
6. Set the **Default** value to be **1.00** as this will be 100%.
7. Lastly, leave the **Add slicer to this page** checkbox selected so the slicer will automatically be created on the current page.
8. Click **OK**.

Advanced options (what-if parameters, Power Query parameters, PBIDS files, and XMLA endpoints) 27

In *Figure 2.4*, we can see how this what-if parameter can be configured:

Figure 2.4 – Example what-if parameter configuration

Once this has been completed, there will be a new table called **Sales Increase** and a slicer is added to the report. The slicer can be used as shown in *Figure 2.5* to select a 'what-if' value for the sales increase:

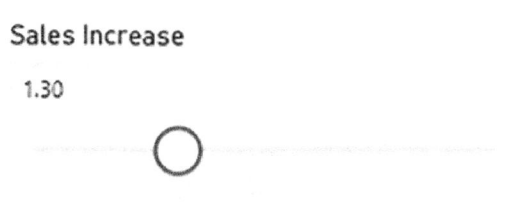

Figure 2.5 – Slicer created for the what-if parameter value

This table contains two fields: **Sales Increase** and **Sales Increase Value**. The **Sales Increase** field stores the generated increments from 1.00, 1.1, 1.2, 1.3, 1.4, and so on up to 2.0, while **Sales Increase Value** contains only the DAX expression using the SELECTEDVALUE function, which correlates to the location of the slicer. Together, these allow a dynamic multiplier to be selected using the slicer visual and another measure to be created that will multiply (or perform other math) against other fields in the data, like this:

```
= [Monthly Sales] * [Sales Increase Value]
```

This simple equation allows us to see what would happen if sales increase by nothing (100%) all the way up to double sales (200%) with this dynamic value set by the user using the slicer.

Power Query parameters

For data connection and transformation, Power BI uses a technology called **Power Query**. Power Query is a key component of Power BI, but it also powers data connection and data shaping in Excel. Power Query provides extensive capabilities, including the ability to create and use parameters that help Power Query become more extensible and maintainable. Power Query parameters allow dynamic values to be used that can be used in a query or queries.

The **Manage Parameters** tool is used from within the Power Query window (**Home** menu | **Transform data**) and allows the creation of new parameters to be used within Power Query. Each parameter has these values:

- **Name**.
- **Description**.
- **Required** or **Not Required**.
- **Type** – This is where the data type is set (decimal number, date/time, text, or binary).
- **Suggested Values** – This is either **Any value**, **List of Values**, or **Query**.
- **Current Value** – Allows for the initial value of the parameter to be set.

We will check out the **Suggested Values** parameter in depth here.

Any Value

A parameter value can be any string of characters or numbers the user desires to enter.

List of Values

This option provides the capability of defining a list of values that can be used as parameters. The user interface shows a table interface to help the user enter the values to be stored as preset options. When **List of Values** is used, the user also selects **Default Value** and **Current Value** from the options defined in the **List of Values** table. It is possible to type values in as a parameter; **List of Values** merely provides the default options that can be easily selected.

Query

This option makes it possible to select a query that contains an output list of values. This is useful when you need to have a dynamically updating list of values and you don't want to hardcode them into the **Manage Parameters** tool. Instead, these could be stored in a database or a file and then included in the data model as a typical query. To use values in a parameter, a list query first needs to be made. To make a list query inside Power Query, take the following steps:

1. Select the column from an existing query that contains the list of values you want to use as the dynamic list of values in a parameter.
2. Right-click the column and select **Add as New Query**.
3. A new query is created in the query list. The icon used is different from the typical table-like icon. Instead, it looks more like a list.
4. The new query can be renamed as needed and then selected as an option in the **Query** drop-down list.

When a query is used for **Suggested Values**, the option for **Current Value** is still available.

Parameters are often used in different ways, but common scenarios include the following:

- A common value used for multiple transformations
- Used as arguments for custom functions

When parameters are configured, they will become a selectable option on transforms such as **Filter Rows**. **Always Allow** may need to be checked under the **View** menu | **Parameters**.

PBIDS files

Sometimes identifying and creating the connections to data sources can be a challenge in larger organizations as there can be many data sources to choose from. In those cases, it may be helpful to create something called a PBIDS file. **Power BI Data Source** (**PBIDS**) files contain the data source connection information only, which will allow beginner report creators to get started quickly with the proper data sources prepopulated.

The PBIDS file format is based on JSON and is fully editable in a text editor but also creatable from an existing **Power BI Desktop file** (**PBIX**).

To create a PBIDS file with Power BI Desktop (from an existing PBIX file that has the needed data source connected), take the following steps:

1. Click **Options and settings** under the **File** menu.
2. Click **Data source settings**.
3. Verify that the connections in the current file look correct, and then click **Export PBIDS**.
4. Select the location where the file will be saved.

The JSON structure of the PBIDS file will look something like this:

```
{
  "version": "0.1",
  "connections": [
    {
      "details": {
        "protocol": "<PROTOCOL USED, SUCH AS TDS FOR SQL SERVER>",
        "address": {
          "server": "<SERVER HOSTNAME OR IP>",
          "database": "<DATABASE NAME>"
        },
        "authentication": null,
        "query": null
      },
      "options": {},
      "mode": null
    }
  ]
}
```

PBIDS files only contain connection information and do not contain credentials. This is an important distinction as PBIDS files can be shared around an organization and for security reasons, data sources (files and databases) are often controlled and set by data governance teams to protect sensitive data.

A PBIDS file will open with Power BI Desktop, and you will be greeted with the final steps for the creation of the connection, such as credentials, Import, or DirectQuery (where applicable), and then the data source will be set up and you will be able to create reports or visuals. The user will not need to specify the details of the connection to the source.

As of the time of writing, PBIDS files only support connecting to one data source in a file. If more than one is specified, an error will result.

XMLA endpoints

XMLA is the communications protocol used by Microsoft SQL Server Analysis Services instances. XMLA is a widely used connectivity option supported by many BI tools as a source for visualization.

Power BI is built off the foundation of Analysis Services technologies, and as part of Power BI Premium, it is possible to connect to a Power BI Premium workspace using XMLA. This happens through an XMLA endpoint that is part of the Premium service.

Common uses of XMLA endpoint clients used include the following:

- **SQL Server Data Tools (SSDT)**/Visual Studio with Analysis Services – Some organizations standardize developer tooling. SSDT has been around a long time and is widely used.
- **SQL Server Management Studio (SSMS)** – Another tool that has been around a while and is widely used, SSMS allows you to create DAX, MDX, and XMLA queries.
- Power BI Report Builder.
- Tabular Editor.
- DAX Studio.
- ALM Toolkit.
- And the perennial favorite data tool: Microsoft Excel.

Many times, an XMLA endpoint will be used for dataset management with write operations. When this is the case, it's recommended to enable large model support in Power BI Premium. Large model support in Power BI Premium will allow data models to grow larger than 10 GB of compressed data size. When write operations need to take place, be advised that XMLA endpoints are enabled as read-only by default, so write capability will need to be enabled.

Tenant-level settings are enabled by default to allow XMLA endpoints and analyzing in Excel with on-premises datasets. This setting is enabled for the entire organization by default. Some organizations will choose to disable this default setting, so it's important to know that this may need to be enabled sometimes.

To enable read-write capability for XMLA endpoints, this option needs to be changed in the Power BI admin portal:

1. Select **Capacity settings**.
2. Select **Power BI Premium**, then select the name of the capacity.
3. Expand **Workloads** and select **Read Write** under the **XMLA Endpoint** setting.

The XMLA endpoint connection URL can be seen for each workspace deployed to Power BI Premium by viewing the workspace settings and clicking on the **Premium** tab.

In addition to client connectivity to Power BI Premium workspaces, XMLA endpoint capability also enables fine-grained data refresh capabilities. By setting up data partitioning, it becomes possible to refresh selected historical partitions without having to reload all data. This is useful for organizations who want to maximize the data stored in the Power BI service (for best report performance) while using large historical datasets.

Summary

In this chapter, we looked at a number of topics related to connecting to and querying data with Power BI. We reviewed some of the popular data sources that are supported by Power BI and how queries to those data sources can be DirectQuery or Import, and how those sources can even be located on-premises. It's very important that Power BI supports as many data sources as possible so organizations can spend more time querying data and using it to answer business questions and less time moving data to a supported data store.

We also learned how Power BI supports the creation of composite data models that use both DirectQuery and Import data. Composite models help enable many new use cases, including performance optimization in some scenarios. We learned how Power BI uses the concept of a dataset to store connection information to a data source and how that connection information can be shared using a PBIDS file that can be shared across an organization to help make getting connected to data easier for new Power BI developers.

Finally, we learned what Power BI dataflows are and also some of the other advanced features of Power BI Premium, such as XMLA endpoints, which allow power users to connect to the backend analysis service running in the Power BI service to enable advanced capabilities. Other advanced topics we reviewed included what-if parameters, which allow the advanced analysis of data using dynamically generated values, and Power Query parameters, which help to extend and provide more flexibility for programming a data connection and transformation queries. These topics are key to having a foundational knowledge of Power BI and how it is used to solve today's BI challenges.

In the next chapter, we will cover the capabilities that Power BI has for data profiling. Profiling data is important to understand more about your data and how the data can be used for data visualization and BI reporting.

Questions

1. Which data sources can Power BI connect to?

    A. Only local, on-premises data sources

    B. On-premises, cloud, and SaaS sources

    C. Only SaaS sources

    D. On-premises and cloud sources

2. What are some ways to tune the performance of Power BI queries?

    A. Running a shrink on the data model

    B. Importing only the required data

    C. Zipping the PBIX file

    D. Removing all queries

3. XMLA is the protocol used for which software or service?

    A. Microsoft Analysis Services

    B. Microsoft Excel

    C. Azure Synapse Analytics

    D. Microsoft SQL Server Management Studio

3
Profiling the Data

After connecting to data and getting it into Power BI, your next step will be to profile your data, or as data scientists and statisticians call it, performing **exploratory data analysis**. This is the process of *getting to know your data*. One of the worst things you can do is to create reports without knowing how the underlying data is structured. This is particularly true of data you work with all the time. It's often a great idea to step back and really look at the data you are working with to make sure you understand what is there and what isn't.

If you have null values in a column of data, how will you handle them? If you are only getting 100 rows when you expected 10,000, what will you do?

Power BI loves working with date fields, but what if your dates are coming in as text? Or as a number?

You will have to learn how to identify these problems and correct them. The PL-300 exam may test you on how to identify and fix these problems.

In this chapter, we will cover the following exam skills:

- Identifying data anomalies
- Interrogating data statistics

Technical requirements

To complete the exercises in the chapter, you will need the following:

- Microsoft Power BI Desktop installed on a Microsoft Windows PC, with the Power Query Editor open.

- Access to some data to use. We've also provided synthetic data that can be used, which is available in the GitHub repository for this book here: `https://github.com/PacktPublishing/Microsoft-Power-BI-Data-Analyst-Certification-Guide/tree/main/example-data`.

Identifying data anomalies

We will start with the same tool, the Power BI Power Query Editor, that we used to connect to and transform our data in *Chapter 2*, *Connecting to Data Sources*. The Power Query Editor provides several tools to help us to identify anomalies.

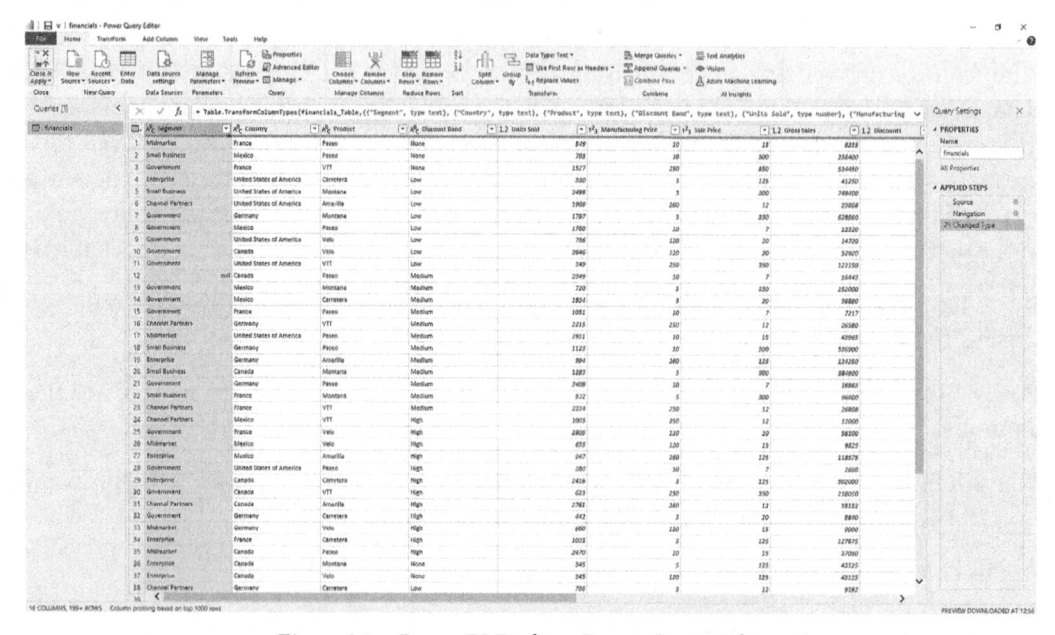

Figure 3.1 – Power BI Desktop Power Query Editor

Identifying data anomalies 37

You will find most of the tools on the **View** ribbon. You may be tested on any or all of these in the certification exam.

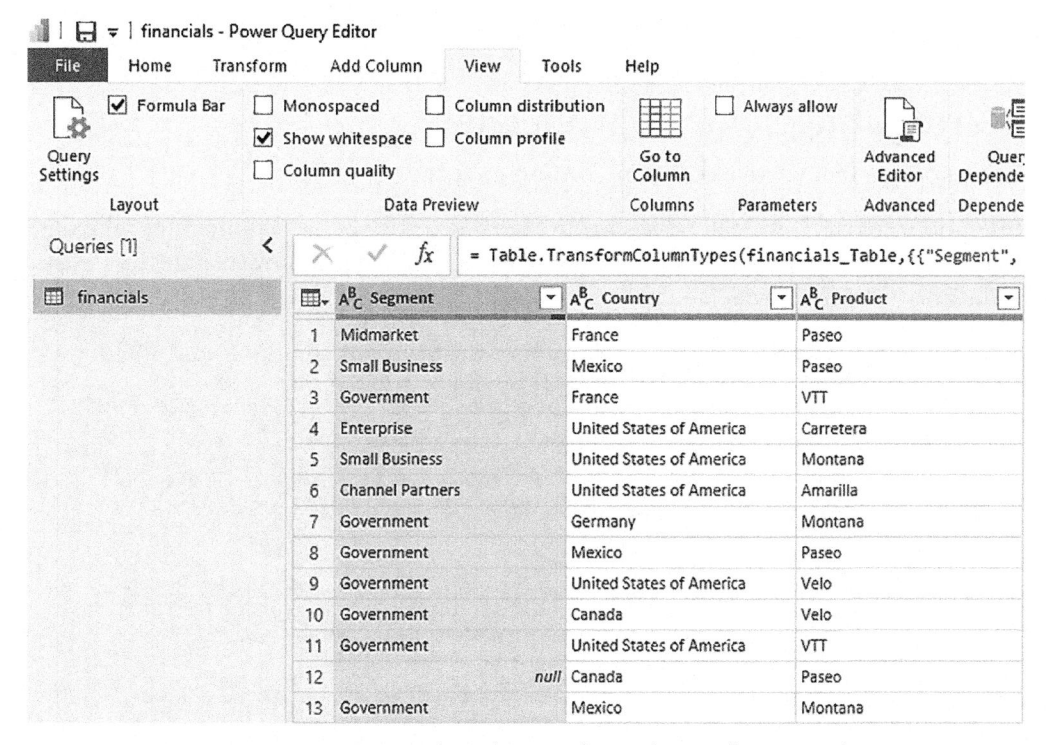

Figure 3.2 – Power Query Editor showing that we have nulls in our column

It is very important to note, and it may come up on the test, that the Power Query Editor only looks at the first 1,000 rows of data. In the lower left-hand corner of the Power Query Editor, you will see a selector to change the Power Query Editor to scan your entire dataset.

Figure 3.3 – Controlling how many columns are profiled

> **Real-World Tip**
>
> You may not want to do this against very large datasets. It will take longer and you may use all your computer's memory before profiling can finish.

Interrogating column properties

The first option that we will look at is **Column quality**.

This option will create a small table showing the percentage of rows containing valid data (green) or errors (red) or are empty (black). Remember, this will only include the statistics for the first 1,000 rows by default.

In the following example, you can see that 1% of the **Segment** column is null, 4% of **Discounts** is null, and 1% of the **Date** data has errors:

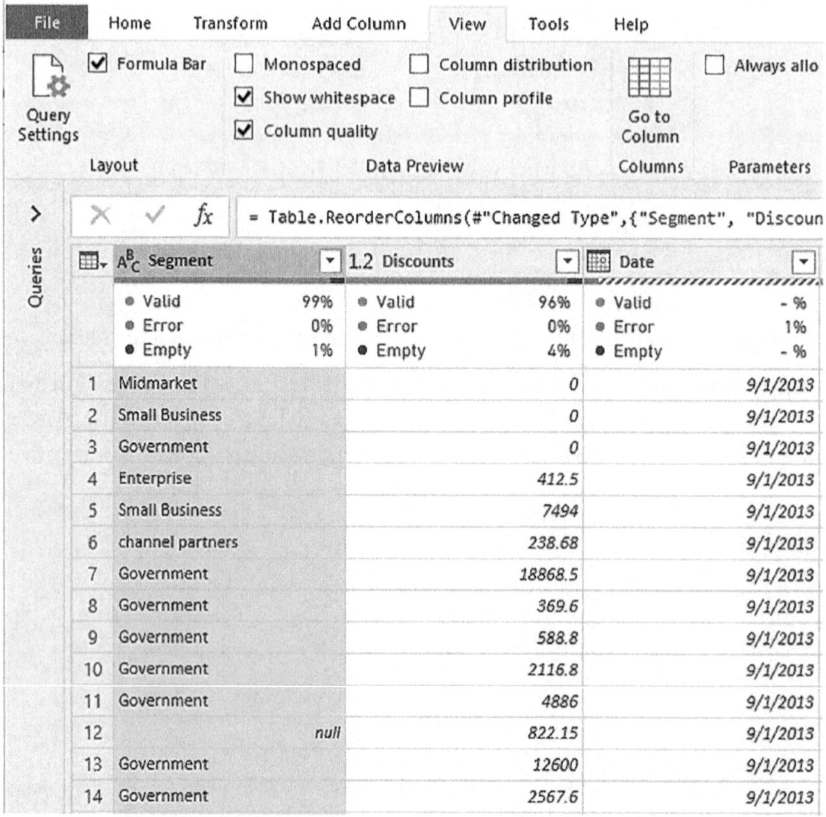

Figure 3.4 – Column quality showing how many rows in your column are valid, will return an error, or are empty

Identifying data anomalies 39

It is very easy and intuitive to see all this information immediately. Once you know about error and null rows, you can set about fixing them, if necessary.

> **Test Tip**
> Errors are often the result of a row having the wrong data type in the column: a text field where Power BI expects a numeric or date value.

For the test, it is important to remember that **Column quality** shows you the percentage of valid, error, and null rows in a column.

Examining data structures

Once you have handled any errors in your columns and decided what to do with null rows, you can start looking at your data structures.

The first thing to look at is **data types**. Your reports will run faster if you have everything set to its its correct type. You can easily change between data types using the **Transform** ribbon.

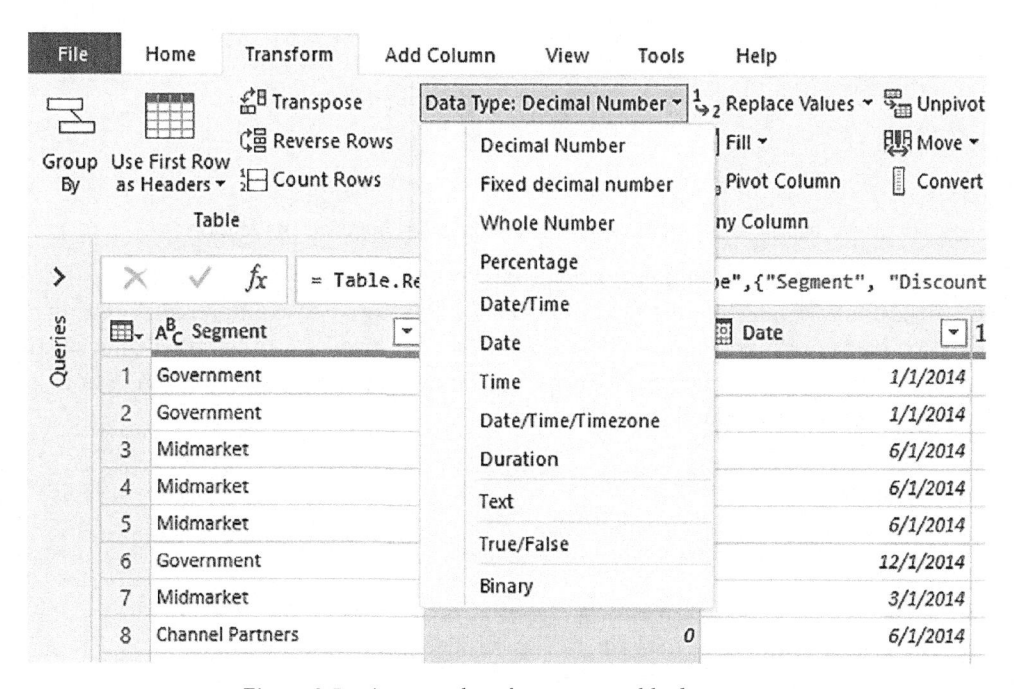

Figure 3.5 – A screenshot showing possible data types

Ensure that your data sources are providing you with data of the types that are expected. You will get errors or anomalous results if there's text where you expect a number or a date.

You can also change the type by clicking on the data type icon to the left of the column name in the **Data Preview** area of the Power Query Editor.

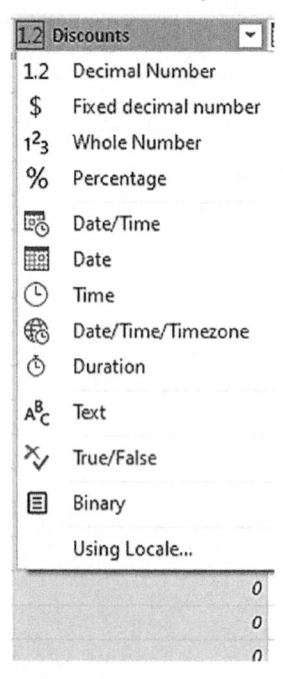

Figure 3.6 – You can also change data types in Power BI Desktop

It is typically best to set data types for fields in Power Query and then only change the categorization or formatting of a field in Power BI Desktop. For example, categorizing the numeric values of 38.889484 and -77.035278 as latitude and longitude rather than simply decimal numbers will help Power BI properly display these decimal values while not inherently changing the way they are stored.

> **Test Tip**
> Changing data can be accomplished from the Power Query Editor or Power BI Desktop.

Next, let's get a closer look at the statistics generated from your data.

Interrogating data statistics

Knowing how your data is distributed within a column can be extremely helpful. It can tell you a large amount of information in a simple, easy-to-understand format. In the Power Query Editor, there are two ways to see summarized data on a column: **Column distribution** and **Column profile**.

Column distribution

Column distribution generates a bar chart for the data in the column. This is particularly good for categorical data, such as countries, market segment, or payment type, for example. Below the bar chart, there will be two numbers, a count of distinct values in the column, including duplicates and nulls, and a count of how many values are unique.

As you can see from the following screenshot, this works better for categorical data than for continuous numbers:

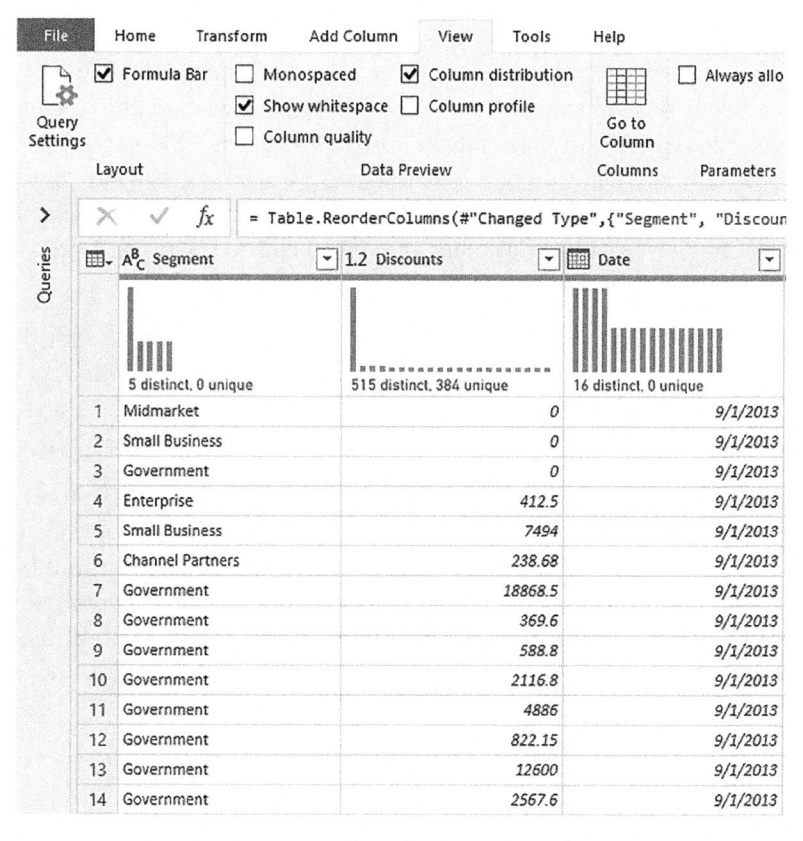

Figure 3.7 – Power Query Editor displaying how data is distributed

> **Test Tip**
>
> Look for weird or unexpected distributions of your data. If you only have five business segments, you should not see any more or any less in the graph.

The **Segment** column has only six distinct values, whereas the **Discounts** column has many distinct and many unique values. For the test, you want to remember that you can use **Column distribution** to see how many distinct and unique values you have in your column. You can also use it to generate a bar chart that shows how those values are distributed.

If we look at the **Discounts** column, maybe there's a better way to see what's going on.

Column profile

This option will give you a more detailed view of how the data is spread in your column. It will provide you with summary statistics for the first 1,000 rows, by default, of your dataset. This includes a count of how many rows Power BI is bringing in. This can give you not only a sense of how large the data in the column is but also whether you are missing data. If your original data source had 500 rows, but you are only seeing 250, then either you filtered out half your data in Power BI or it's not being retrieved from the source for some reason. This row count will also show how many rows are outliers, how many are null, and how many are empty text. It will also show the minimum value and the maximum value. If the column is marked as a text column, Power BI determines the minimum and maximum alphabetically.

If the column is marked as a numeric column, then along with all those statistics, you will see how many rows are zero, the average for the column, and the standard deviation. There is also an entry for **NaN**, which stands for **not a number**. This is the count of rows that have some non-numeric character in them.

The bar chart will show you how the values are distributed. This is a larger and easier-to-read visualization of the same data from the **Column distribution** option. The main differences, aside from the size, are that you can easily compare distributions between columns in **Column distribution**, and you can easily create a filter of your data in **Column profile**. In **Column profile**, you can hover over or click one of the bars and choose to either exclude all the rows it represents from the report or filter the report to just those rows.

Here, you can see a column profile for a numeric column. Notice that the column statistics include **Average**, **Standard deviation**, **Zero**, and **NaN**. Also, note that by hovering over one of the columns, you are presented with the **Equals** or **Does not Equal** options. Choosing either one will add a **Filtered Rows Step** to **Applied Steps** and filter the report according to which you choose.

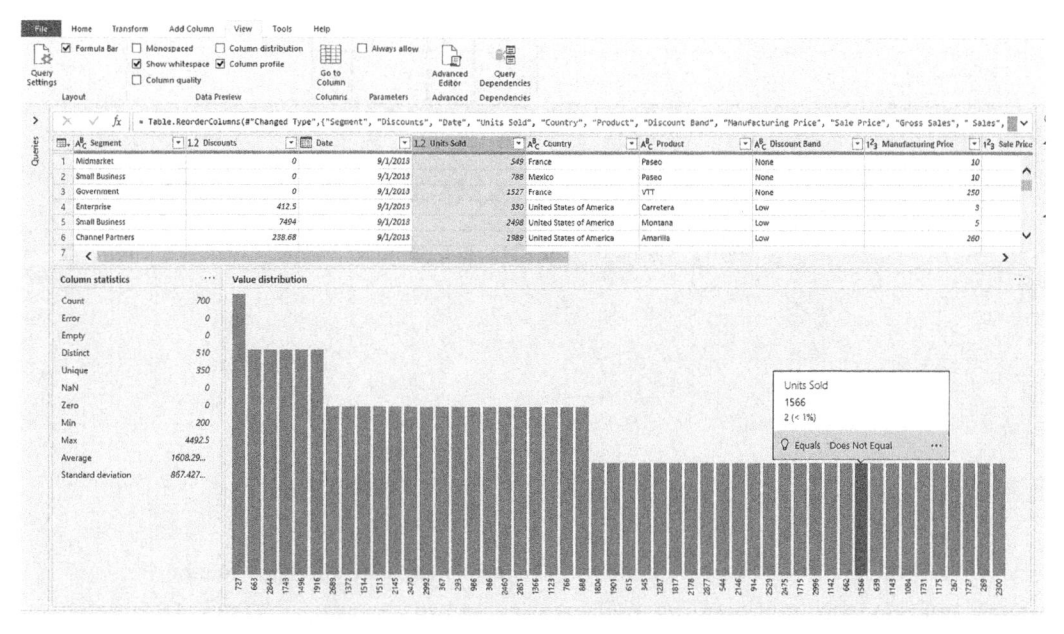

Figure 3.8 – Summary statistics and distribution for a single numeric column

Looking at the summary statistics and distribution for a single column will let you get a feel for your data, giving you a preview of what you can report on when you start adding visualization to the report page. For example, *Figure 3.8* shows us the minimum, maximum, and average values that can be used as summary values on a table visual in your report.

44 Profiling the Data

The following screenshot shows the column statistics for a text-type column. Notice that there are fewer statistics available:

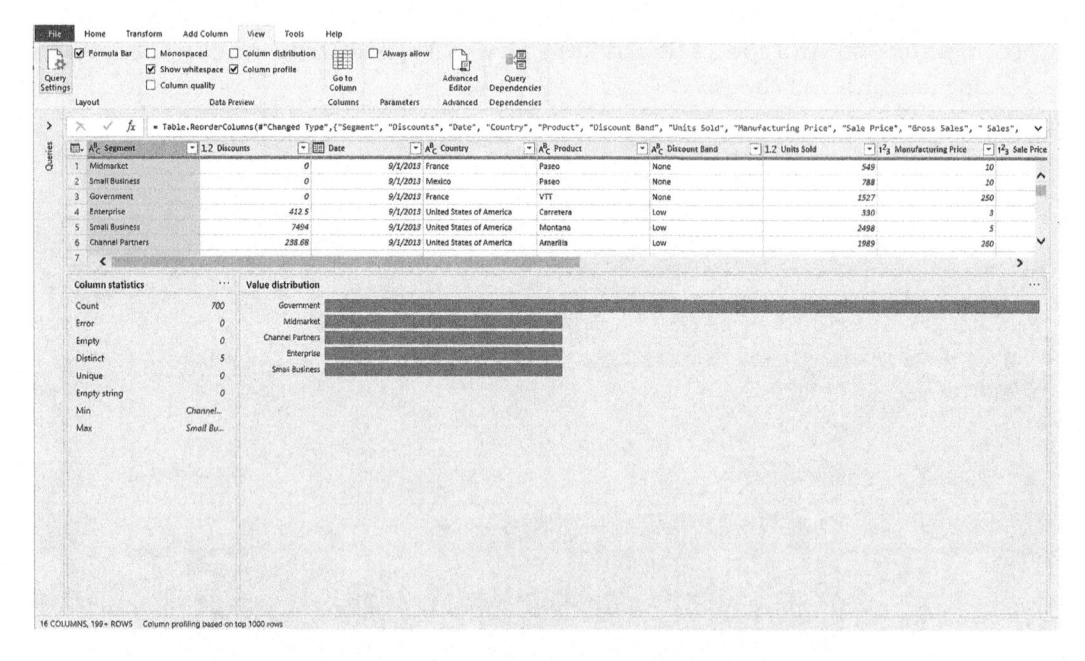

Figure 3.9 – A screenshot showing column statistics for a text type column

Notice this text column does not have an average or other number-based statistics.

Date columns have one more statistical field than text. A date column will have all the statistics as a text column, but will also have an average.

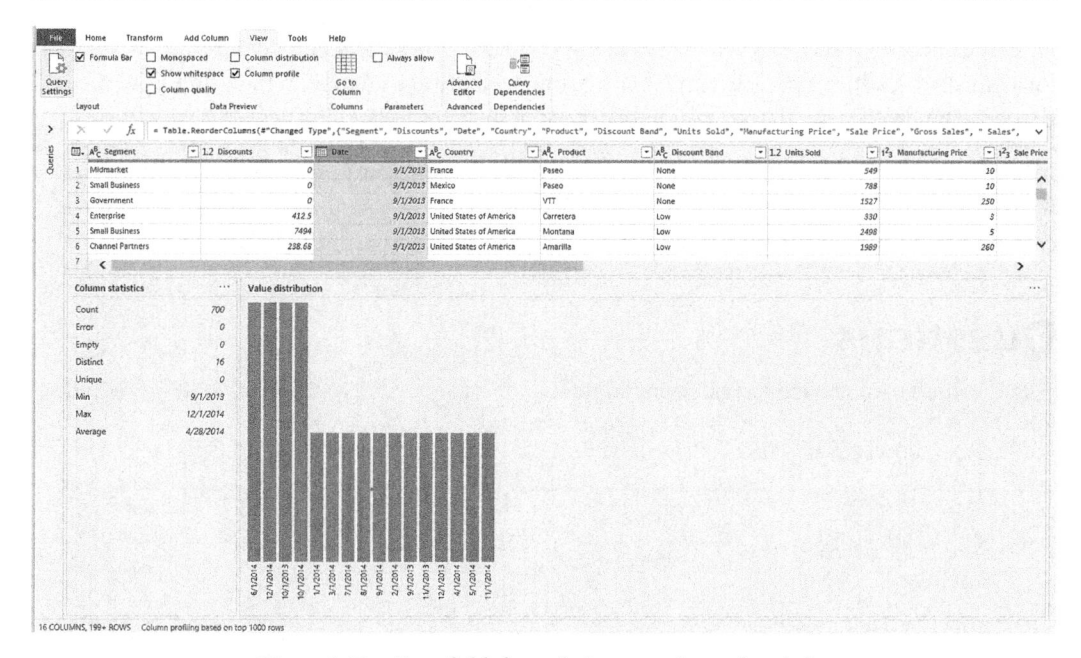

Figure 3.10 – Date fields have their own subset of statistics

Looking at individual column statistics can help you ensure that the data you are reporting on is correct. It can also provide you with some information on what to expect when you start adding visualizations to the reporting page.

Summary

In this chapter, we looked at how Power BI can help us identify data anomalies by viewing column quality. We looked at how to examine data structures and data types in the Power Query Editor. We interrogated the properties of our columns by enabling the **Column quality** setting. Finally, we explored the data statistics associated with our columns by using **Column distribution** and **Column profile**. Power BI Desktop is an easy-to-use exploratory data analysis tool. **Column quality** can quickly alert you to possible problems in your data. Having a tool that shows you how much of your data is valid, how much is null, and how much will generate errors lets you know at a glance about possible problems.

Looking at how the data is distributed in your columns can alert you to missing data. The distribution can also let you know at a glance if your data is unexpectedly skewed.

One-click access to summary statistics using **Column profile** lets you get an immediate feel for your data. **Column profile** can let you know what kind of data you have and how it is shaped. The profile can also let you know if you may want to keep or get rid of a column.

In the next chapter, we will look at cleaning and organizing your data for reporting. You will learn about cross-filter direction and security filtering, calculated tables, hierarchies, calculated columns, row-level security, object-level security, and the Q&A feature.

Questions

1. Which tool is used to transform data?

    A. Power Edit
    B. Transform Data
    C. Query Tool
    D. Power Query

2. By default, the Power Query Editor will use how many rows of data?

    A. 100 rows
    B. 1,000 rows
    C. 2,000 rows
    D. Entire dataset

3. Column distribution view can be enabled by selecting the checkbox under which tab on the ribbon?

    A. Tools
    B. Statistics
    C. View
    D. Home

4

Cleansing, Transforming, and Shaping Data

For data to be used effectively in any kind of reporting, analytics, or AI use case, it must be clean and ready to be joined or shaped with other data. When data is viewed only in the context of the source system that creates it, we're often limited in how we can use it.

For example, if we have sales data coming from point-of-sale terminals, then we can draw conclusions about the total amount of sales completed on any given day, week, or month by simply summing the sales for a given time period. However, if we could join the sales data with weather data, then we could possibly draw conclusions about the impact weather has on sales. Perhaps we believe that rainy weather will have a negative impact on the sales for a given location. In order to test this hypothesis by correlating sales data with weather data, we'll need to ensure things such as that the date and time fields in the weather data can be joined with the date and time fields in our sales data (since weather and sales both change from day to day). If the sales data represents a date and time in the format "2021-10-14T11:03" but the weather data represents the same date and time in the format "10-14-2021 11:00am," then we must do some shaping of the data in order to help test our hypothesis. Likewise, after we've profiled our data, if we discover we are missing data or it has become corrupt, we'll need to be able to cleanse the data in order to make it usable.

Power BI includes a component called Power Query that allows us to not only connect to data but also apply data transformations, cleansing operations, and shaping to data to enable the creation of new datasets that are used as part of the Power BI data model. This chapter will get you familiar with Power Query so you can use it to shape and transform data. By learning how to use Power Query, you will be able to build data models to use for interactive Power BI reports and dashboards.

In this chapter, we're going to cover the following topics:

- Accessing Power Query in Power BI Desktop
- Sorting and filtering
- Managing columns
- Column transformations
- Row transformations
- Combining data
- Enriching data with AI
- Advanced operations

Technical requirements

For this chapter, you'll need the following:

- Microsoft Power BI Desktop installed on a Microsoft Windows PC.
- Access to some data to use. We've also provided synthetic data that can be used, which is available on the GitHub repository for this book here: https://github.com/PacktPublishing/Microsoft-Power-BI-Data-Analyst-Certification-Guide/tree/main/example-data.

Accessing Power Query in Power BI

Power Query is accessible inside the Power BI Desktop tool by connecting to a data source and then clicking **Transform Data** (rather than **Load** or **Cancel**). For existing data models, Power Query can be accessed by right-clicking on the query in the **Fields** pane and clicking **Edit query**.

The Power Query window provides a ribbon at the top with tabs for **Home**, **Transform**, **Add Column**, **View**, **Tools**, and **Help**. There is also a **Query Settings** pane on the right-hand side that shows the name of the query and the steps applied to the data that get built up as you transform the data. The **Applied Steps** pane makes it easy to undo or redo different transforms and immediately see the impact of those transforms on the data, which is shown in the center of the window. The last part of the user interface is the **Queries** pane on the left-hand side of the window. This shows all queries that make up the data model and allows you to flip back and forth between them as you're transforming and shaping data in your data model.

Unless stated otherwise, all data transformation capabilities discussed in this chapter will happen in Power Query. Let's start with sorting and filtering data after we've connected to it.

Sorting and filtering

Sorting data is a key capability that helps us understand more about the data. When data is displayed in Power Query, it is shown in tabular format with rows and columns and sorting is easily accomplished by clicking the ▼ button on the column you want to sort on. From there, you can select **Sort Ascending** or **Sort Descending**. When this happens, a step gets added to the **Applied Steps** pane and you can instantly see the data sorted in the center of the window. Sorting can also be achieved by clicking the name of the column and then clicking the appropriate button under the **Home** ribbon under **Sort**.

To filter data in a column, you also use the ▼ button on the column you want to filter on and you see some options for **Remove Empty** and data type-specific filtering. The data type filtering options are shown in the following table:

Data Type	Filtering Options
Decimal Number Fixed Decimal Number Whole Number Percentage	Equals Does not Equal Greater Than Greater Than Or Equal To Less Than Less Than Or Equal To Between
Text	Equals Does not Equal Begins With Does Not Begin With Ends With Does Not End With Contains Does not Contain
True/False	Equals Does not Equal

Data Type	Filtering Options
Date/Time Date Time Date/Time/Timezone Duration	Equal
	Before
	After
	Between
	In the Next
	In the Previous
	Is Earliest
	Is Latest
	Is Not Earliest
	Is Not Latest
	Year
	Next/This/Last
	Year to Date
	Quarter
	Next/This/Last
	Specific quarter 1-4
	Month
	Next/This/Last
	Specific month January – December
	Week
	Next/This/Last
	Day
	Tomorrow
	Today
	Yesterday
	Hour
	Next/This/Last
	Minute
	Next/This/Last
	Second
	Next/This/Last
	Custom Filter

Figure 4.1 – Filtering options by data type

A core capability of working with tabular data as we have in Power Query is managing the columns and rows of data. In the next section, we'll explore how we can manage columns.

Managing columns

There are many kinds of transformations that can be done on columns. The first step for columns is often identifying which columns are needed and whether there are any that are not needed for the given data model.

Power Query makes it easy to change the order of columns; just simply drag and drop by clicking on the column name. It's also possible to remove columns by right-clicking and selecting **Remove**. Other column operations on the right-click menu include **Remove Other Columns**, **Duplicate Column**, and **Add Column from Examples**.

It's also possible to make these changes using buttons on the **Home** ribbon under **Manage Columns**. The **Choose Columns** capability under **Manage Columns** is an efficient way of selecting many columns to be removed at once because it presents you with a full list of all columns preselected with a checkbox and you only need to uncheck the columns you'd like to remove and click **OK**. After the operation completes, you'll be left with only those columns where a checkbox remained.

Once we've ordered, removed, or possibly duplicated columns in our dataset, we also need to know how to perform more advanced transformations.

Using column transformations

Columns in a query can be transformed in multiple ways. The simplest transform that can take place on a column is to rename it. Often, columns in source systems are named in a meaningful way within the context of the source system. For example, within a point-of-sale system, there might be a table to record each sale transaction. This table would contain a column named `UnitPrice`, which is used to record the price of each item in a sales transaction. When this data is summed to get total sales for the hour or for the day, then the name `UnitPrice` no longer makes sense in the context of an analytical data model, so it would be best to rename this column to be `TotalSales`.

To rename a column, right-click the column name and click **Rename**. Columns can also be renamed by selecting the column (clicking on the column name) and then clicking **Rename** under the **Any Column** group in the **Transform** tab on the ribbon.

Another key aspect of column transformations in Power Query is ensuring the proper data type is set for each column to enable the needed data transformation or shaping required. Power Query considers the source systems when deciding on the data type to set by default; for example, if you connect to a relational database that will have defined data types, then this is used to help define the data types set in Power Query. For some data sources, Power Query needs to make its own guess on the data type, although it's important to understand that this default data type can be changed. It is also possible to force Power Query to detect the data type of a column using the **Detect Data Type** button under the **Any Column** group in the **Transform** tab on the ribbon.

To change the data type of a column, right-click the column and select the type you'd like to change to under the **Change Data Type** submenu. This can also be accomplished under the **Transform** tab in the ribbon by clicking the **Data Type** drop-down menu under **Any Column** and selecting the type you'd like to set.

Now, we'll look at the other column transforms.

Transforming any data type columns

First, let's look at column transformations available for any data type:

- **Replace Values** – Replaces a defined value in the selected column with another value. This is used to replace values in the data, like how Find and Replace is used to replace values in a text file.

- **Replace Errors** – Replaces error values in the selected column with another value. This is used like Replace Values except it's looking for error values in the data.

- **Fill** – Replaces empty or null values in a column with the value from the adjacent row, the adjacent row being defined as either **Fill Up** or **Fill Down**.

- **Pivot Column** – Similar to how pivot works in Microsoft Excel, this will create new columns using values in the selected column and turn values for each row into new rows for the newly created columns.

- **Unpivot Columns** – Generates **Attribute** and **Value** columns for selected or unselected columns.

- **Convert to List** – Converts the selected column into a list. Lists are another M query language primitive and useful for things such as parameters.

Transforming text columns

Column transformations for text data type columns include the following:

- **Split Column** – This allows you to split a column of text by delimiter, number of characters, positions, lowercase to uppercase, uppercase to lowercase, digit to non-digit, and non-digit to digit.
- **Format** – This provides formatting options that are applied to every row of the selected column. Options include changing all text to lowercase or uppercase, capitalizing each word, and trimming spaces at the beginning or end of the text. This can also be used to add a prefix or suffix to text or remove control characters.
- **Extract** – **Extract** is like split column capability, but it just leaves the extract value in the existing column rather than splitting a new column into two. For example, if there are delimiters in your text and you only need the text before the delimiter, then this can be used rather than splitting and then removing the unneeded column.
- **Parse** – When working with XML or JSON data, this is used to transform the embedded XML or JSON data and turn it into tabular data.

Transforming number columns

Number data type columns can be transformed in these ways:

- **Statistics** – Provides basic statistical functions to perform against the selected number column. Functions include sum, minimum, maximum, median, average, standard deviation, count values, and count distinct values.
- **Standard** – Performs standard mathematic operations such as adding, subtracting, multiplying, dividing, integer-divide, modulo, percentage, and percentage of a value you enter against each data value in the column.
- **Scientific** – Performs scientific mathematic operations such as absolute value, power (square, cube, n), square root, exponent, log (base-10, natural), or factorial against each data value in the column.
- **Trigonometry** – Calculates trigonometric functions against each data value in the column. Functions include sine, cosine, tangent, arcsine, arccosine, and arctangent.
- **Rounding** – Calculates the rounded value of each data value in the column. Specified as rounding up, down, or to a specified decimal place.
- **Information** – Transforms a number into a true/false type based on whether the data value is odd or even. Can also change data values into 1 or -1 depending on the sign of the numeric value.

Transforming date and time columns

Lastly, these are the date and time column transformations available in Power Query:

- **Date** – Changes the date values in the data to specific dates that relate to the date in the data or an age in days or finds the earliest or latest date in the data. It's also possible to change it to just the year, month, or day or day of the week, quarter, and so on using the **Date** transform.

- **Time** – Changes, extracts, or aggregates the time values. This also works on columns with the date/time data type.

- **Duration** – Extracts components (such as just the seconds or just the minutes) from a duration in the data. This also allows for the transformation into decimal forms of the duration in years, days, hours, minutes, and seconds. You can also multiply or divide each value in the data by a value entered or perform mathematical functions (sum, min, max, average, or median) against the values in the data.

Adding columns

There are multiple ways to add columns to a query using Power Query. New columns can be created using typed-in examples in a low-code experience or new columns can be created using Power Query M formula functions (`https://docs.microsoft.com/powerquery-m/quick-tour-of-the-power-query-m-formula-language`) to derive new columns from existing or generated data. These commands are available under the **Add Column** tab in the ribbon of Power Query:

- **Column From Example** – This allows you to simply start typing the values you'd like to see in the new column, and from there Power Query will generate new column data using column operations in the examples you manually provide. This is useful if you're not aware of other column transform capabilities because it shows you the detected transform.

- **Custom Column** – This is where you can specify the specific M formula to transform data from other columns into the new column. The full syntax reference for the Power Query M formula is available on the Microsoft documentation website (`https://docs.microsoft.com/powerquery-m/power-query-m-function-reference`).

- **Invoke Custom Function** – This is used when you've created custom functions either directly from M query code or by generating a function from a query that uses parameters. This provides reusability across custom functions for multiple queries and columns.

- **Conditional Column** – This provides the ability to create a new column of data values based on values from another column using IF, ELSE IF, and ELSE logic to determine the values of the new column. For example, this would allow you to make a new column based on unique values in a column and do it using a low-code GUI interface to define the logic.
- **Index Column** – Index columns are used when you need to generate a column of increasing numbers for each row. This is often used when generating surrogate keys for a table or query. Values can start at 0 or 1 or be custom-defined along with the incremental value for each row.
- **Duplicate Column** – This simply duplicates the selected column.

It is also possible to add a new column using the same text, number, and data and time transforms discussed previously by invoking these under the **Add Column** tab in the ribbon. Some column transformations are also accessible from the right-click menu when clicking on a column name.

Next, we will discover row transformations. The ability to transform rows when needed is important as it helps ensure data quality and helps us build analytics that can be trustworthy.

Using row transformations

In addition to the row transformations mentioned in the *Sorting and filtering* section, there are row transformations that can be helpful under the **Transform** tab of the ribbon:

- **Replace Values** – This provides a user interface where you define the value being searched for and the value you want to replace. It works the same as Find and Replace works on most text editors, such as Notepad.
- **Replace Errors** – This is similar to **Replace Values** where it provides an option for the replacement of rows that contain error values. The definition of an error will depend on the data type.
- **Reverse Rows** – This is a way of sorting the rows such that the data is shown or stored in reverse order. The first row becomes the last, the last row becomes the first, and all order in between is preserved.
- **Transpose** – Transpose functions as both a row and a column transformation as it turns each row into its own column and each column into a row.

In addition to the data cleansing and transformation capabilities of Power Query, there is also the ability to combine data from multiple queries or sources. In the next section, we'll see how we can combine data using Power Query.

Combining data

Data can be combined from multiple queries or even multiple source files depending on the nature of the data connected in the data model.

Power Query uses different terminology compared to technologies such as relational databases, so it's important to understand both the concepts as well as the terminology used for the PL-300 exam.

Using merge queries

Merge queries are used when we want to merge or combine columns from multiple queries where some columns are different. This often happens in **data warehouse** environments as data tends to be **normalized** or split across multiple tables (imported into a Power BI data model as a query). For more information on why data is normalized in a data warehouse, we recommend reading *The Data Warehouse Toolkit: The Definitive Guide to Dimensional Modeling* by Ralph Kimball. Tables contain key columns that allow individual records to be merged or joined together when needed. Normalizing data is standard practice for properly designed data warehouses. For more information on **data warehouse design**, we recommend looking at resources on **dimensional modeling**, such as `https://wikipedia.org/wiki/Dimensional_modeling`.

In order to use merge queries in Power Query, you need to have at least two queries that contain data that you'd like to merge into one query by bringing together columns from both queries. Ideally, these queries contain columns that allow the data to relate to each other, typically called **key** or **join key** columns. If the queries don't contain a key, then it may be possible to use other data transformation capabilities (as discussed earlier in the *Using column transformations* section) to create keys that would allow the data to be merged properly.

Using merge queries requires one of the two queries to be selected from the **Queries** pane on the leftmost side of the Power Query Editor window. Then, you click the **Merge Queries** button under **Combine** on the **Home** tab of the ribbon. There is the option to just merge the queries or merge the queries as a new query.

The selected table will show at the top of the merge user interface that is shown and the second query can be selected from the drop-down menu in the center. Now both queries are shown in the preview, and you only need to select the key column or join columns from both queries and then select **Join Kind**. There are six types of joins supported by merge:

- **Left Outer** – Brings all rows from the first query and only matching records from the second query.
- **Right Outer** – Brings all rows from the second query and only matching records from the first query.
- **Full Outer** – Brings all rows from both queries, no matter whether they are matching or not. If there are any rows that do not match, this will create null values for some columns.
- **Inner** – Brings only rows that match from both queries.
- **Left Anti** – Brings only rows from the first query that don't have matching rows in the second query.
- **Right Anti** – Brings only rows from the second query that don't have matching rows in the first query.

Additionally, you can use **fuzzy matching** for the join, which means the values in the key columns do not need to match exactly. Fuzzy matching can be configured using these settings:

- **Similarity threshold** – This setting needs to be a decimal value between 0.00 and 1.00. A value of 1.00 means every value needs to match exactly, while a value of 0.00 means any values will match.
- **Ignore case** – Without this checkbox enabled, values will have to match exactly, while this checkbox will enable values to match even if the case in the text does not match.
- **Match by combining text parts** – When this option is enabled, Power Query will try to match parts of the text to find matches. For example, if one column contains "wind" and another contains "mill," then Power Query will try to use these two parts to match against "windmill."
- **Maximum number of matches** – This option can be used to enforce a limited number of matches to take place during the merge. For example, if you only want to return the first match (not all matches), then using "1" in this option should be used.

- **Transformation table** – This option will keep track of fuzzy matches and record instances where "wind" and "mill" match to "windmill." This table needs to contain **To** and **From** columns.

Append queries

Append queries are used when you want to combine rows from multiple queries into a single query. For example, a point-of-sale database might keep track of sales for each store in unique tables. After connecting to the sales database and each table getting a unique query in the Power BI data model, an append query can be used to append or add the rows from one query to another. Append queries need at least two queries to combine; however, it is possible to select *three or more tables* and Power Query will combine them all.

Append queries work best when the columns between all the queries match exactly. Differing column names will result in some rows having null values as they don't have a corresponding value for the column in the other table. Append queries can sometimes handle different data types in matching columns by allowing whole numbers and text to be presented in the append output. If this occurs, it is advised to manage the column and set a unified data type across all rows in the column. In the relational database world, we often call this type of query a `UNION` query, as it combines records from multiple tables into a single table.

To use append queries, just click **Append Queries** under **Combine** on the **Home** tab of the ribbon. Then, you just need to select the queries you'd like to append and click **OK**.

Combine files

Sometimes, data is stored as files in a filesystem. In cases like that, it may be ideal to simply select an entire directory or folder of files as a data source, especially when all files have a similar layout or structure. For example, we may receive an extract of sales data from an external partner and that extract may come in CSV files partitioned by month. All the extracted files came from the same source system at the partner, so they all have the same structure. We can use the folder data source in Power BI to connect to the folder of files, which will set up a query in Power Query that lists each file, the extension of the file, and the folder path to each file, among other attributes.

Once the query to the folder is in place, we can then use the **combine files** capability to bring the data from all these files together into one query in a manner like append queries (records from each file get combined into a single query with data in matching columns stored together).

To use combine files, just open a folder of files that can be read by Power BI (see *Chapter 2, Connecting to Data Sources*, for supported data file formats) and then click **Combine Files** under **Combine** on the **Home** tab of the ribbon. Power Query will evaluate the files and start with showing a preview and the detected file attributes (**File Origin, Delimiter, Data Type Detection**, and so on). For CSV and Excel data types, each file found can be examined before the combine action executes to ensure proper configurations (delimiter, worksheet, and so on) are set.

> **Note**
> Data files in the folder need to be of the same data type and the same structure for combine files to be most successful. Different data types will be met with an error, while differing file structures will result in null values where column names do not match.

We've now explored many methods for combining or mashing up data, correcting errors in our data, and performing data analysis. The next section will uncover how we can use advanced AI tools available in Power BI and other services that unlock even more value from our data.

Enriching data with AI

Power Query also includes ways to enhance data using AI services from Microsoft. These features integrate with **Microsoft Azure Cognitive Services** and require a **Power BI Premium** capacity or per-user license. The options for **AI Insights** include the following:

- **Language detection**
- **Key phrase extraction**
- **Sentiment analysis**
- **Image tagging**

Let's consider why each of these would be useful.

Language detection

When data contains free-text fields, and we want to use those in analysis, it's important to first ensure we know the language used in the text. The accuracy and usability of subsequent text analysis are enhanced when the language of a given text block is known. AI Insights provides capabilities to detect language and it is recommended to start with language detection before performing key phrase extraction or sentiment analysis. AI Insights can detect up to 120 languages and returns both the name of the language as well as the ISO code of the identified language. For example, the ISO code of the English language is "en."

Key phrase extraction

When analyzing text, especially larger-sized groupings of text, it's valuable to shorten or break down the key phrases from that text to better understand it. For example, if we have the sentence *"Well!" thought Alice to herself, "after such a fall as this, I shall think nothing of tumbling downstairs!"* from Lewis Carrol's *Alice's Adventures in Wonderland* we can see that the **key phrases** or **keywords** are *tumbling*, *stairs*, *Alice*, and *fall*.

Key phrase extraction is useful for categorizing text. For example, if there are multiple customer surveys that contain the same key phrases or keywords, then it's possible that multiple customers are commenting on the same topic or idea. This makes it easier to identify the most important topics from a customer survey based on the contents of a free-text field in the data. This analysis can be reliably completed by the AI Insights capability without having to rely on a human to read each survey response and manually come up with the keywords.

Sentiment analysis

A sentiment is a feeling or judgment of something and in the field of analytics, sentiment analysis is a type of language or **text-processing algorithm** that will break down parts of a text grouping into at least three categories: *positive*, *neutral*, and *negative*.

In Power Query, the sentiment analysis capability will evaluate a text input and return a score. For example, if you have a query of customer survey results, there might be a free-text field where customers write down their thoughts about your retail organization. The survey takers will complete the survey and might respond with text such as "*This was a wonderful shopping experience*" or "*You didn't have the product I wanted*." When the survey results are compiled, these free-text values will be stored in a text field and the sentiment analysis feature can decide whether the sentiment of the text entered is positive, negative, or neutral. If there are 500 survey responses, then it's possible to use this capability combined with other aggregation and transformation capabilities to determine the sum of positive, negative, and neutral results based on the free-text field alone.

The sentiment analysis capability takes the entire input field as input into the pretrained algorithm so, as with any text analytics process, it's important to understand how this works, as there may be blocks of text such as "*At first, I didn't find the product I wanted but there was a very helpful associate who showed me where the product was and helped ensure I had everything I needed.*" In this example, there are parts that could be interpreted as negative and others that could be interpreted as positive; if analysis is performed on the entire block of text, then it's likely to have a positive sentiment.

Sentiment scoring will return a decimal value between 0 and 1, where negative sentiment can be interpreted as being between 0 and 0.5 while positive sentiment is 0.5 and greater. When sentiment is detected as neutral, a value of 0.5 is returned.

It's also important to note that support for this feature varies by language. Currently, English, German, Spanish, and French are supported, with others in preview.

Image tagging

Sometimes, data in a query contains an image (Base64 encoded) or a URL of an image. In those cases, we can use the **image tagging** capability of AI Insights. The image tagging capability uses a pretrained algorithm that is trained to identify over 2,000 objects for general object recognition. It is not trained to identify specialized objects or non-widely known objects. For example, the image in *Figure 4.2* of a bicycle returns the tags "grass," "outdoor," "bicycle," "tree," "red," "parked," "transport," "sidewalk," and "walkway":

Figure 4.2 – Public domain image of a bicycle
Source: https://live.staticflickr.com/3954/15655615295_3a46e83728_b.jpg

With these tags, we can draw conclusions that this is a photo of a red bicycle that is outdoors and parked near trees, grass, and a sidewalk or walkway. If we remove all the words that are not product descriptions, we can understand that this is a "red bicycle." The way this could be useful for our retail business example would be to enrich product information with additional metadata that can help categorize products.

To use the AI Insights capabilities in Power Query, you simply need to click the **Text Analytics** button under **AI Insights** on the **Home** or **Add Column** tabs of the ribbon. You will then be asked to sign into your account used for Power BI. This will perform the checks to ensure you have access to Power BI Premium. Then, you'll see the three options for **Text Analytics**: **Detect language**, **Extract key phrases**, and **Score sentiment**. At the bottom, there is a drop-down menu to select which Premium capacity should be used to execute this AI process and on the right-hand side, there are options for each algorithm. For each algorithm, you just need to select the column that contains the text to be used as input for the selected algorithm. The ISO code for the language used in the text data is an optional parameter for **Extract key phrases** and **Score sentiment**. After clicking **OK**, new columns will be added to the query:

AI Insights algorithm	New column(s) added to query
Detect language	Detect language.Detected Language Name
	Detect language.Detected language ISO Code
Extract key phrases	Extract key phrases
	Extract key phrases.KeyPhrase
Score sentiment	Score sentiment
Tag images	Tag images.Tags
	Tag images.Json
	Tag images.Tag
	Tag images.Confidence
	Tag images.ErrorMessage

Figure 4.3 – List of output columns from each AI Insights function

These built-in AI capabilities make enriching data very easy with minimal expertise needed. Now, we will look at how we can enrich data further using advanced, integrated capabilities with the Azure **Machine Learning** (**ML**) service.

Azure ML

Like how AI Insights allows integration with the pretrained text analytics and computer vision models previously described, it is also possible to use custom-trained models from Azure ML within Power Query. Many organizations use the Azure ML cloud service to build custom ML models for scalable predictive analysis.

To use the Azure ML capability, you must not only be a Power BI Premium user but also have a **Reader role** for deployed models in the Azure ML service. The Azure ML integration works like the **Cognitive Services** (text analytics, computer vision) integration we used for language detection, key phrase extraction, sentiment scoring, and image tagging, where a desired model or algorithm is selected along with an input column. Output columns will vary depending on the nature of the model used.

The AI capabilities of Power Query can be useful and provide a unique set of capabilities not offered by other data transformation tools in Power Query. In the next section, we'll discuss advanced operations that allow you to fine-tune your data in Power BI using different programming languages.

Using advanced operations of Power Query

Power Query is truly a powerful tool for data transformation that helps to enable capabilities that often meet all the needs for modern reporting, analytics, and visual storytelling. While this is true, there may be cases where advanced operations need to take place to meet the business needs. For these cases, Power BI provides additional capabilities that we'll discuss now.

Using the Advanced Editor

At the heart of Power Query is the data mashup engine. This engine uses the Power Query M language for defining inputs, transformations, and outputs. The M language is a case-sensitive and functional language that is like **F#** (https://fsharp.org/). The Power Query user interface provides a fast and efficient way of generating Power Query M code that allows developers to be productive. At the same time, the **Advanced Editor** functionality also allows the generated M code to be viewed and edited if needed. It's also possible to create a Power BI dataset using Power Query and only write the M code manually, using the Advanced Editor.

Microsoft provides a full reference of the Power Query M formula language at this website: https://docs.microsoft.com/powerquery-m/. The PL-300 exam is not an exam on the Power Query M language, but it is advised to know the basic structure of a Power Query M formula.

Power Query M formulas contain values made up of variables and expressions. These components are contained within a `let` expression that also uses `in`. For example, this is a basic method of manually entering three records of sales ID and sales date data into a query:

```
let sales = Table.FromRecords({
    [SaleID = 1, SaleDate = "2021-10-16"],
    [SaleID = 2, SaleDate = "2021-10-16"],
    [SaleID = 3, SaleDate = "2021-10-17"]})
in
    sales
```

Once the data is in the query, it's possible to transform it using the variety of available functions, such as transforming a text data type to a date data type for the `SaleDate` column in our data:

```
let
    sales = Table.FromRecords({
    [SaleID = 1, SaleDate = "2021-10-16"],
    [SaleID = 2, SaleDate = "2021-10-16"],
    [SaleID = 3, SaleDate = "2021-10-17"]}),
    #"Changed Type" = Table.TransformColumnTypes(sales,{{"SaleDate", type date}})
in
    #"Changed Type"
```

By adding the line after our data, we can use the `TransformColumnTypes` function to transform the `SaleDate` column from a text type to a date type. The value after `in` also changes as this defines where we are in the stage of transformation. As more transformations get added to the code, `in` will typically define the latest changes to the data. This enables easy undoing and navigation of the list of transformations within the Power Query window.

Microsoft provides a full reference of the Power Query M functions available here: `https://docs.microsoft.com/powerquery-m/power-query-m-function-reference`.

To access the Advanced Editor in Power Query, click **Advanced Editor** under the **Advanced** section on the **View** tab of the ribbon.

Using the Query Dependencies tool

For complex data models, it's very helpful to understand the relationship between different queries, staging queries, and transformations. While the data model view in the main Power BI window provides a nice relationship view of the different queries in a data model, it shows the end-product of the work completed in Power Query. To see the full picture of what is happening with Power Query, the **Query Dependencies** tool can be used. The **Query Dependencies** tool gives a graphical picture of all data sources, merge and append queries, AI functions, and other transformations that take place within a data model.

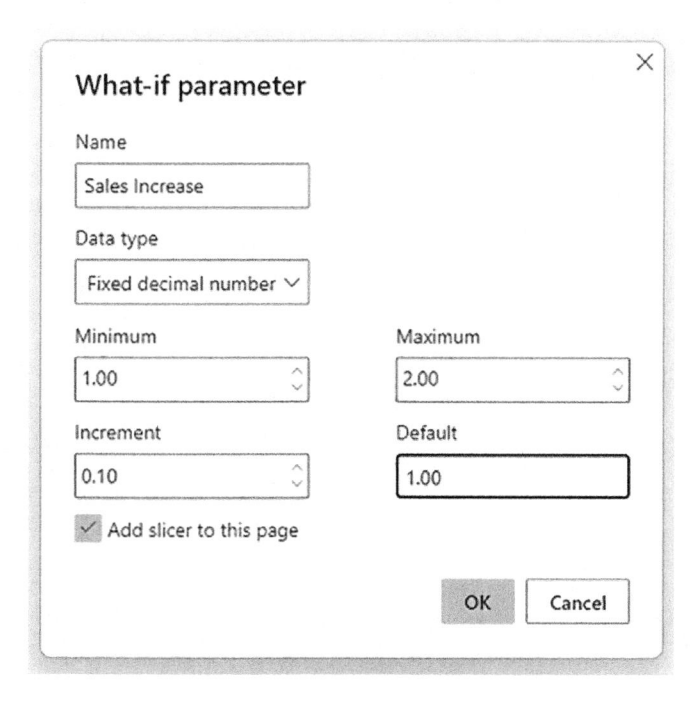

Figure 4.4 – Query Dependencies tool

To access the **Query Dependencies** tool, click **Query Dependencies** under the **Dependencies** section of the **View** tab on the Power Query ribbon, as shown in *Figure 4.4*.

R and Python scripts

In addition to all the capabilities of Power Query, there is also an option to utilize Python or R to help transform data in Power Query. **Python** (https://www.python.org/) is an **open source**, interpreted, and general-purpose programming language that is often used in **data science**, **data visualization**, and **ML** applications today. **R** (https://www.r-project.org/) is an **open source** statistical programming language that is also used in data science and data visualization applications.

This requires the computer running Power BI Desktop/Power Query to also have the R or Python execution environment installed. To execute Python scripts in Power BI, there are required libraries that must be installed in our Python environment: `pandas` (https://pandas.pydata.org/) and `matplotlib` (https://matplotlib.org/). `pandas` is an open source library for data transformation and analysis, while `matplotlib` is an open source library for data visualization. Installation of these libraries in your Python environment may vary but is usually accomplished by running the following commands:

```
python -m pip install pandas
python -m pip install matplotlib
```

Or, run the following commands:

```
pip3 install pandas
pip3 install matplotlib
```

Once the required environment and/or libraries are installed, you can configure Power BI to use these on the **Options** screen under **Options and Settings** on the **File** tab of the ribbon. Set the location of the R or Python environment you'd like to use with Power BI by selecting it in the drop-down menu under the appropriate setting.

With the R and Python scripting capabilities, it's possible to use these additional data transformation and analysis languages to prepare data in Power Query for reporting and visualization with Power BI.

Summary

In this chapter, we learned about the vast array of data transformation and mashup capabilities that are provided by Power Query inside Power BI. We started with sorting and filtering, which allow data to be ordered and filtered as required. After that, we looked at managing columns and the transformations we can make to those columns to help shape the structure of the data in our data model. Row transformations also played a key role in our understanding of how data quality impacts the overall value of the data model, because if we have null or error values in our data, we won't be able to draw many conclusions from the data; row transformations in Power Query allow us to handle those cases.

Then, we looked at how Power Query can be used to combine data. Data can be combined using merge queries and append queries. We also looked at how data can be enriched using pretrained AI capabilities as well as integration with the Azure ML service.

Lastly, we looked at advanced data transformation capabilities using the Power Query M language, R, and Python scripting. These advanced capabilities make the data transformation possibilities endless.

In the next chapter, we will look at designing a data model. A well-designed data model will help make creating dynamic and impactful reports and dashboards easy. A properly designed data model is also required to ensure reports and dashboards meet business requirements.

Questions

1. If you need to transform a column by adding a prefix to every record, which transform would you use?

    A. Format

    B. Pivot

    C. Replace Values

    D. Parse

2. What is used to combine data from multiple queries or tables?

    A. Merge query

    B. Join query

    C. Append query

    D. Left Outer query

3. What are some of the ways Power BI can be used to enrich data using AI?

    A. Linear regression, language detection, key phrase extraction, and sentiment analysis

    B. Language detection, key phrase extraction, and sentiment analysis

    C. Language detection and key phrase extraction

    D. Image tagging, key phrase extraction, language detection, and sentiment analysis

Part 2 – Modeling the Data

This section showcases how, to make clean and trusted data that is effective to use for an organization, it needs to be modeled such that it aligns with how the business operates.

This section comprises the following chapters:

- *Chapter 5, Designing a Data Model*
- *Chapter 6, Using Data Model Advanced Features*
- *Chapter 7, Creating Measures Using DAX*
- *Chapter 8, Optimizing Model Performance*

5
Designing a Data Model

Once you have connected to your data, done a bit of analysis, and organized it for reporting, the next step is to create a data model.

A good data model will provide faster and more accurate reporting. If the data model is easy to understand, report developers will take less time to generate reports, and it will make those reports easier to maintain. We'll see how to do that in this chapter.

In this chapter, we will cover the following topics – each using the same names you'll see in the exam:

- Define the tables
- Flatten out a parent-child hierarchy
- Define role-playing dimensions
- Configure table and column properties
- Define quick measures
- Resolve many-to-many relationships
- Create a common date table
- Define the appropriate level of data granularity
- Design the data model to meet performance requirements

Technical requirements

You will need the following:

- Microsoft Power BI Desktop installed on a Microsoft Windows PC, connected to some data to use: https://github.com/PacktPublishing/Microsoft-Power-BI-Data-Analyst-Certification-Guide/tree/main/example-data

Define the tables

As mentioned in the introduction, once you've acquired your data, cleaned it, and organized it, you can start to model it. Usually, a simpler model will perform better than a complicated model. As every situation is different, there are a few hard-and-fast rules for simplifying your data model. This is good news for you, as you will encounter a few questions about this and most are common sense.

When creating tables, what you leave out can be as important as what you keep. Typically, if a column or table is not necessary for a visual or a calculation, do not include it in the model. If you bring in more tables and columns than you need, not only will the reports based on the model be slower but it can also lead to confusion. If you import all the tables from your database, report creators will have to search through all the tables to find the columns they need to report on. This can lead to frustration, especially if the end result is a slow-running report. Slow-running reports are usually bad reports. No one wants to wait for a report to finish showing their data, especially Power BI reports. Power BI reports are known for their interactivity, that is, the slicing and dicing of data in real time. There is an immediacy to working with Power BI reports that is diminished when the report is slow to render.

Let's explore parent-child hierarchies next.

Flatten out a parent-child hierarchy

Where possible, you should strive for simpler models. When your report builders see fewer tables, they will be able to use the model more effectively. The simpler the model, the fewer problems you will have with it. We are not saying leave out important data, but we are saying, again, *if it's not necessary, don't include it*.

The most common way to do this is by using a star schema.

Star schema

A **star schema** organizes your data into **fact** and **dimension tables**. You can use dimension tables to filter the fact table. Dimension tables contain information that is repeated over and over again, for example, in the `Sales` table. If you think of a product dimension, it can hold all the information about a product, such as the name, color, SKU, size, and weight. Instead of repeating that information over and over, you can represent the product by an SKU number or even an integer in the `Sales` table. You can then filter the `Sales` table by selecting a product name, or even filter it to all products sold that are purple.

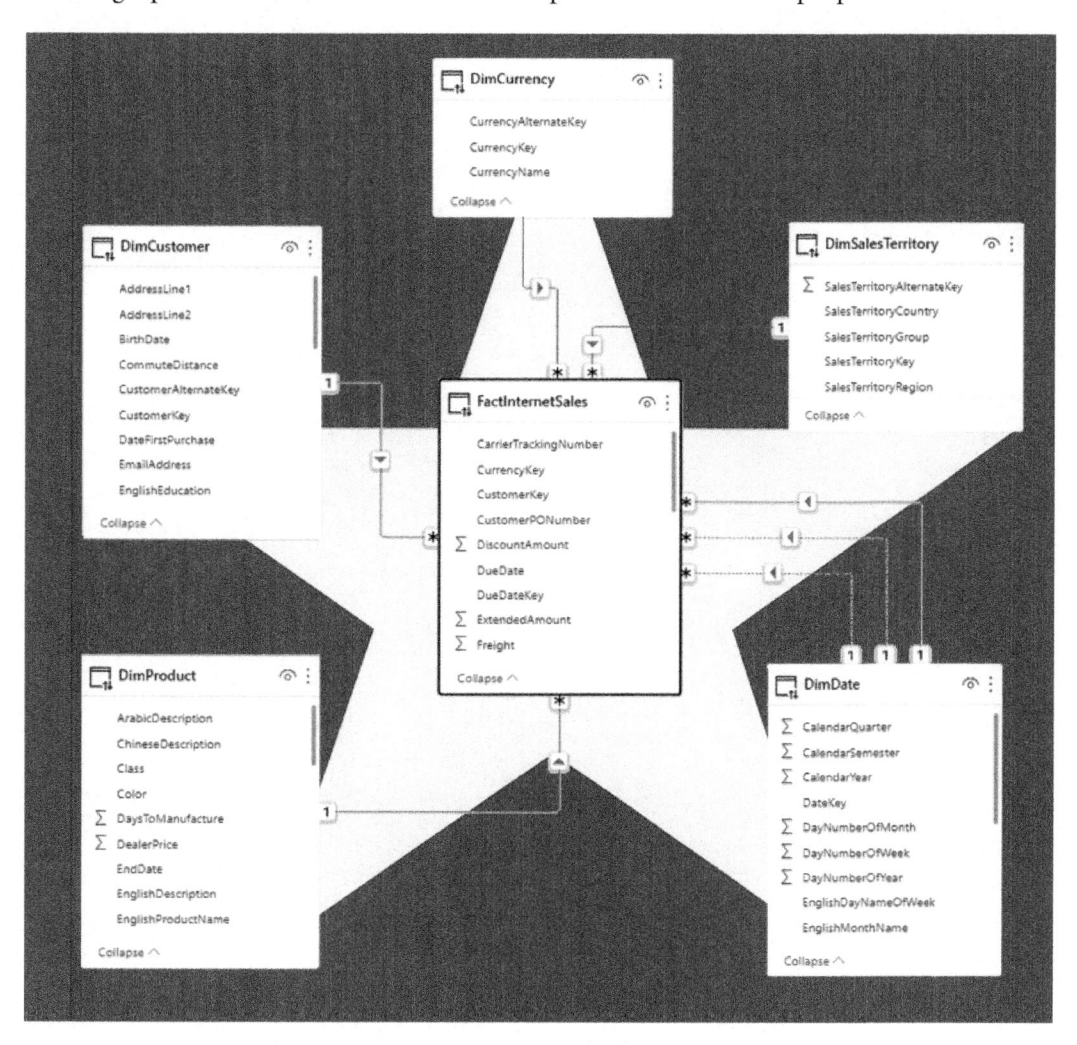

Figure 5.1 – An example of a star schema

Complicated models

A complicated model is confusing for report designers and slower for Power BI to refresh and render.

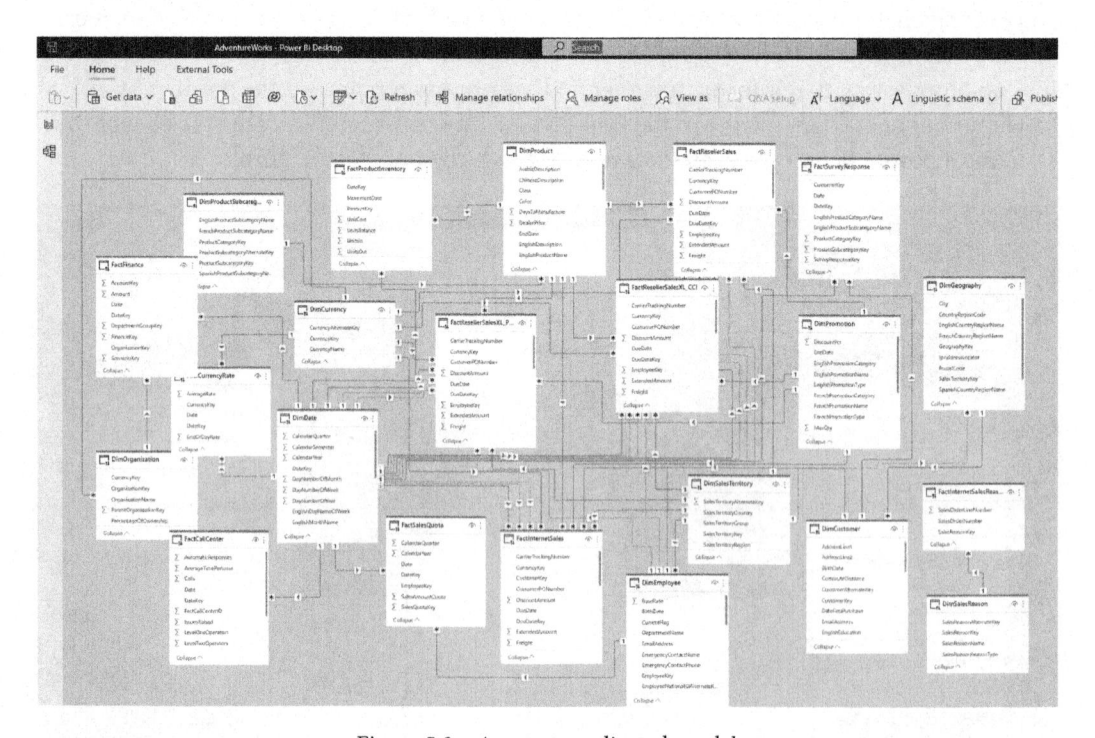

Figure 5.2 – A very complicated model

Notice how hard it is to read and follow the relationships.

Simple model

A simpler model is easier to maintain, create reports on, and refresh.

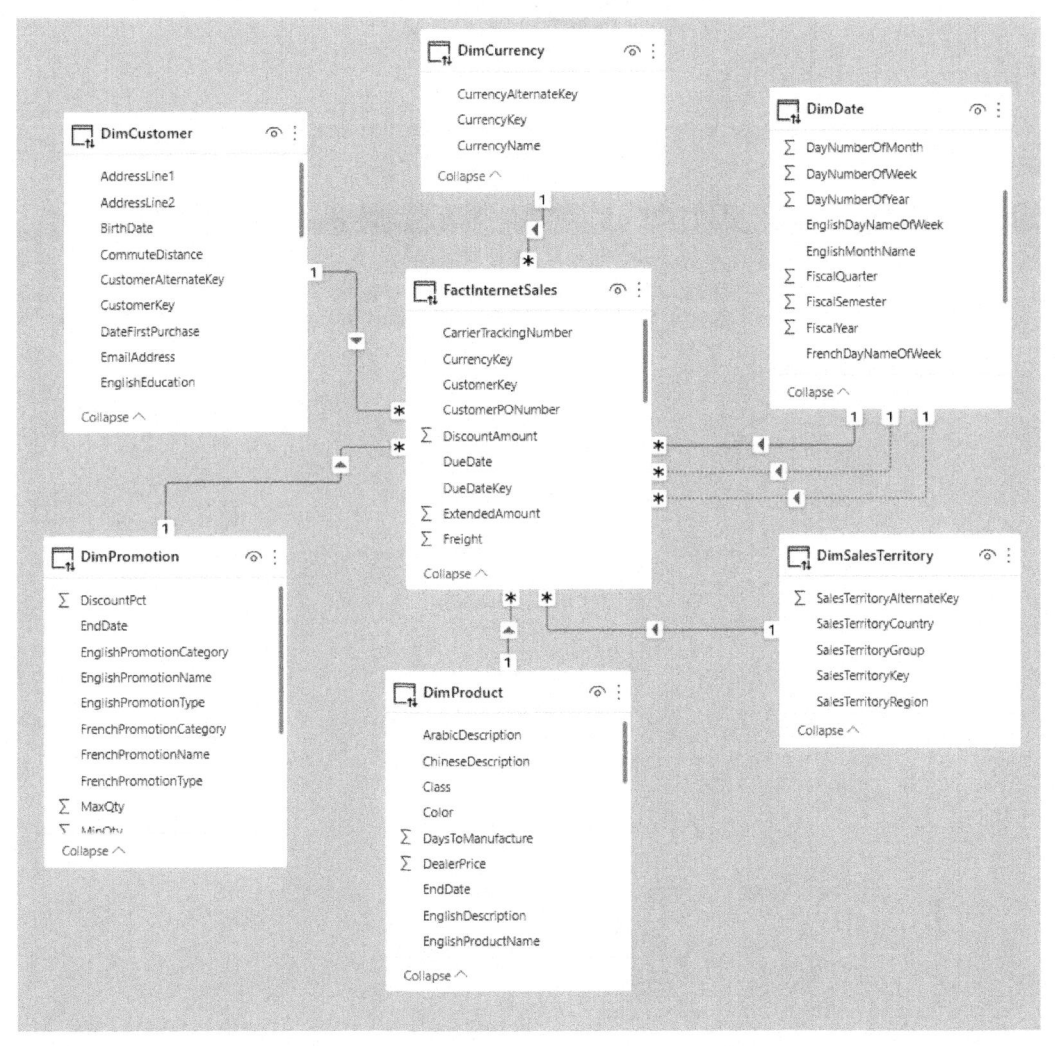

Figure 5.3 – A simpler model

A simpler table structure should be simple to navigate. The columns and tables should have friendly names, not obtuse system-defined ones. Whenever possible, you should merge or append tables to minimize relationships. Those relationships should also make sense.

Defining relationships

As you can see in both *Figure 5.2* and *Figure 5.3*, there are lines connecting the tables in the modeling view. These lines define the relationship between the tables.

Manage relationships

You can manage relationships by selecting the **Manage relationships** button on the modeling tab.

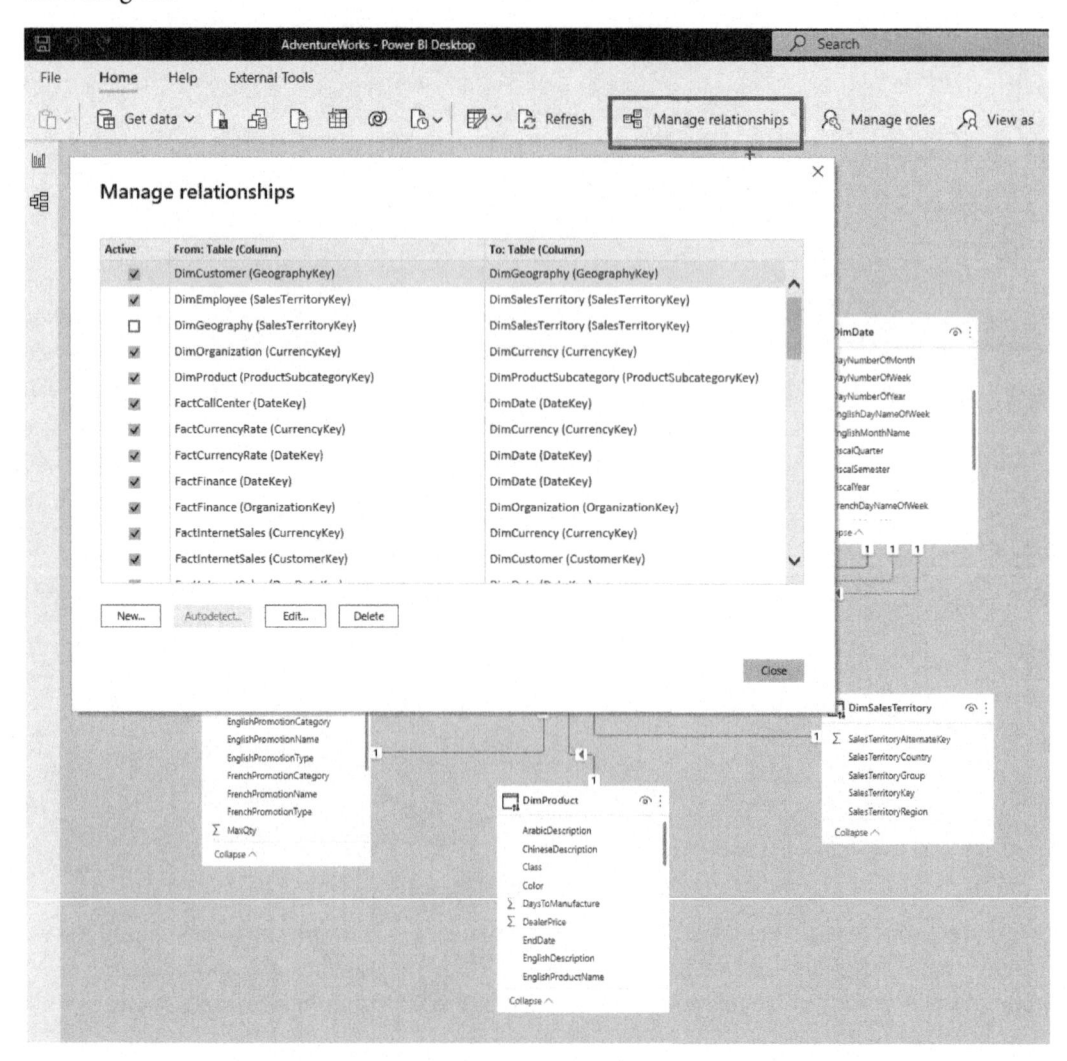

Figure 5.4 – Manage relationships window

Using this window, you can create, edit, and delete relationships between tables. You can also choose the **Autodetect...** button, which will try to find relationships in your data.

Edit relationship

You can choose to edit relationships from **Manage relationships** or by right-clicking on one of the relationship lines in the model and selecting **Properties**. You can set or change the properties of any relationship in the **Edit relationship** dialog window.

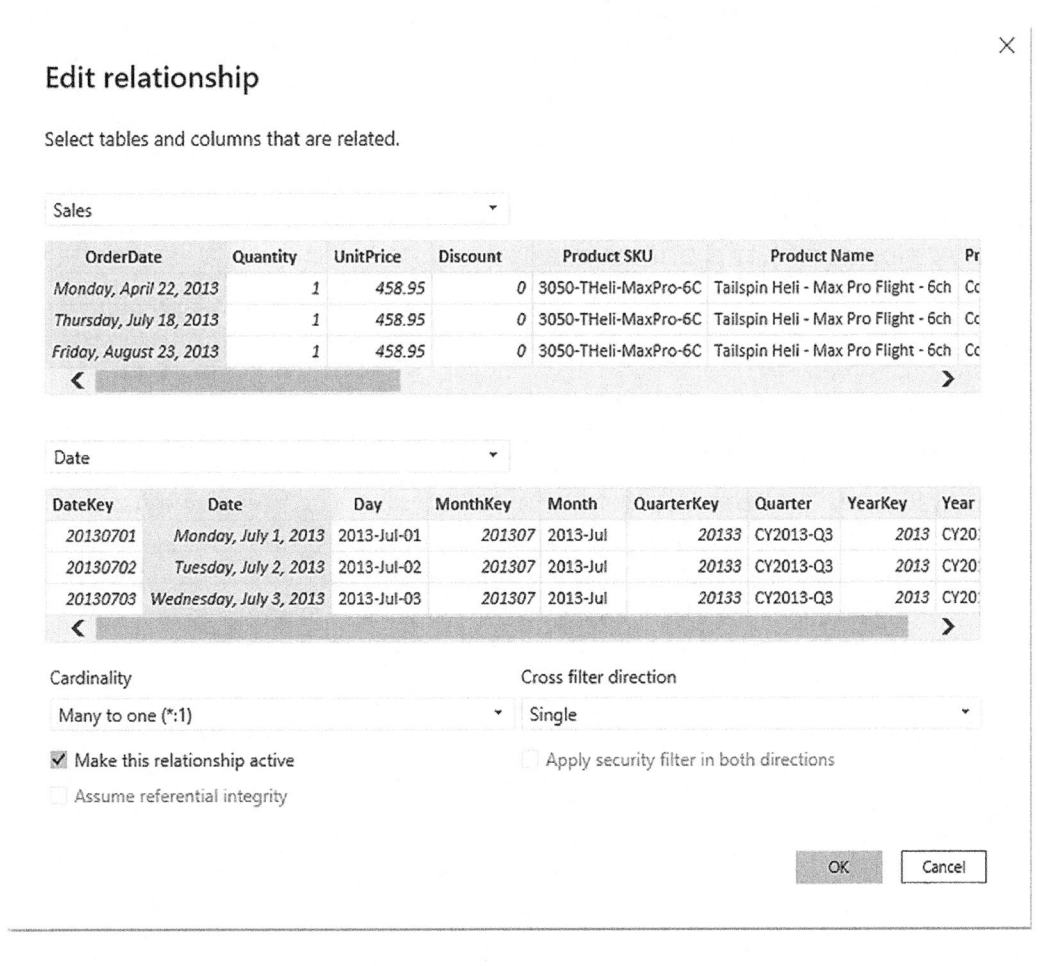

Figure 5.5 – Edit relationship dialog

Relationships control filtering and can change the behavior of calculations. They are at the heart of how a Power BI data model works and are one of the key differentiators between Power BI and its competitors. Choosing a subset of data from one side of the relationship can filter what data is available on the other side. If you have a `Date` table and filter it to today, if that `Date` table has a relationship with your `Sales` table, the `Sales` table will also be filtered.

Within the **Edit relationship** dialog, you can change how the tables interact in two ways: with cardinality or cross-filter direction.

Cardinality

Power BI relationship **cardinality** decides which table filters the other. There are three possible cardinalities.

Many-to-one (*:1) and one-to-many (1:*)

This is a relationship where you have one unique instance of each value in a column in one table and many instances of those same values in another table. This is the default type of relationship in Power BI.

Many-to-many (*:*)

In this type of relationship, you have many values in common between two columns in two different tables, so it does not require one side to be unique. This is not recommended. The lack of unique values can lead to confusion and your report developers may not know which value represents which table. In the *Resolve many-to-many relationships* section later in this chapter, you will learn how to represent a many-to-many relationship with many-to-one and one-to-many.

One-to-one (1:1)

This is the easiest relationship to describe. If you have a unique set of values in a column in a table and another unique set of values in a column in another table, and they are the exact same set of values, you can create a one-to-one relationship. This is not recommended, as you are storing duplicate data, and if your data ever changes, you could end up generating errors unless both tables receive the data change and thus maintain the exact same value sets.

The top table in the dialog box corresponds to the left-hand side of the cardinality. The many-to-one and one-to-many options are identical if the table you want on the *one* side is in the correct location in the dialog box. For one-to-many, the *one* side should be listed at the top of the box; for many-to-one, the *one* side should be the second table listed.

Cross-filter direction

We use relationships to filter data. **Cross-filter direction** determines whether that filter works in a single direction or both directions.

Single direction

In a single direction, one table in the filter is used to filter the data. For instance, products can filter sales, but sales cannot filter products. For a one-to-many or many-to-one relationship, the *one* side, the side with the unique values, will be used to filter the *many* side.

Both directions

If you enable **Both**, then either table can filter the other. So, in our example, the `Products` table can filter the `Sales` table, but the `Sales` table can also filter the `Products` table. If we add a third table of `Region`, we can then use the `Region` table to filter the `Sales` table to *then* filter the `Products` table. This would allow us to generate a report telling us what products are sold in each region. Be careful about using **Both** on all your relationships, though, as it may add ambiguity to your model and may also lower performance.

You will not be allowed to create a circular dependency. This means that if we have **Both** enabled on all our relationships, there's a strong possibility that eventually you will try to link to a table that's already referenced by another table that your first table has a relationship with. This might be a table that references a table that then references another table that you have a relationship to. If all those relationships are marked as **Both**, then when you try to create a new relationship, you will get an error message telling you to deactivate relationships. We will talk more about active and inactive relationships later in this chapter.

You can avoid this by having all relationships marked as **Single** or by using a star schema. In a star schema, dimension tables only ever have a relationship with the fact table.

Relationship test tips

Here are some tips for managing table relationships:

- Relationships can only connect two tables together.
- Relationships do not have to be between columns of the same data type, though it is advised.
- Relationships have direction, either **Single** or **Both**.
- Cardinality defines which table in the relationship the filter is applied to.

- Relationships can help reduce the model size, but too many relationships can make models confusing and hard to work with.
- You can never create a circular relationship.
- Two tables can have more than one relationship between them, but only one can be active.

Define role-playing dimensions

If you are used to using star schemas, one of the features is the idea of a **role-playing dimension**. This does not mean that your dimension will be out LARPing somewhere; it means we can use a dimension in multiple ways.

Power BI doesn't directly support role-playing dimensions; instead, it mimics the capability by utilizing active and inactive relationships. A table can only have one active relationship with another table, but it can have multiple inactive relationships. We just tell Power BI when we want to use the inactive relationship instead of the active one.

Date table as a role-playing dimension

In this diagram, our Date table has two relationships between it and the Sales table: one on the order date and one on the shipping date. This allows this Date table to filter the Sales table by order date or shipping date, or both! It allows the Date table to pretend to be the "order date dimension" or the "shipping date dimension."

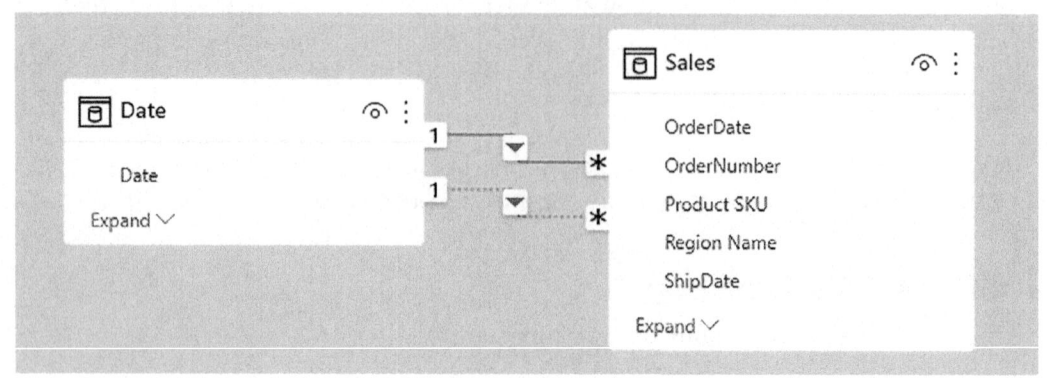

Figure 5.6 – Date table playing multiple roles

Date dimensions are some of the most common types of role-playing dimensions you will use. We will explore this more in the *Create a common date table* section later in this chapter. For now, we're moving on to table configuration.

Configure table and column properties

Once we have our relationships sorted, we can take a peek at our table and column properties. In Power BI Desktop, you can view and make changes to these properties in Model view. You can multiselect columns or tables using the normal Windows shortcuts of *Ctrl*-clicking or *Shift*-clicking.

The properties pane is organized into three sections: **General**, **Formatting**, and **Advanced**.

The General section

There are many properties that can be set on a column or table. Probably the most common one is to hide a column or table for Report view. Think about a relationship, as we discussed in the previous sections. You will often end up with two columns that contain the same data. You will usually want to hide one or both of those columns. You can control hiding/unhiding a column or table with the toggle.

The most common table and column property operations are in the General section.

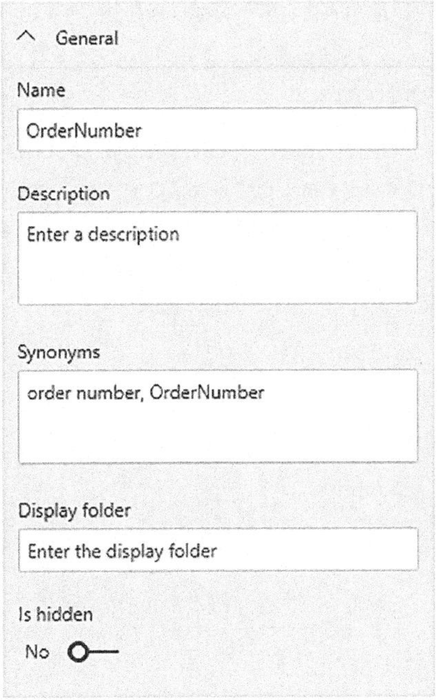

Figure 5.7 – The General section of the properties pane

Another cool feature you can set under the properties is **synonyms**. Synonyms let you query the model using natural language and let various business entities keep their own nouns. You may call it a purchase order number, another group may just call it a purchase, and another just an order number. Synonyms let everyone use their own natural language for querying.

Organizing your columns and measures into display folders can make it easier for report builders to find the columns and calculations they need to display on the report. This is done by simply typing in the name of the display folder. If you want a deeper path, you can separate each subfolder with a \ character.

The Formatting section

The Formatting area lets you control the formatting of the column when it is used in a report. Your choices here will be determined by the data type of the column. There are not many choices for text columns.

You can also change the data type of the column here. But be careful: if you set a column with text data to be a fixed decimal number, you will get an error.

Numeric formatting options

For numeric columns, you set the format to **Currency**, **Decimal number**, **Whole number**, **Percentage**, or **Scientific**. If those aren't enough, you can specify a custom format. You can even choose whether you want a thousands separator. The actual separator chosen will be determined by the region format you have chosen for your PC.

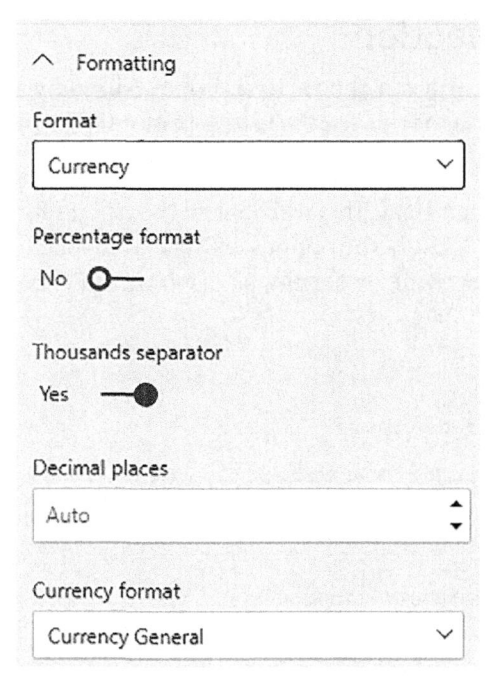

Figure 5.8 – Numeric formatting options

Date formatting options

As with numeric data, you can set how you want your dates to be displayed. There is a format dropdown, just like for numbers, but it only contains date formatting options. If none of those work for you, you can define a custom date format.

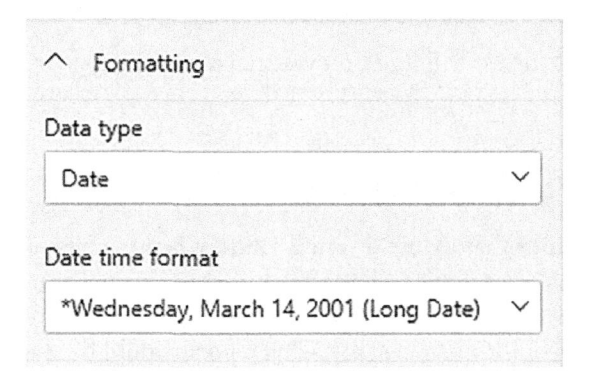

Figure 5.9 – Date formatting options

The Advanced section

In the **Advanced** section, you can choose to sort one column by another column in the same table. A common use for this feature is to sort months by their dates, as opposed to alphabetically.

You can also categorize your data. This will control the default for how the data is displayed in your report. Most of the options are related to locations, and data categorized as an address or a continent will, by default, be displayed on a map.

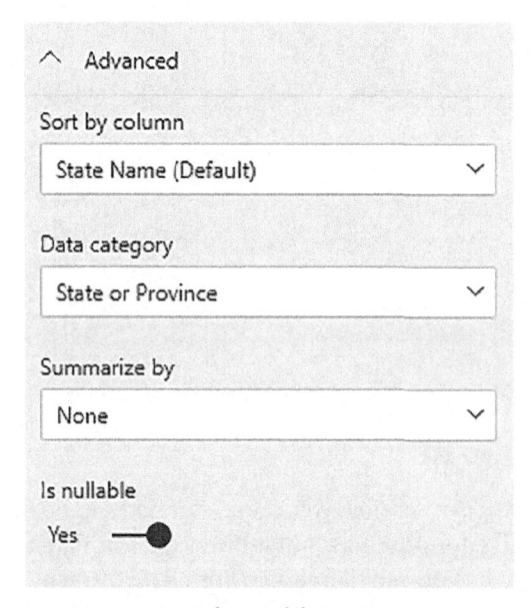

Figure 5.10 – Advanced formatting options

This is only the default, as we will find out: you can always change the visual once it's on the report.

Define quick measures

Measures are calculations that define business rules. It is not a business rule if we cannot define it mathematically. We don't say "We need most of our customers to like us"; we say "We need a 90% or better score on all customer surveys returned." We don't say "We need to create reports for people to use"; we say "This report should be used at least once a week by 73.4% of managers in finance."

There is a whole Excel-like language for creating measures. But the **quick measures** feature allows you to build calculations without knowing DAX.

The available calculations are organized into six categories:

- Aggregate within category
- Filters and baselines
- Time Intelligence
- Running Total
- Mathematical Operations
- Text

Start by right-clicking on a table or column in the **Field** pane to create a calculation. Select the calculation you want from the list, then drag and drop in the fields you want to base your calculation on, and then click **OK**. You've now created a measure.

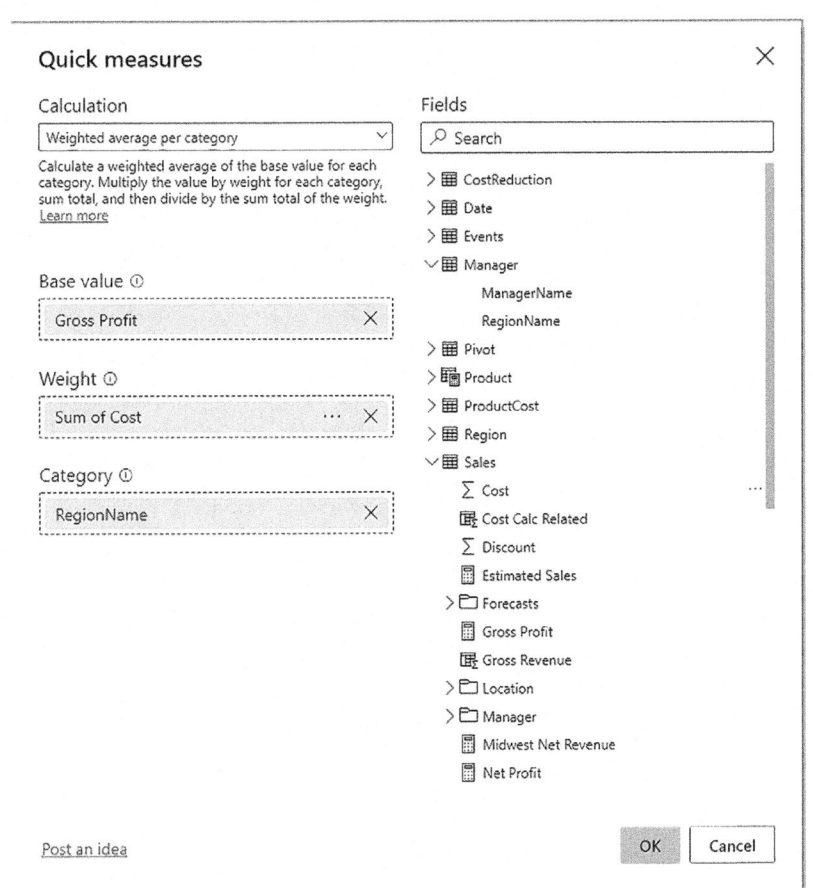

Figure 5.11 – Creating a weighted average of gross profit by region weighted by cost

Quick measures are a great way to not only create business calculations but also learn DAX. You can look at the calculation once it is created and see how Power BI does it.

Resolve many-to-many relationships

Many-to-many relationships are *not* recommended. As mentioned earlier in this chapter, the lack of a column with unique values can lead to performance issues and possible confusion about which column to filter on.

For instance, the following diagram shows a many-to-many relationship between my `Manager` table and my `Sales` table. I track sales by region, not manager, so I have a region on my `Sales` table:

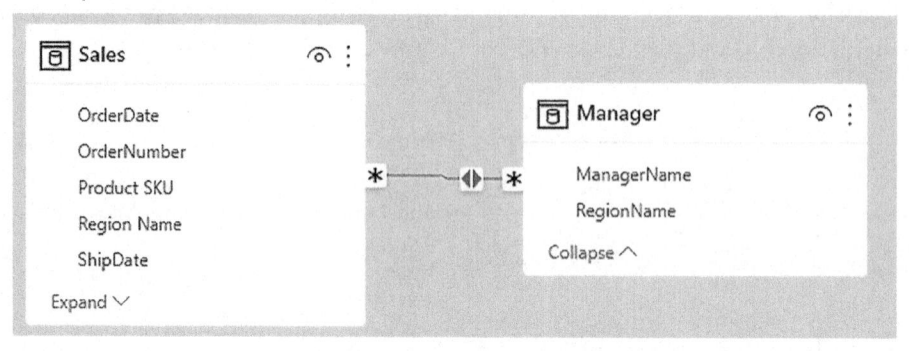

Figure 5.12 – Many-to-many relationships are slow and bad

I can easily fix this by creating a new "bridge" table named `Region` of the unique region values from my `Manager` table. I can do this in Power Query or DAX, with one query.

I can then delete the many-to-many relationship and create two new relationships: a many-to-one from the `Sales` table to the new `Region` table and a one-to-many from the `Region` table to the `Manager` table.

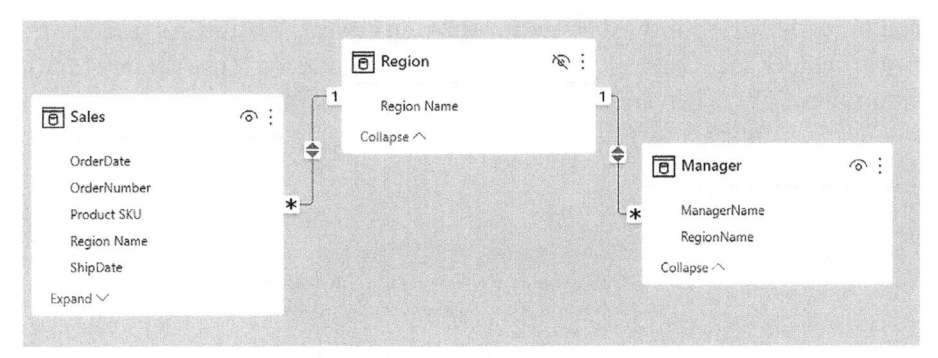

Figure 5.13 – Creating a bridge table solves our "many" problems

For the exam, understand that, although available, many-to-many relationships should be avoided. One method to remove them is to just create a table of the unique values you need and create many-to-one and one-to-many relationships to it.

Create a common date table

Date tables are *awesome*. We already discussed them briefly in the *Define role-playing dimensions* section, but now we will talk more about them.

Many, if not most, reports have a date-based aspect to them. "How many widgets did I sell last month?" followed by "Was that better than the previous month?" or "How about the same month last year?" are common questions asked about our data. A date table will help you answer these questions.

You have two options for creating date tables.

Power BI date hierarchy tables

You can let Power BI look for every date column in your model and create a hidden hierarchy table for every column. This will allow you to use those hierarchies when you want to be able to report by day, month, quarter, or year. You can also use these hierarchies in quick measures, slicers, or filters. All you must do is use the date column in your report; Power BI takes care of the rest using the hidden table.

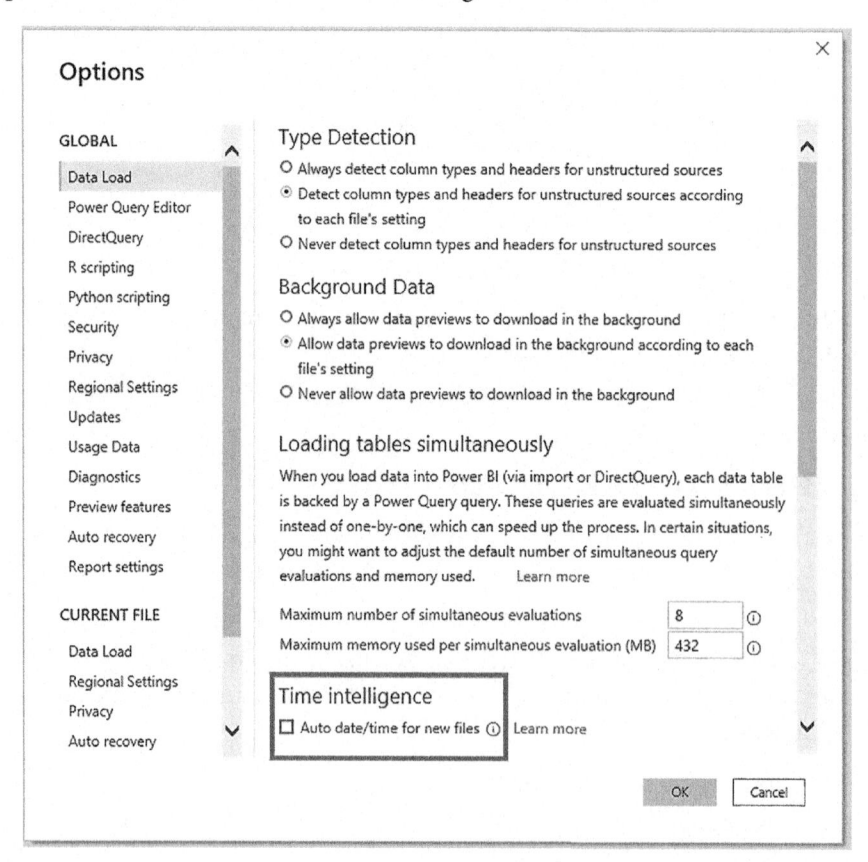

Figure 5.14 – Uncheck this box and use your own date table, please

There may be times when you don't want to use this built-in date hierarchy capability; for example, when you want to build this yourself, then automatic date tables can cause extra storage and complexity to your data model. Additionally, there can be scenarios when date and time are stored together, so defining relationships between fields with date and time to those with only the date will result in poorly related data because time is still being considered.

Using your own date table

You can either create a date table in Power BI or use a date table already in your data source. Many data sources are time-based and contain a date table. But if your data source doesn't provide one, you can create one in Power BI, by using either Power Query or DAX. DAX has a built-in function called CALENDARAUTO that can generate a date table for you, which we will implement as follows:

1. Once you have your date table, you have to mark it as a date table. To mark a table as a date table, you must have a table in your model that has the following:

   - A column with the date data type.
   - That column must contain unique values.
   - That column can have no blank or null rows.
   - The column must have a contiguous date span; it cannot have any missing dates in the middle.
   - The column must span a full year, but it does not have to be a calendar year.

2. If you have a table that meets those requirements, you can mark it as a date table by selecting the three dots (ellipses) next to the table name in the modeling view and selecting **Mark as date table** from the selection.

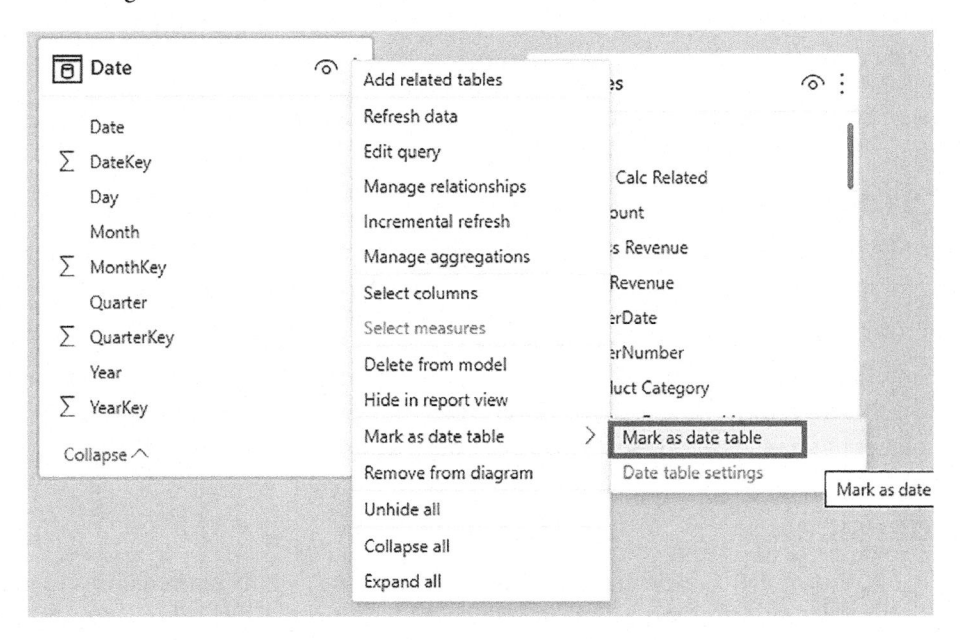

Figure 5.15 – Let's make that a date table!

3. That will bring up the **Mark as date table** dialog, where you can tell Power BI which column you want to use as your date column. If the column meets all of the criteria, you will get a green validation checkmark and the **OK** button will become active.

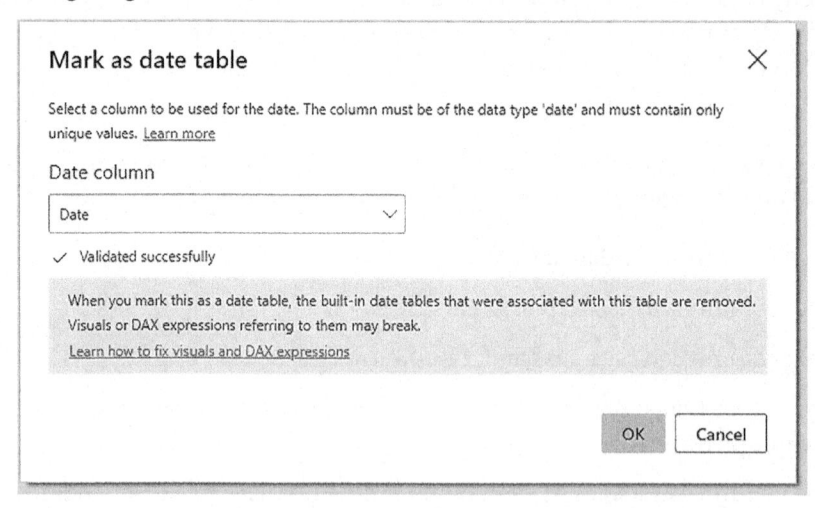

Figure 5.16 – Power BI will only let you pick a column that meets the requirements

Congratulations, you now have a date table!

4. The next step is to ensure that all of your date columns are in a one-to-many relationship with the date table. The "one" side of the relationship must be the date table.

Now we can talk about what wonders a date table can unlock.

Date math

Power BI has some really powerful time intelligence functions that require a date table to work. These functions allow you to create calculations based on time periods such as days, months, quarters, and years.

Currently, there are 35 time-based calculations that require a date table to work. I will not list them all here, as my editor hates long, bulleted lists. If you are using a date table, then the date column in the calculation *must* come from the date table for these calculations to work.

Model size

Creating your own date table and creating relationships with all the date columns in your model will reduce the model size, sometimes significantly. This will speed up both refreshes and report load times. I have seen reports go from load times of more than 5 minutes to under 30 seconds, just by removing the hidden date tables.

For many smaller reports, these date tables are great. They speed up development and allow less-savvy report creators to get going with a shallower learning curve.

For larger reports, these date tables can be a performance killer. They slow down large datasets and can make date math confusing. Using a date table allows you to standardize on one date across all your data.

Role-playing with our date table

We already touched on this when we talked about role-playing dimensions, but I want to reiterate it here. Date tables are awesome to role-play with; they provide a single date field for all reporting but can pretend to be any date field in your report.

> **Note**
> Make certain all the relationships with the date table are marked as **Single direction**. This way, our order date won't filter out the shipped date.

Define the appropriate level of data granularity

One key way to establish what your report can contain is establishing its granularity, or grain. The grain is the smallest level your report can go to. It is not uncommon for data in a fact table to be stored as a daily or monthly total. If you are storing sales by store by day, you should not divide that number by 24 to get hourly totals. That number implies a degree of certainty that is not actually in the data.

I'm going to present a screenshot from earlier, but this time talk about *what* we are relating, not *how*.

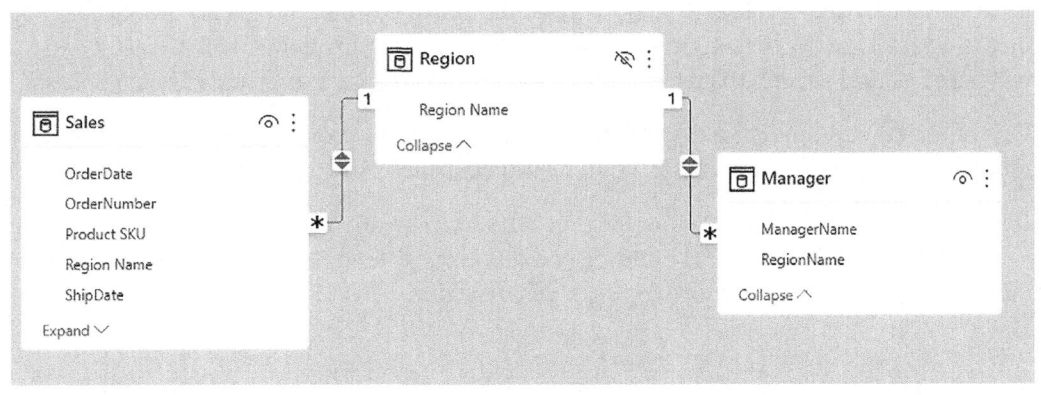

Figure 5.17– The grain of the Sales table is product by Region Name and OrderNumber

Here, you can see that our `Manager` table can filter our `Sales` table through the `Region` table, and the other way around: `Sales>Region>Manager`. If I filter the `Manager` table by `ManagerName`, it will filter the `Sales` table by `Region`. So, if Ted and Ananya both manage the Midwest region, both will end up showing the exact same revenue.

RegionName	ManagerName	Net Profit
Midwest	Ananya Kumar	4,684,310
Midwest	Ted Baker	4,684,310
Total		**4,684,310**

Figure 5.18 – This is incorrect

If you noticed that the total is not a summation of the `Net Profit` column, you are correct. Power BI calculated the net profit total separately; it doesn't just add the columns above it. We will talk about filter context later in this book, in *Chapter 9, Creating Reports*.

Just remember, you can never have more detail than your model allows. When it comes time for me to hand out my bonuses, I can't just give half credit to each manager. That would not be fair if the bulk of my profit come from one of them. That's a quick way to lose a good manager.

Design the data model to meet performance requirements

As mentioned previously, model performance is extremely important. A faster rendering report is a much more enjoyable experience for your consumers than one that takes minutes to show data. A report that refreshes faster places much less strain on source systems, thus making the owners of those systems much more likely to remove access to them.

Many of the preceding topics in this chapter, and in previous chapters, have dealt with this issue. Gathering and organizing your data and then correctly designing a data model on that data is what all the chapters up to this point have been about. By doing it all correctly, you will have fast data models that are simple and clear and concise to use, and easy to maintain.

One of the keys to modeling data in Power BI is creating the correct relationships between tables. As with many things in life, good relationships lead to good performance.

In larger models, removing the hidden date tables can greatly improve performance. Using a date table will simplify report building and allow consistency across your reports. Date tables also allow the use of more complex date functions.

Many of our "fast, simple, and clear" reporting requirements can be accomplished by using a star schema. A star schema helps us to implement good relationships while avoiding circular ones. It will usually enable faster reporting because we filter the fact table based on data in our smaller dimension tables.

Summary

This chapter was all about creating the best data model for our reports. We covered a lot of ground and hit many topics, all of which might be in the exam.

The important takeaways are as follows.

Simpler is better. Simple models are easier to create reports on and usually result in faster rendering. That means your report consumers will be happier and you will receive fewer complaints from them!

The star schema pattern is a great tool. Star schemas usually lead to smaller, faster models, as Power BI is built to consume star schema-type models natively. Also, star schemas lead to good relationships. Which brings us to the next point.

It's all about good relationships. As you will find out in almost every chapter of this book going forward, relationships are the key to Power BI reporting. Good relationships lead to good, interactive reports. Good relationships lead to accurate slicing and dicing of data.

Use your own date table. Dates are extremely important to reporting. Creating your own date table will result in a smaller dataset footprint and allow you to use data time intelligence features. We will see in *Chapter 9, Creating Reports*, that one date table can role-play as many different date tables.

To really take advantage of your date table, make sure all the date columns in your report have a relationship with the date table. We will explore this more in *Chapter 9, Creating Reports*.

Quick measures help you use complicated calculations with minimal effort. Using quick measures will help you develop your report quicker and can be used as a training tool, teaching you how to create more complicated calculations. You will learn more about measures in *Chapters 6, 7, 8, 9, 10*, and *11*.

Remember the grain of your report. You can't report on anything lower than your grain. Remember, the grain of your report is defined by the smallest piece you can report on. If you have sales data per store per day, you cannot report on sales per store per hour by dividing the day into 24 hours. You could roll your report up to weekly or a region; you just cannot go any lower than per day or per store.

In the next chapter, you will learn how to develop your data model to make it more effective for reporting.

Questions

1. Which type of table relationship describes a scenario where each unique value in one table occurs only once in another table?

    A. Many-to-many

    B. One-to-one

    C. One-to-many

    D. Unique relationship

2. What is the DAX formula needed to build a quick measure to calculate the weighted average per category?

    A. `AVG(CATEGORY)`.

    B. `AVGW(CATEGORY)`.

    C. `AVERAGE([QUERY].[CATEGORY])`.

    D. DAX isn't needed for a quick measure.

3. If your data has sales by store by day, are you able to find sales by hour?

    A. No.

    B. Yes.

    C. Sort of, it will be averaged by store by day.

    D. Sort of, it will be averaged by store by hour.

6
Using Data Model Advanced Features

Now that we've designed a **data model** that incorporates a **star schema**, uses **fact and dimension tables**, and links them together with **surrogate keys**, we can make use of some of the advanced capabilities of data models in **Power BI**. We'll be exploring these capabilities in this chapter.

In this chapter, we're going to cover the following topics:

- Using sensitivity labels
- Implementing row-level security
- Applying natural-language Q&A capability

Technical requirements

To best understand the topics covered in this chapter, it is advised that you have the following available:

- Microsoft Power BI Desktop installed on a Microsoft Windows PC
- A Power BI data model where we can apply the advanced features covered in this chapter

Using sensitivity labels

As part of the holistic data protection capabilities, Power BI includes integration with **Microsoft Information Protection** (**MIP**). MIP provides **sensitivity labels** as a way of making it easy for users to classify critical content and data while not making this a burden for the user or restricting collaboration.

Sensitivity labels allow users to classify datasets, reports, dashboards, and dataflows as having a specific sensitivity so that data can be protected. For example, some data used in Power BI reports might be publicly accessible data, and this feature allows those datasets to be labeled as such. In the same way, internal sales data might need to be protected and labeled as confidential; when this happens, the data is protected by the service from being accessed by those who do not have permission to access data labeled *confidential*. It can also enforce encryption, restrict forwarding, and, in some cases, printing as well.

In Power BI, sensitivity labels are persistent wherever the data is used. There is a concept known as **downstream inheritance** that will enforce downstream data products to adhere to the defined sensitivity label. For example, if the sales data is labeled as confidential, then a downstream aggregation of that data in a new table or query will also be labeled as confidential if this feature is enabled. This helps ensure that data is protected throughout its life cycle. Downstream inheritance works when data is exported as a PDF from the Power BI service or Excel from the Power BI service or Power BI Desktop. It does not support exporting to CSV files.

The requirements for sensitivity labels in Power BI are as follows:

- **Azure Information Protection** (**AIP**) Premium P1 or Premium P2.
- AIP, which uses the MIP unified labeling platform.
- The user applying labels must have a Power BI Pro or Premium per-user license.
- Defined and published sensitivity labels for your organization in Microsoft 365.
- An up-to-date version of Power BI Desktop.

For sensitivity labels to be used in Power BI, MIP sensitivity labels need to be enabled on the tenant. Administrators can enable sensitivity labels in the **Power BI admin portal**.

Within the Power BI admin portal, the sensitivity labels setting can be found under **Tenant settings** and then **Information Protection**. This capability can be enabled for an entire organization or specific security groups within the organization.

Sensitivity labels are an expanding capability for Power BI where additional features, such as default labeling, mandatory labeling, and downstream inheritance capabilities, are being added. Through expanded integration, such as **Cloud App Security**, **sensitivity labels** are also used to prevent **data exfiltration** by blocking the exporting of data from reports.

In the next section, we'll look at how we can further enhance the security of data in a data model by using row-level security.

Implementing row-level security

A common security need for customers building reporting solutions with Power BI and needing to simplify the data model is a way to build multitenant data models. This means that data can be stored in a single table but only be viewable by the designated users who should have access to it. This capability is called **row-level security**.

Row-level security allows filtering to happen at the table level in a data model based on the user accessing the data. For example, an entire table might contain all the sales data for the organization across different regions or countries and some users of the report might only need to access data from their region or country. Without row-level security, we'd have to manually set up different tables for each region or country as well as a combined table with data from all regions for senior leadership. With row-level security, we can define the roles needed and apply a **DAX expression** to the table that will handle the filtering for each role. This way, all data can be stored in the same table and the filtering criteria set up for row-level security ensure each user sees only the appropriate data.

Setting up row-level security

After connecting to data in Power BI Desktop and creating a report that shows sales by country, your report might look like this:

CountryRegion	TotalDue
United Kingdom	$572,496.5594
United States	$383,807.0355
Total	**$956,303.5949**

Figure 6.1 – Example Power BI report visual showing sum of TotalDue in sales per country, for the United Kingdom and the United States

In the following steps, we will set up row-level security so each team member can only see the data for their respective country:

1. On the **Modeling** tab, click **Manage roles**. In the **Manage roles** window, we create all the roles within our organization that will need to view data in the report.
2. Click **Create** to create a new role.
3. Type a name for the role that corresponds to one of the groups of users that will access the data. For example, there may be a group of sales leaders in the United States, so we'll call this role `US Sales`. We'll also create a role for `UK Sales`.
4. Select the address table. The address table is used as a single place in our data model where all addresses (shipping and billing) are stored. A relationship is established between our address table and our sales and customers table, which allows cross-filtering between the tables. This will be required for the data to be filtered properly by the DAX expression we set up in the row-level security.
5. Type in the `[CountryRegion] = "United States"` and `[CountryRegion] = "United Kingdom"` DAX expression for each role created.

We can verify that the roles and filtering are set up properly by using the **View as** button on the ribbon under **Modeling**.

	Now viewing as: US Sales	
CountryRegion	TotalDue	
United States	$383,807.0355	
Total	**$383,807.0355**	

Figure 6.2 – The same Power BI report visual showing sum of TotalDue in sales per country filtered to only show the United States

1. Click **View as**.
2. Select one of the roles we just created; try **US Sales**.
3. View the filtered data in the report.

Next, let's look at managing this security.

Managing row-level security

In Power BI Desktop, you can manage roles and the DAX expression applied to each role by clicking **Manage roles** under the **Modeling** tab on the ribbon. In the Power BI service, you can view the row-level security roles that have been created for a dataset by clicking **More options** under a dataset. From there, select **Security** on the **More options** menu.

In the Power BI service, members can be added to the row-level security roles that have been created. Typically, groups of users would be added to each defined role. Row-level security roles can contain groups such as **distribution groups**, **mail-enabled groups**, or **security groups**. **Office 365 groups** cannot be added. Additionally, it is possible to add specific users to a role as well but as a security best practice the use of groups is advised.

It's also possible to use a **dynamic variable** called `username()` and `userprincipalname()` with the DAX query of a role. This will be dynamically populated for the user logged in and viewing the report. This corresponds to the `DOMAIN\user` or `user@domain.com` value for the current user or viewer of the report.

When it comes to the dynamic capabilities of reporting in Power BI, one of the best features to help with the creation of reports and understanding data models is the Q&A feature, which we'll look at next.

Applying natural-language Q&A capability

The **Q&A** feature of Power BI allows you to use **natural language** to ask a question of the data and return a visual providing the answer. This can be useful when users are learning about the dataset and can also provide a way for less experienced users to build complex visuals.

Q&A is useful for report designers to explore data, create visuals, and build reports in a quick way using natural language. Even for experienced report designers, Q&A provides a way to start with a basic question and then still have the same visuals that could be created manually with the same fine-tuning adjustments possible on the visual after it's been created by Q&A.

Q&A is also useful for report viewers, allowing them to quickly get to the most important questions they want to ask of the report data. After viewing the Q&A-created visuals, they can easily pin the created visuals to a new or existing (if they have the required permissions) dashboards in the Power BI service.

Using Q&A in reports and dashboards

An easy way to get started using Q&A is to add the visual to a report.

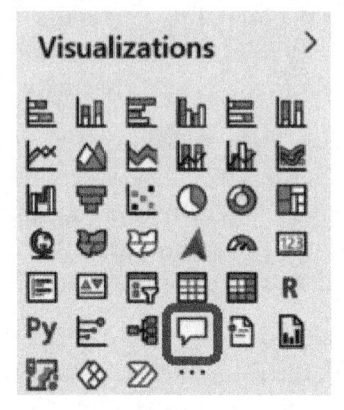

Figure 6.3 – Button to add a Q&A visual to a report

The first time this visual is added to a report, you may see the following message:

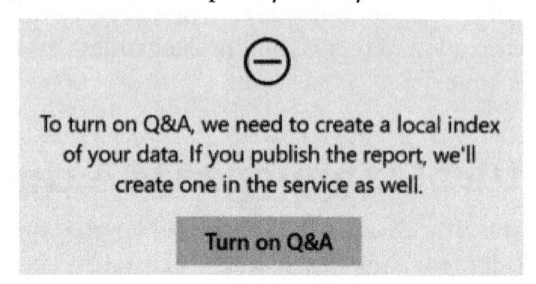

Figure 6.4 – New Q&A visual added to a report

This indicates that the Q&A feature is not yet enabled for this Power BI file. From here, click **Turn on Q&A** to enable the feature. When Q&A is enabled for a file, an index of the data will be created. This index is updated regularly when a file is open in Power BI Desktop and when reports are published to the Power BI service, they require no maintenance by the user. After this happens, the visual will load and you may see something like this:

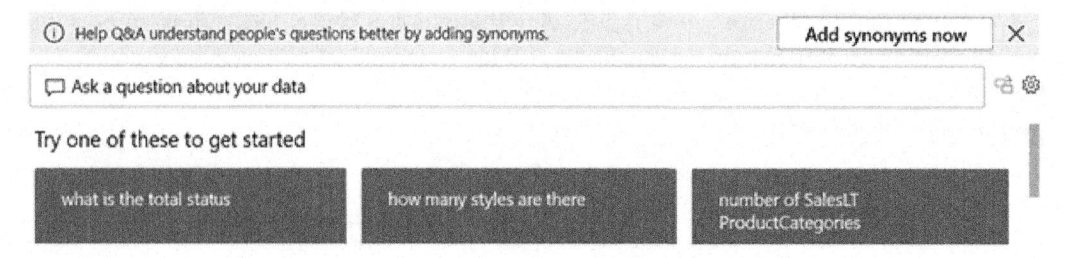

Figure 6.5 – Example Q&A visual on a report

Upon the first load, Q&A will attempt to show example questions to help users get started asking natural-language questions of this dataset. Those are shown in the blue boxes near the bottom of the visual, as seen in *Figure 6.5*. When the example queries are selected, the text is populated in the search text box and then a few seconds later, the query runs against the data. This gives the user time to see the query and make changes if desired.

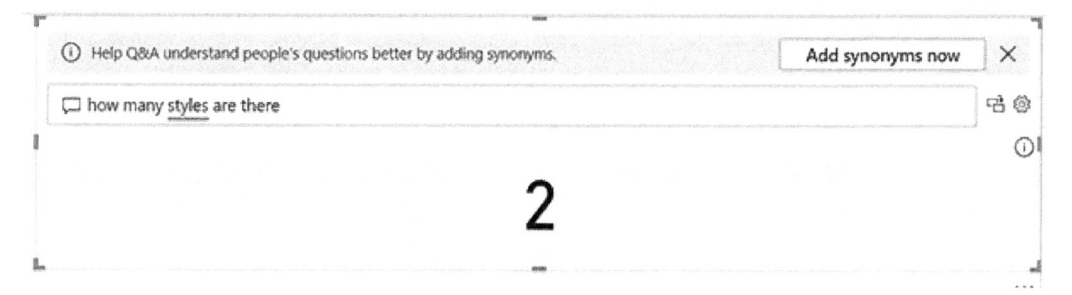

Figure 6.6 – Example Q&A query showing blue underline

When Power BI understands that a word in a natural-language query relates to a field in the dataset, the word gets underlined in blue, as seen in *Figure 6.6*.

When users type in natural-language queries, Q&A provides autocompletion to help the user navigate the data and find questions that can be asked of the data. For example, if we have a dataset containing only customer contact information, we could probably ask *how many customers do we have in each state?*, but we need to ask this in a way that aligns with the data model.

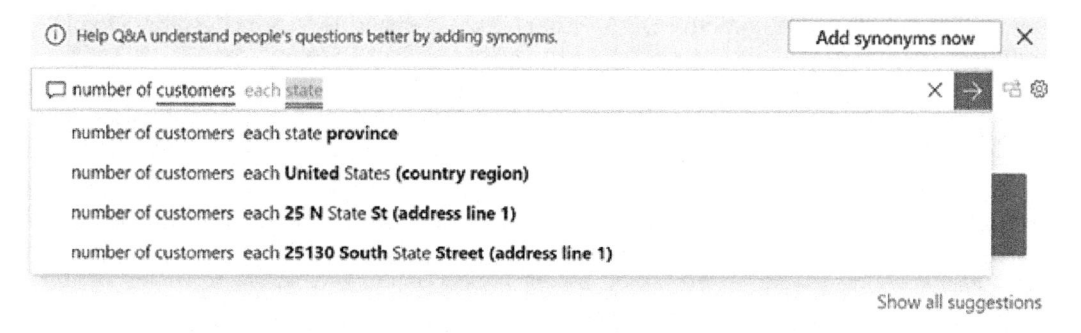

Figure 6.7 – Q&A visual showing suggestions for a query

102　Using Data Model Advanced Features

We can see in *Figure 6.7* that Q&A is making autocomplete recommendations based on the word state and that it seems like a field in our **StateProvince** data model. After accepting the top suggestion, we're able to instantly see the visual created for us by Q&A.

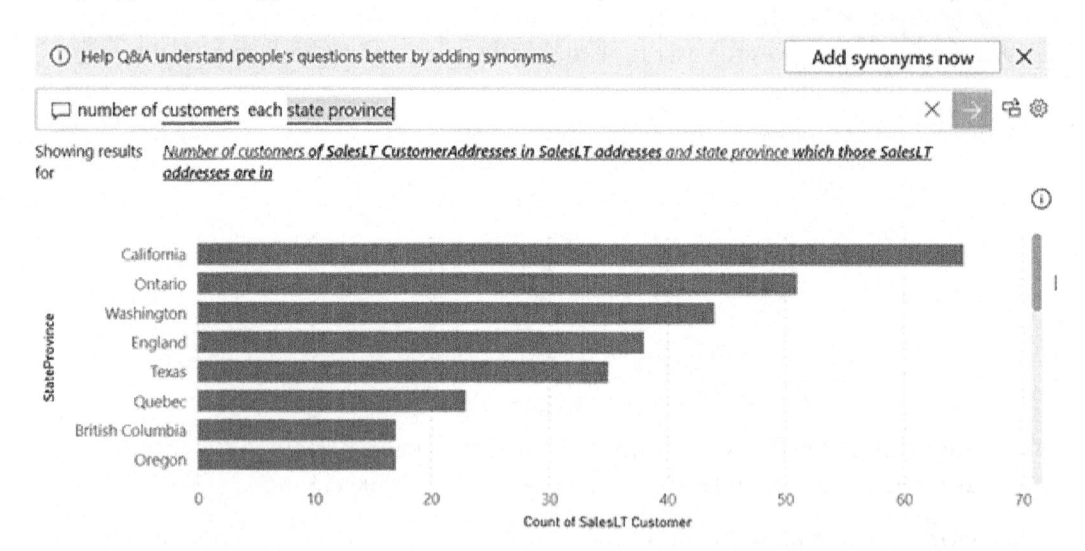

Figure 6.8 – Q&A visual showing count of customers from each state ordered from most to least in a bar chart

At any time while querying with natural language, the resulting visual is shown below it, and the button can be clicked to turn the visual shown into a standard visual in the report. This is one of the ways the Q&A visual makes it easier for report designers to build reports.

At the top of the visual, we can see that we can help Q&A better understand the data model by providing **synonyms**. In the example query used previously, *how many customers do we have in each state?*, we noted that the word **state** was not immediately recognized as the **StateProvince** field in our data model. While sometimes autocomplete suggestions will help us here, it's also possible the autocomplete doesn't recognize the words used in your data model. If you're using a word that is domain-specific, then you may need to provide synonyms that will help Q&A better understand your data model.

In addition to synonyms, there are more advanced capabilities by providing a **linguistic schema** in the form of a *.yaml (**YAML**) file, which is possible from Power BI Desktop. We'll cover that in the next section.

Q&A linguistic models

A **linguistic model** is like a regular Power BI data model in that it is a way to describe the data and relationships between columns and tables. A linguistic model also describes the terminology used in a data model. This helps Q&A to better relate words used in a **natural-language query** to tables, columns, and relationships in the data model.

Linguistic models in Power BI are represented as a YAML file and allow the report designer to define the relationship between specific words, phrasings, and the data in the data model. For example, by editing a custom YAML file, you can specify that both a bicycle frame and a bicycle wheel are part of a bicycle. This would help Q&A to be able to support natural-language queries when a user asks about sales of bicycle components, as opposed to all products, which would include things such as bicycle helmets and gloves.

Importing linguistic models happens in Power BI Desktop under the **Modeling** tab on the ribbon.

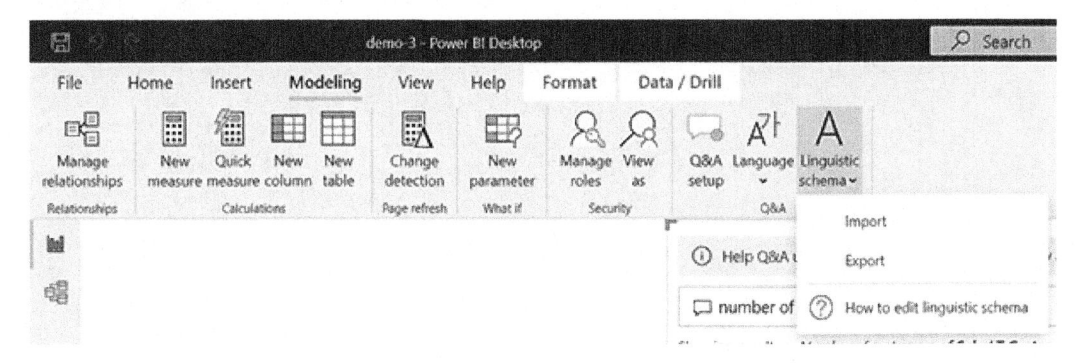

Figure 6.9 – Editing a linguistic schema in Power BI Desktop

Full details of the linguistic schema will not be covered in the exam, but for some more information, let's consider how they work.

Linguistic models in Power BI use a basic structure in the YAML file:

- General information, such as the version and language
- Entities
- Relationships

Within the **entities** section, there is a description of each table and each column in every table of the data model. Each entity (table or column) is described with a binding tag (if it is a table or a column belonging to a table) as well as a state tag (if it was generated by Power BI) and then tags that further define the entity with terms. For example, a linguistic model will start out with the following:

```
Version: 3.3.0
Language: en-US
DynamicImprovement: HighConfidence
Entities:
  table_1:
    Definition:
      Binding: {Table: Table1}
    State: Generated
    Terms:
    - table 1: {State: Generated}
    - Table1: {Type: Noun, State: Generated, Weight: 0.99}

  table_1.column_1:
    Definition:
      Binding: {Table: Table1, Column: Column1}
    State: Generated
    Terms:
    - column 1: {State: Generated}
    - Column1: {Type: Noun, State: Generated, Weight: 0.99}
```

This section defines the entities that will be used in the next section, relationships.

The **relationships** section is where **phrasings** are defined. Phrasings are how you define relationships between things. For example, it's where you can define that *purchase orders* contain *products* or that *airplane wings* contain *parts*. Q&A can make good guesses on entries that relate to each other when it comes to general knowledge domains, but when it comes to domain-specific knowledge, this is where a custom linguistic model can help users be able to ask domain-specific questions.

Phrasings are made using the building blocks of basic grammar:

- **Nouns** – A person, place, or thing
- **Verbs** – An action or state of being
- **Adjectives** – A description of a noun
- **Prepositions** – A word that governs a noun and expresses a relationship to another noun, verb, or adjective

To get an idea of how phrasings work, let's look at attribute phrasings.

Attribute phrasings are used when a noun is made up of another noun. For example, if orders are made up of items, then the attribute phrasing would be as follows:

```
orders_has_items:
  Binding: {Table: Orders}
  Phrasings:
  - Attribute: {Subject: order, Object: order.item}
```

Other types of phrasings include the following:

- **Name phrasings** enable the use of product names in Q&A.
- **Adjective phrasings** allow the mapping of a generic term, such as *satisfied customers*, to a numeric value, as would be the case in a survey requesting a *rating of 10*.
- **Noun phrasings** define nouns that use domain-specific language, such as "winning season" being defined as winning more games than losing in professional sports.
- **Preposition phrasings** create relationships between things using prepositions. For example, some products may be books and those books might be about business intelligence. So, creating preposition phrasings would allow Q&A to answer questions such as *How many books are about business intelligence?*
- **Verb phrasings** create relationships between nouns using verbs, for example, *customers submit orders*. This allows Q&A to answer questions such as *Which customer submitted orders for business intelligence books?*

The Power BI documentation (`https://docs.microsoft.com/power-bi/natural-language/q-and-a-tooling-advanced`) contains more details on creating linguistic models.

Optimizing Q&A in data models

Q&A works best when table relationships are set up so the service can fully understand how data from one table relates to another table. Using the previous example, if the relationship between *Customers* and *Addresses* is not set up, then it will not be possible for Q&A to understand that each unique customer has an address that lives in the Addresses table. This relationship is defined by a **many-to-one** relationship in our data model between the *CustomerAddress* table and the *Customer* table.

Another area that often needs optimization work in the data model is field names and data types. It's not uncommon for fields to use different names, especially across different data sources that are often needed to build meaningful reports. You should always be sure to rename fields to be consistent across all tables/queries in the data model. Remember, renaming fields in the Power BI data model does not impact the name of a column or field in any underlying data stores. Similarly to field names, field data types should match and be set optimally based on the type of data stored. For example, if a date field is stored as a numeric type, it will be challenging for Q&A to answer questions about data for a specific month.

If you're still not able to ask questions that you'd like to ask of Q&A, then additional recommendations include the following:

- Review which numeric columns should and should not be automatically aggregated (**Properties** on the **Modeling** tab).
- Categorize data properly for geography and date columns (**Properties** on the **Modeling** tab), choosing a column for sorting (**Sort by Column** on the **Modeling** tab).
- Normalize the data model. As a general rule, use **Third Normal Form** (**3NF**) database normalization principles when building a Power BI data model. Adjustments to your data model can be made using Power Query.
- Append queries when data has been partitioned.

Add synonyms and/or edit the linguistic model appropriately to meet the needs of the data. Natural-language Q&A queries can bring a new level of usability and discoverability to Power BI data. When properly configured, Q&A can be a powerful tool for fast and simple analysis.

Summary

In this chapter, we learned about the advanced data modeling features of Power BI.

We learned how we can protect sensitive data in our data model by using sensitivity labels, and how sensitivity labels integrate with a holistic data protection suite across Microsoft products and services. We learned that sensitivity labels can be configured to follow the data even when it is exported from Power BI into other data stores, such as Microsoft Excel.

We also learned how row-level security can be implemented and used. We learned that row-level security can be used to tailor the data in a report to the specific users or groups of users who are consuming the reports, so we don't need to make costly data model changes.

Lastly, we learned about Q&A and how it can be used to dynamically create report and dashboard visuals from natural-language queries written by report designers or report users. We learned that Q&A can be used to help users explore data made available by the data model. We learned how using synonyms and custom linguistics models can make Q&A tailored to technical or domain-specific words used in a data model.

In the next chapter, we will look at how the DAX language can be used to create measures and columns in your data model. This will be helpful as you improve your data model to meet increasing demand from report users.

Questions

1. Which of the following does Power BI use as the default sensitivity labels?

    A. Top secret, secret, official, public

    B. Confidential, official, public

    C. Confidential, general, public

    D. Whatever your organization uses for MIP sensitivity labels

2. If the data model for sales data includes columns for **Country**, **State**, and **Postal code**, what are some potential ways we can implement row-level security to filter data?

    A. Use a DAX expression to filter by **Country**, **State**, or **Postal code**.
    B. Use a DAX expression to filter by **State** or **Postal code**.
    C. Use a DAX expression to filter by **Country** or **State**.
    D. Use a security filter by **Country**.

3. What kind of model (or YAML file) is used for domain-specific natural-language querying in Power BI?

    A. Data model
    B. Super model
    C. Linguistic model
    D. Dimensional model

7
Creating Measures Using DAX

Once you have connected to your data, done a bit of analysis, and organized it for reporting, the next step is to create a data model.

A good data model will provide faster and more accurate reporting. If the data model is easy to understand, report developers will take less time to generate reports and it will make those reports easier to maintain. The data model is a crucial component of any Power BI solution, so ensuring you have effective and efficient use of measures will be a key factor. In this chapter, we will take a deep dive into the powerful **Data Analysis Expressions** (**DAX**) programming language, which will unlock dynamic and useful capabilities for solving reporting challenges.

In this chapter, we will cover the following topics:

- Building complex measures with DAX
- Using CALCULATE to manipulate filters
- Implementing time intelligence using DAX
- Replacing numeric calculated columns with measures
- Using basic statistical functions to enhance data
- Implementing top N analysis
- Creating semi-additive measures

Creating Measures Using DAX

Technical requirements

For this chapter, please make sure you have the following:

- Microsoft Power BI Desktop installed on a Microsoft Windows PC.

- Access to some data to use. We have also provided synthetic data that can be used, which is available in the GitHub repository for this book here: https://github.com/PacktPublishing/Microsoft-Power-BI-Data-Analyst-Certification-Guide/tree/main/example-data.

Building complex measures with DAX

Power BI uses a programming language called DAX for creating calculated columns, calculated tables, and measures. This language can be used to easily create complex expressions to implement business rules.

As we discussed in the previous chapter, measures are calculations that define business rules. It is not a business rule if we cannot define it mathematically. We don't say "We need most of our customers to like us"; we say "We need a 90% or better score on all customer surveys returned." We don't say "We need to create reports for people to use"; we say "This report should be used at least once a week by 73.4% of managers in finance."

DAX uses a Microsoft Excel-like language for these calculations. That means if you have ever created a formula in Excel, you are already well on your way to learning DAX! If you haven't, know that millions, if not billions, of people around the world use Excel every day; it's one of the most common programs on the planet.

A DAX formula starts with a name, the name of the calculated column or table or the name of the measure. The name can contain most characters or numbers, including some special characters. What the name *cannot* contain is an equal sign, =. The equal sign is used to mark the end of the name and the beginning of the formula. After the equal sign, a function, or combination of functions, is applied, which returns a value. In the case of a measure or calculated column, this has to be a single value; in the case of a calculated table, this can be a range of values.

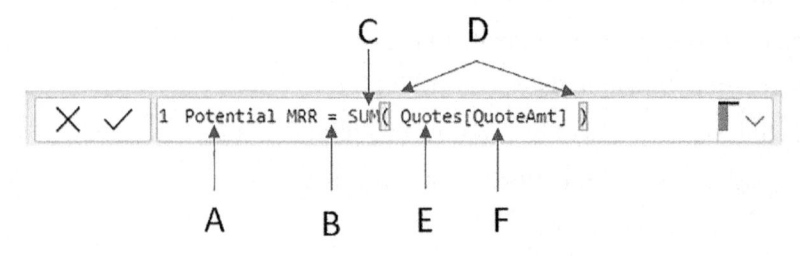

Figure 7.1 – A basic DAX measure

In the preceding example, you can see the following:

- A. is the name of the expression.
- B. is the equal sign that indicates the beginning of the formula.
- C. is the function we are using. This could be one or more functions, but they must return a single value.
- D. is the argument of the function; this can be columns or other functions.
- E. is the table that is being referred to.
- F. is the column of that table.

It is important to note that a function always references a column or a table. You can add filters to the function to limit it to some set of rows, but it will always reference a column or table. This is not the same behavior as Excel, where a function references a specific cell.

A calculated column or measure function will always return a value or a table. If a table is returned, further functions must be applied so you return a single value.

A calculated table will return a table of data, but that kind of goes without saying.

Although DAX is simple to learn, as we talked about before, Power BI provides a quick and easy way to get started with DAX by using quick measures, which we will explore next.

Quick measures

Quick measures are a capability that allows you to use a drag-and-drop interface to quickly create measures with a minimal amount of code. Quick measures are a great way to not only easily create measures but also learn DAX. You can look at the code produced by quick measures and see some of the more esoteric functions, such as how to calculate a weighted average of the base value for each category.

See *Chapter 5*, *Designing a Data Model*, for more information about quick measures.

Creating your own measure

So, how do we create these DAX calculations? We already touched upon quick measures, but you may have noticed that you can right-click on a table in the **Fields** list and choose the **New measure** option. Alternatively, you can select the **Modeling** tab from Report view or the **Table tools** tab from Data view to create a new measure.

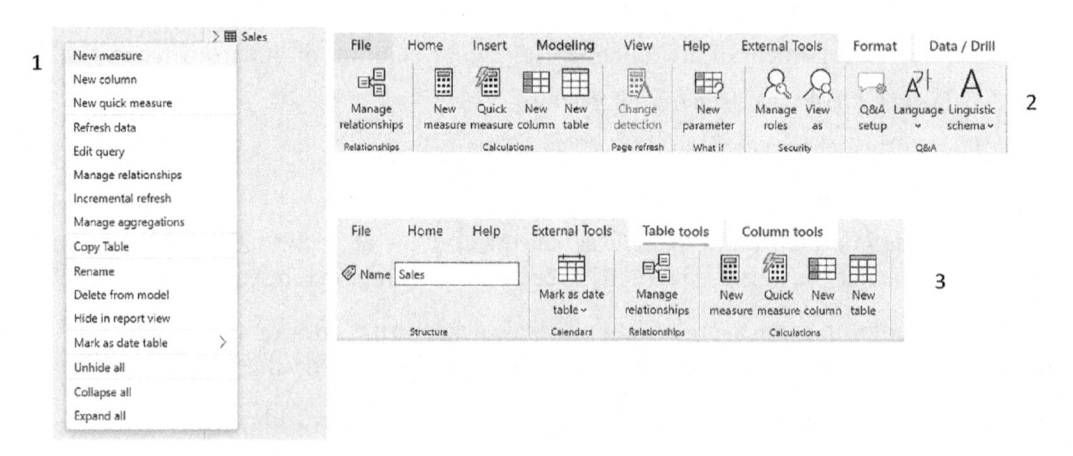

Figure 7.2 – How to create a new measure. 1 is the context menu. 2 is the Modeling tab from Report view. 3 is Table tools from Data view

Once you have selected one of these options, the formula bar will appear and you can start typing your new measure.

Measures versus calculated columns

DAX provides a way to add or generate data using data brought in from other data sources. This provides a way to build a more complete picture using the data you have. Both measures and calculated columns can do this but there are nuances and pros and cons to each, which we'll look at later in this chapter.

Suppose you want to create a new column in a sales table for gross revenue. As some of you may know, gross revenue is usually calculated as *quantity * unit price*. What we can't do is sum up the number of things sold for the day and multiply it by the sum of the unit prices of the things sold for the day. That would not lead to an accurate number. If I sold one widget for $3 and two gadgets for $6, I did not have $18 worth of sales; I had only $15. I must go line by line with this calculation:

```
Gross Revenue = Sales[Quantity] * Sales[UnitPrice]
```

This is the classic use for a calculated column.

Later in this chapter, in the *Replacing numeric calculated columns with measures* section, we will explain why the best answer for this may not be calculated columns and how to craft a measure that goes line by line.

Default summarization

It is also important to know that every numeric field has a default summarization that will be applied to it when it is added to a visual in a report. You can see the default summarization for your column in the **Column tools** tab. You can change the default summarization to another calculation from the dropdown, or even choose **Don't summarize**. This last choice is good for things such as ZIP codes, which are numeric columns we want to display as text.

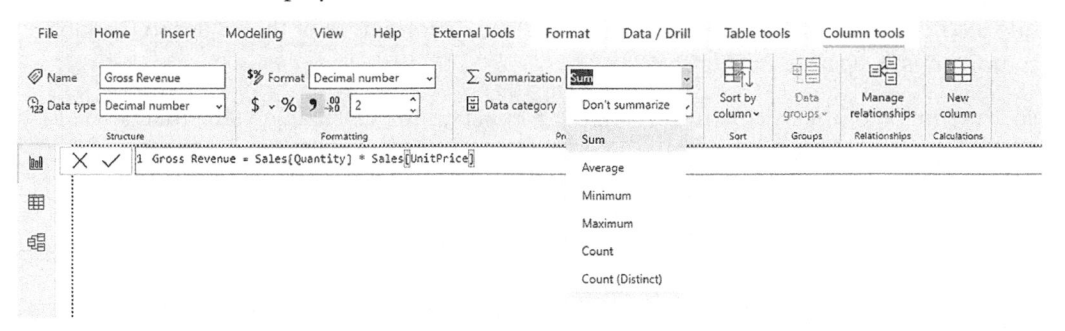

Figure 7.3 – Choosing the default summarization for your column

Next, we will look at how measures use filtering context to calculate the needed value dynamically.

Context is everything!

One of the most powerful things about Power BI is that it does all the calculations of measures in context.

Take the gross revenue calculation we previously discussed. That calculation returns one value per row of my `Sales` table. But if I use that column in a visual, it will automatically be filtered in the row context of the visual.

Figure 7.4 – Data is summarized depending on its context

This behavior is the same for measures. This is a good thing, else we would have to create one measure per scenario, such as the sum of gross revenue by state or the sum of gross revenue by demographic. Instead, we can have one gross revenue and use it in multiple visuals.

Calculations can be applied in both the row context and the filter context. As you can see from the preceding screenshot, **Gross Revenue** in the table has one value per line of my **Sales** table. This is the row context. If I drag it onto a visual, it will sum in the filter context of the visual. This is the default summarization of the **Gross Revenue** field working in conjunction with the filter context.

The two rows of my table visual, **Helicopter** and **Airplane**, each shows the correct gross revenue for their filter context. The total is the gross revenue calculated, ignoring the row filter of **Product Item Group**. The total is *not* a summation of the values in the table column; it is a separate calculation.

So, the context of the calculation will have an effect on the calculated value that is displayed.

Using CALCULATE to manipulate filters

Often, we want to add to or override the filter context of a value. For that, we have the CALCULATE function. This is one of the most important functions to learn to pass the exam.

Suppose we want to create a measure that calculates the gross revenue for just our Midwest region. This will allow us to see the Midwest gross revenue. I have created the measure using the **Calculate** function and added it to the table we saw before.

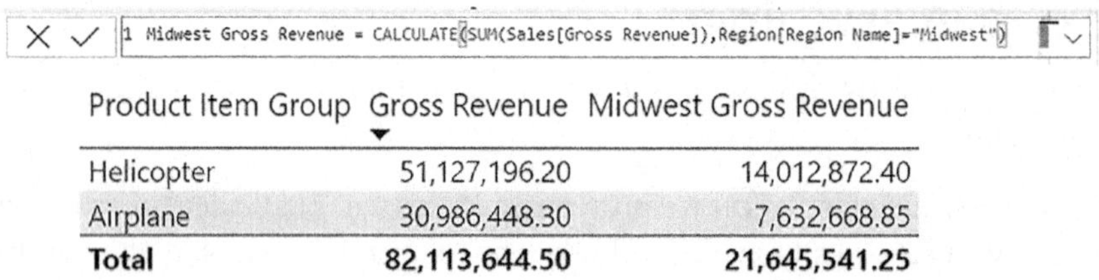

Product Item Group	Gross Revenue	Midwest Gross Revenue
Helicopter	51,127,196.20	14,012,872.40
Airplane	30,986,448.30	7,632,668.85
Total	**82,113,644.50**	**21,645,541.25**

1 Midwest Gross Revenue = CALCULATE(SUM(Sales[Gross Revenue]),Region[Region Name]="Midwest")

Figure 7.5 – Using Calculate to change the context filter

Notice that our Midwest net revenue is filtered to both **Midwest** and **Product Item Group** when in the filter context.

Simple filtering

The `Calculate` command syntax is as follows:

```
CALCULATE (<measure expression>, <filter1>, <filter2>, …)
```

The first argument in the CALCULATE function must be an expression that returns a single value. Each filter is separated by a comma. You can have none, one, or multiple filters. Filters can be a table. All the `<filter>` arguments in a single CALCULATE() behave as if they are wrapped in an AND() function. In other words, a row must match every `<filter>` argument to be included in the calculation. If you need an OR() style of operation, you can use the || operator.

If your filter is a simple comparison, such as =, <, >, <=, >=, or <>, then you do not have to use the FILTER() command.

The FILTER function

Say you are trying to compare one of the following:

- `<column> = <measure>`
- `<column> = <formula>`
- `<column> = <column>`
- `<measure> = <measure>`
- `<measure> = <formula>`
- `<measure> = <fixed value>`

Then, you are required to use the Filter() command.

The filter command requires a table as its first argument. This does not have to be an actual table; you could create one as part of the statement.

The CALCULATE syntax with the FILTER argument looks like this:

```
CALCULATE(<measure expression>, FILTER(table,
<expression),<filter2>, …) .
```

116   Creating Measures Using DAX

If we were trying to get a row count of our products by name, we could create this measure:

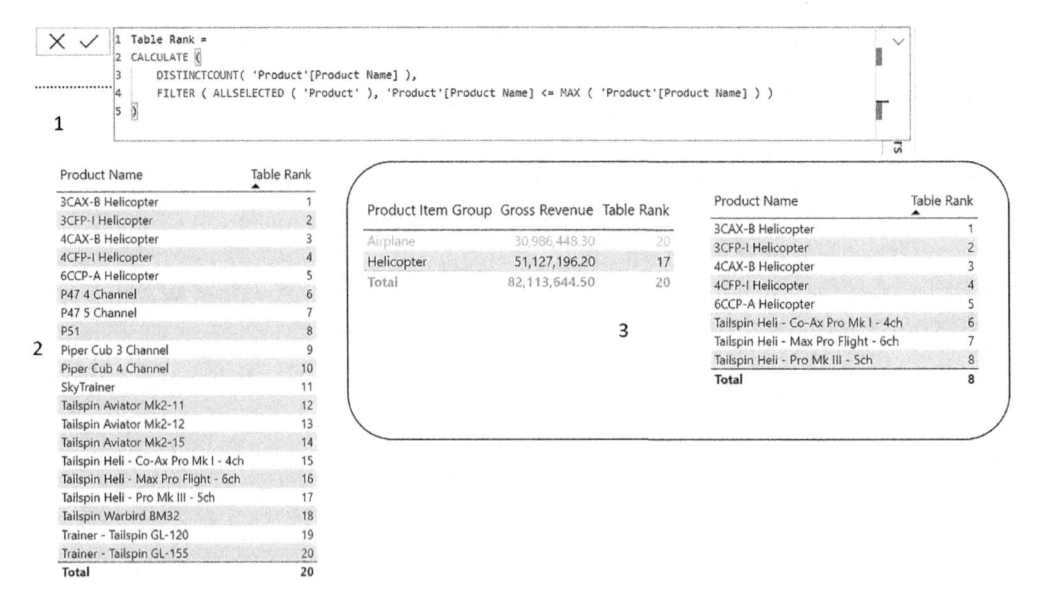

```
1 Table Rank =
2 CALCULATE (
3     DISTINCTCOUNT( 'Product'[Product Name] ),
4     FILTER ( ALLSELECTED ( 'Product' ), 'Product'[Product Name] <= MAX ( 'Product'[Product Name] ) )
5 )
```

Figure 7.6 – By using CALCULATE and FILTER together, you can access much more complex filtering

The following list shows the various elements seen in this screenshot:

1. The measure definition. We must use the filter statement because we are comparing a column against a measure expression, MAX.

2. The table rank with the **Product Name** column. Notice it is just an alphabetical ranking.

3. (Outlined) The table rank in two different tables. Notice it makes no sense in the left-hand table, but in the right-hand table, it changes the ranks based on our selecting **Helicopter** in the left-hand table. The table rank is correct in this context filter.

Understanding how the CALCULATE function works will be important for passing the exam and working with Power BI in the future.

The ALL function

The ALL function instructs the surrounding function to ignore the execution context for the table or column within the function.

What if you wanted to know what percentage of gross revenue each product provided? It should add up to 100% however you sliced and diced your data.

If you simply divide your gross revenue for a product by the sum of gross revenue for all products, you can get that answer. But the filter context will make that result 1:

```
% Product Gross Revenue =
DIVIDE(
  SUM(Sales[Gross Revenue]),
  SUM(Sales[Gross Revenue])
    )
```

You can use CALCULATE with ALL to ignore any context filters:

```
% Product Gross Revenue =
DIVIDE(
 SUM(Sales[Gross Revenue]),
 CALCULATE(SUM(Sales[Gross Revenue]),ALL('Product'[Product Name]))
    )
```

If you use the `Product Name` column from the `Product` table, this will work.

Product Item Group	Product Name	% Product Net Revenue
☐ Airplane	P47 5 Channel	20.52%
	Piper Cub 4 Channel	19.44%
	Tailspin Aviator Mk2-15	17.21%
	Tailspin Warbird BM32	9.12%
	Tailspin Aviator Mk2-12	8.99%
	P51	6.47%
	SkyTrainer	6.06%
	Piper Cub 3 Channel	3.34%
	P47 4 Channel	2.95%
	Tailspin Aviator Mk2-11	2.39%
	Trainer - Tailspin GL-155	2.06%
	Trainer - Tailspin GL-120	1.45%
	Total	**100.00%**
☐ Helicopter	Tailspin Heli - Max Pro Flight - 6ch	71.72%
	6CCP-A Helicopter	17.14%
	Tailspin Heli - Co-Ax Pro Mk I - 4ch	5.75%
	4CAX-B Helicopter	2.64%
	3CAX-B Helicopter	2.05%
	3CFP-I Helicopter	0.39%
	Tailspin Heli - Pro Mk III - 5ch	0.16%
	4CFP-I Helicopter	0.15%
	Total	**100.00%**
Total		**100.00%**

Figure 7.7 – With CALCULATE and the ALL filter option, you can ignore filter context

You can use CALCULATE to change the filter context of a value or even ignore the filter context entirely.

Next, we'll look at a special kind of calculation – time intelligence calculations, which Power BI has built-in capabilities for to ease implementation.

Implementing time intelligence using DAX

Most reports have a time quality; we often need to compare now versus some previous point in time to see whether we are trending in the right direction. Power BI offers many powerful time intelligence functions to handle this kind of reporting.

In *Chapter 5, Designing a Data Model*, we covered how to create a date table. This chapter explains how to use its awesomeness.

Time intelligence functions fall into one of two types:

- Functions that require CALCULATE.
- Functions that return a scalar value on their own. This is sometimes referred to as **syntactic sugar**, which is an awesome name.

A function that uses the DATESYTD call requires CALCULATE:

```
Products Ordered YTD = CALCULATE(COUNT(Sales[Product SKU]),DATESYTD('Date'[Date]))
```

Syntactic sugar has an aggregate value in its name, such as TOTALYTD or CLOSINGBALANCEMONTH. We will get the same results as the CALCULATE measure using the following:

```
Total Products Ordered YTD = TOTALYTD(COUNT(Sales[Product SKU]),'Date'[Date])
```

It may take generating some error messages before you get a feel for which type of function you are trying to use.

Date tables

To get the most out of your time calculations, you need to use the date column from your date table. This will allow for consistency in analysis, can lead to a smaller and faster data model, and allows you to use DAX time intelligence functions, such as Year-over-Year and Same Period Last Year.

The most important thing when working with a date table is that every date in your data model has a relationship to the date column of your date table. I cannot stress this enough. Here, I have my date table with two relationships, one to **OrderDate** and one to **ShipDate**:

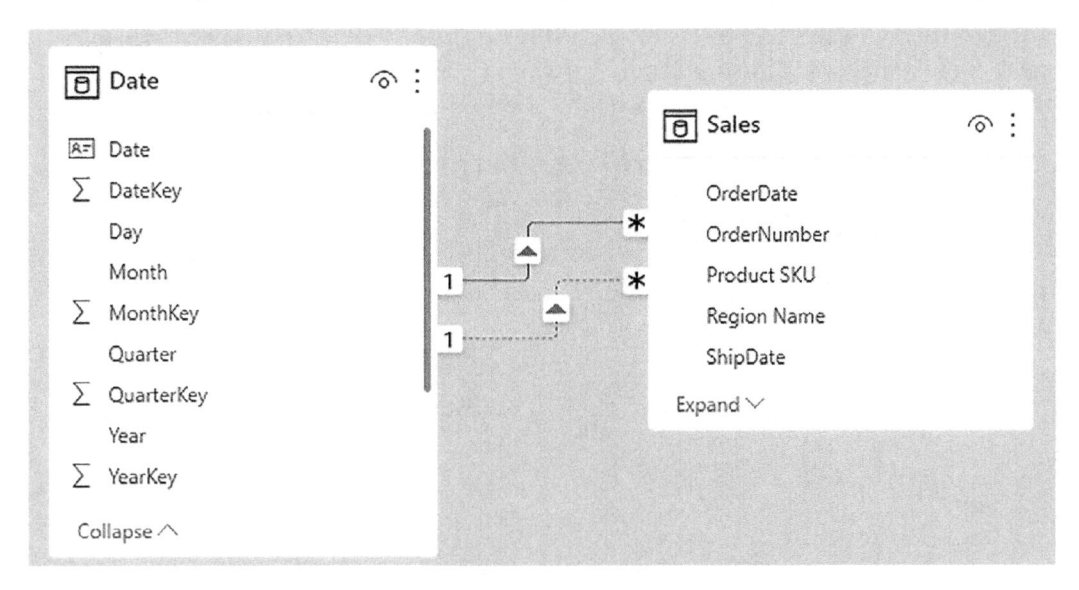

Figure 7.8 – OrderDate is the active relationship (solid line) between the tables; ShipDate is the inactive relationship (dotted line)

To use the date table, use the date column in the date table in all your calculations. The date table simply becomes another table with the referenced values that are used to filter records in other tables, such as filtering the **Sales** table in *Figure 7.8*.

Role-playing dimensions

In *Chapter 5*, *Designing a Data Model*, we talked about role-playing dimensions and how they allow a dimension to be used in multiple ways. Now, we are going to use our date table as a role-playing dimension to filter data based on different dates and against different columns.

The first role our date table will play is going to be the `OrderDate` dimension.

We can use the time intelligence measure we created earlier to count how many products were ordered each day. Notice we are using the syntactic sugar TOTALYTD call:

```
Total Products Ordered YTD = TOTALYTD(COUNT(Sales[Product SKU]),'Date'[Date])
```

Also notice we are not even mentioning `OrderDate`. The relationship between the `Sales` table and the date table defaults to using `OrderDate`. You can think of the date table as being the `OrderDate` dimension table in this context.

The next role our date table will play will be the `ShipDate` dimension table. We will create almost the same measure as our `Products Ordered` measure but tell Power BI to use the `ShipDate` relationship instead of the `OrderDate` relationship:

```
Total Products Shipped YTD = TOTALYTD(COUNT(Sales[Product
  SKU]),DATESYTD('Date'[Date]),USERELATIONSHIP('Date'[Date],
  Sales[ShipDate]))
```

This allows us to show both the number of products ordered by Year-to-Date and the number of products shipped by Year-to-Date.

Figure 7.9 – In this quarter, I shipped 999 fewer products than were ordered. That's what I get for giving the shipping department the week after Christmas off!

So, here you have a very talented date table, able to jump in and pretend to be a dimension for any date in your model. Wow, what a table!

Now, let's explore how numeric calculated columns can be replaced with measures.

Replacing numeric calculated columns with measures

Calculated columns and measures are different in the way they are stored and calculated within Power BI. When calculated columns are added to a data model, the values are calculated and stored for every row. This means that if there are 1,000 rows in a table and you add a calculated column for `Margin` (using a formula taking sales minus production costs), then for each row of the table, the data model would store a value for `Margin`. This data would be stored and updated whenever the model was refreshed so there are storage and performance implications when using many calculated columns.

Measures are not stored but instead calculated when used on the fly. Instead of creating a calculated column for Margin, you could instead create a measure that performs the same calculation, but the value would not be stored in the data model but instead be computed when the measure is used in a report visual.

For Power BI to use a measure to replicate what a calculated column does, the measure would have to be calculated row by row.

Normal Power BI statistical functions use a single table column as the only argument for their calculations, functions such as SUM, COUNT, and AVERAGE.

The X functions

Statistical functions also have a separate X function, such as SUMX, COUNTX, and AVERAGEX, and these take two arguments, a table and an expression. The expression is calculated in row context for the provided table.

We could recreate our gross revenue calculation using the SUMX function like so:

- Original:

    ```
    Gross Revenue = Sales[Quantity] * Sales[UnitPrice]
    ```

- SUMX:

    ```
    Gross Revenue X = SUMX(Sales, Sales[Quantity] * Sales[UnitPrice])
    ```

This gives us the following table:

Product Item Group	Gross Revenue	Gross Revenue X
Airplane	30,986,448.30	30,986,448.30
Helicopter	51,127,196.20	51,127,196.20
Total	**82,113,644.50**	**82,113,644.50**

Figure 7.10 – Both calculations return identical results

Note that there is a cost associated with the X functions, as we do not have the data already calculated, so Power BI will have to calculate it every time. But in many situations, the savings in model size, especially the model's memory footprint, may be worth it.

So, when do we use a calculated column and when do we use a measure?

When to use calculated columns

Calculated columns are ideal for fixed values. For example, if you want the fixed value of the year number parsed out from an entire column storing the date, the value in the calculated column would always be the same based on the date. Parsing and calculating the year value 2022-06-01 would always return 2022.

Likewise, if you want to add any text values to a table, then it's best to use a calculated column. For example, if you wanted to parse the name of the month from the date, then the calculated value would be the same based on the date. Parsing and calculating the text month value 2022-06-01 would always return July.

Calculated columns must be used if you plan to filter by a value stored. You can add a calculated column to a visual, page, or all pages filter in a Power BI report.

When to use measures

Measures are best used when values can or need to change based on the context. For example, the sum of revenue would change depending on the region we selected. Total revenue might be $1,000,000 with revenue across three different regions. Some visuals will need to show total revenue, while other visuals for regional managers might need to be filtered to only show revenue for their region.

Measures can be used to minimize the size of data in a data model as they don't add to data stores since they are calculated on the fly. This increases CPU load but reduces data size and refresh time.

Measures cannot be added to a filter in Power BI, so if you need to filter by the value in a measure, it will instead need to be a calculated column.

Using basic statistical functions to enhance data

Like many programming languages DAX has built-in capabilities for statistical and aggregation functions, such as sum, count, and averages. If you've used these functions in Microsoft Excel, you will pick up how to use these functions quickly in DAX.

Often our reports use statistics to explain and explore our data. Statistics can show you how your data is distributed, explain trends, or identify outliers. Using statistics to summarize your data can provide a quick and easy way to not only describe your data but also help find new insights or heretofore undiscovered trends. We saw this in *Chapter 3*, when we used data profiling to help us understand our data in Power Query.

Generating a statistical summary can provide you with a high-level view of your data. The advantage of doing this in DAX over Power Query is that we can use the relationships in our model and generate statistics that cover more than one table. This will help you gain even deeper insights into your data and provide you with a better foundation for your data storytelling.

Many times, you will be asked how often something happens or at what frequency. You may be asked to give the net revenue of the top 10 products by region. Power BI makes answering complex questions such as this much easier. In this example, the net revenue data needs to be grouped by both product and region. Using the statistical functions in Power BI and DAX, this challenge becomes much easier.

More often, you may be asked to return the minimum, maximum, or average of a column. If so, you do not need to create a new measure; you can override the default summarization of a column on a per-visual basis.

Changing the default summarization

Power BI has many statistical functions. In fact, many of them are similar to their Excel counterparts. Many times, they can be accessed by right-clicking on the **Values** field in the **Visualizations** pane. In the dropdown, you can change the visual to use a different summarization from whatever was set as the default.

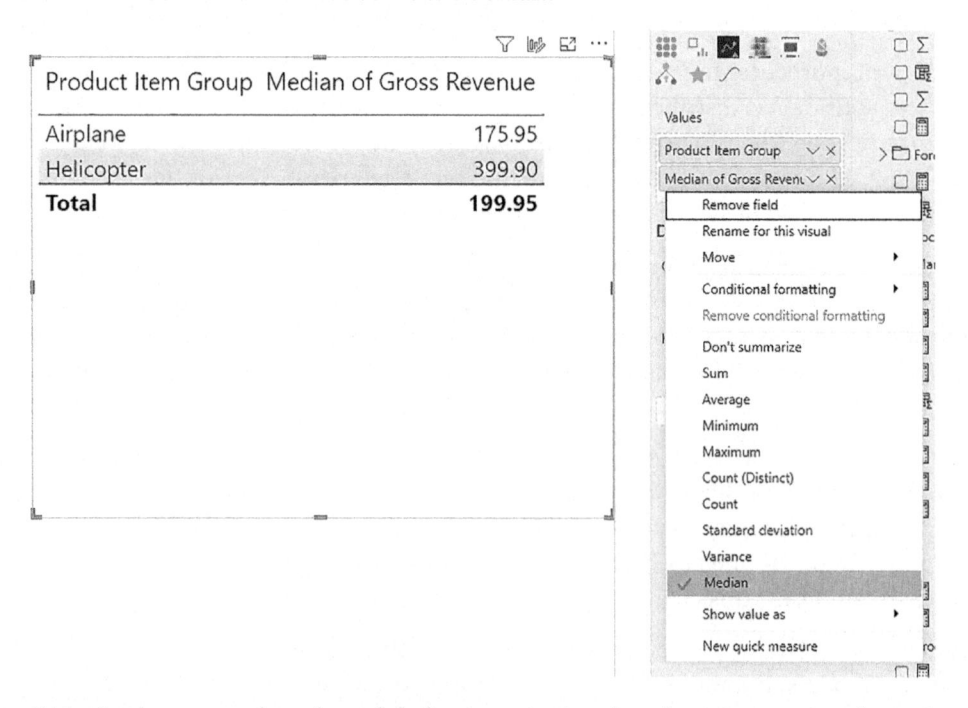

Figure 7.11 – Just because a column has a default summarization, doesn't mean we cannot change it on a visual-by-visual basis

Here, you can see that instead of using the default summarization of **Sum** for gross revenue, we changed this table to use **Median**. This is even easier than quick measures.

It is better, from a performance standpoint, to create the statistical measure instead of changing the default summarization of a column. Also, it is important to note that this feature only works on columns, not measures. It could be a native column or a calculated column, but it must be a column. Measures are already aggregated, so there is no way to change them on the fly; you have to either change the measure or create a new one.

Binning and grouping histograms

One of the more common ways to display data is with a histogram. This is a fancy term for any one of the many varieties of bar or column charts that are available in Power BI. The simplest bar chart will show the relationship between two data points, usually a dimension and a measure:

1. A histogram usually displays just one data point that has been broken down into bins. We can do this by creating a new group on a column.
2. Sticking with our **Gross Revenue** column, if we add that to the report surface, it will create a bar chart with a single bar.

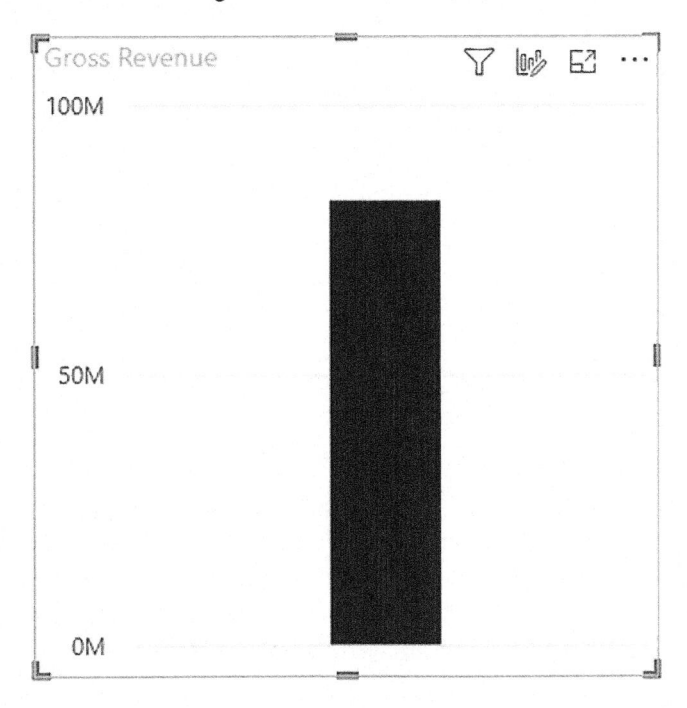

Figure 7.12 – This is a very smooth histogram. If we break it up into parts, it might become more interesting

126　Creating Measures Using DAX

3. We can then right-click on the **Gross Revenue** column in the field area and select **New group**.

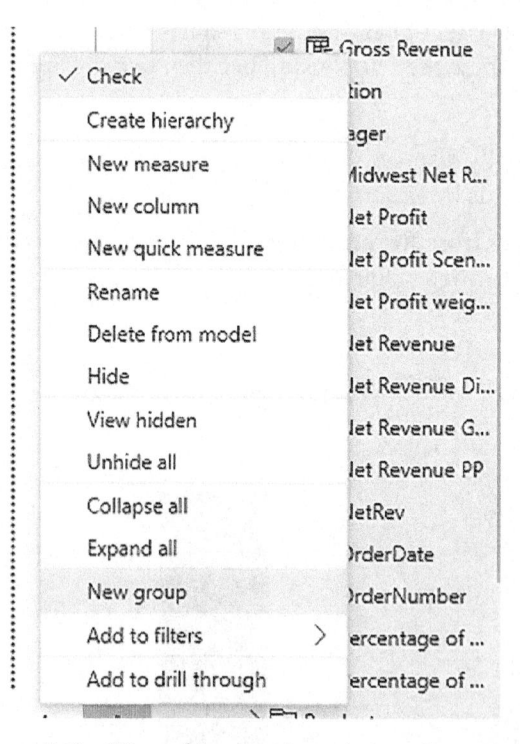

Figure 7.13 – We can bin our column by creating a group

This will open the **New group** dialog, where we can define our group. By default, binning splits a numeric or date/time column into equally sized groups. We can override this behavior by changing **Bin Type** to **Number of bins** and selecting a bin count. The fewer bins you have, the less likely you are to see trends in your data, but having too many bins can also lead to the same problem.

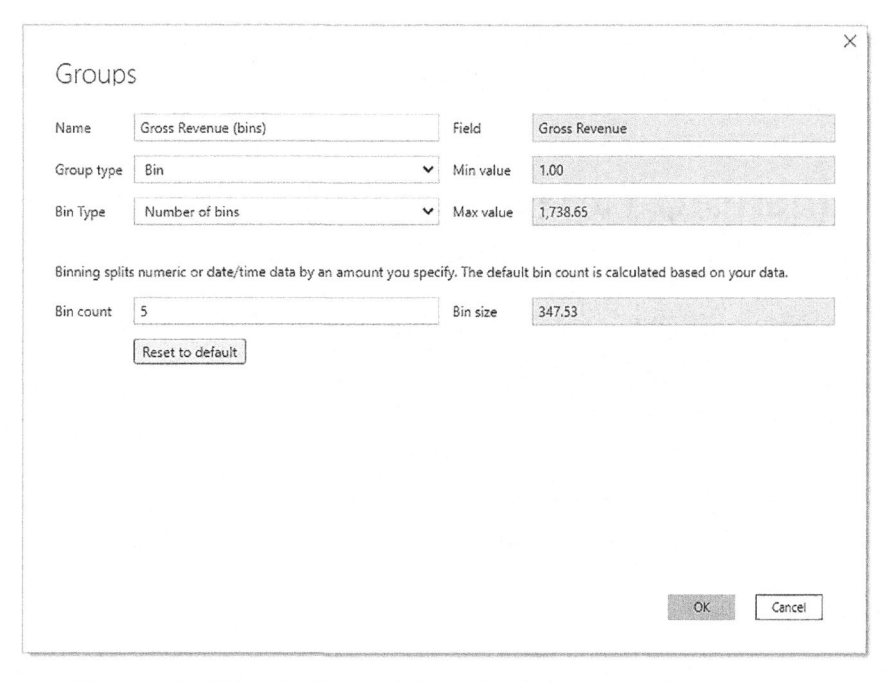

Figure 7.14 – Using the Groups dialog to break down our column into parts

4. After choosing our bin count, we can click **OK**. We now have a new group that we can add to the axis of our column chart.

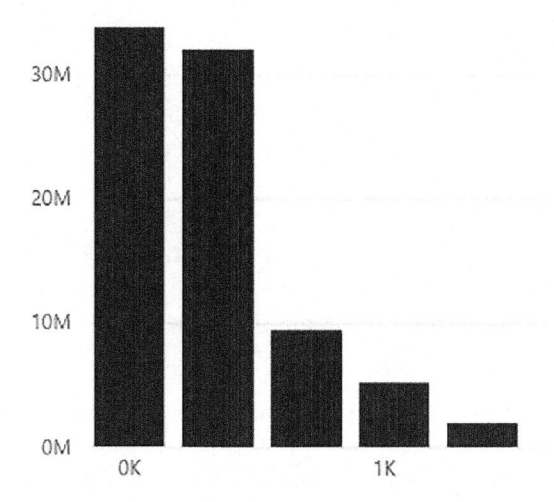

Figure 7.15 – This is a much more interesting histogram than we started with! We have grouped our single value into five separate sums

We have now produced a histogram that displays the gross revenue by the bucket size that we selected. This allows us to see that most of our gross revenue comes from smaller transactions.

Implementing top N analysis

People and companies love top N lists. There are whole websites dedicated to *The top 10 foods that celebrity data analysts like to eat* and *Top 25 ways to make your Power BI data model faster*. Not really, but I would definitely sign up for the first one!

Top N lists can provide useful information for organizations. Data consumers like to see what the company's top-selling products are. What is the most popular color widget? How do I compare my top 10 product's revenue against the rest?

There are actually two different problems here. One is to generate a ranking function and display it, and the other is to create a top N table to use a filter in a measure.

Ranking function

You can create a rank and ordered list by using the RANKX function. This is another one of those X functions that aggregate over a table. It will produce a numerical ranking of a category by an expression:

```
RANKX(<table>, <expression>[, <value>[, <order>[, <ties>]]])
```

As with all the X functions, RANKX takes a table as its first argument. It then has an expression that is evaluated for each row of the table in the first argument and returns a single scalar value for ranking. The next three arguments are optional. The value argument returns a single value whose rank is to be found. This is usually skipped and the value from the expression is used. The order can be descending or ascending, with descending the default. Finally, we can tell RANKX how to handle ties. If you choose SKIP, then the next rank value, after a tie, is the rank value of the tie plus the count of tied values. For example, if three values are tied with a rank of 11, then the next value will receive a rank of 14 (11 + 3). If you choose DENSE, then the next rank value after a tie is the next value. For example, if three values are tied with a rank of 11, then the next value will receive a rank of 12.

Here's an example of a ranking function to number our product names by gross profit:

```
Product Rank = RANKX(ALL('Product'[Product Name]),Sales[Gross Profit],,DESC,Skip)
```

The table we are ranking over, `ALL('Product'[Product Name])`, uses the `ALL` filter. This means that even if we filter our report down to one product name, it will retain its rank against all product names and not just become rank 1.

Product Item Group	Product Rank	Gross Revenue
Airplane	1	30,986,448.30
Piper Cub 4 Channel	1	6,030,480.35
P47 5 Channel	2	6,364,165.90
Tailspin Aviator Mk2-15	3	5,319,784.85
Tailspin Warbird BM32	4	2,825,737.10
Tailspin Aviator Mk2-12	5	2,784,730.30
P51	6	2,005,801.70
SkyTrainer	7	1,879,770.55
Piper Cub 3 Channel	8	1,034,387.10
P47 4 Channel	9	916,093.20
Tailspin Aviator Mk2-11	10	739,019.60
Trainer - Tailspin GL-155	11	637,316.20
Trainer - Tailspin GL-120	12	449,161.45
Helicopter	1	51,127,196.20
Tailspin Heli - Max Pro Flight - 6ch	1	36,688,985.05
6CCP-A Helicopter	2	8,746,778.70
Tailspin Heli - Co-Ax Pro Mk I - 4ch	3	2,938,161.55
4CAX-B Helicopter	4	1,345,678.60
3CAX-B Helicopter	5	1,049,130.10
3CFP-I Helicopter	6	200,990.60
Tailspin Heli - Pro Mk III - 5ch	7	79,099.60
4CFP-I Helicopter	8	78,372.00
Total	1	82,113,644.50

Product Item Group	Product Rank	Gross Revenue
Airplane	6	2,005,801.70
P51	6	2,005,801.70
Total	9	2,005,801.70

Figure 7.16 – Ranking is easy in Power BI!

Notice that each product item group gets its own ranking, and that's even when we filter down to one product; it maintains its ranking.

Top N functions

There is nothing in the `RANKX` function to limit the number of rows returned. We will see in this section how to limit our calculations to the top N.

We will start with the easiest way: just asking.

Q&Aing our way to a top N list

As we saw in the previous chapter, we can use Power BI's impressive natural-language capabilities to help us create reports. Using the Q&A visual, we can ask Power BI to answer the question *What are my top 5 product names by gross revenue?*

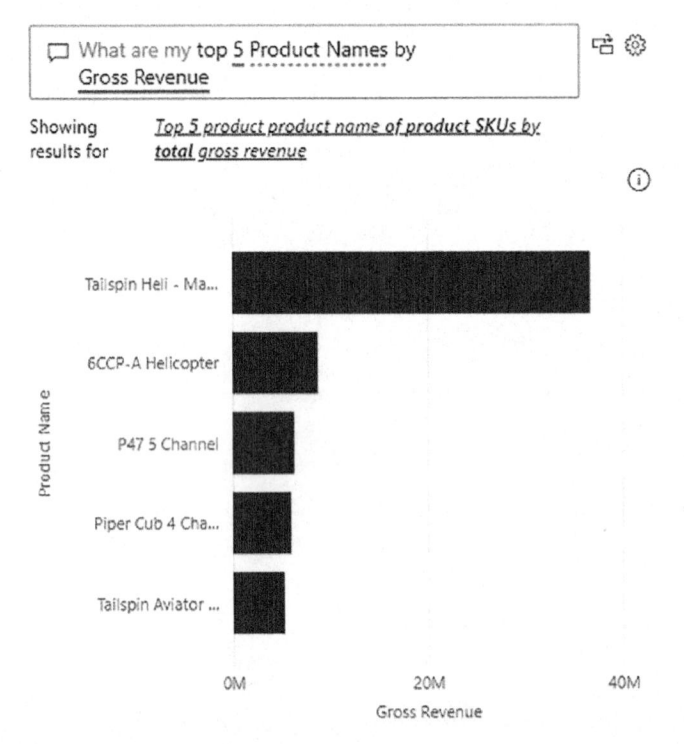

Figure 7.17 – When you are not certain how to do something in Power BI, just ask!

And with zero coding on our part, we get a top 5 chart!

Top N filter

In the filters pane, there is an option for a top N filter on a visual. Click on the visual you want to filter and select the category you want to filter on.

Then, in the filters pane, expand the **Filter type** list and select **Top N**. In the **Show items** settings, select **Top** and however many you want to display. Then, select a numeric column or measure as the value that you want to filter the field by. The visual updates accordingly.

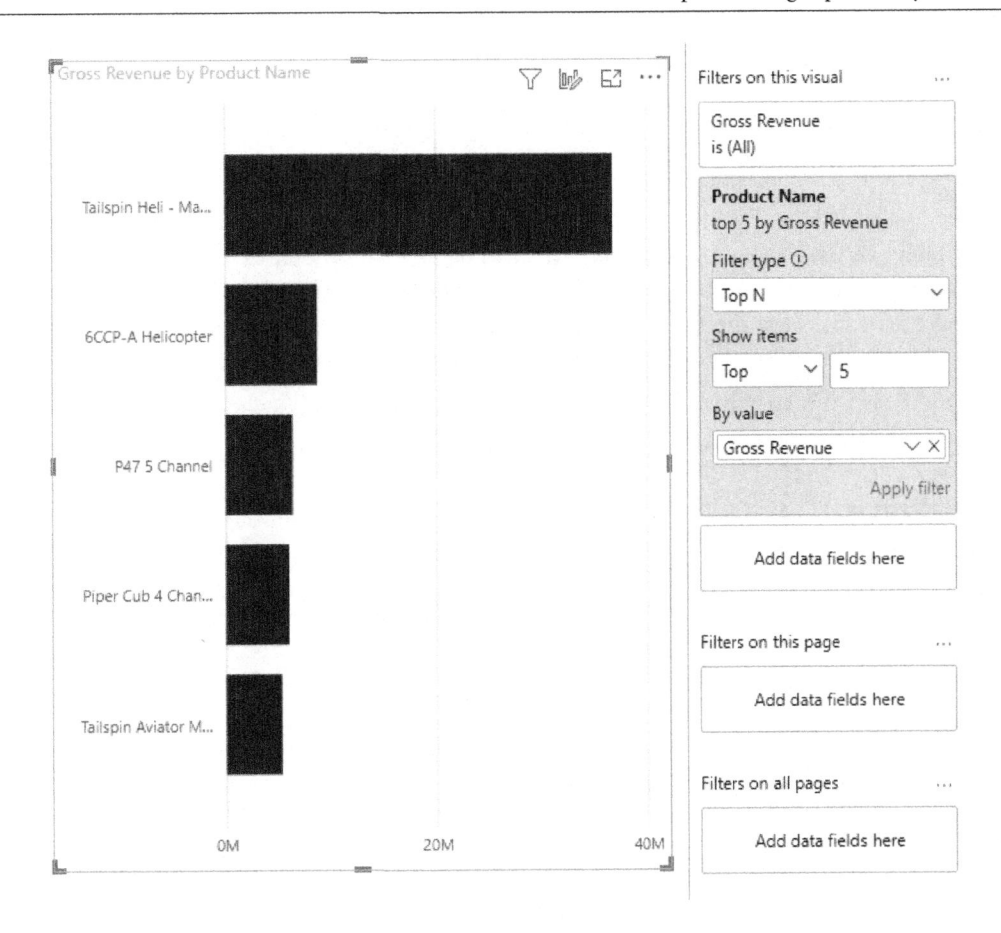

Figure 7.18 – Using the filters pane to limit a visual to the top 5! Easy!

We can use this type of filter to limit our RANKX functions as well, though it would be easier to create a filter on the RANKX field and limit it to 5 or 10 or whatever we choose.

Top N function

Another option to calculate the top 10 products using DAX is to use the TOPN function. Using TOPN, you can discover the top 10 values in different filtering contexts, such as the impact the top 10 products made on the total sales.

The `TOPN` function returns a table, not a single scalar value, and you can use it as follows:

```
TOPN(<n_value>, <table>, <orderBy_expression>, [<order>[,
<orderBy_expression>, [<order>]]…])
```

The first value is where we tell `TOPN` how many rows we want in our table, while the next is the table we want to run `TOPN` over. This can be any valid DAX expression that returns a table, or just a table. `orderBy_Expression` is the value we want to order our table by, and the order is the direction, descending or ascending, that we want the table to be ordered in. We can repeat `orderBy_expression` and order if we want to use more than one expression in our calculation.

Here is an example where we use `TOPN` to generate a table to filter our data by:

```
Top Product Gross Revenue =
CALCULATE([Gross Rev],
TOPN(1,ALL('Product'[Product Name]),[Gross Rev],DESC)
)
```

We can use this calculation in visuals or other calculations. We can use this in another measure to compare how other products compare against our best-selling product:

```
% Product Gross Revenue vs Top=
DIVIDE(
        [Top Product Gross Revenue],
        SUM(Sales[Gross Revenue])
        )
```

We can now create a visual comparing our top product revenue versus everything else.

Product Item Group	Gross Revenue	Top Product Gross Revenue	% Product Gross Revenue vs Top
Airplane	30,986,448.30	6,364,165.90	486.89%
P47 5 Channel	6,364,165.90	6,364,165.90	100.00%
Piper Cub 4 Channel	6,030,480.35	6,364,165.90	94.76%
Tailspin Aviator Mk2-15	5,319,784.85	6,364,165.90	83.59%
Tailspin Warbird BM32	2,825,737.10	6,364,165.90	44.40%
Tailspin Aviator Mk2-12	2,784,730.30	6,364,165.90	43.76%
P51	2,005,801.70	6,364,165.90	31.52%
SkyTrainer	1,879,770.55	6,364,165.90	29.54%
Piper Cub 3 Channel	1,034,387.10	6,364,165.90	16.25%
P47 4 Channel	916,093.20	6,364,165.90	14.39%
Tailspin Aviator Mk2-11	739,019.60	6,364,165.90	11.61%
Trainer - Tailspin GL-155	637,316.20	6,364,165.90	10.01%
Trainer - Tailspin GL-120	449,161.45	6,364,165.90	7.06%
Helicopter	51,127,196.20	36,688,985.05	139.35%
Tailspin Heli - Max Pro Flight - 6ch	36,688,985.05	36,688,985.05	100.00%
6CCP-A Helicopter	8,746,778.70	36,688,985.05	23.84%
Tailspin Heli - Co-Ax Pro Mk I - 4ch	2,938,161.55	36,688,985.05	8.01%
4CAX-B Helicopter	1,345,678.60	36,688,985.05	3.67%
3CAX-B Helicopter	1,049,130.10	36,688,985.05	2.86%
Total	82,113,644.50	36,688,985.05	223.81%

Figure 7.19 – Comparing our top product gross revenue against all our products

TOPN is a great way to compare parts of your data against the rest of the data. Next, let's look at how we can use semi-additive measures to enhance our data model.

Creating semi-additive measures

Power BI has three different types of measures it can perform: additive, non-additive, and semi-additive. We will check each of them out in the following sections.

Additive measures

An additive measure, such as sum, aggregates over an element. Our gross profit calculations are examples of additive measures. The gross profit for each product item group adds up to the gross profit for *all* product item groups.

Non-additive measures

Non-additive measures do not aggregate over anything. `DISTINCT COUNT` is a good example of this. The `DISTINCT COUNT` value of product SKUs ordered over a month does not equal the sum of distinct counts of every day of that month.

Semi-additive measures

Semi-additive measures use `SUM` to aggregate over some of the elements and different aggregations over other dimensions.

One common scenario that uses a semi-additive calculation is inventory.

Let's say we need to perform an inventory count in our warehouse. If we have 100 helicopters in the warehouse on Monday, and then we have 95 on Tuesday, we can't add those numbers up. We do not have 195 helicopters in our warehouse, we have 95.

If want to get an inventory count for a specific date, we could write a measure like this:

```
Last Inventory Count =CALCULATE(SUM( 'Warehouse'[Inventory
Count]), LASTDATE('Date'[Date]))
```

This calculation will prevent `SUM` from aggregating across all the dates; the function will only sum for the last date in the period. This will, effectively, create a semi-additive measure.

Summary

In this chapter, we covered a lot of ground! We talked a lot about DAX, the programming language to implement business rules in Power BI.

We went over the basics of DAX, how it looks a lot like Microsoft Excel formulas, and how those formulas are applied in either the row or filter context. We compared measures to calculated columns.

We then discussed one of the most powerful functions in DAX, `CALCULATE`. We used `CALCULATE` to manipulate the filter context of our formulas to create more complex equations. We saw how `CALCULATE` can be used with simple filtering or be combined with the `FILTER` function for more powerful operations.

We discussed date tables and how they can be used with time intelligence calculations and how the date table becomes a role-playing dimension to be used across many related tables. We learned that Power BI includes time intelligence functions to make aggregations such as Year-over-Year much easier.

When comparing measures and columns, we learned that there are pros and cons to each. We explored how by using both in your data model, you can best optimize for your business needs, by using calculated columns when you need to calculate a value that you can use in a filter. This can also be used while using measures to calculate a value on the fly based on the filtering context. We also covered statistical functions, including RANKX and TOPN. These and other functions will help bring out more value from the data in your Power BI data model. We finished by looking at additive, non-additive, and semi-additive measures to round out our understanding of measures.

In the next chapter, we will explore how we can optimize our Power BI data model for performance.

Questions

1. What are quick measures?

    A. Measures that move around the screen quickly

    B. Calculated fields that can be added without coding

    C. Measures that can quickly be added by writing DAX code

    D. Custom visuals added from Microsoft AppSource

2. What is used to evaluate an expression in the context of a modified filter?

    A. COMPUTE

    B. APPRAISE

    C. SUM

    D. CALCULATE

3. If you only have the Sales Amount and Total Product Cost fields, which function would be best to use to calculate the sum of margin?

    A. SUMX

    B. MARGIN

    C. DISTINCTCOUNT

    D. FILTER

8
Optimizing Model Performance

The data model is a key component of any Power BI solution. Data models require data structures to be imported and relationships set up so that business questions can be answered using the data contained in the model. Often, data sizes grow, and performance can become a challenge when this happens. Optimizing the data model for performance becomes a necessary exercise to ensure expectations for performance can still be met.

Optimizing data model performance is a component of the PL-300 exam and is also important to consider when using Power BI in a production environment. Additionally, it's important to optimize Power BI data models for performance in order to ensure users have the best experience with the solution. Having a performant data model will ensure you are able to answer questions in an efficient manner that leads to positive outcomes for the organization.

In this chapter, we're going to cover the following topics:

- Optimizing data in the model
- Optimizing measures, relationships, and visuals
- Optimizing aggregations
- Query diagnostics

Technical requirements

For this chapter, you will need the following:

- Microsoft Power BI Desktop installed on a Microsoft Windows PC.
- A Power BI data model where we can apply the optimization techniques covered in this chapter. If you've been following along with the book, you should have one ready to go!

Optimizing data in the model

We've covered, in previous chapters, how Power BI supports directly connecting to a data store, such as connecting to an **Enterprise Data Warehouse** (**EDW**) that has billions of records and years of sales history. When configured with DirectQuery performance, Power BI becomes dependent upon not only the calculations and rendering of visuals in the report but also the performance of the underlying data store. If the EDW takes a long time to query, then the Power BI report that uses the query will also take a long time.

To help, Power BI also supports importing data, which reduces the performance dependency on the underlying data store to increase the performance of report visuals. Data imported into the Power BI data model is stored both in memory and on disk using the VertiPaq **Storage Engine** (**SE**). VertiPaq will compress data, sometimes by as much as 10x, so even with limitations on the amount of data imported, it's often able to store large datasets.

To best optimize import datasets, we recommend taking a layered approach and reviewing each characteristic of your data, starting with removing unnecessary rows and columns.

Removing unnecessary rows and columns

Often, when connecting to data sources, there will be additional data (both in rows and columns) that is not needed for the reports and dashboards that you want to create. In these cases, you will be best served by removing these rows and columns from the dataset using the Power Query Editor.

Data is stored in the VertiPaq engine in a columnar format, which is highly compressed. However, if it's possible to remove columns of data, it will successfully reduce the size of your dataset. Due to how data is stored in VertiPaq, it is recommended to remove all unnecessary text columns since they will take up more storage space in the data model. To remove unnecessary columns from a dataset in the Power Query Editor, simply right-click the column to be removed and click **Remove**. It's also possible to select multiple columns, right-click, and then select **remove columns** to remove multiple columns at the same time.

To remove unnecessary rows of data, you'll need to add a filter to a query. To best execute a filter, you'll need to understand the basic characteristics of the data, which is easy to do using the data profiling capabilities of Power Query (see *Chapter 3*, *Profiling the Data*, for more details). Filtering rows of data is dependent upon the data type of the column being filtered. For example, if you want to filter using the `ListPrice` column of a `Products` table, then you'll need to supply a numeric or currency value to the filter criteria. If you want to filter by a text value (such as removing all products that have a `Color` value of `Red`), then you'll need to apply the filter to a column that is set to a data type of text. To apply a filter to a column, simply click the ▼ button for the column.

For text filters, select **Text Filters** and then select the type of operator you'd like to use:

- **Equals**
- **Does Not Equal**
- **Begins With**
- **Does Not Begin With**
- **Ends With**
- **Does Not End With**
- **Contains**
- **Does Not Contain**

For numeric or currency filters, select **Number Filters** and then select the type of operator you'd like to use:

- **Equals**
- **Does Not Equal**
- **Greater Than**
- **Greater Than Or Equal To**

- **Less Than**
- **Less Than Or Equal To**
- **Between**

For date filters, select **Date/Time Filters** and then select the one needed. Different column data types will have different criteria for applying filters.

Removing unnecessary columns and rows is often a quick and easy way to reduce the amount of data in your Power BI data model. Next, we will look at some more complex ways of reducing the data model size.

Splitting numeric and text column data

In the VertiPaq engine, data is stored in a columnar data format. This means for a given query or table, each column is given a data type and all records for each column are stored independently from each other, allowing for optimized compression for each data type.

Numeric data type data in the data model uses **value encoding** to store the data in an optimized way. Value encoding is where data gets stored on disk or in memory based on a mathematical operation in order to gain compression. For example, say we have a table of numeric values, as follows:

ZipCode
45674
45675
45677
45678
45679

Figure 8.1 – Example ZIP code table with data values without value encoding compression

Using value encoding, the data stored might look more like this:

ZipCode
0
1
3
4
5

Figure 8.2 – Example ZIP code table with value encoding compression

To arrive at the value-encoded data, we simply subtract the lowest value from the table: 45674. This means that the underlying numeric type can often be changed from long (64-bit integers), to integer (32-bit integers), to short (16-bit integers), which can have a dramatic impact on the amount of memory or disk storage needed to store the data. Power BI can use much more advanced mathematic algorithms to do value encoding.

Text and non-numeric data type columns use hash encoding. Hash encoding is similar in that it replaces the original value with another value that takes up fewer bytes for storage; however, the algorithm used to store the values tends to need to store an entire dictionary in order to encode and decode the values (rather than a simple mathematical formula). Hash encoding tends to be less efficient than value encoding so it is important to use tools such as Tabular Editor to provide hints to the VertiPaq engine to ensure the best encoding is used.

In some cases, you may have text data type columns that store both text and numeric data. In some cases, it can be helpful to split a column such as this into two columns, setting one as the text data type and the other as numeric. This allows the VertiPaq engine to use hash encoding on the text component and value encoding on the numeric component. Even greater efficiency can be achieved when there is high cardinality in the text component (reducing the size of the dictionary-needed hash encoding) of the column.

Splitting columns is a feature of the Power Query Editor, and it's possible to split columns by the following:

- Delimiter
- Number of characters
- Positions
- Lower- and uppercase characters
- Digit and non-digit characters

Next, we'll look at other ways of optimizing using measures, relationships, and visuals.

Optimizing measures, relationships, and visuals

Measures in Power BI are driven by DAX queries. To optimize DAX queries (and measures), we must understand how Power BI uses both a **Formula Engine** (**FE**) and an **SE**, which make up the backend technology. Simply put, the SE is where imported data is stored in the highly compressed columnar VertiPaq format, and the FE is where data can be calculated based on the requirements in DAX queries.

The SE provides a single interface for the FE to query and retrieve data. It functions to store data or provide a conduit for underlying data stores in cases where data is connected using DirectQuery. The SE is built into Power BI Desktop and is also part of the underlying technology used in SQL Server Analysis Services and Azure Analysis Services.

The FE is the query processor that takes DAX queries as input, interacts with the SE, and then returns data to Power BI visuals in reports and dashboards. The FE does not have direct access to every kind of data source that Power BI supports; instead, the FE *only* interacts with the SE. It's the SE that has both the ability to store data in-memory in VertiPaq storage and the myriad of different data stores supported by Power BI. The FE serves the purpose of understanding DAX queries, converting to **xmSQL** (the SQL dialect used by VertiPaq), and performing calculations on data received from the SE to get to the end result as directed by the DAX query.

When optimizing measures, you will want to use an open source tool called **DAX Studio** (available for free from `https://daxstudio.org`). DAX Studio is an open source DAX client tool that allows you to do an in-depth analysis of DAX queries and how they are executed in the Power BI environment:

1. To use DAX Studio, you will need the DAX query used by the specific operation of the report in Power BI Desktop. You can acquire this query easily using the **Performance analyzer** pane in Power BI Desktop, accessed from under the **View** menu on the ribbon. Click **Performance Analyzer** and then click **Refresh visuals**, select a slicer, or apply a filter. Power BI will generate and run the DAX query (or queries) to generate the requested data for each of the visuals on the report being analyzed.

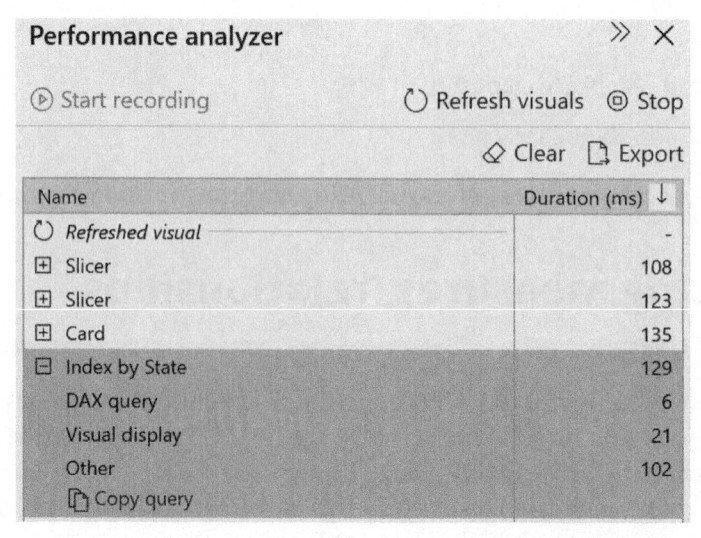

Name	Duration (ms) ↓
↻ Refreshed visual	-
⊞ Slicer	108
⊞ Slicer	123
⊞ Card	135
⊟ Index by State	129
DAX query	6
Visual display	21
Other	102
📋 Copy query	

Figure 8.3 – Results of Performance analyzer after refreshing visuals

Optimizing measures, relationships, and visuals   143

2. After the operation has completed, you will be able to click **Copy query** in the **Performance analyzer** pane. Copy the query and then open DAX Studio.

3. Open DAX Studio, and ensure you connect to the PBI/SSDT model that is currently running in Power BI Desktop (the name of your Power BI file will show under **PBI / SSDT Model**).

Figure 8.4 – Connection screen in DAX Studio

4. Copy your query into the main or largest query pane shown in the DAX Studio interface, where it shows **Start by typing your query in this area.**.

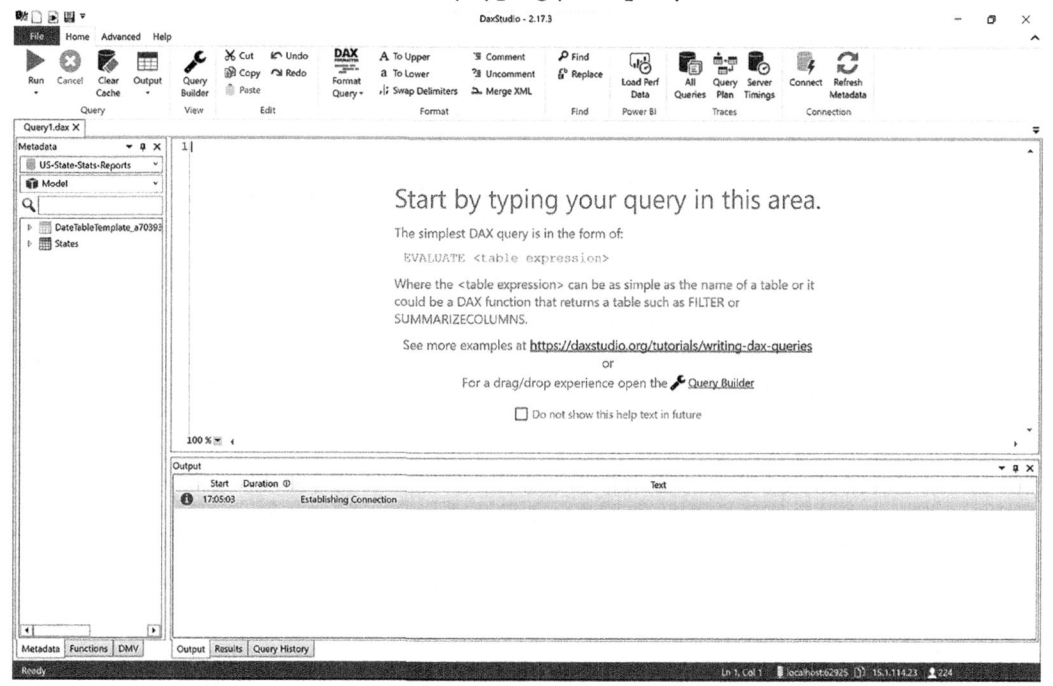

Figure 8.5 – DAX Studio window showing various panes, including the main query pane

5. After pasting your query, be sure to select **Server Timings** and then **Clear Cache and then Run** under the **Run** menu shown under **Home** on the ribbon.

6. Once these settings have been selected, click **Run** (which should run **Clear Cache and then Run**), and then click the **Server Timings** tab on the bottom pane. The bottom pane should now show something like this:

Total	SE CPU	Line	Subclass	Duration	CPU	Par.	Rows	KB	Query
4 ms	0 ms x0.0	2	Scan	1	0		54	1	SELECT

FE: 3 ms 75.0%
SE: 1 ms 25.0%

SE Queries: 1
SE Cache: 0 0.0%

```
SET DC_KIND="AUTO";
SELECT
'States'[State],
SUM ( 'States'[Index] )
FROM 'States'
WHERE
    'States'[R/B] = 'Blue';

'Estimated size ( volume,
marshalling bytes ) : 54, 864'
```

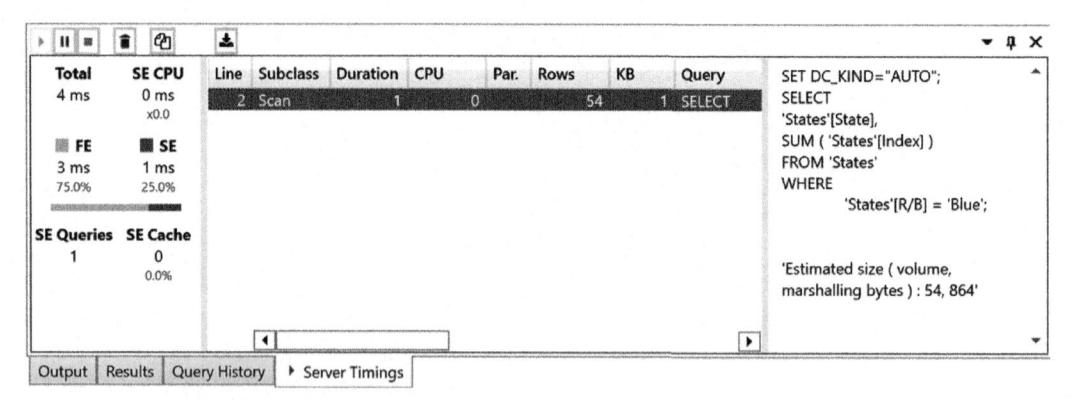

Figure 8.6 – Server Timings tab showing details of the DAX query

From this screen, we can see information about our DAX query that tells us the following:

- How much time was spent in total to run the DAX query (**4 ms**)
- How much time was used by the FE to run the DAX query (**3 ms**)
- How much time was used by the SE to run the DAX query (**1 ms**)
- How many SE queries were generated by the FE (**1**)
- What the SE query looks like (shown in the right-hand side subpane)

This information will help us determine where we can spend time optimizing the DAX query used by the measure. In the previous example, we can see that the majority of the 4 ms time is spent in the FE, so it would make the most sense to optimize that as the remaining portion (1 ms consumed by the SE) will have less time to optimize. Ideally, you want to see more time spent in the FE or equally balanced between the FE and SE.

Here is an example of a DAX query used by a visual that contains two SE queries and is relatively balanced between FE and SE time:

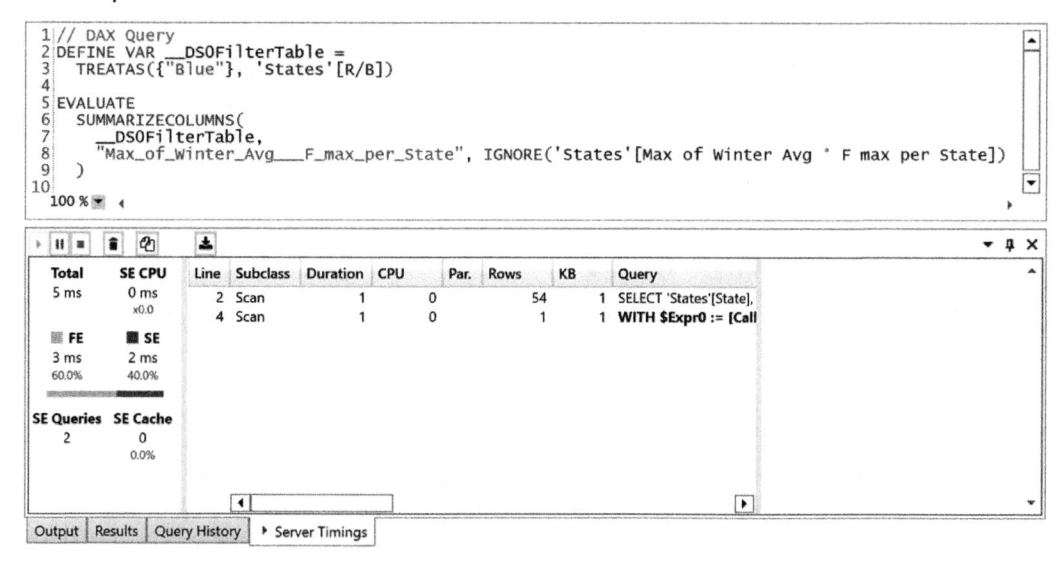

```
// DAX Query
DEFINE VAR __DS0FilterTable =
    TREATAS({"Blue"}, 'States'[R/B])

EVALUATE
    SUMMARIZECOLUMNS(
        __DS0FilterTable,
        "Max_of_Winter_Avg___F_max_per_State", IGNORE('States'[Max of Winter Avg ° F max per State])
    )
```

		Line	Subclass	Duration	CPU	Par.	Rows	KB	Query
Total	**SE CPU**	2	Scan	1	0		54	1	SELECT 'States'[State],
5 ms	0 ms x0.0	4	Scan	1	0		1	1	WITH $Expr0 := [Call
■ FE	■ SE								
3 ms	2 ms								
60.0%	40.0%								
SE Queries	**SE Cache**								
2	0 0.0%								

Figure 8.7 – DAX query with two SE queries

SE queries are composed of xmSQL and are viewable by clicking each one in the middle-bottom pane. In this case, the SE query from line 2 is as follows:

```
SET DC_KIND="AUTO";
SELECT'States'[State],MAX ( 'States'[Winter Avg ° F] )
FROM 'States'
WHERE 'States'[R/B] = 'Blue';
'Estimated size ( volume, marshalling bytes ) : 54, 864'
```

The SE query from line 4 is as follows:

```
SET DC_KIND="AUTO";
WITH $Expr0 := [CallbackDataID ( MAX ( 'States'[Winter Avg °
F]] ) ) ] ( PFDATAID ( 'States'[State] ) )
SELECT
MAX ( @$Expr0 )
FROM 'States'
WHERE 'States'[R/B] = 'Blue';
'Estimated size ( volume, marshalling bytes ) : 1, 16'
```

The PL-300 exam will not require in-depth knowledge of tuning FE or ST queries (or SE queries that get pushed down to DirectQuery data sources) but it is important to understand the dynamics of how DAX is executed (the relationship between the FE and the SE and how to troubleshoot these operations to increase performance).

Recommended reading for in-depth study on this topic is the book *The Definitive Guide to DAX: Business intelligence with Microsoft Power BI, SQL Server Analysis Services, and Excel* by Marco Russo and Alberto Ferrari.

Optimizing relationships

When report visuals are configured with fields from multiple queries or tables and expected results are not seen, then it's possible there are issues with the relationships that have been set up (or autoconfigured by Power BI).

When optimizing relationships, it's important to understand the true cardinality of the tables involved (this may require analysis using Data view) and how that has been configured in Power BI (properties on the connecting line between queries in Model view). It's also important to verify that the filter direction supports propagation (shown by the arrows on the connecting lines in Model view).

Some other things to look out for that will make for suboptimal relationships include blank values matching columns between the tables and mismatching or incompatible data types for the matching columns between the tables.

Now, let's look at how we can optimize visuals.

Optimizing visuals

When optimizing visuals, it's important to think about all the ways visuals are used in Power BI. Visuals can be used in the following:

- Reports
- Dashboards
- Paginated reports

Let's look at how we can uniquely optimize visuals in each case in the next sections.

Optimizing visuals in reports

To optimize visuals in reports, we need to follow a layered approach. First, review each visual and determine whether it is required. Limit the visuals used to only those required to meet business requirements. Adding additional visuals that are not needed will have a negative impact on report performance. Next, apply the most restricted data filtering to the visuals. This is accomplished by using filters for all pages, only the selected page, or only a specific visual. Lastly, you should consider performance when adding each visual to the report canvas. Each visual used has the potential to decrease the overall performance of the report, especially third-party or custom visuals, as they may not have gone through extensive performance testing before becoming available for use.

Optimizing visuals in dashboards

To optimize visuals in dashboards, you need to remember that Power BI keeps a cache of data in order to serve dashboards in the Power BI service. The cache used by the Power BI service helps to enable consistent performance across multiple users (unless row-level security is used, in which case a per-context cache will be built). Live report tiles and streaming tiles will not use a cache since they are used to serve very up-to-date information.

By default, the dashboard cache will be updated automatically by the service every hour, but this can be configured manually in the dataset settings. This should be set to the default setting or optionally configured per business requirements.

Optimizing visuals in paginated reports

The optimization of visuals in paginated reports centers around the performance of the data retrieval settings and Premium capacity memory allocation. The optimization of paginated report data retrieval settings includes concepts such as limiting data used by the paginated reports, using expression-based fields, and using filters (applied to a dataset in Power BI) or parameters (filtering injected to underlying data sources). All these techniques go back to the idea of limiting the amount of data in the dataset used by the report. More details on using paginated reports will be covered in the chapter on paginated reports.

Additionally, since paginated reports rely on the Power BI Premium service, it's important to monitor the capacity resource usage using tools such as the Power BI Premium Capacity Metrics app. The use of the Metrics app is important for Power BI Premium administrators since it is possible to overload a Premium capacity with too many Premium workspaces for the specified SKU size. Paginated reports are run within a protected sandbox per Premium capacity to help ensure the isolation of resources. But it's also important to ensure only trusted publishers in your organization have access to publish paginated reports.

Next, we will look at optimizing using group by and summarize aggregations.

Optimizing with aggregations

Any time you want to optimize your data model, in addition to reducing the data storage by removing unnecessary columns and rows, it's also important to consider removing data by summarizing or using group by to reduce the number of rows and/or columns in your data if the additional grain is not needed.

For example, the data warehouse we use to store the data of historical sales and inventory data needed by our organization may contain highly detailed information, such as every sale made for every day of the business year. Additionally, it may contain multiple years of data. This kind of detail may be needed for some analysis, but other reports and analytics may only need total sales per month. So, in those cases, we can simply summarize the data by grouping the data by calendar year and month. Aggregating by month can reduce millions of rows of data into less than 100 rows, which can dramatically increase performance.

To illustrate this concept, let's look at a simple example of a table with 10 sales records:

Sale ID	Sale Date	Sale Amount
619	2021-06-01	$ 9.87
517	2021-06-02	$ 83.33
107	2021-07-06	$ 28.91
394	2021-07-20	$ 6.38
348	2021-08-10	$ 98.54
478	2021-08-12	$ 7.38
376	2021-08-23	$ 63.67
314	2021-09-16	$ 33.29
394	2021-09-28	$ 87.97
816	2021-09-29	$ 89.44

Figure 8.8 – Example table of 10 sales

If we want to answer questions about monthly sales, then we can aggregate the 10 records shown in *Figure 8.8* into only 4 records, as shown in *Figure 8.9*:

Sale Month	Total Sales Per Month
2021-6	$ 93.20
2021-7	$ 35.29
2021-8	$ 169.59
2021-9	$ 210.70

Figure 8.9 – Example table of aggregated sales by month

In this example, we lose some data fidelity, but we reduce our data size from 3 columns and 10 rows to just 2 columns with 4 rows. If we normally aggregate this data and do not drill down into each sale or drill down into data by day or week, then we can use this method to reduce the size of data in the data model while still being able to answer questions about the sales amount each month.

Last, we will look at how the built-in query diagnostics tool can be used to help optimize model performance.

Query diagnostics

The **query diagnostics** tool that is built into Power Query allows us to see additional information related to each operation that Power Query performs. Many times, these Power Query operations will be data refreshes or when data is retrieved the first time; however, Power Query may perform other operations, such as retrieving a list of tables that can be used to source data. The information provided will provide more information on query steps, their duration, and other details that will allow you to understand which parts of the query take the longest time. Query diagnostics run in a trace fashion where the monitor needs to be started and stopped. When query diagnostics is running, it is recording the operations performed by Power Query to help you gain new insights.

There are two types of diagnostics that can be executed: **step diagnostics** and **session diagnostics**. Step diagnostics will provide details on only the selected step from a list of steps in the **Query Settings** pane. Session diagnostics can be used to start recording multiple steps, and then details will be recorded for multiple steps.

Diagnostics are recorded in special-purpose queries (or tables) inside Power Query and show up as tables designated as follows:

- **Counters** – This table stores diagnostic data containing processor and memory usage while the step or the session recording took place.
- **Detailed** – This table stores diagnostic data for each query, step, operation, and data source query, and the duration for each. This is the table with the most verbose information.
- **Aggregated** – This table is like the detailed table but is aggregated to improve readability.
- **Partitions** – This table provides information related to the logical partitions used for data privacy.

Once the diagnostics tables have been created, they can even be used in report visualizations once the **Enable load** setting has been enabled for the table from the right-click menu.

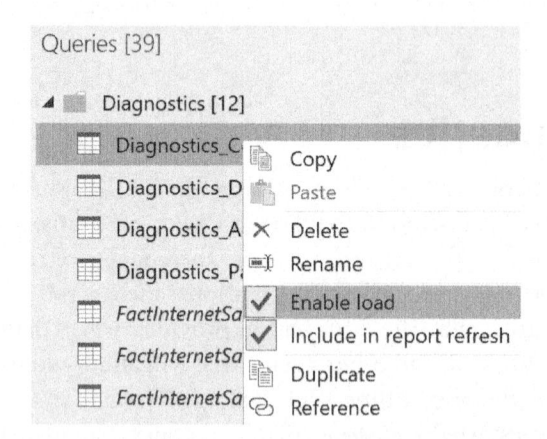

Figure 8.10 – Right-click menu on a query showing the Enable load option

Now, we'll look at how diagnostics tables can be generated for both sessions and steps.

Session diagnostics

To generate session diagnostics tables, click **Start Diagnostics** under the **Tools** tab on the ribbon in the Power Query window. Once the session has been started, perform the steps in Power Query for which you want the diagnostic data. Once the steps have completed, go back to the **Tools** tab on the ribbon and click **Stop Diagnostics**. Upon stopping the session, the diagnostics tables will show up in the **Queries** pane of the Power Query window under a new group called **Diagnostics**.

Step diagnostics

To generate step diagnostics tables, select the step under **Applied Steps** of the **Query Settings** pane in Power Query. Then, click **Diagnose Step** under the **Tools** tab of the ribbon. Once the diagnostics have executed, you'll see new diagnostic tables created for just this step in the **Queries** pane list, under a new group called **Diagnostics**.

Understanding query diagnostics

When reviewing or analyzing the details or aggregations of query diagnostics data, it's important to understand what each step is doing and which ones are happening inside Power BI and which ones might be steps where Power BI is going back to underlying data sources (which is typical for data refreshes even for import scenarios). Some of the important columns to look at include the following:

- query (so you know which query or table the operations pertain to)
- operation (to distinguish between opening a connection, sending a query, or evaluating, among other things)
- start time
- end time
- exclusive duration

The last few columns will help you understand which operations are taking the longest time during the query execution.

Once you know where the time is being spent, then you will be able to focus on that operation. For example, you may find that the data refresh is taking a long time because Power Query is waiting for the underlying database to return data to a query – so you'll end up with better performance in Power BI if you scale up the underlying database to make a better-performing data refresh in Power BI.

Summary

In this chapter, we learned about optimizing model performance. We learned how some of the easiest ways to increase data model performance include only keeping data that is necessary for reports and either removing the additional rows and columns using Power Query, aggregating the data to reduce it, or simply removing the data in the underlying data store (sometimes accomplished with a view in a database). We also learned how to use tools such as DAX Studio to investigate the inner workings of measures to best optimize those components of our data models for the best performance. We learned how we can optimize relationships and visuals and how we can use the query diagnostics tools in Power BI to better understand the operations that take place in Power Query.

In the next chapter, we will learn about creating dynamic and engaging reports using Power BI Desktop.

Questions

1. Which technique will increase the performance of data models?

    A. Adding more memory to Power BI Desktop

    B. Changing the data source to Microsoft Excel

    C. Publishing reports to Power BI Premium

    D. Removing unnecessary data from the data model

2. Aggregating data will do what?

    A. Reduce the number of columns and rows.

    B. Reduce the number of columns only.

    C. Increase the number of rows only.

    D. Both b and c.

3. Filtering in a Power BI report can be applied to what?

    A. All pages in a report file, a single page, only a visual.

    B. Filtering can only be applied to visuals.

    C. A single page or a visual.

    D. A dashboard, a page, or a visual.

4. Which tool or capability should be used to determine how much of a query duration uses the formula engine or the storage engine?

   A. Query diagnostics

   B. Query analytics

   C. DAX Studio

   D. Tabular Editor

5. When using query diagnostics, which kind of diagnostics should be used to analyze multiple steps in a query?

   A. Multiple-step diagnostics

   B. Session diagnostics

   C. Step diagnostics

   D. Model diagnostics

Part 3 – Visualizing the Data

This section explores the visualization capabilities of Power BI to create reports and dashboards using data from previous parts. The visualization capabilities allow insights to be unlocked from data.

This section comprises the following chapters:

- *Chapter 9, Creating Reports*
- *Chapter 10, Creating Dashboards*
- *Chapter 11, Enhancing Reports*

9
Creating Reports

Finally! Yes, in our book about Microsoft's awesome reporting tool, Power BI, it's not until *Chapter 9* that we're talking about creating reports!

There's a reason for that: to *tell a story with data*, you need to have data. Once you have the data, measures, hierarchies, security, and all the other things that go into modeling your data, the storytelling becomes very easy.

Power BI provides an easy-to-use canvas for you to tell your data story. It has a wealth of visualizations that can be added to reports from an easy-to-use application, Power BI Desktop.

Power BI has numerous visuals you can use to tell your story. From tables and matrixes to pie and donut charts, to scatter plots and histograms, odds are that Power BI has the perfect visual to tell your story.

In this chapter, we will cover the following:

- Understanding the reporting capabilities of Power BI
- Adding visualization items to reports
- Choosing an appropriate visualization type
- Formatting and configuring visualizations
- Importing a custom visual
- Configuring conditional formatting

- Configuring small multiples
- Applying slicing and filtering
- Adding an R or Python visual
- Adding a smart narrative visual
- Configuring the report page
- Designing and configuring for accessibility
- Configuring automatic page refresh
- Creating a paginated report
- Using Power BI datasets in Excel PivotTables

Technical requirements

The following are the prerequisites in order to complete the work in this chapter:

- Microsoft Power BI Desktop installed on a Microsoft Windows PC.
- Access to some data to use. We've also provided synthetic data that can be used, which is available in the GitHub repository for this book here: `https://github.com/PacktPublishing/Microsoft-Power-BI-Data-Analyst-Certification-Guide/tree/main/example-data`.

Understanding the capabilities of Power BI

Reporting and visualization capabilities are the core functionalities of Power BI. After sourcing data and modeling the data, you are now well positioned to take full advantage of it.

Imagine you want to show your boss gross revenue by state by product item group. You could create a table of data, much like what you would see in Excel.

Product Item Group	State Name	Gross Revenue
Airplane	California	$4,967,218.05
Helicopter	California	$3,384,371.95
Airplane	Florida	$2,201,335.35
Helicopter	Florida	$1,936,433.65
Airplane	New York	$1,801,496.80
Helicopter	Minnesota	$1,614,087.15
Helicopter	New York	$1,584,893.60
Helicopter	Delaware	$1,483,751.00
Helicopter	Oregon	$1,457,334.65
Airplane	Illinois	$1,456,043.00
Helicopter	New Jersey	$1,417,643.05
Airplane	Texas	$1,396,501.00
Helicopter	Arkansas	$1,319,437.25
Helicopter	Nebraska	$1,299,812.20
Helicopter	Pennsylvania	$1,267,843.70
Helicopter	West Virginia	$1,259,671.40
Total		**$82,113,644.50**

Figure 9.1 – Data represented as a table

This is a decent way to show data, but it is not compelling. We could instead use the data storytelling capabilities in Power BI and create something like this:

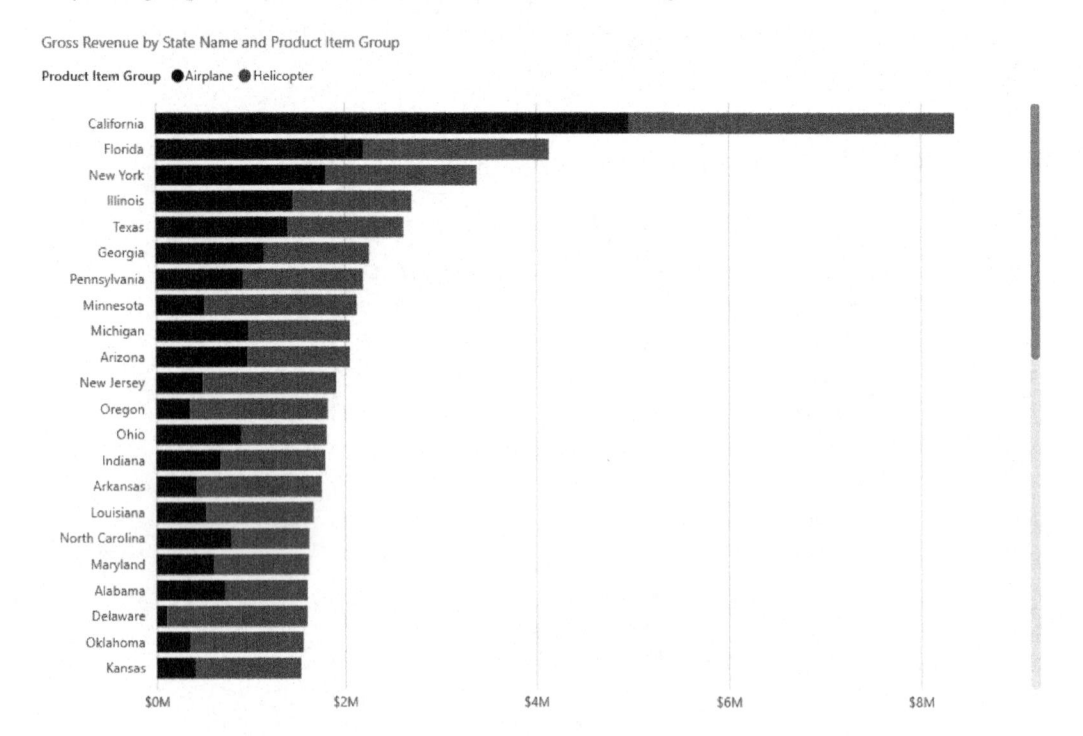

Figure 9.2 – Data represented as a bar chart

Notice how you get a much better "feel" for the data when it is visualized like this. It's less confusing and drives your eyes and brain to understand how gross profit changes between states.

Or, even better, we could use the map visualization and have something such as this:

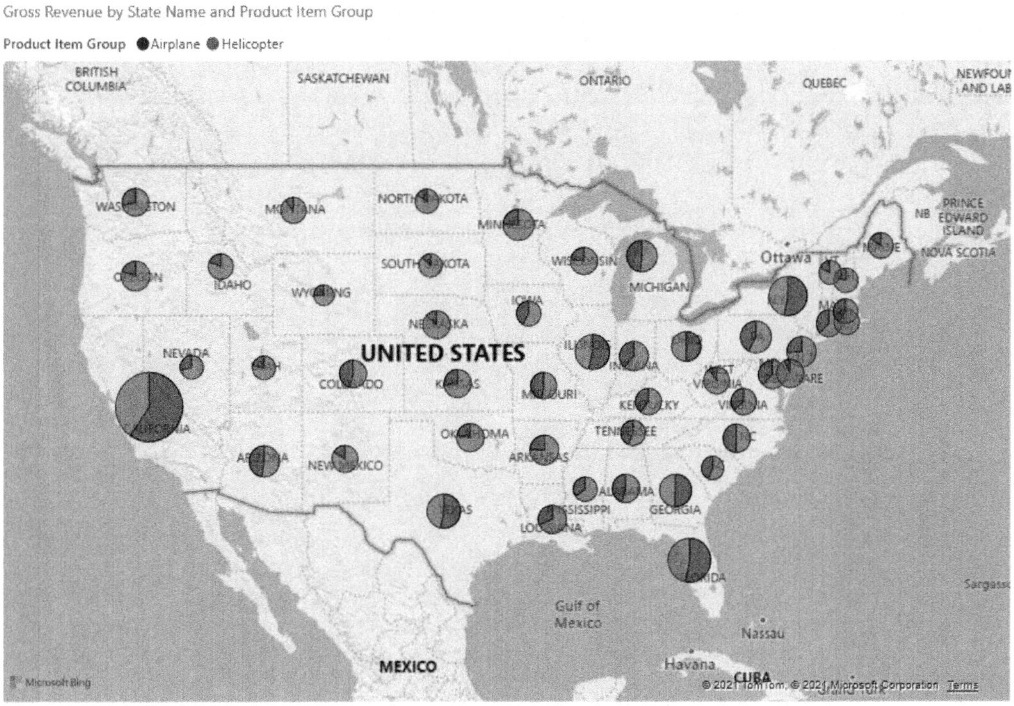

Figure 9.3 – Data represented as a map

This allows us to visualize our sales across the entire United States.

The great thing about all three choices is you get to choose. It's your story to tell. Sometimes a table of data is the correct choice, while sometimes you need a more visual way of displaying your data.

Adding visualization items to reports

Power BI installs with many visuals you can use to tell your data story. These visuals allow you to highlight the data you want in order to explain insights you have discovered in your data that lead to actions your business can take.

Reporting is a lens on your data, allowing non-technical people to understand your business's data. By visualizing your data, you make that data more accessible to a wider audience.

162 Creating Reports

In Power BI, each visual you can use, from pie charts to funnel charts to some of the more esoteric visualizations, such as decomposition tree and key influencers, are all represented by their own icons in the **Visualizations** pane.

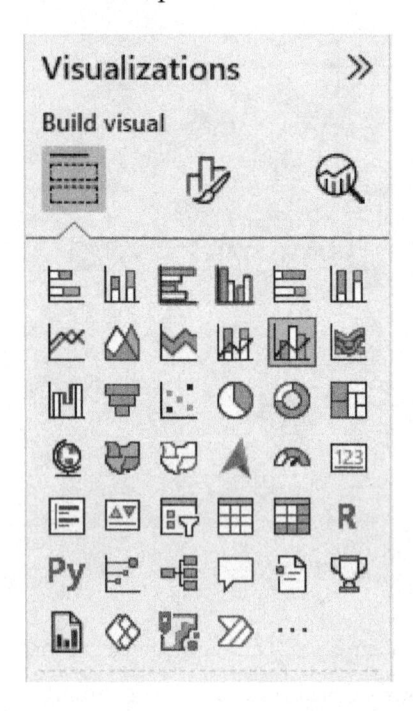

Figure 9.4 – Built-in visuals for building Power BI reports

The interface is often referred to as a clicky-clicky, draggy-droppy interface. The way you visualize your data is you select the visualization you want from the **Visualizations** pane. This will place the visualization on the reporting surface. Then, you add the columns you want to visualize.

If you want to visualize **Gross Revenue** by **State Name** and **Product Item Group** as a stacked bar chart, you can start by selecting the stacked bar chart visual from the **Visualizations** pane.

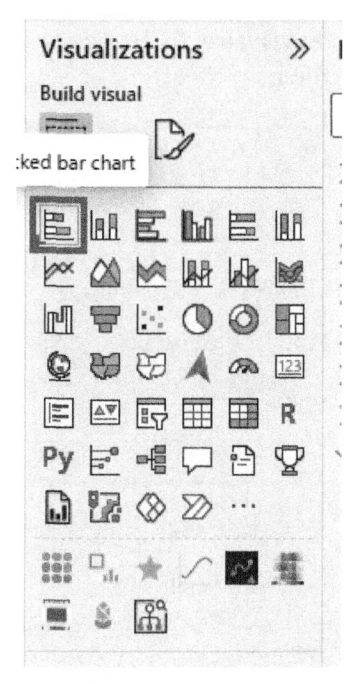

Figure 9.5 – Adding a stacked bar chart

This will place an empty stacked bar chart visualization on the reporting surface.

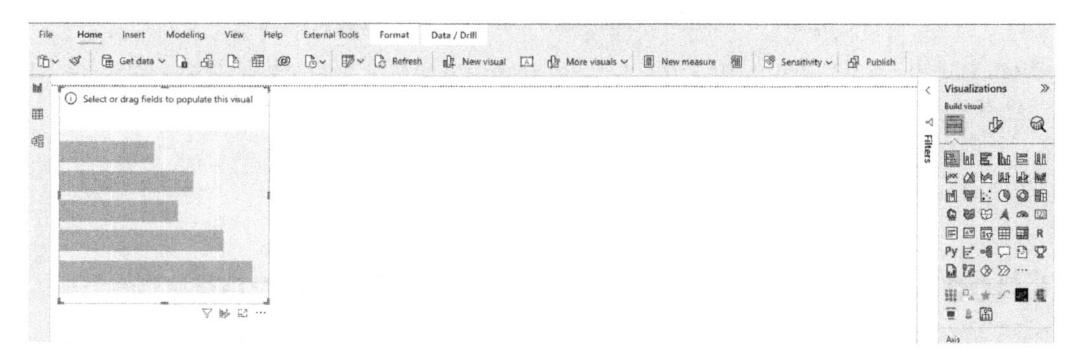

Figure 9.6 – Empty stacked bar chart added to report canvas

164   Creating Reports

You then add the field you want to visualize to the values area. These options will change depending on the visualization you have chosen.

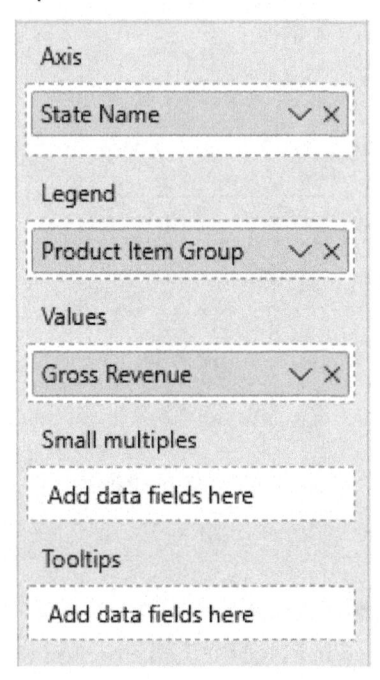

```
Axis
  State Name              ∨ ×

Legend
  Product Item Group      ∨ ×

Values
  Gross Revenue           ∨ ×

Small multiples
  Add data fields here

Tooltips
  Add data fields here
```

Figure 9.7 – Adding data fields to the stacked bar chart visual

Then, you will end up with the same visualization you saw in *Figure 9.2*. Power BI makes it easy and quick to visualize your data and tell your data story.

Now that we have learned how to add visualization items to reports, let's learn how to choose the appropriate visualization for any report.

Choosing an appropriate visualization type

Power BI offers many options for visualization using out-of-the-box capabilities that are available directly in the **Visualizations** pane. By selecting the fields you'd like to use in the visualization, you can drag and drop the fields to the various configurations and quickly see the outcome in the visualization displayed in the report canvas to find the visualization and configuration that best tells the data story you'd like to communicate.

Additionally, there are visuals available in Microsoft AppSource that provide further visualization beyond the capabilities built in. You can even create your own custom visuals if you cannot find the exact visualization that tells your story the way you want it to be told.

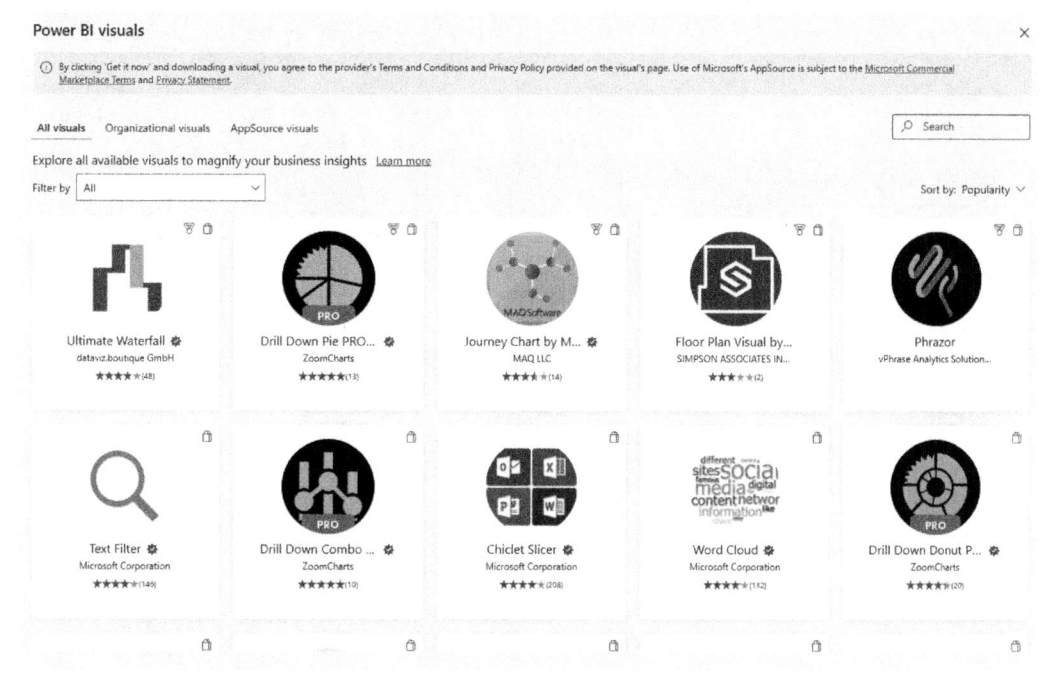

Figure 9.8 – Custom Power BI visuals in Microsoft AppSource

When selecting the visualization type, it's best to consider the data being presented. For example, geographic data may not be best displayed using a pie or line chart. Some data can be presented in multiple ways, such as geographic data being displayed in a map visual but also in a table. The best visual in a scenario such as this will depend on the specific story you're telling with the data.

Selecting the best visualization type may take some time to get optimized but it can make a big impact on the way your data is communicated.

Table and matrix visualizations

Tables and matrixes are some of the most elemental reporting visualizations. They provide the report consumer with a nice grid of data. As you will see later in this chapter, you can "decorate" your tables and matrixes with conditional formatting, making "boring" data grids quite informative.

166　　Creating Reports

The table visual is a rectangular grid that displays data in rows and columns. The table has two dimensions. It has headers and, by default, a row for totals. It looks like a table in an Excel spreadsheet.

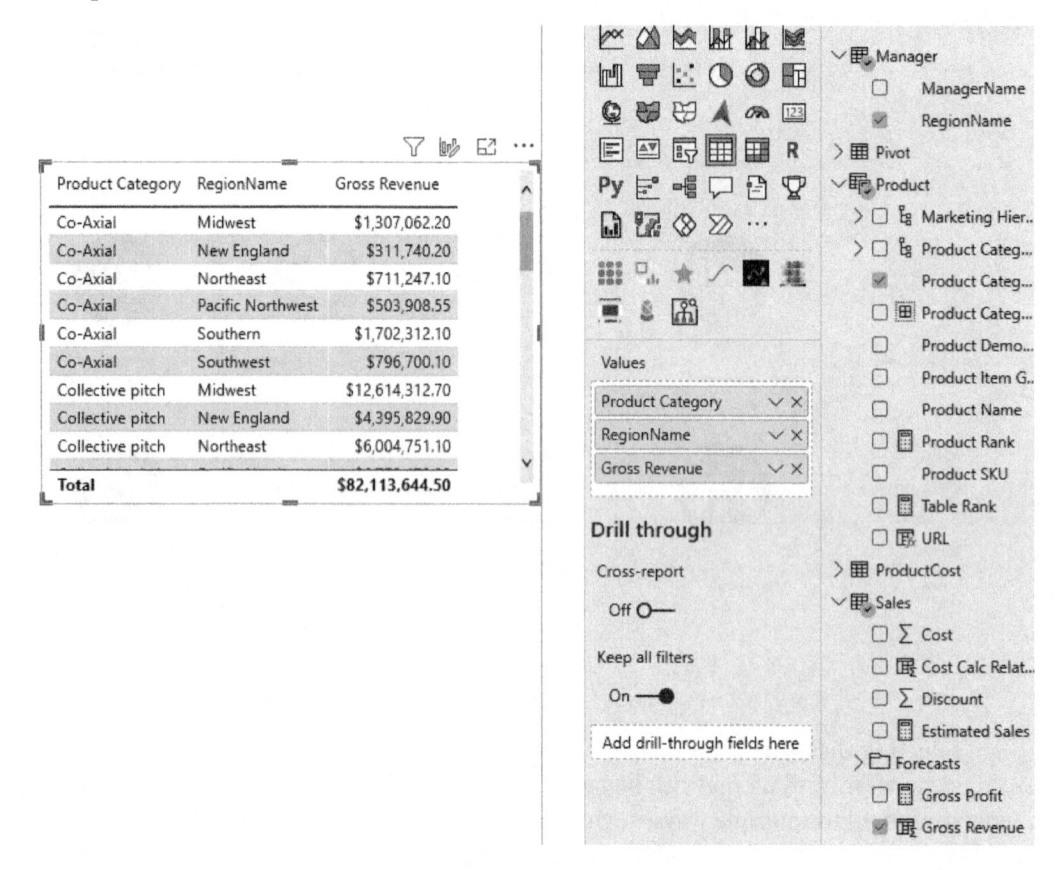

Figure 9.9 – The table visual and its configuration

The matrix visualization looks similar to the table visualization; however, it allows you to display rows, columns, and values. It looks and acts much like a PivotTable from Excel.

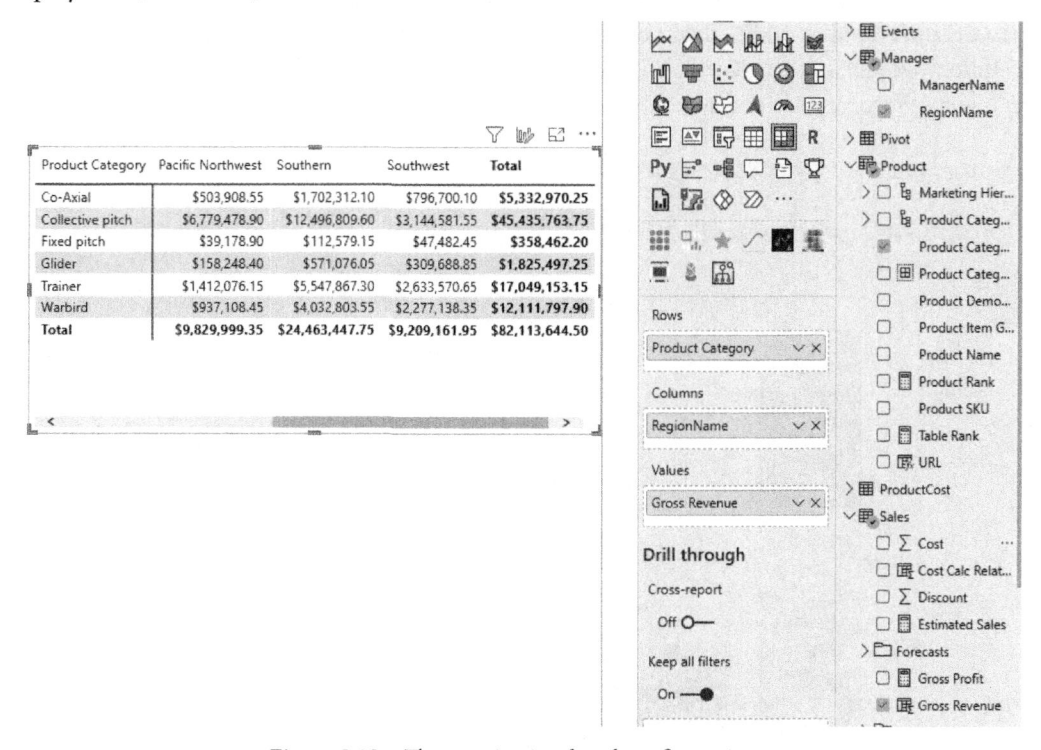

Figure 9.10 – The matrix visual and configuration

Bar and column charts

Another set of fundamental visualizations is the bar and column charts. Power BI provides several different bar and column chart visualizations that allow you to present data in different ways using clustered and stacked formats. The stacked bar chart will group data categories into single bars, as shown in *Figure 9.11*:

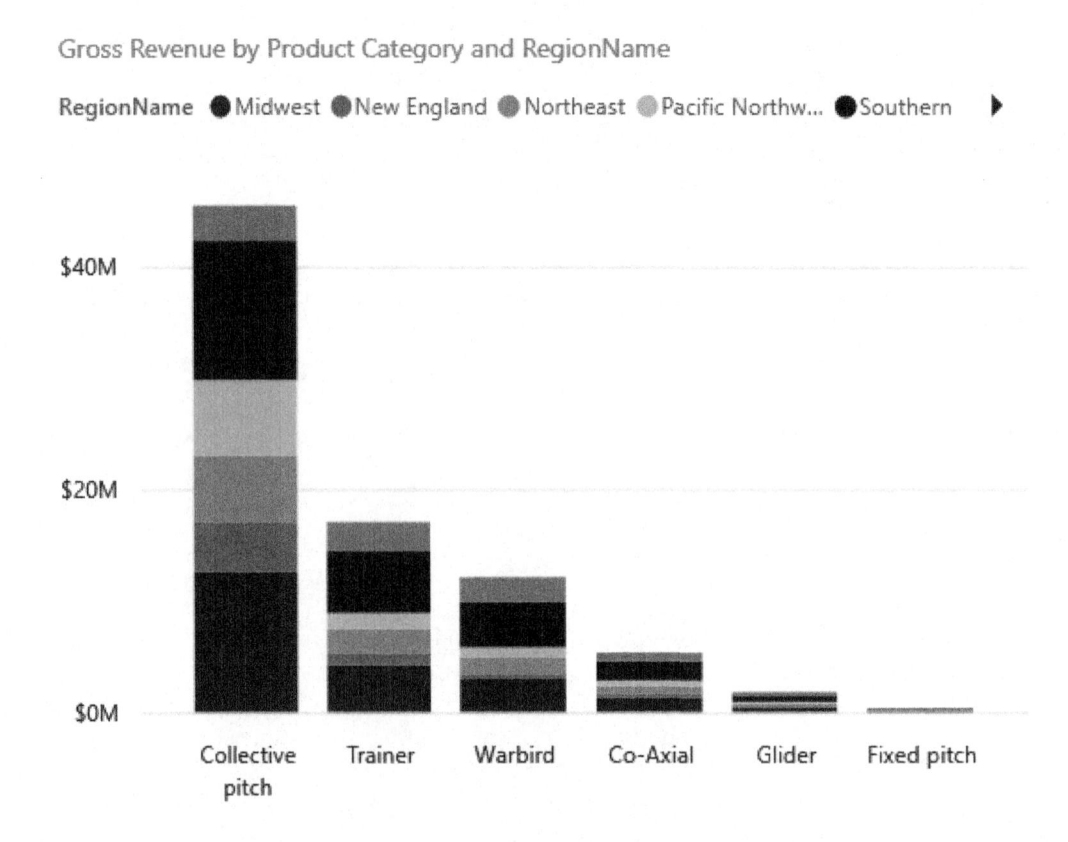

Figure 9.11 – Stacked column chart visual

The clustered column chart visual will group categories of data in multiple bars rather than stacking. *Figure 9.12* shows an example clustered column chart showing the same data as *Figure 9.11*, but you can see how the data is presented in both stacked and clustered formats:

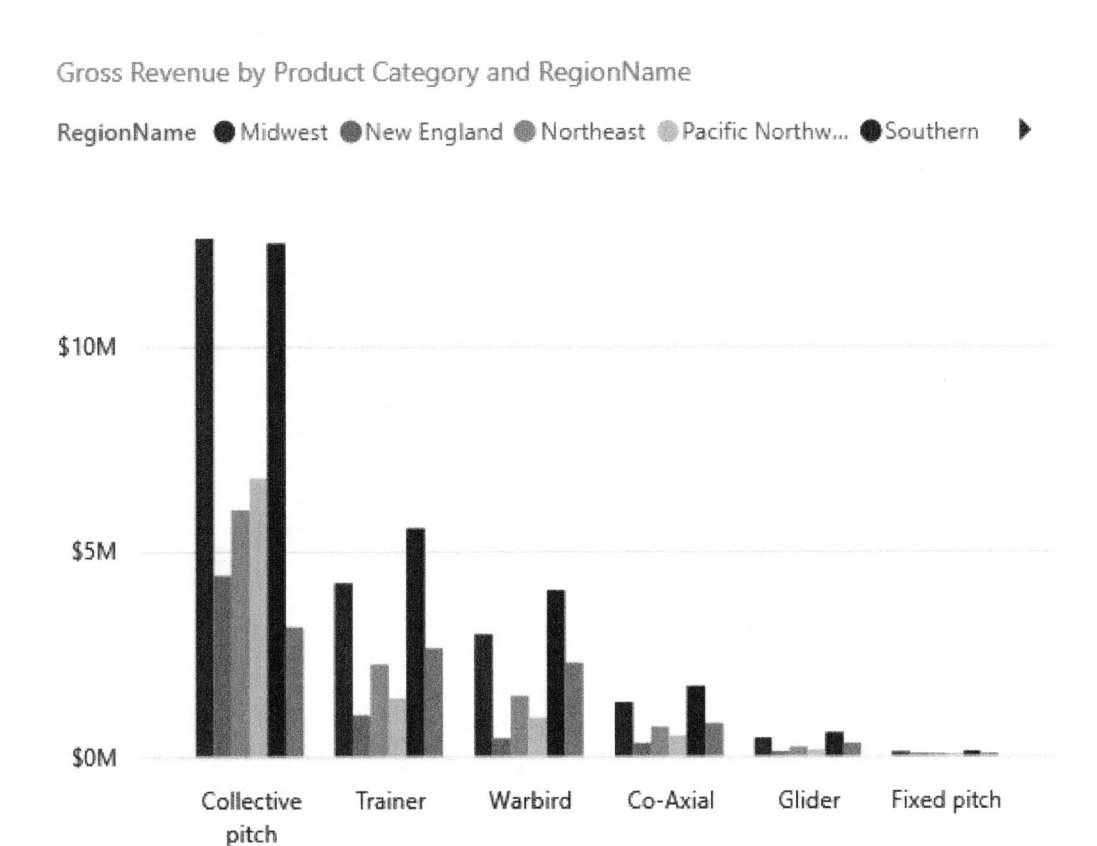

Gross Revenue by Product Category and RegionName

RegionName ● Midwest ● New England ● Northeast ● Pacific Northw... ● Southern ▶

Figure 9.12 – Clustered column chart visual

Stacked and clustered bar and column charts can be used in many cases, but they present the data differently, so it's good to experiment with both to best determine which is best to use in your use case.

Line and area charts

The line chart and area chart visuals are useful for displaying data over time. The area chart is like the line chart, with the addition of the area between the line and the *x* axis filled in. You will see similarities between the line and area charts but sometimes area becomes the best visual to use if you need to emphasize change over time.

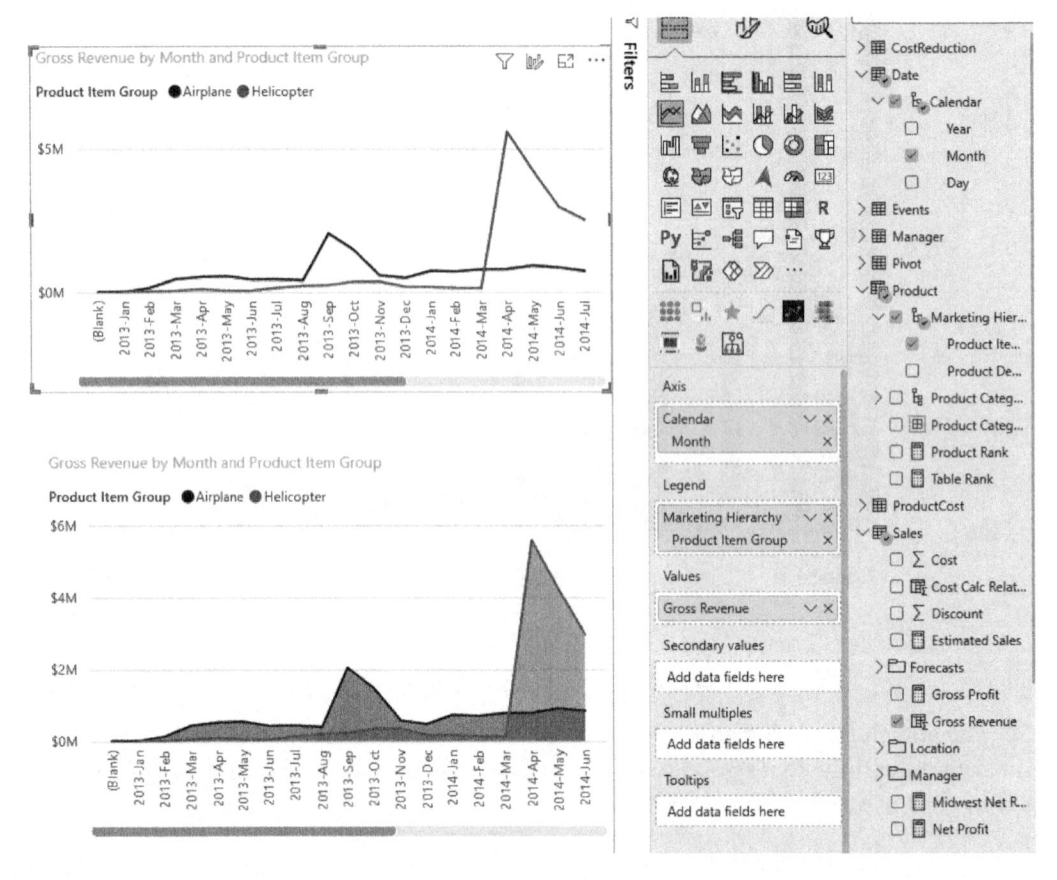

Figure 9.13 – Line and area chart visuals

Pie chart, donut chart, and treemaps

The pie treemap, donut chart, and pie chart visuals allow you to depict the relationship between subsets of data and the whole. These visuals can be very colorful and are useful when portraying percentages of a whole, such as which regions of the country make up the majority of the total sales for a country.

The pie chart is like pie charts in any other plotting tool, made up of a filled-in circle, while the donut chart is a circular bar that plots the size of each value based on the size of the whole circle. It is slightly easier for most people to see the percentage differences in a donut chart compared to a pie chart.

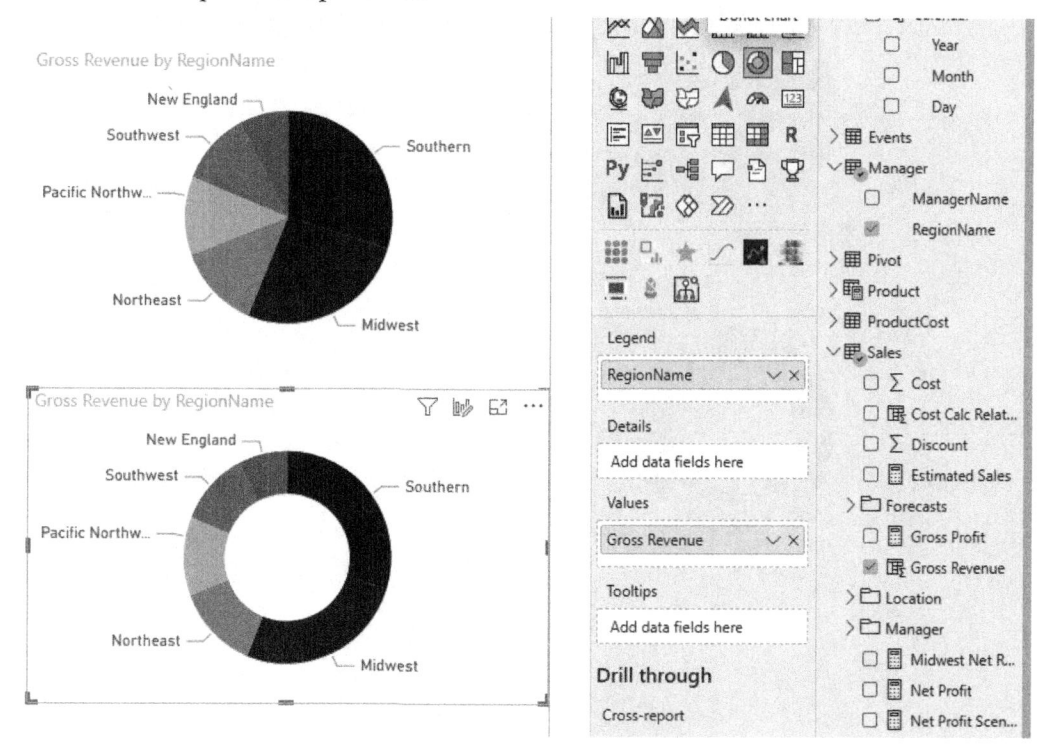

Figure 9.14 – Pie and donut chart visuals

172 Creating Reports

A common problem with these visualizations is trying to present too many categories at once. It is recommended to refer to your requirements to ensure that you're only adding categories that are needed and that you're not adding additional categories of data that will make the visuals overly complex. When presenting many categories of data, it's recommended to use multiple visuals and typically use another kind or style of visual.

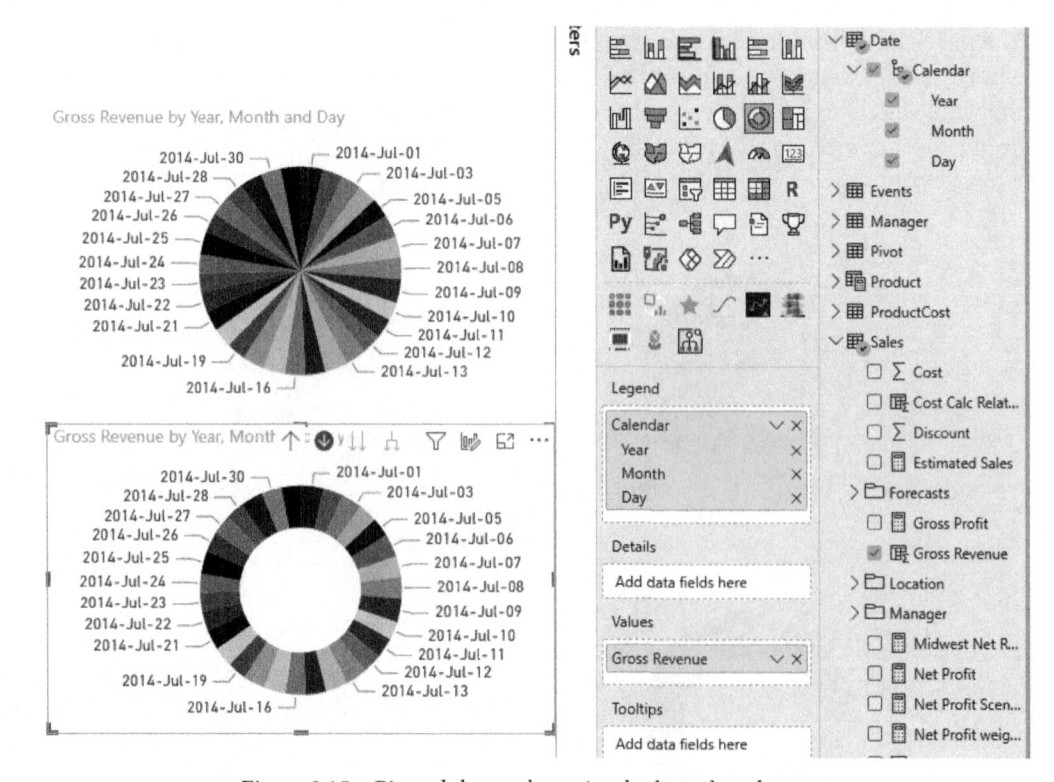

Figure 9.15 – Pie and donut chart visuals show date data

While the pie and donut charts use circles to represent an entire dataset, the treemap visual instead uses a box or rectangle. Like the pie and donut charts, the treemap also uses colors to represent different categories of data and likewise, the treemap is useful when depicting a part of the whole. For example, if the whole box represents the total sales for the country, the colored boxes inside will be sized to represent each region and each region will use different colors to distinguish between them. The treemap visual will arrange the boxes inside from top left to lower right in largest to smallest order.

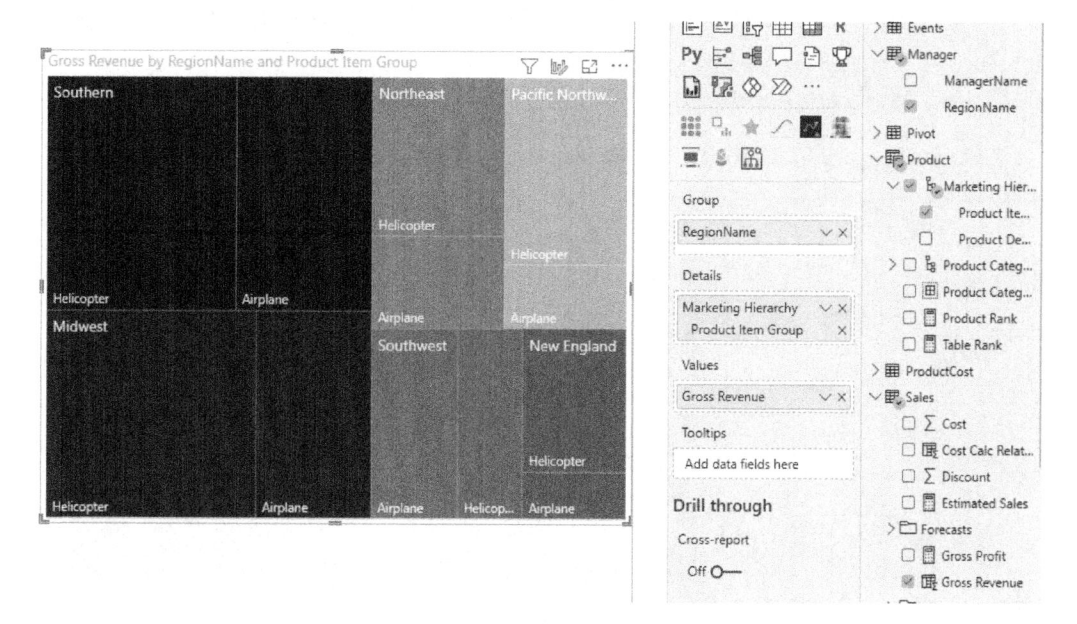

Figure 9.16 – Treemap visual

We can see in *Figure 9.16* how a treemap visual is used to represent gross revenue by region and product item group.

Combination charts

There are multiple combination chart visuals that pair line and column charts into one visual. This allows you to see multiple values plotted over a common axis. For example, *Figure 9.17* shows gross revenue in different product categories over time and shows us gross profit across the same time periods. This is useful because we can now not only see the impact of sales (revenue) for each product category but also link those sales to profit. Using a combination chart visual like this can sometimes allow you to save space by combining the data and using one visual to show what might normally need two visuals to show:

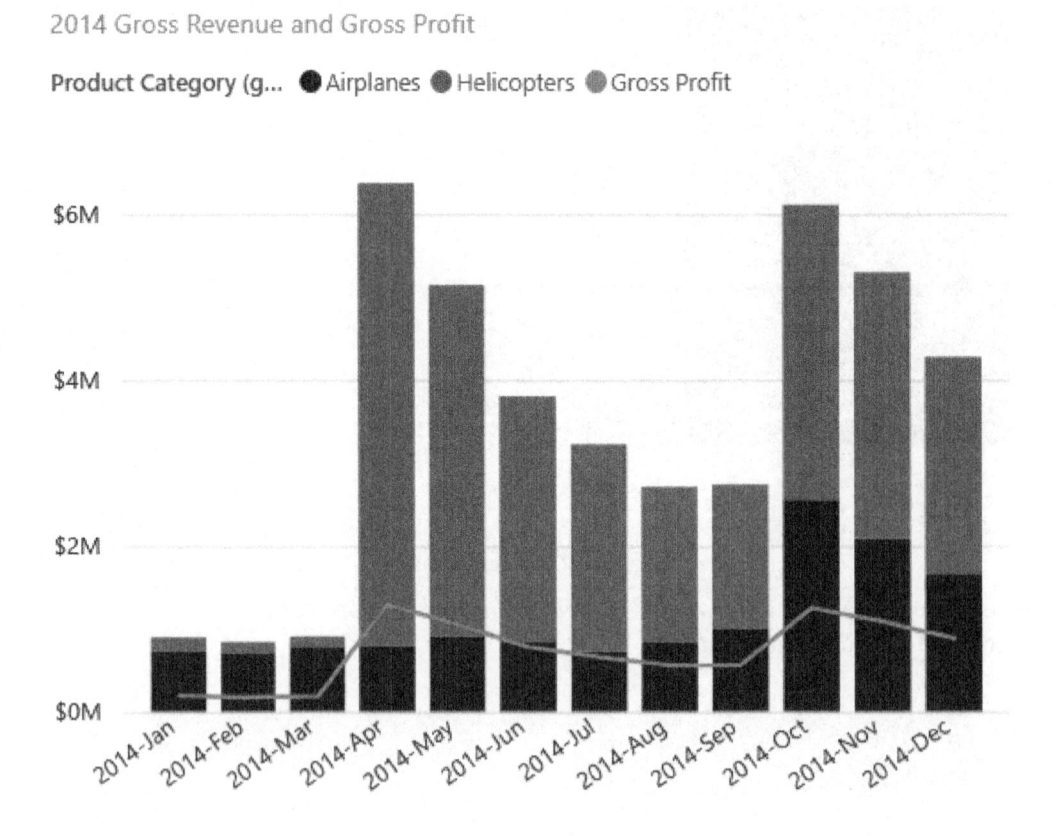

Figure 9.17 – Combo chart with bars and lines

Card visualization

Sometimes you just want to display a single value. For that, Power BI has the card visualization. This is great for displaying important data that you want to keep an eye on with your Power BI report, such as YTD sales, gross revenue for different product categories, or year-over-year manufacturing output. For multiple values, there is the multirow card visualization. When multiple values are used with the card visualization, the visual will show multiple rows for each data point.

Figure 9.18 – Card visual showing $82.11M in gross revenue

The following figure shows another card visualization that shows various revenues:

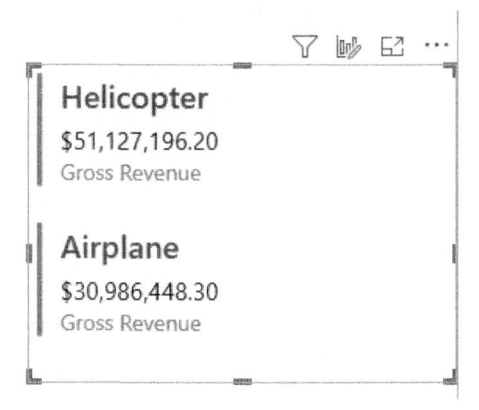

Figure 9.19 – Card visual showing gross revenue for multiple rows (Helicopter and Airplane)

Funnel visualization

The funnel visual is great for displaying steps in a linear process over time. Funnel charts are most often seen displaying workflows or processes such as an order being fulfilled or a sales opportunity moving through various stages from envisioning with a potential customer to onboarding the product to the customer.

Though that is what it is designed for, that does not mean you have to use it that way. If a funnel chart can add context to your data story, use it.

Gross Revenue by Year

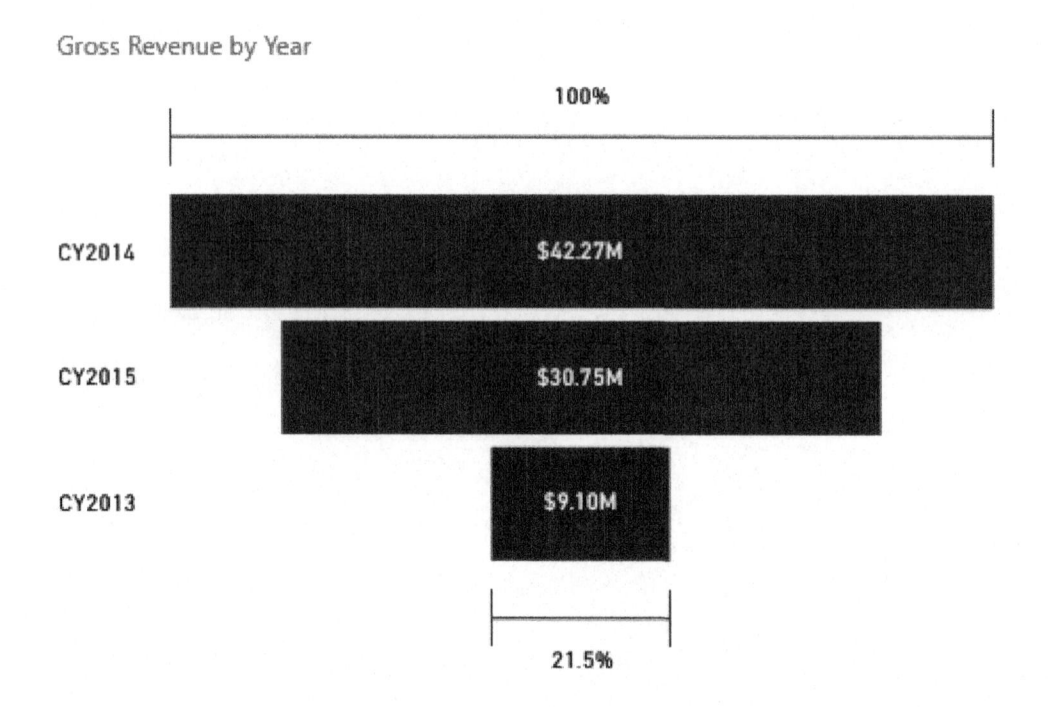

CY2014	$42.27M
CY2015	$30.75M
CY2013	$9.10M

100%

21.5%

Figure 9.20 – Funnel visual showing gross revenue by year

Funnel charts can be useful in these contexts:

- Depicting staged or sequential movement of data through a process
- Illustrating the work to be done in various stages, such as when work items increase or decrease across multiple stages
- Showing challenges that might occur in a linear process

Gauge chart

Often, business reports need to tell the report consumer what is happening at a glance. The gauge chart is designed to do just that. Much like a dial you might find on the dashboard of your car, the gauge chart is a semi-circular arc showing a single value that progresses toward a target value.

Minimum, maximum, and target values are set using the visual configuration where data fields are applied to each on the **Visualizations** pane. You can use conditional formatting to change the color of the gauge depending on whether it is higher or lower than the **Target** value.

The data value compared to the minimum, maximum, and target is shown by color shading on the gauge. The visual is plotted such that the left-most side of the gauge will show the minimum value, while the right-most side of the gauge will show the maximum value. The target value and the current value will be shown somewhere between the minimum and maximum values.

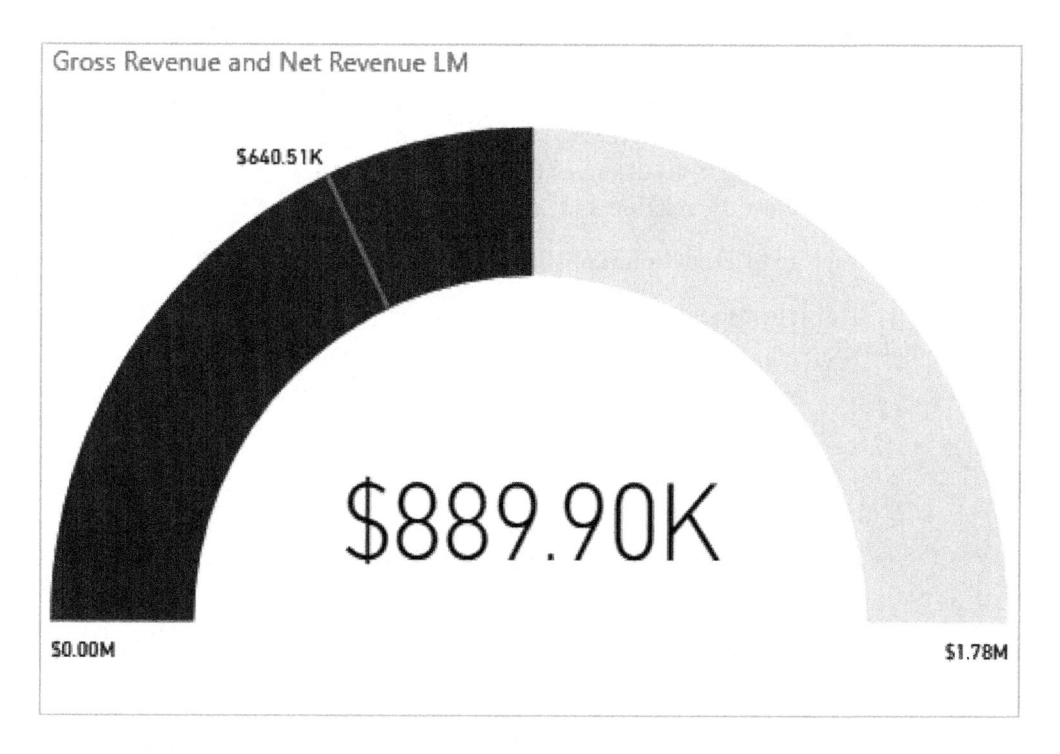

Figure 9.21 – Gauge visual showing gross and net revenue

While gauge visuals only really show one value, they communicate things such as progress toward a goal. It's important to have a balance of different visuals so as not to overwhelm the report consumers and use the best visual for the requirements in your data story.

Waterfall chart

The waterfall chart visual is similar to a line chart; however, it combines bars to indicate increases or decreases in value. Typically, the *x* axis shows time, such as months in a fiscal year, while the *y* axis is used to show increases or decreases in value that happen during those months. For example, you can show changes to revenue each month using the waterfall visual, where the first month may have an increase and the second month has a decrease, both from a starting value and then ending at a value shown on the *y* axis. The columns are color-coded for increases and decreases, so this visual is useful to communicate these changes in a value over time.

Scatter chart

A scatter chart is a visual that plots many data points using an *x* and *y* axis for typically two categories or variables that you select. Scatter charts are the same as scatter plots, which are often used in statistics for visualizing data. Scatter charts can also be color-coded to show different categories of values that can be plotted across the same *x* and *y* axes, which will help show the relationship between the two categories of values.

Power BI can render up to a maximum of 10,000 data points in a scatter chart.

Scatter charts can also be used instead of a line chart when you want to change the scale of the horizontal axis.

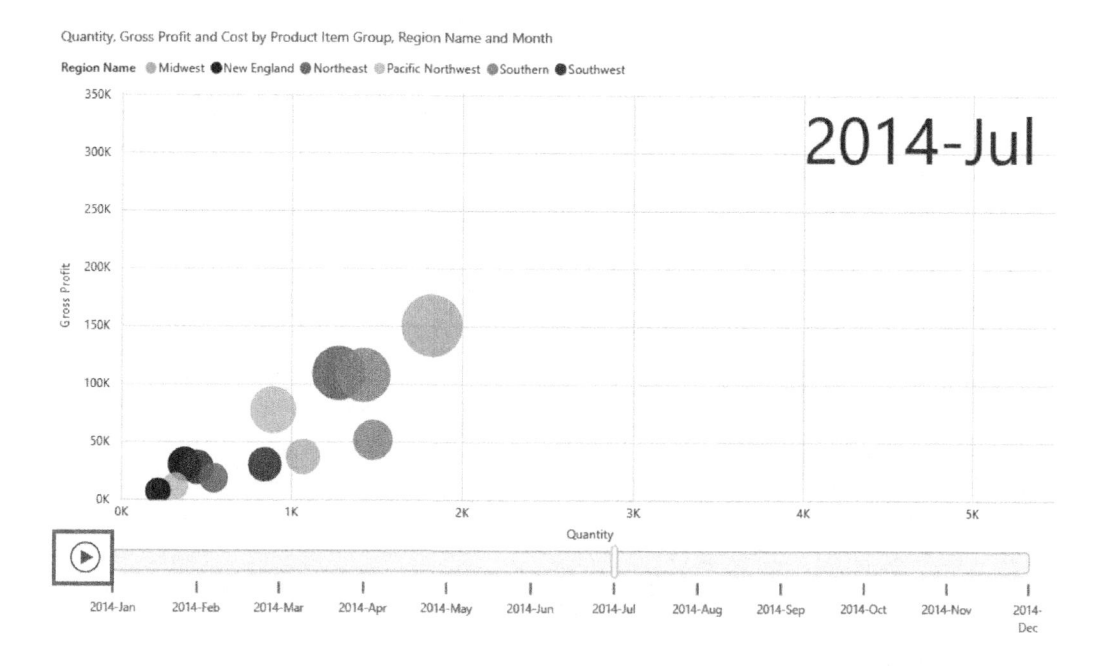

Figure 9.22 – Scatter chart showing gross profit across date and regions

You can also have a date field as a play axis. This will allow you to "play" your data. The play will change over time and the data points will move as the data changes by date.

Map visuals

Power BI provides multiple ways of communicating geographical information. The first is the map visual, which allows you to plot data on a map in a very straightforward way, where numeric values or a percentage of the whole values can be overlayed on a map showing a geography. The map visual uses Microsoft Bing Maps as the core geography data.

There are also other map visuals, such as filled map, shape map, Azure map, and ArcGIS map visuals, which allow plotting data on a map in different ways. The shape map, for example, is useful when you only want the shape of a geographical region and not the whole map. For example, when plotting values by state in the United States, the map visual will show both Alaska and Hawaii on a map and then plot the values over the map. The shape map will start with just the outline of the contiguous states and then add Alaska and Hawaii to the corners of the visual, as shown in *Figure 9.23*.

180   Creating Reports

The filled map visual combines the shape map's ability to fill in space in a mapped geographic region but overlays it on top of the Bing map of the regular map visual. The Azure map visual uses the Azure service **Azure Maps** and uses supplemental data from other parties, such as road, satellite, night, and terra layers, for displaying maps. ArcGIS Maps for Power BI uses the **ArcGIS service** developed and maintained by **Esri**.

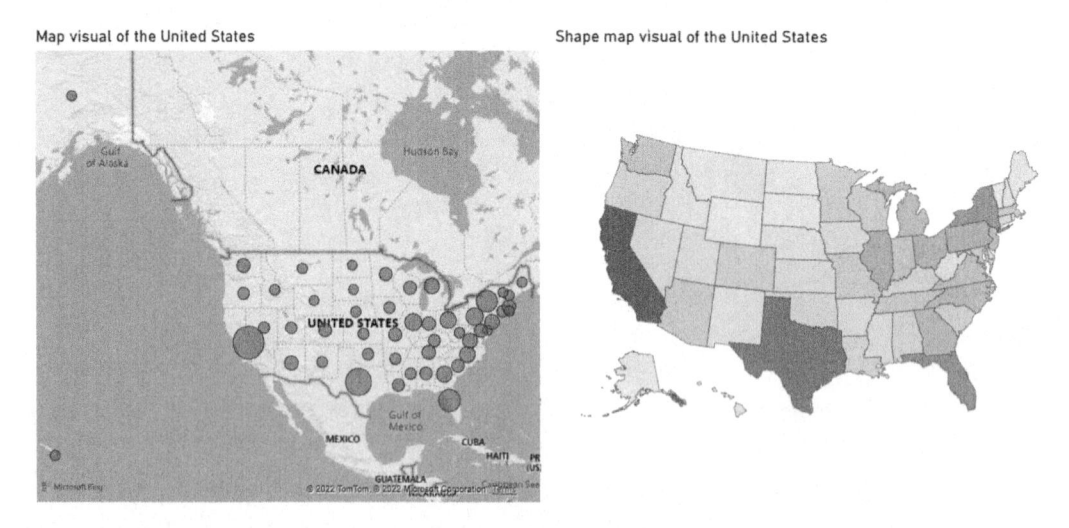

Figure 9.23 – Map and shape map visuals showing population data for the United States

Q&A visualization

The Q&A visual provides a question-and-answer interface that uses natural language processing to generate visual representations of your data. By asking questions in natural language, this makes it easier for report consumers or even report designers to quickly generate insights from the data used in this report.

Power BI will attempt to choose the "best" visual to display your data. As with all visuals, you can choose to change the visual just by highlighting the visual and choosing another one from the build visual area.

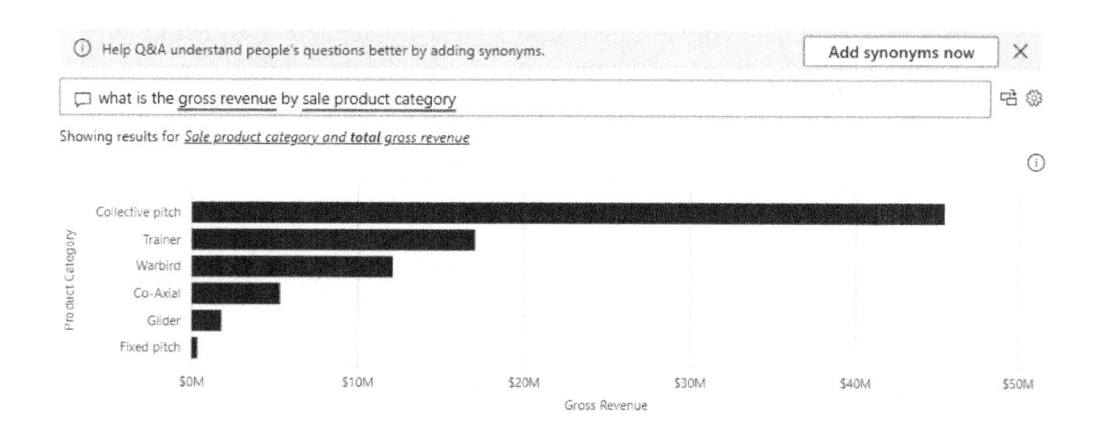

Figure 9.24 – Q&A visual showing gross revenue by sale product category

The Q&A visual has these core characteristics:

- A question entry box where the natural-language query is entered.
- A list of suggested questions will be generated based on the data model.
- A button that takes the query result and generates another visual displaying the same information.
- A settings button that allows you to change the Q&A settings. For more information on this, please see *Chapter 6, Using Data Model Advanced Features*.

Now that we've reviewed the different kinds of visualizations, let's look at how we can configure those visualizations to meet the reporting needs of our organization.

Formatting and configuring visualizations

There are many ways you can customize the visuals in Power BI. There are options for fonts, colors, and sizes to name a few. There are near-constant improvements in visual customization, so be sure to take the time to explore the options that are available for each visual.

To get better acquainted, look at the clustered column chart visual and see how the formatting options are grouped; notice the default configurations. It's helpful to know the defaults for the visual and how each can be customized.

Each visual can be configured independently, so select a visual on the canvas and then click the **Format** button to view the **Format** pane and change the configuration of the selected visual.

Formatting options for a visualization

Each visual will have different options for formatting. The new **Visualizations** pane separates visual-specific formatting from formatting options that apply to most, if not all, visuals.

General formatting

In the **General** formatting option area, you will find the following:

- **Properties**
- **Title**
- **Effects**
- **Header icons**
- **Tooltips**
- **Alt text**

Each section has options under it that we will explore.

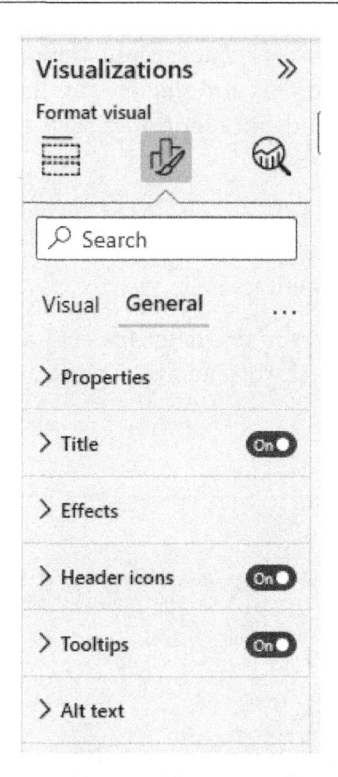

Figure 9.25 – General formatting for visuals

The **Properties** section allows you to specify the size and location, in pixels, of the visualization. These options allow you to place the visual where you want it to be on the canvas. It can also help when it comes to aligning visuals on the canvas. You can also lock the aspect ratio here as well. The advanced options are not covered as part of the exam, but they let you control responsiveness and layer order.

The **Title** section is where you make modifications to the title of the visual. The title describes the visual using text, which can help communicate the relevance and differentiate visuals on the report page. Titles can be formatted by selecting the text size, color, and font as well as styles such as bold and italic.

The **Effects** section allows you to select background options, such as color and transparency, as well as visual borders and shadows for the visual. In many cases, you will want to follow corporate style guidelines for things such as colors and shadows as well as fonts and text styles.

As with **Title**, the options in the **Effects** section can be defined by the value of a measure. You can easily create a measure that changes the border of a visual to red or green depending upon the measure's value.

Defining the header icons allows you to change the colors of the icons that appear when you hover over or click on a visual. You can even choose which icons to display, if any.

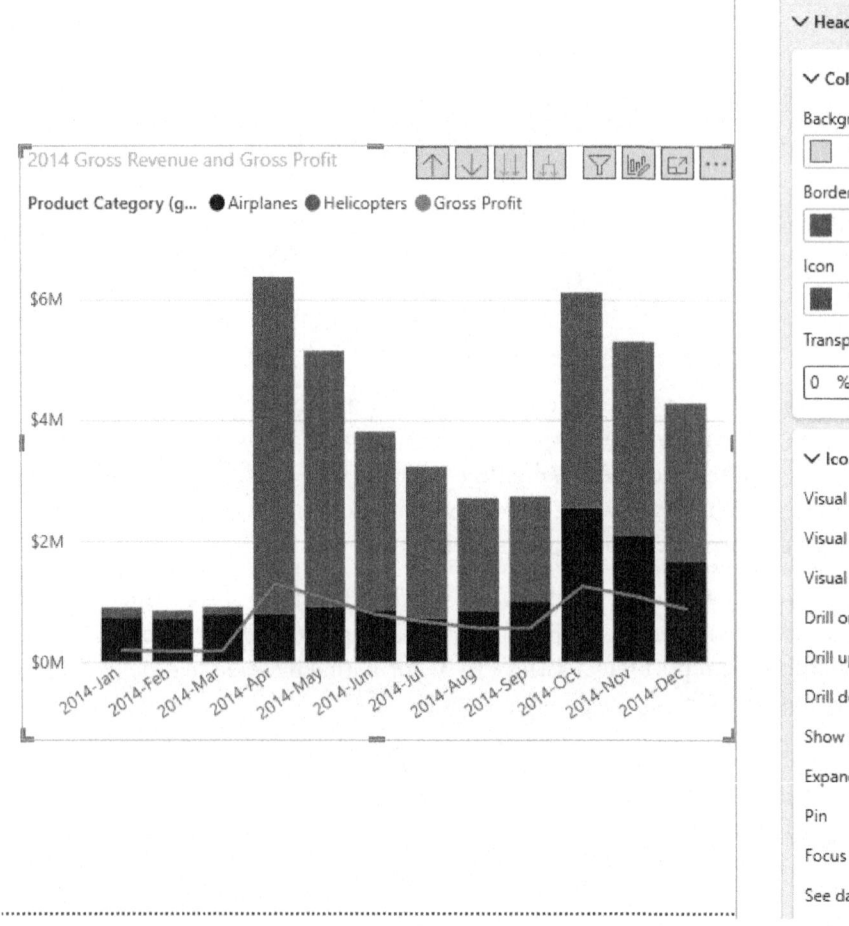

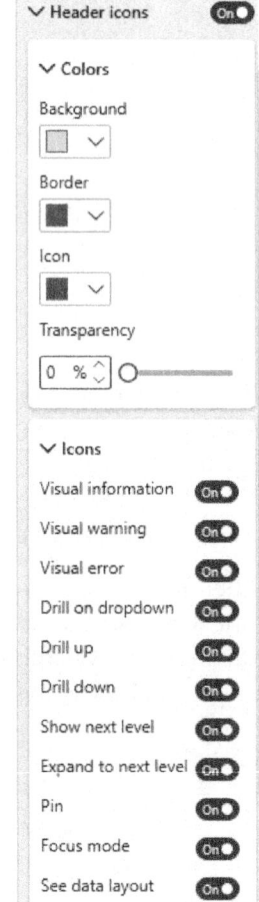

Figure 9.26 – Color formatting for a visual

The **Tooltips** section provides a way to customize the tooltip that appears when the mouse cursor hovers over a visual. Tooltips provide more context and detail to data points on a report visual. Power BI will automatically generate a tooltip based on the visual and fields selected, but in this area, you can customize this to fit your needs. You can even have a tooltip that displays other visuals.

Visual formatting

The **Visual** tab allows you to customize items that are specific to the visual selected. The categories of settings in this section will vary for each type of visual but most of the time, you can modify things such as the colors used. As previously mentioned, it's best to stick to consistent styling for colors and also to be inclusive of those who may have challenges distinguishing between some colors.

If there is a section called **Data labels**, then you can change fonts, size, and colors for the labels used for data points in the visual. Using solid colors is usually recommended but depending on the use of the visual or report, other options may be required. Keep in mind the background that will be behind the data label in order to ensure that they will stand out.

Every visualization will have options that apply only to that visualization. If you have selected a slicer visual, you can change the slicer orientation to horizontal. In a pie or donut visual, you can rotate the visualization, if needed. It wouldn't make any sense to change the orientation of a pie chart to horizontal, so you will not see that option.

When changes are made in the **Visualizations** or format pane you will instantly see the changes made to the visual on the canvas.

Importing a custom visual

The visuals included in Power BI out of the box will cover many use cases and be enough for most scenarios. If there are scenarios where the built-in visuals are not solving the requirements, then you should explore the custom visuals that have been made by many different developers found in AppSource, Microsoft's marketplace for Power BI visuals. If you can't find a visual you like, it is also possible to build your own custom visual for Power BI.

186   Creating Reports

Microsoft AppSource contains visuals that have been created by Microsoft and Microsoft partners. Visuals can go through a certification process, so some visuals in AppSource have been certified and some have not. A certified visual has been tested and investigated by the Microsoft Power BI team to ensure it doesn't access external services or resources and that it follows secure coding patterns and guidelines. Certification is not a required process, but many custom visual developers will choose to go through the process to further validate their work.

To create your own custom visual, you should start with the custom visual **Software Development Kit** (**SDK**), which is open source and based on **Node.js** (a JavaScript programming language). The development kit is available on GitHub. For the exam, you need to know that it is possible to create a custom visual but actually creating one is not required.

To add custom visuals from AppSource, click **Get more visuals** in the ellipsis menu on the **Visualizations** pane. The **Power BI visuals** window will display, where you can search and filter to find the visual you'd like to import into your report. Once the visual is located, click **Add** to add it to your report.

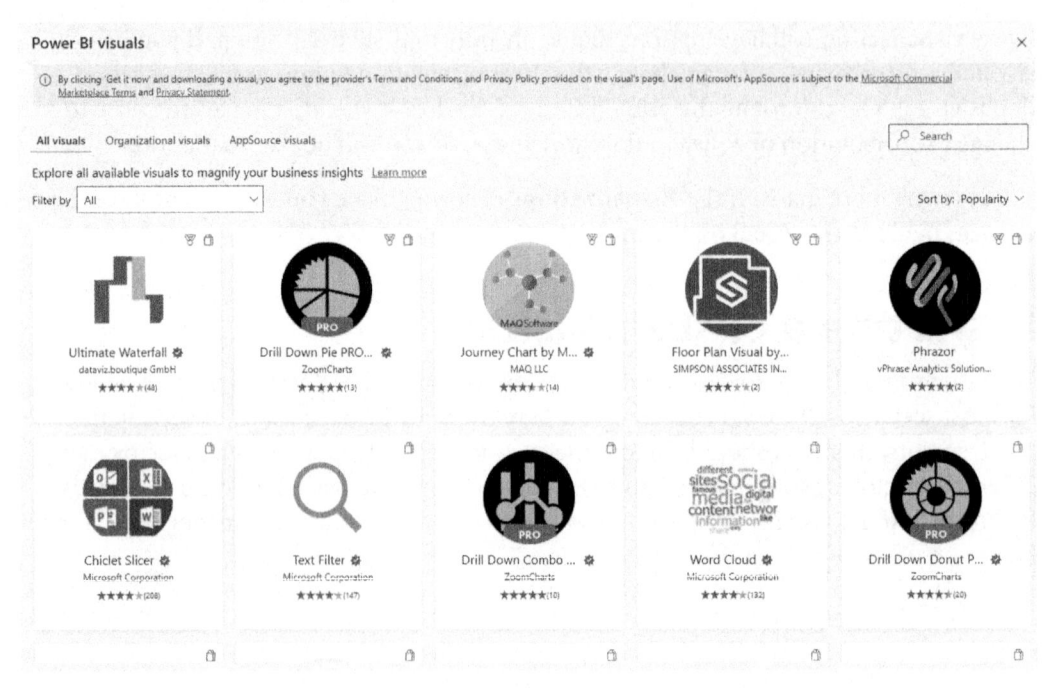

Figure 9.27 – Power BI visuals in Microsoft AppSource

Newly added custom visuals appear below the built-in visuals on the **Visualizations** pane. Once added to the report, visuals are added to the report canvas and configured similarly to the built-in visuals. In addition to built-in and custom visuals, each visual has formatting options that can be configured, but another powerful feature is conditional formatting based on data values. In the next section, we will explore how conditional formatting can be configured.

Configuring conditional formatting

Power BI allows you to apply conditional formatting visuals. In table and matrix visualizations, you can customize cell colors, including gradients, that are based on field values. Conditional formatting can also be used to represent data values with bars, icons, or web links.

You may use this to draw your report consumer's attention to outlier data or to differentiate different parts of the business based on performance.

You can configure conditional formatting on a table or matrix by right-clicking on the column in the **Values** area and then selecting **Conditional formatting** and what you want to format.

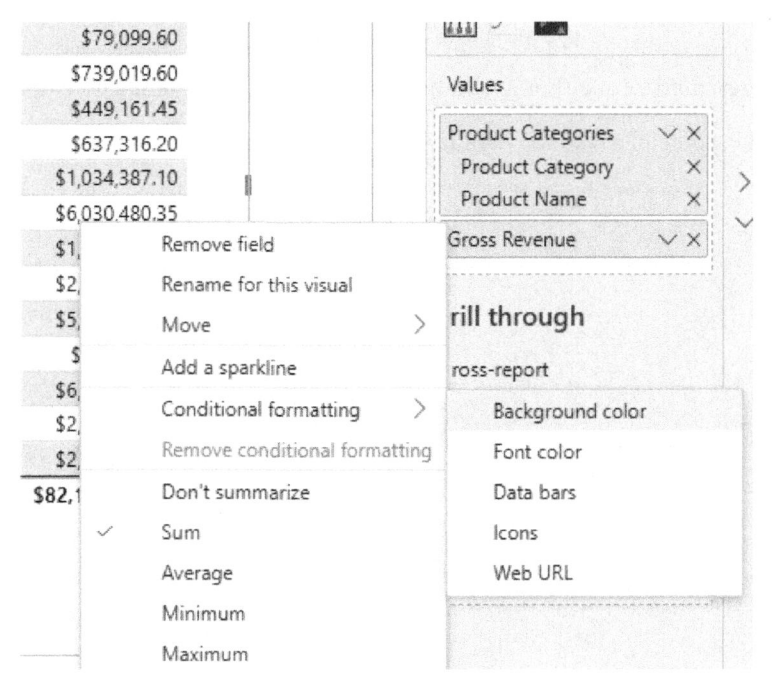

Figure 9.28 – Changing the summarization setting for values in a visual

188   Creating Reports

You can change the background color or font color and add data bars or KPI icons. You can even dynamically generate a web URL, sending your report consumers to other reports or web pages, depending on the values.

Figure 9.29 – Changing color configuration for a visual

You will be presented with either a rule-based option or a divergent series option.

As you can see, you can make the data in a table really stand out:

Product Category	Product Name	Gross Revenue
Co-Axial	3CAX-B Helicopter	$1,049,130.10
Co-Axial	4CAX-B Helicopter	$1,345,678.60
Co-Axial	Tailspin Heli - Co-Ax Pro Mk I - 4ch	$2,938,161.55
Collective pitch	6CCP-A Helicopter	$8,746,778.70
Collective pitch	Tailspin Heli - Max Pro Flight - 6ch	$36,688,985.05
Fixed pitch	3CFP-I Helicopter	$200,990.60
Fixed pitch	4CFP-I Helicopter	$78,372.00
Fixed pitch	Tailspin Heli - Pro Mk III - 5ch	$79,099.60
Glider	Tailspin Aviator Mk2-11	$739,019.60
Glider	Trainer - Tailspin GL-120	$449,161.45
Glider	Trainer - Tailspin GL-155	$637,316.20
Trainer	Piper Cub 3 Channel	$1,034,387.10
Trainer	Piper Cub 4 Channel	$6,030,480.35
Trainer	SkyTrainer	$1,879,770.55
Trainer	Tailspin Aviator Mk2-12	$2,784,730.30
Trainer	Tailspin Aviator Mk2-15	$5,319,784.85
Warbird	P47 4 Channel	$916,093.20
Warbird	P47 5 Channel	$6,364,165.90
Warbird	P51	$2,005,801.70
Warbird	Tailspin Warbird BM32	$2,825,737.10
Total		**$82,113,644.50**

Figure 9.30 – Data bars added to a table visual

Now that we know how conditional formatting can be applied, in the next section, we will look at how we can configure small multiples.

Configuring small multiples

Sometimes you want to show multiple visualizations that all share a common axis, or you want to break a crowded line chart into smaller, more easily understood pieces.

The small multiples option will allow you to do just this on some visuals. If the option is available, just add the common axis you want to break your data into.

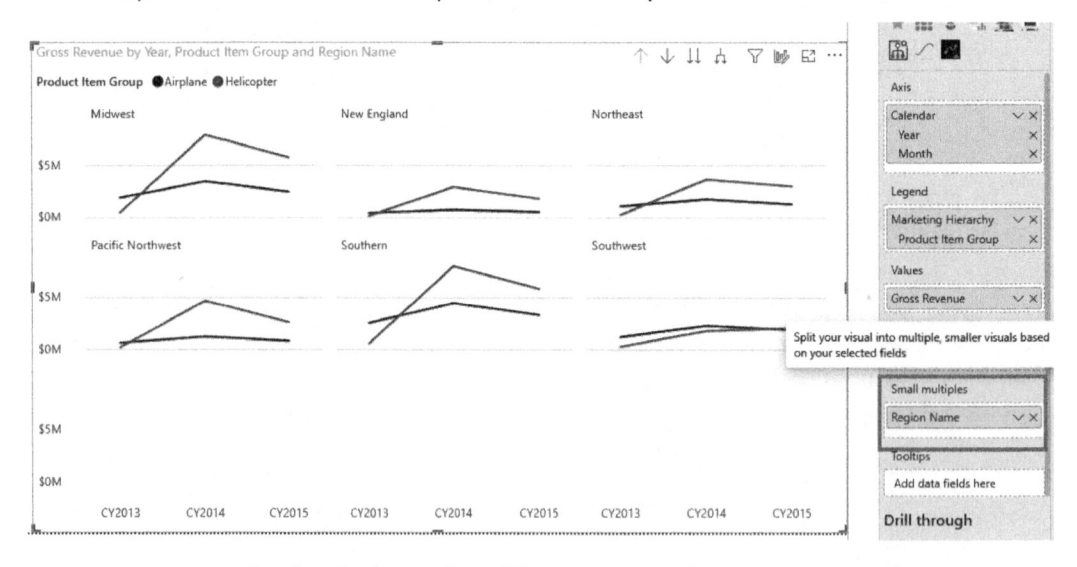

Figure 9.31 – Small multiples configured for gross revenue by year, product, and region

Small multiples are a great capability to help users think about data in smaller subsets and also make it easier for report designers to build multiple-visual reports without having to manually configure each visual. For example, breaking up by **Region Name**, as shown in *Figure 9.31*, allows you to see the same visual by each region in a simple step.

Applying slicing and filtering

The ability to focus your report to show exactly what you want to see is one of the biggest advantages of using a modern reporting platform. Filtering allows you to remove data so you can focus on the data that is needed for a particular scenario. Filtering can be applied directly to all pages in the report, only the current page, or only the selected visual. Additionally, you can use a slicer visual to build custom filtering directly on the report page.

Applying slicing and filtering   191

Slicers and filters are similar; both will enable you to filter data in your report. Though both are similar, filters are generally faster and do not take up space on the report page. Slicers, though slower, can have conditional formatting and some users find them more intuitive, as they *do* appear on the report page. Slicers can have more advanced filtering options than the filters pane, which is designed for more basic operations.

Slicers can be customized to include lists, drop-down selectors, or button selectors, and they can be formatted to allow the single-selection or multi-selection of values.

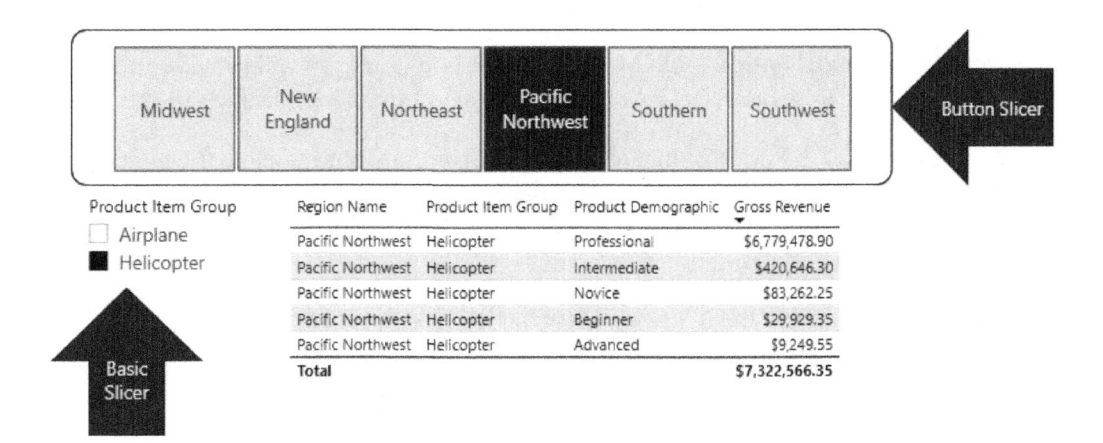

Region Name	Product Item Group	Product Demographic	Gross Revenue
Pacific Northwest	Helicopter	Professional	$6,779,478.90
Pacific Northwest	Helicopter	Intermediate	$420,646.30
Pacific Northwest	Helicopter	Novice	$83,262.25
Pacific Northwest	Helicopter	Beginner	$29,929.35
Pacific Northwest	Helicopter	Advanced	$9,249.55
Total			$7,322,566.35

Figure 9.32 – Slicer configured for a report

Slicers are great for the following cases:

- You want the report user to be able to apply commonly used filters.
- Filtering on fields that have been hidden from the data.
- Making filtering easier for your end users by prepopulating the fields and the values to filter by.
- Showing slicer visuals on the report, making a more focused experience for the report user.

> **Tip**
> Drop-down format slicers can help improve performance by deferring the queries sent to the dataset.

Slicers can be configured in many ways, and this happens the same way it does with other visuals, on the **Format your visual** tab of the **Visualizations** pane. Options for slicers include the following:

- **Single select** – Off by default. This option allows the slicer to be configured to only allow one selection at a time.
- **Multi-select with CTRL** – On by default. This option allows the slicer to be configured to allow the selection of multiple values by holding down the *Ctrl* key while clicking.
- **Show "Select all" option** – Off by default. This configuration will provide another value that the user can select to automatically select or check all values in the slicer.

While slicers are useful, Power BI includes basic filtering capabilities using the filters pane as well. The filters pane can handle basic slicer operations. Using the filters pane allows you to maximize the use of the report canvas for visuals rather than using the canvas space for slicers.

The filters pane will enable the filtering of visuals that have been added to the report canvas and have configurations for filters that can be applied to the visual, the page, or all pages in the report.

Report designers can customize the filters pane by doing the following:

- Adding or removing fields users can use to filter
- Adjusting the fonts and colors of the filters pane
- Setting the default state of the filters pane (open or closed)
- Making the filters pane or specific filters visible or hidden
- Setting a lock on filters that you don't want users to change

Next, let's look at how we can use R or Python visuals to add additional visualization capabilities to Power BI reports.

Adding an R or Python visual

In addition to Power BI, the open source R and Python programming languages can also be powerful tools for transforming and visualizing data. Power BI has built-in capabilities to use R and Python environments to visualize data and use those visualizations in reports.

This is not the book to get into R or Python, but there are some things you should know for the test. If you would like to go deeper with data analysis with Python, then we suggest the Microsoft Learn module *Explore and analyze data with Python*, available here: `https://docs.microsoft.com/learn/modules/explore-analyze-data-with-python/`. For data analysis with R, we suggest the module *R developer's guide to Azure*, available here: `https://docs.microsoft.com/en-us/azure/architecture/data-guide/technology-choices/r-developers-guide`.

- You must have R or Python installed on the same computer as Power BI Desktop.
- If you have multiple versions of R or Python installed, Power BI Desktop will use the **Path** variable to identify the default version. You can change this in the **Settings** pane in Power BI Desktop.
- You can only use one version of R or Python for the report; different visualizations cannot use different versions of R or Python.
- Power BI Desktop can open your preferred integrated development environment for you to write your code in.
- You will need to install R or Python for R or Python visuals from the marketplace to work.

Adding a smart narrative visual

They say that a picture is worth a thousand words. That may be so, but sometimes you just might want some words to explain what is happening in your data. The smart narrative visualization will quickly summarize visuals and reports and put that summarization into text. It provides relevant innovative insights that you can customize.

Smart narrative summaries will build key takeaways and trends, and you can edit the language and format so the insights can be tailored to a specific audience. With smart narrative visuals, your report users will better understand the data, arrive at key points faster, and be able to explain the insights to others.

There are two different ways to generate a smart narrative summary. The first is to right-click on a visual in Power BI Desktop and select **Summarize** from the context menu. This will create a new smart narrative visualization.

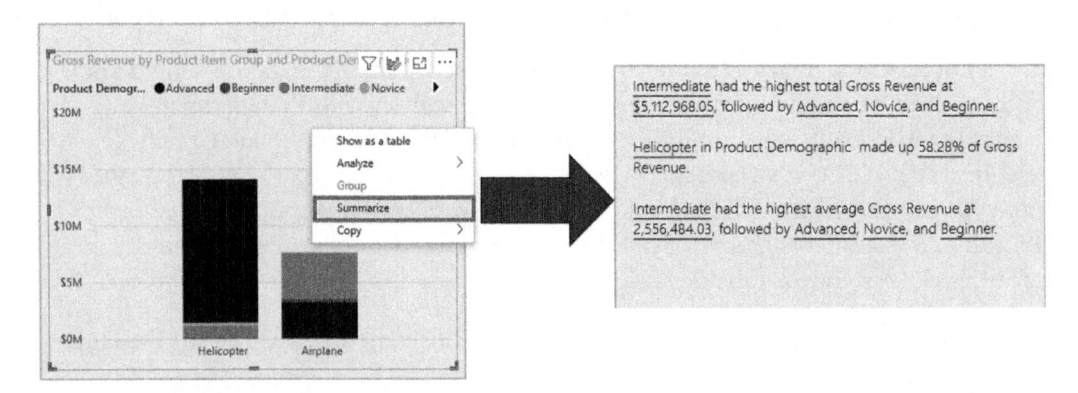

Figure 9.33 – Smart narrative visual

If you have many visualizations on the page and you want a summary of all the data, you can select the smart narrative visualization from the **Visualizations** pane and it will generate a summary of all the visualizations on the page.

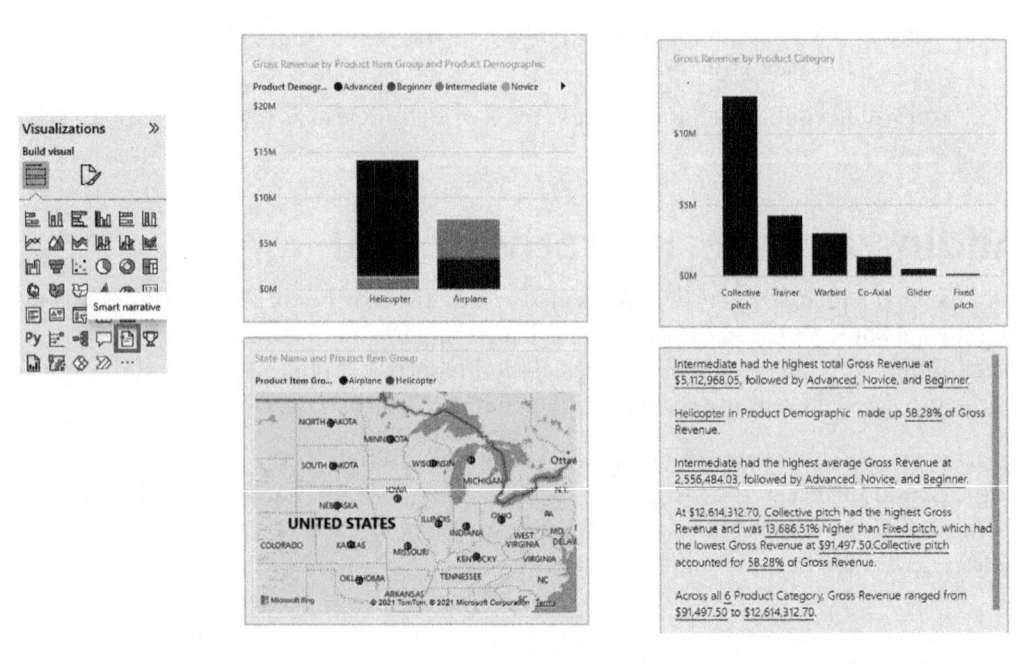

Figure 9.34 – Smart narrative visual summarizing all visuals on the page

Adding a smart narrative visual   195

You can edit the resulting text, adding text and configuring the formatting or any other text option you want. You can also add your own insights dynamically by adding your own values or calculations.

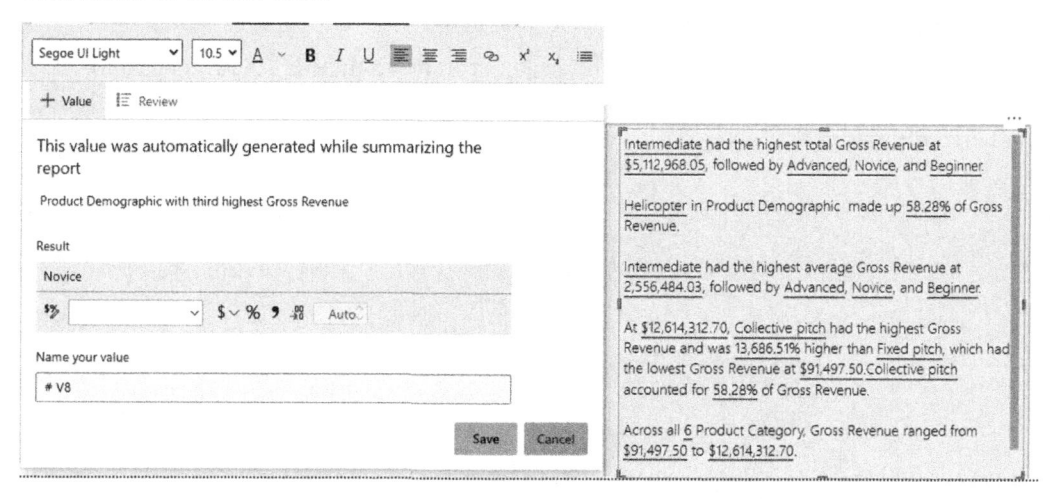

Figure 9.35 – Editing the smart narrative text

The smart narrative visualization will react to cross-filtering. For example, if you highlight **Helicopter** in the stacked column chart, the smart narrative will rerun, filtering for **Helicopter**.

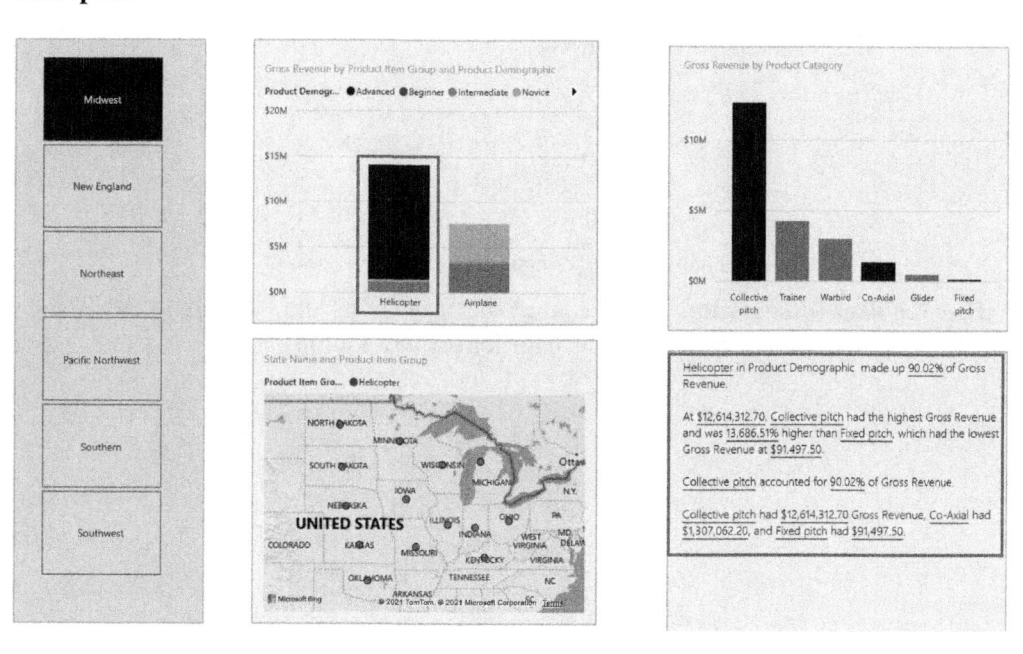

Figure 9.36 – Smart narrative visual reacting to cross-filtering

We'll now check out how we can configure the report page so that we can customize it.

Configuring the report page

Much like visualizations, report pages themselves can be configured. As you are only configuring the page, you will not see a **General** or **Visual** area; instead, you will only see the **Format page** area.

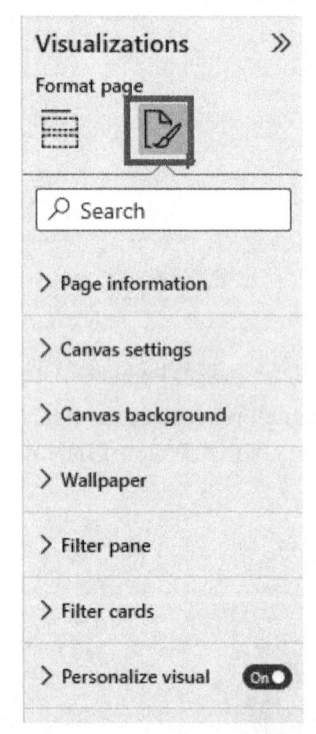

Figure 9.37 – Configuration of report pages

You use the **Page information** area to change the page name, allow for use in Q&A by just double-clicking on the canvas, or set the page for use as a tooltip.

Figure 9.38 – Page information configuration

The canvas settings allow you to set the page size, in one of the preset configurations. The default is a 16:9 ratio, as most computer monitors are set to that. You can change the setting to **4:3**, **Letter**, **Tooltip**, or **Custom**, which is a count of pixels.

The **Tooltip** option will shrink the page down to a size that is great to display a chart instead of just a grid of data in a tooltip. You don't have to turn **Tooltip** on in the **Paging information** settings, but it makes sense if you do.

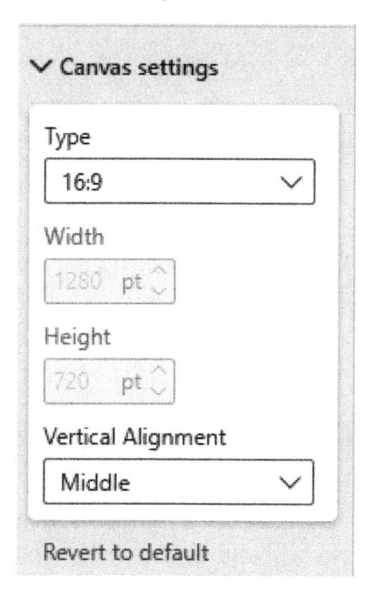

Figure 9.39 – Canvas settings

You can also change the alignment of the report page in Power BI Desktop here. Your choices are **Top** or **Middle**, with **Middle** being the default.

Much like changing the background of a visual, you can change the background of the entire report page. The same ideas apply; follow the style guidelines of your organization and ensure colors, images, and shapes follow inclusive patterns so all users will be able to read and understand your reports.

As this is the entire page, you could choose a background image that "divides" the reporting area into sections.

Figure 9.40 – Dividing the canvas into areas

You can then layer your visuals on this grid and make your report really stand out. I created the preceding layout in PowerPoint and saved it as a JPG, then imported it as my background image.

This is also a great place to add a watermark, to identify whether the report is managed by a BI team or a data warehousing team. Watermarking reports can help your report consumers develop a level of trust that the report is accurate and follows your corporate guidelines. Just don't take up too much real estate with your watermark.

Designing and configuring for accessibility

It is important to think of all the different types of users and the methods with which users will interact with your Power BI reports. Some users may have visual or physical impairments and Power BI has the capabilities to make reports inclusive, as well as features to help ensure that building reports is also an inclusive activity.

Microsoft has recommendations for using Power BI with a screen reader that include turning scan mode or browse mode off.

Designing and configuring for accessibility 199

To help in scenarios where screen reader software is used, context menus are available. You can move fields up and down in the list using the context menu. You can also move fields around between entries such as **Value** or **Legend** depending on the visual.

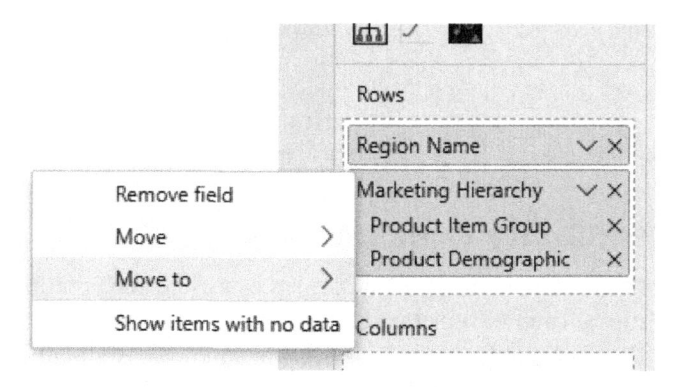

Figure 9.41 – Moving fields up and down

It's possible to build accessible reports in Power BI but it takes attention and effort by the report designer to make that a reality.

Power BI accessibility features can be either of the following:

- Built-in (no configuration required)
- Built-in (configuration required)
- Other tips and considerations

The built-in with no configuration required features include the following:

- Navigation using the keyboard
- Compatibility with screen reader software
- Viewing in high-contrast colors
- Showing data tables

These features require no special attention by the report designer but are available for all reports created in Power BI. These are basic features of Power BI and require no configuration by the report designer.

Accessibility features that do require configuration by the report designer include the following:

- Report themes
- Tab order
- Alt text
- Titles and labels

Report accessibility checklist

Power BI provides a checklist that report designers can use when creating reports. By using this checklist, you can help ensure your reports are accessible and usable by the largest audience. The checklist is available at the official Power BI documentation here: `https://docs.microsoft.com/en-us/power-bi/create-reports/desktop-accessibility-creating-reports#report-accessibility-checklist`.

> **Tip**
> For the exam, you should know that these features exist. Microsoft is making accessibility a key component of all its products going forward.

Configuring automatic page refresh

Reports are often only as valuable as the data they display. The frequency in which data is updated in the report can be critical to the value the report provides. When the most up-to-date data is required, it's best to consider using the automatic page refresh feature of Power BI.

When you enable automatic page refresh, you will be presented with an option of when to refresh the page. You can either select a fixed time interval or have Power BI detect changes in the underlying data source.

When using the fixed interval refresh type, all visuals in a report page will be updated at the same interval. You can refresh as often as every second or go as long as 5 minutes or more.

Another option besides fixed interval is to use change detection. Change detection will refresh visuals on a page when changes are detected in the data. This feature polls for changes to DirectQuery sources. When this is set up, you have defined how Power BI will detect changes by selecting the measure and you also have to select the frequency at which Power BI will check for changes. For published reports, this refresh type is only supported in workspaces that are part of a Premium capacity. LiveConnect data sources, such as Analysis Services and Power BI datasets, are not supported as they use LiveConnect. By using change detection, you may put less stress on the source system and on Power BI, as you only refresh the page if the underlying data changes.

When using either fixed interval or change detection, your Power BI tenant admin can set a minimum number of seconds or minutes that you can specify. If you publish your report with a lower value set, it will be reset to the tenant minimum.

Automatic page refresh is configured on the report page in the **Format page** pane, the same place where you can set the page background and name.

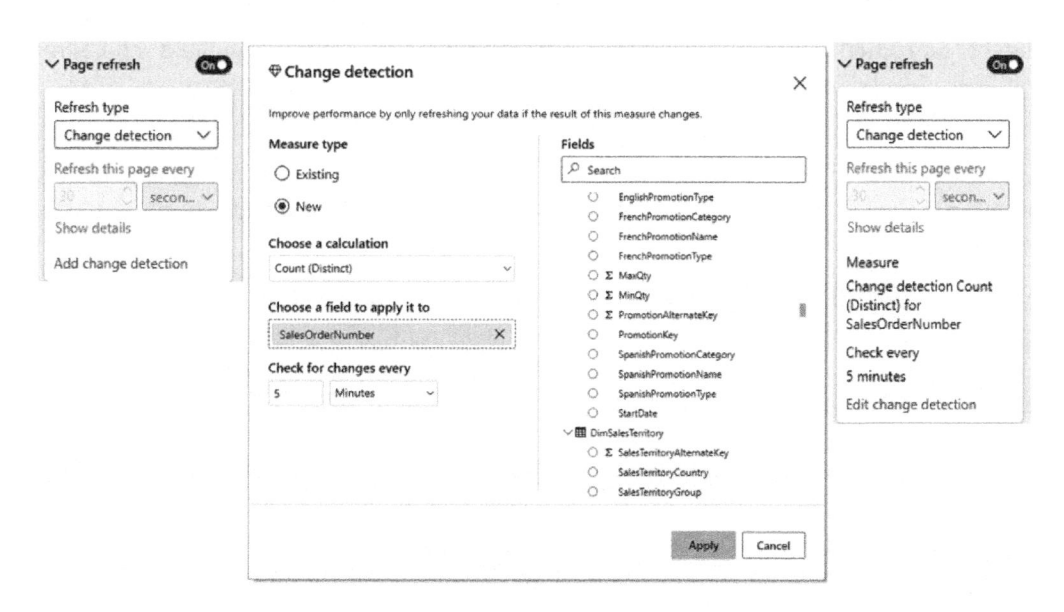

Figure 9.42 – Configuring change detection for page refresh

Change detection here is set to detect whether a new `SalesOrderNumber` field is added.

Creating a paginated report

Paginated reporting is another style of reporting than the interactive reports you can produce with Power BI. Paginated reports are reports that are meant to be consumed in a tightly controlled way. Often, this is referred to as "pixel perfect" because it allows reports to be rendered onscreen and printed on pages without losing the fidelity of the original design made by the report designer. Paginated reports are not meant to be interactive like typical Power BI reports.

Paginated reports can have headers and footers on every page and typically follow the design of reports that have been created for decades by enterprises and organizations using tools such as SQL Server Reporting Services.

When report requirements include user stories such as printing reports, or the data being displayed often includes dozens of columns or perhaps hundreds of rows of data, then it's typically a good idea to explore the use of Power BI paginated reports as the capability is well suited for those use cases.

Some organizations you are familiar with may already be generating paginated reports for you, either electronically or in the mail. Think of your bank statements, your credit card statements, or an itemized receipt. All of these are examples of paginated reports.

To create paginated reports in Power BI, you need to use an additional tool that is free to download called Power BI Report Builder. In order to publish paginated reports, you will need to publish to a workspace hosted in Power BI Premium.

Power BI Report Builder allows you to connect to data sources and create paginated reports. Although the number of data sources Report Builder can connect to is limited, it can connect to Power BI datasets, so the entire list of Power BI data sources and the refresh capabilities built into Power BI become immediately available.

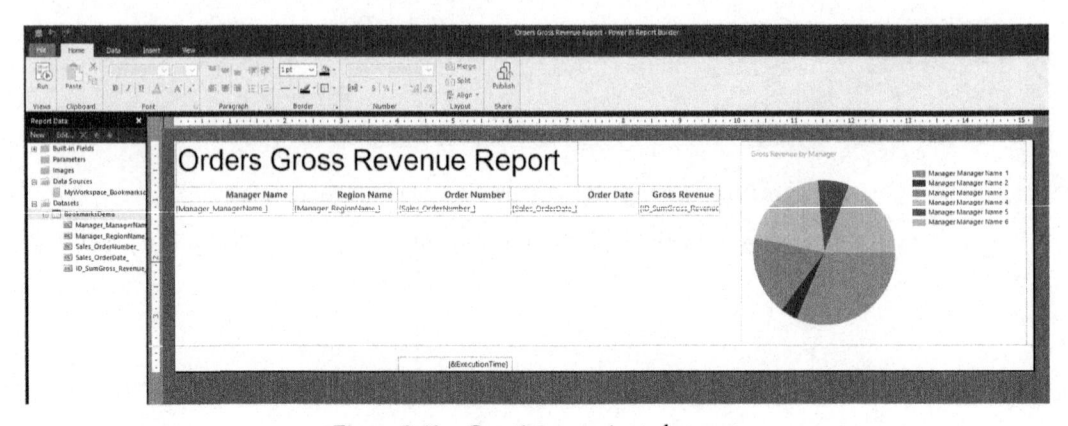

Figure 9.43 – Creating a paginated report

Once you have created your report in Report Builder, you can publish it directly to the Power BI service from within Power BI Report Builder.

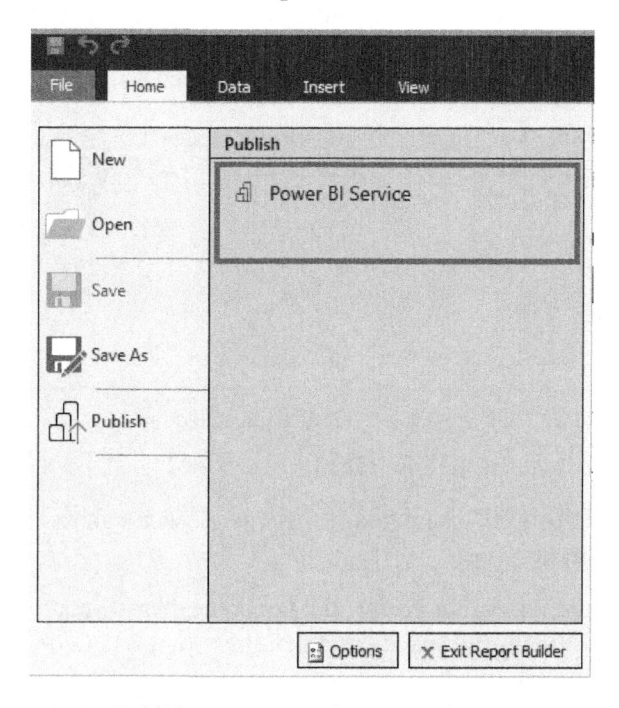

Figure 9.44 – Publishing a paginated report to the Power BI service

You will need to select a workspace that is backed by Premium capacity. Look for the diamond icon next to the workspace name.

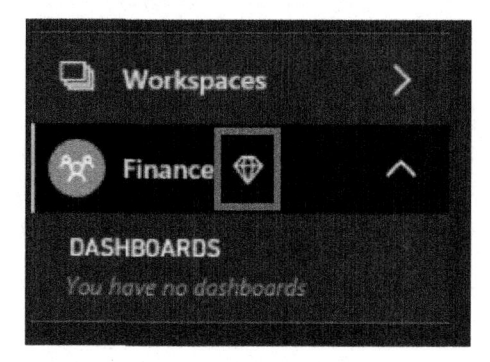

Figure 9.45 – Diamond icon designating a Power BI Premium workspace

Once you publish your report, you can view it online.

Figure 9.46 – Published paginated report

Paginated reports are used throughout the business world.

This is not a book on Power BI paginated reports, so we won't go too deep into these extremely powerful report types.

For the test, you should know that Power BI paginated reports must be published to a workspace backed by Premium capacity and that these reports are designed for pixel-perfect rendering and interactivity.

Using Power BI datasets in Excel PivotTables

You can bring Power BI datasets into Excel with **Analyze in Excel**. You can then view and interact with your Power BI dataset using PivotTables, charts, slicers, and other Excel features.

To do this, you must go to the Power BI dataset in the Power BI workspace you want to connect to. Once there, click on the ellipsis and select **Analyze in Excel**.

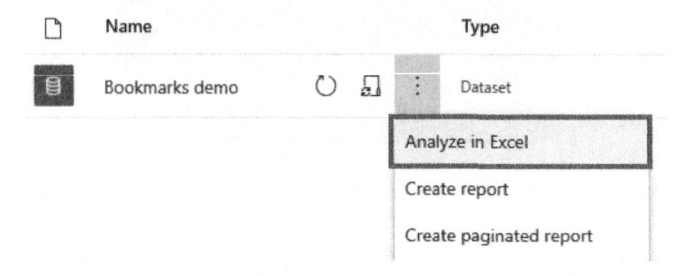

Figure 9.47 – Analyze in Excel option for Power BI datasets

The **Analyze in Excel** feature should install automatically, if not already installed. Then, an Excel workbook will be downloaded. Once you open the workbook, you may need to select **Enable Editing** and **Enable Content** in Excel.

At this point, your Excel workbook is connected to the Power BI dataset and you can use the data as you need.

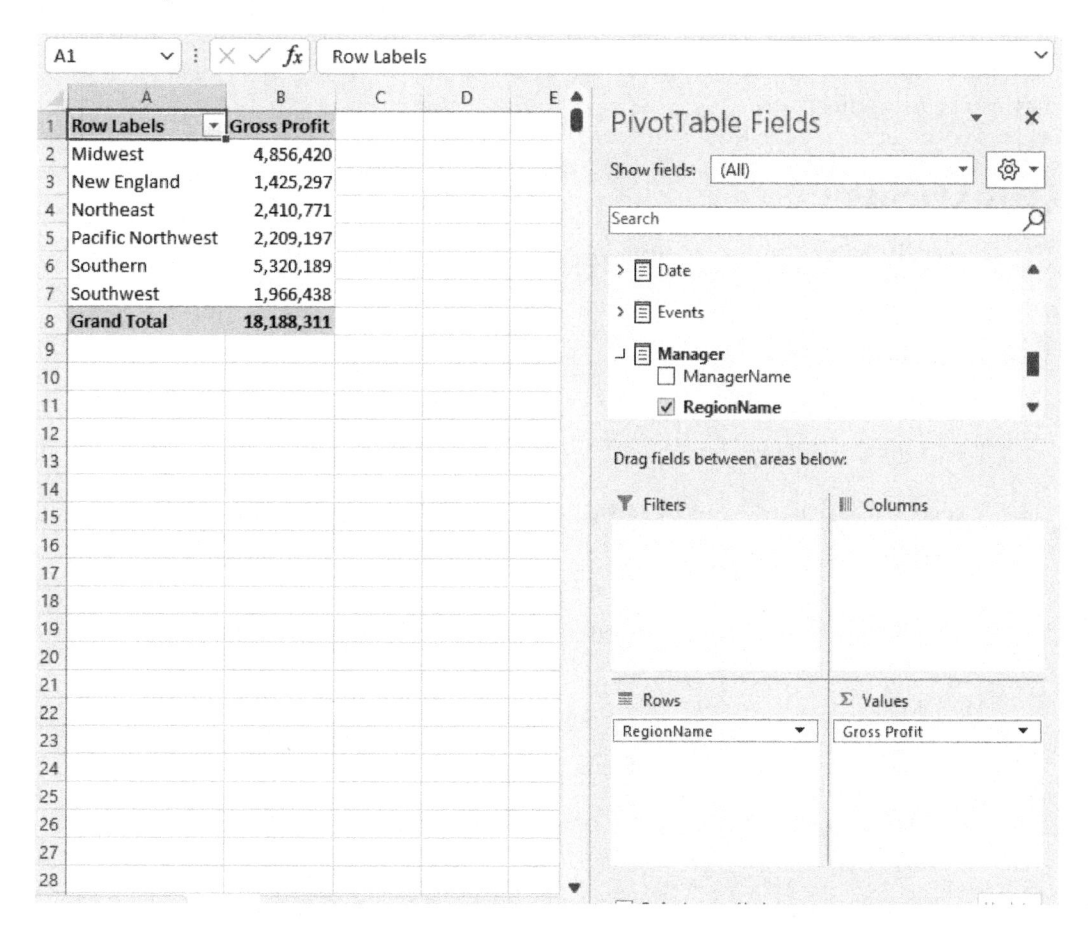

Row Labels	Gross Profit
Midwest	4,856,420
New England	1,425,297
Northeast	2,410,771
Pacific Northwest	2,209,197
Southern	5,320,189
Southwest	1,966,438
Grand Total	18,188,311

Figure 9.48 – Excel workbook connected to Power BI dataset

You get all the data cleaning, organization, and security of Power BI, and your data analysts get to use a tool they may be more comfortable with.

Summary

In this chapter, we checked out the reporting capabilities of Power BI. We explored various charts, custom visuals, and also learned how to format and configure visualizations to show what we need. We also checked out conditional formatting, and various advanced techniques in Power BI.

In the next chapter, we will explore Power BI dashboards, how dashboards are created from published Power BI reports, how they are different from Power BI reports, and how they can be used effectively.

Questions

1. Power BI reports can use custom visuals added from what resource?

    A. Microsoft AppSource

    B. Microsoft Store

    C. Power BI VisualStore

    D. Office 365 templates

2. Which visual makes the most sense to use for geographical information?

    A. Clustered bar chart

    B. Stacked bar chart

    C. Scatter chart

    D. Map

3. If you want to make the color of data change based on its value, what feature will you use?

    A. The Edit tab

    B. Conditional formatting

    C. Bold formatting

    D. Conditional settings

10
Creating Dashboards

One of the main reasons organizations adopt Power BI is to enable dynamic storytelling using data with vibrant visuals. Report designers create reports using specific datasets and sometimes, to tell a whole story, you need to use data across different datasets and reports. This is where Power BI dashboards become useful.

A dashboard is one place where you can see all the relevant information about something. In a car, the dashboard contains information about the speed of the car, what gear it is in, whether the lights are on, the temperature of the cabin environment, and even the volume of the sound system. All the data from this example comes from different systems and some inputs can vary when it comes to importance while driving the car, but all of them are going to be important to the person operating the car.

When used properly, dashboards become an integral component of a Power BI solution.

In this chapter, we're going to cover the following topics:

- Introducing Power BI dashboards
- Pinning tiles
- Optimizing dashboards

Technical requirements

The following are the requirements for this chapter:

- Access to the Power BI service (https://www.powerbi.com) using a work or school account
- Power BI reports and data published to the Power BI service where we can apply the features covered in this chapter

Let's begin by introducing the concept of Power BI dashboards and how they work.

Introducing Power BI dashboards

Dashboards in Power BI are where users of the business intelligence solution can go to see all the important information without having to switch between multiple reports. A dashboard is a type of content that is created and used from a Power BI workspace. Dashboards are only created with the Power BI service (https://www.powerbi.com) and not with Power BI Desktop. Dashboards tend to rely on visuals created in reports; however, it is possible to use tools such as Q&A to dynamically create visuals and directly pin them to a dashboard. Dashboards rely on the underlying datasets and data models used in reports, and they provide a new way of consuming the data, which provides some unique advantages over reports.

It should also be said that it's important to understand the distinction here between what Power BI refers to as a dashboard and what Power BI calls a report. Reports are typically created using the Desktop tool (sometimes can be created on the Power BI service) and can be saved as a PBIX file, while a true dashboard content type is only created on the Power BI service and there is no file format for dashboards. We're drawing this distinction because sometimes, users will create a Power BI report and refer to it as a "dashboard" due to the use of interactive visuals in the report. To Power BI, these are two different types of content and have different features, capabilities, and uses.

On the Power BI service, you can tell the difference between reports and dashboards by looking at the workspace and noticing the different icons and type designations, as shown in *Figure 10.1*:

	Name	Type
◎	dashboard1	Dashboard
ıll	report1	Report

Figure 10.1 – Difference between a Power BI report and a dashboard

Reports are best used when they can be focused on a specific topic of data or set of questions about a particular dataset or related datasets.

For example, when looking at product sales, we might have visuals showing sales by product categories, regions, sellers, or fiscal period (years, quarters, or months). Sales information will be curated into a sales data model and used within a sales report that allows business users to drill into the details of the sales information.

Likewise, inventory data would also be curated into an inventory data model and reports created showing historical and up-to-date inventory information for various warehouses, regions, and store locations. Inventory reports might also contain information from shipping and supply chain partners to answer critical questions about having products at the right place and time. Since a retail business needs to have products to sell them, inventory and supply chain information is also vital to a business.

Sales managers and inventory managers will likely use the reports on a frequent basis as their primary responsibility is for those areas (sales and inventory). However, the **Chief Financial Officer** (**CFO**) might need to have an understanding of both functions of the organization. The CFO will be interested in not only the margin being made on the sale of products but also the cost of the raw materials and third-party products that are being sold. So, the CFO will need to ask questions about the sales data as well as the inventory and supply chain data, and this is where Power BI dashboards become powerful tools that allow data from both to be included on a single page for easy information consumption.

In *Figure 10.2*, we can see how sales data and inventory data both end up being inputs to the leadership dashboards through the use of both Power BI reports and dashboards. Different content will have different audiences:

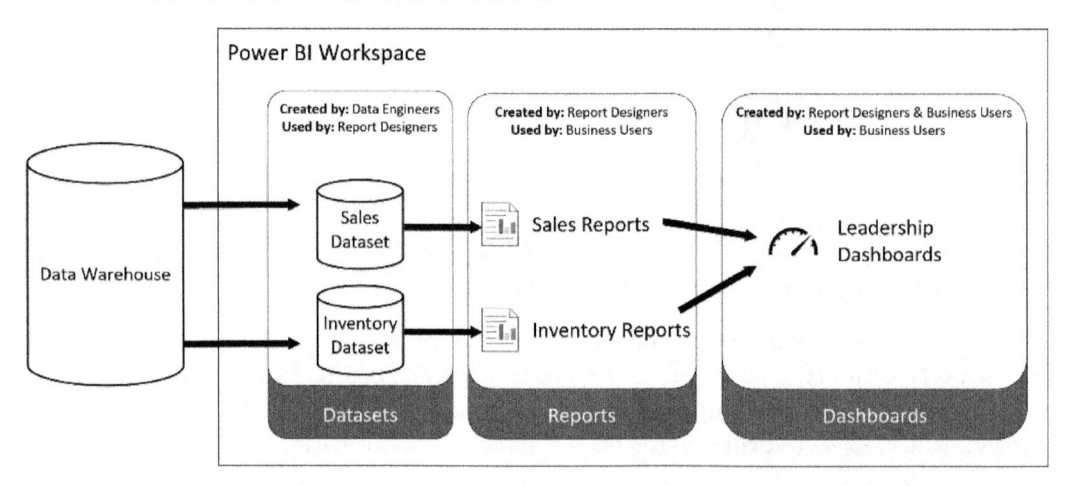

Figure 10.2 – Diagram showing the relationship between datasets, reports, and dashboards

Now that we know how dashboards can be useful, let's explore how they can be created and used.

Creating a dashboard

To create a dashboard, first log into the Power BI service at https://www.powerbi.com. This requires a work or school account with Microsoft to use Power BI. The Power BI service is where workspaces are hosted and where Power BI apps are created, shared, and hosted as well.

Once logged into the Power BI service, navigate to the workspace you'd like to create a dashboard in and then select **New** under the menu at the top:

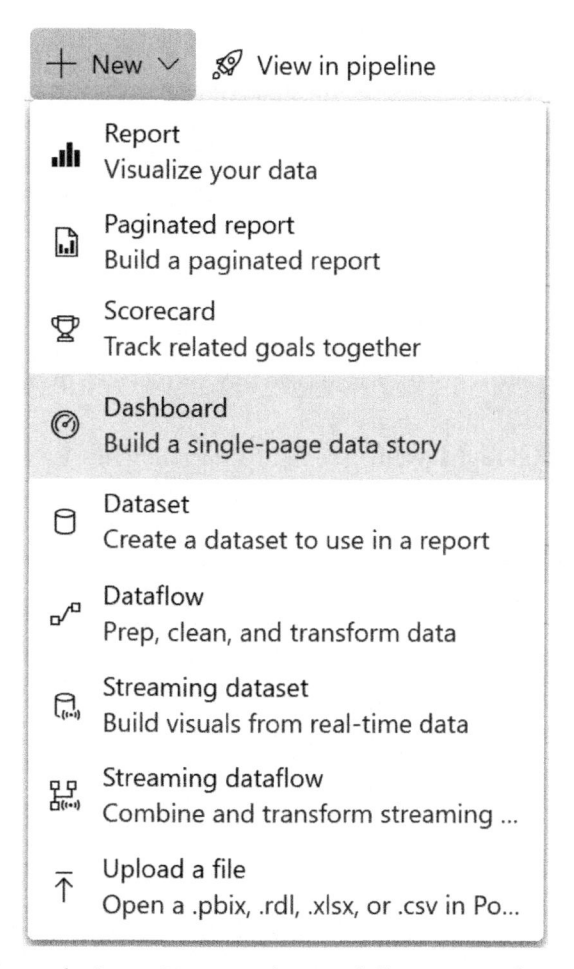

Figure 10.3 – New menu on the Power BI service showing different types of content that can be created, including dashboards

Next, provide a name for the dashboard and click **Create**. If your organization requires setting a sensitivity label, then be sure to select the value for this option when asked. A newly created dashboard will be a blank or empty canvas to which visuals from any report in the workspace can be pinned and organized. Dashboards can be viewed on the Power BI service as part of a Power BI app or from the various Power BI mobile apps, which makes the consumption of Power BI insights easy from nearly any device or location. Dashboards are organized into workspaces the same as reports and datasets.

While the data contained in a dashboard may be the most valuable component, if the data is not presented in a visually appealing way, it won't be as useful to the organization. Colors used in visuals play a big role in the impact they make; so, let's next look at how we can use themes with dashboards.

Setting a dashboard theme

Dashboards are meant to be a single canvas that shows the most important information the user needs to see. As such, visual aspects such as themes are important to best convey the information. Dashboards support theming either with light, dark, color-blind-friendly, or custom themes. When using a theme, every visual on the canvas will use the colors of the theme.

> **Note**
> See the limitations list at the end of this subsection to best understand how dashboard themes work and what you can and can't do with them.

The built-in theme called **Light** will have a light-gray and white background with black text, while the **Dark** theme provides a dark-gray and darker gray background with white text. The color-blind-friendly built-in theme will force visuals to use colors that are easier to distinguish for users who are color-blind.

If you'd like to match your organization's color theme or use seasonal colors, this is possible by using a custom theme with a JSON template file. For example, the JSON file of the **Light** theme looks like this:

```
{
    "name": "Light",
    "foreground": "#000000",
    "background": "#EAEAEA",
    "dataColors": ["#01B8AA", "#374649", "#FD625E", "#F2C80F", "#5F6B6D", "#8AD4EB", "#FE9666", "#A66999"],
    "tiles": {
        "background": "#FFFFFF",
        "color": "#000000"
    },
    "visualStyles": {
        "*": {
            "*": {
                "*": [{
                    "color": {
                        "solid": {
                            "color": "#000000"
                        }
                    }
```

```
                }
            }]
        }
    }
}
```

Using this template, you can define a custom color theme for dashboards to meet your requirements.

Limitations for applying themes to dashboards include the following:

- Dashboard themes will not cascade to live reports, paginated reports, web, workbooks, or image tiles.
- Dashboard themes can only be set using the Power BI service from a web browser, not the mobile app.
- Custom themes only work with tiles containing visuals pinned from reports.

Now that we understand how dashboards can be created, let's discover the functionality they provide when using deployed dashboards.

Using a dashboard

Dashboards are meant to be used for information consumption, and typically in a less interactive way compared to reports. This means that when you click a visual in a dashboard, you're not going to slice or filter data in other visuals, as they may use different data models that may not have relationships set up to enable cross-filtering. When you click a visual in a dashboard, you will be taken to the source report from which it was pinned. In a way, the dashboard is the first place to go to see the most important data, but it is also a switchboard of sorts that allows you to navigate to reports if you want more information after viewing the top-level important information. Therefore, dashboards become a great tool for senior leaders of an organization.

Additionally, dashboards and reports both offer **focus mode**. Focus mode is a feature of Power BI reports and dashboards where the selected visual takes over the entire canvas of the report or dashboard to allow the user to temporarily get a more detailed look at the data used for that visual. You can exit focus mode by clicking **Exit focus mode** or **Back to the report** in the top left-hand corner of the canvas.

214   Creating Dashboards

To set up dashboards that your users will want to use, you'll want to add content to them. This is achieved by pinning tiles that contain visuals and other content, which we'll cover in the next section.

Pinning tiles

Content on a dashboard is referred to as a **tile**. Tiles can be visuals from a report in the workspace, web content, images, text, video, or real-time streaming data. After creating a blank dashboard, it is possible to add any of these content types from the **Edit** menu by clicking **Add a tile**, except report visuals. To add a visual from an existing report, you need to first navigate to the report and select the **Pin visual** option that pops up after hovering the mouse over a visual, as shown in *Figure 10.4*:

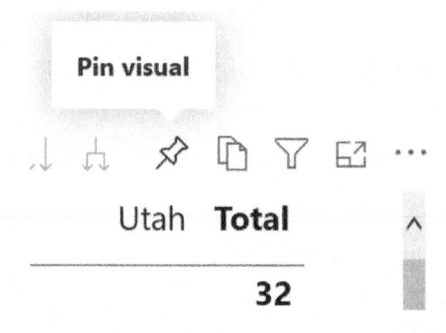

Figure 10.4 – Pin button used to pin a visual to a dashboard

When visuals are pinned to a dashboard, they can have filters applied. Reports provide interactivity where users can filter or even select values from other visuals to cross-filter the display of information, which changes with the user's selection. Dashboards, on the other hand, will provide a static representation of the data you want to use to tell the story. For example, you might have product sales data representing sales in the United States, Canada, and the United Kingdom, but for the dashboard used by the president of the United States subsidiary, you want to tell the story of product sales in the United States only. From the global sales report, you would apply the filter to the `CountryRegion` field to only show data from the United States. Once this filter has been applied (using a filter or a slicer visual), the visual with filtered data can then be pinned to the dashboard.

The Power BI service stores a cache of data to enable performant dashboards with various filters applied for the pinned visuals. More information on optimizing the cache of data used for dashboard tiles will be covered in the *Optimizing dashboards* section.

After clicking the **Pin visual** button, you'll get the option to pin this visual to an existing dashboard or a new dashboard, as shown in *Figure 10.5*. Selecting the name of the existing dashboard will add this visual to the dashboard:

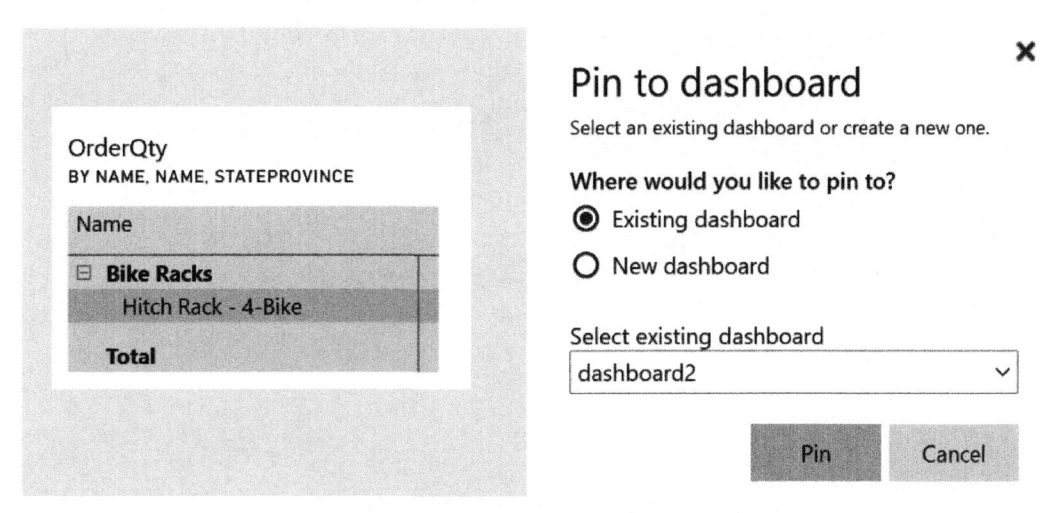

Figure 10.5 – Pin visual to dashboard selection

After the dashboard has been selected (or a new dashboard created) and the visual has been pinned, the notice shown in *Figure 10.6* will appear in the top right-hand corner of the window. This lets you know that the pinning was successful and allows you to quickly go to the impacted dashboard or create a mobile layout for the dashboard. We will cover mobile layouts in detail in the next section:

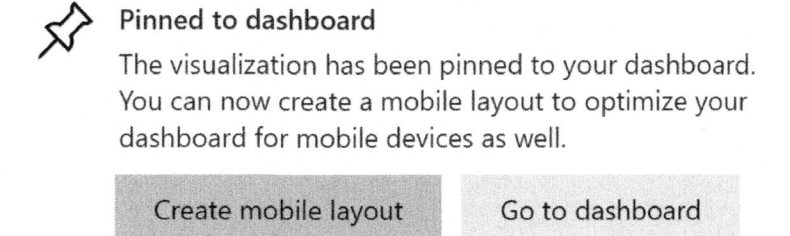

Figure 10.6 – Notice that the visual has been pinned to the dashboard

Since it is possible to use themes when building reports, it's possible that visuals being pinned to dashboard tiles will start with a theme. When you pin visuals from reports that use a theme to dashboards that use a theme, you'll see this message asking for confirmation for the theming of the dashboard tile to either use the destination theme or the current theme, as shown in *Figure 10.7*:

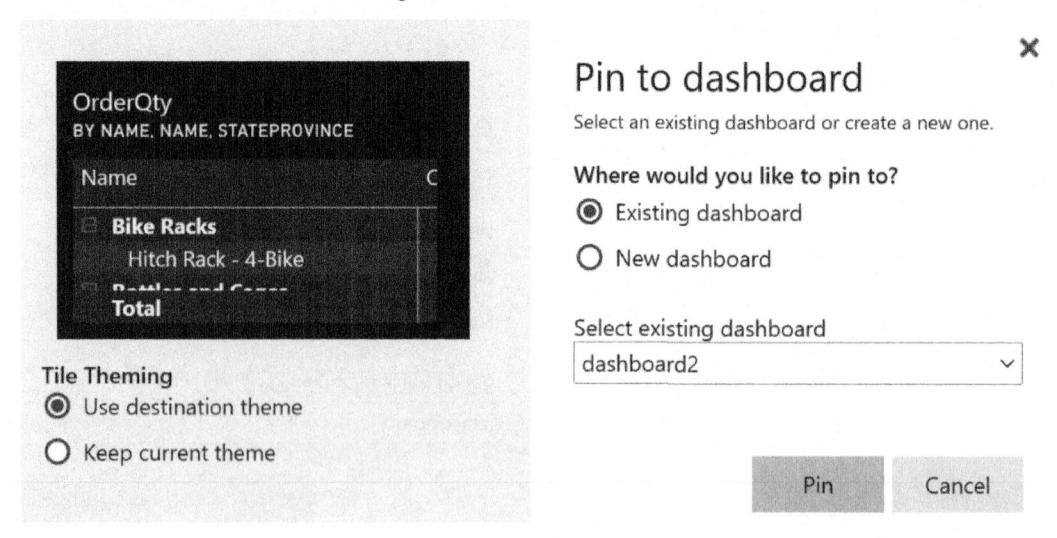

Figure 10.7 – Selection of tile theming when pinning a visual

After visuals have been pinned to a dashboard, it's important to review the dashboard and potentially adjust how the visuals or other elements have been pinned. If you open the dashboard you've created, you'll be able to drag and drop the pinned tiles, as well as resizing them and adjusting things such as adding comments, adding functionality such as displaying the last refresh time, setting custom links, and changing the title and subtitles.

While most often, visuals will be pinned to dashboards, it is also possible to pin a whole report page to a dashboard. When this happens, the entire report becomes a tile in the dashboard and retains the live interactivity and cross-filtering capabilities of the report. Reports pinned to dashboards are not visible in the mobile layout and they may have performance implications; both of these topics will be covered in the next section as part of optimization.

Optimizing dashboards

Dashboards are a useful way to tell a story using data and visuals in Power BI but if they are not optimized to the screen they are being presented on or if the dashboard takes a long time to load, they lose their effectiveness. In this section, we'll see how we can optimize dashboards for these scenarios to make them the most useful starting place for Power BI information consumers.

Configuring views of a dashboard

To recap, Power BI is an online service that allows organizations to see the most important information from anywhere. This is accomplished using a **Software-as-a-Service** (**SaaS**) website at `https://www.powerbi.com` as well as mobile apps for iOS and Android phones and tablets and Windows devices.

However, since these device screens can range from small hand-held sizes to very large, dashboards being created can be consumed optimally for every screen size. Large screen devices such as desktop web browsers and tablets will use the same layout, but mobile phones need an optimized dashboard layout to increase their usability due to the screen size.

To optimize a dashboard to a mobile screen, select **Mobile layout** from the **Edit** menu.

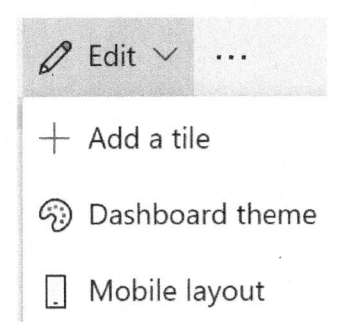

Figure 10.8 – Mobile layout under the Edit menu

You'll now be taken to the **Edit mobile layout** screen, where you can arrange the order in which tiles will be shown when viewing the dashboard on a mobile device. Since most dashboards tend to have KPI visuals all in a row at the top of the default or web layout, the mobile layout allows you to pick the order in which they will be presented when viewing from the Power BI mobile apps.

218 Creating Dashboards

While editing the mobile layout, you can reorder the tiles and or also unpin visuals from the mobile view. This is useful when you want a tile to be shown when viewing on the web but not shown when viewing on a mobile device.

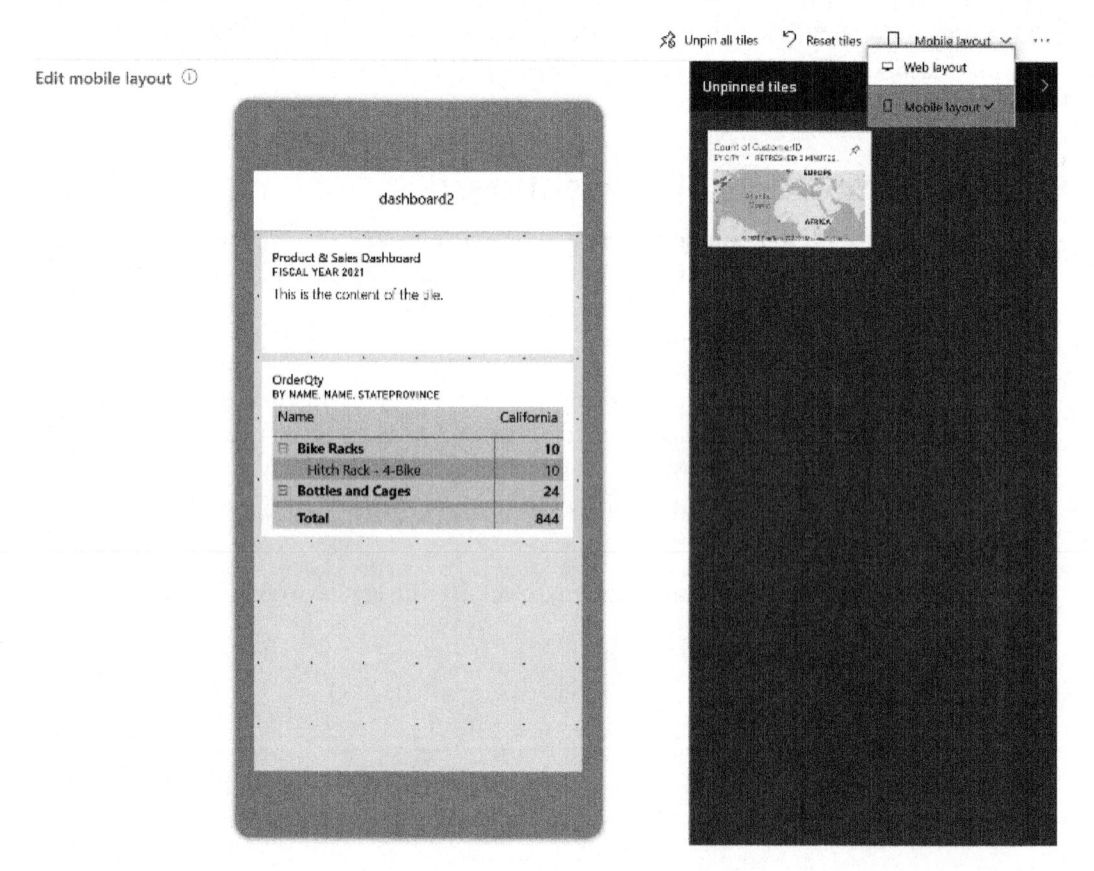

Figure 10.9 – Edit mobile layout

To exit editing the mobile layout, simply select **Web layout** under the **Mobile layout** menu on the top right-hand side of the screen.

It is important to note that if report tiles are used (pinning an entire report page to a dashboard), then they will not be visible on the mobile layout or able to be consumed in the Power BI mobile app. This is due to how report tiles provide additional interactivity, as well as performance impact, which will be discussed in the next subsection.

Once the layout has been optimized for the devices used by the intended consumers, next, you need to make sure the performance is optimized.

Optimizing the performance of a dashboard

The Power BI service includes the ability to diagnose poor performance in dashboards. The **performance inspector** will review the dashboard that has been created and make recommendations to increase the performance of the dashboard.

To open the performance inspector, click **Performance inspector** under the **File** menu when viewing the dashboard.

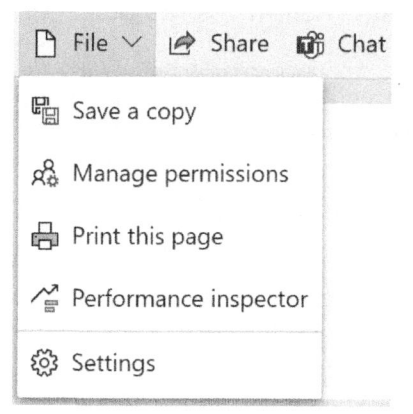

Figure 10.10 – Launching performance inspector from the File menu when viewing a dashboard

When the performance inspector opens, you'll see items that are scored green, yellow, or red, as shown in *Figure 10.11*:

Performance inspector

NEED ATTENTION

- Avoid single-visual report tiles

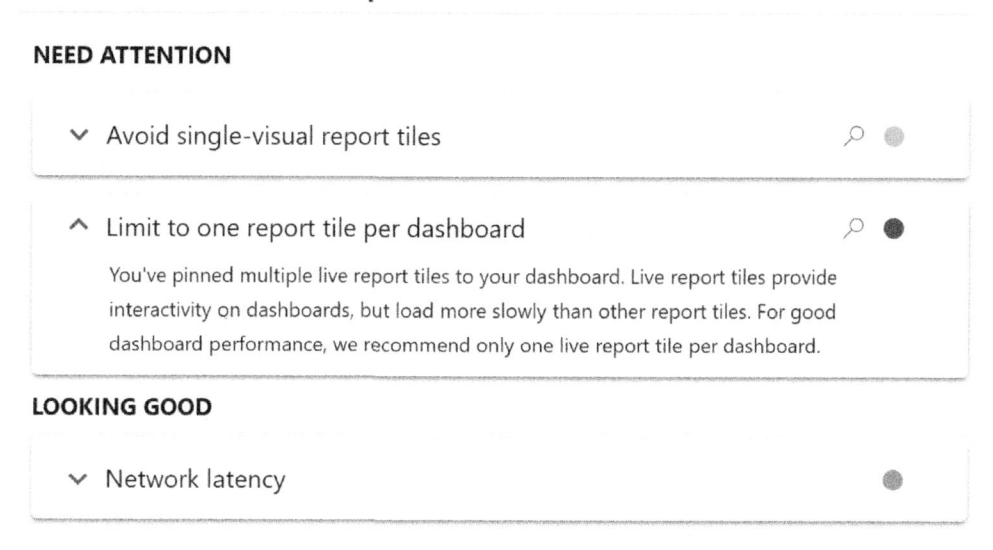

- Limit to one report tile per dashboard
  You've pinned multiple live report tiles to your dashboard. Live report tiles provide interactivity on dashboards, but load more slowly than other report tiles. For good dashboard performance, we recommend only one live report tile per dashboard.

LOOKING GOOD

- Network latency

Figure 10.11 – Dashboard performance inspector findings

These scores will give you an indication of which items will have the most impact on the performance of your report. Under the **NEED ATTENTION** section be sure to review the performance inspector findings and make changes to your dashboard as suggested. Some common findings include the following:

- **Limiting the use of report tiles to one per dashboard** – When multiple report tiles are used, the dashboard can show multiple pages of reports of live data and cross-filtering at the same time. This isn't possible with reports, so it is not advised to do this on dashboards.

- **Removing the use of single-visual report tiles** – It is possible to create a report with one visual and then pin that entire report to a dashboard. In this case, it is suggested to pin the visual rather than the whole page as this will remove the requirement for live interactivity back to the report data.

The Power BI service keeps data in dashboards up to date by keeping a cache of the data needed for the dashboard, which aids in performance. When data in the underlying dataset gets refreshed, the service will update this cache. It is also possible to force this cache to update by clicking the refresh button on the toolbar (upper right-hand side) when viewing the dashboard.

You can also set the service to automatically refresh the cache used for dashboard tiles by enabling automatic tile refresh in the dataset options and setting the refresh frequency, as shown in *Figure 10.12*:

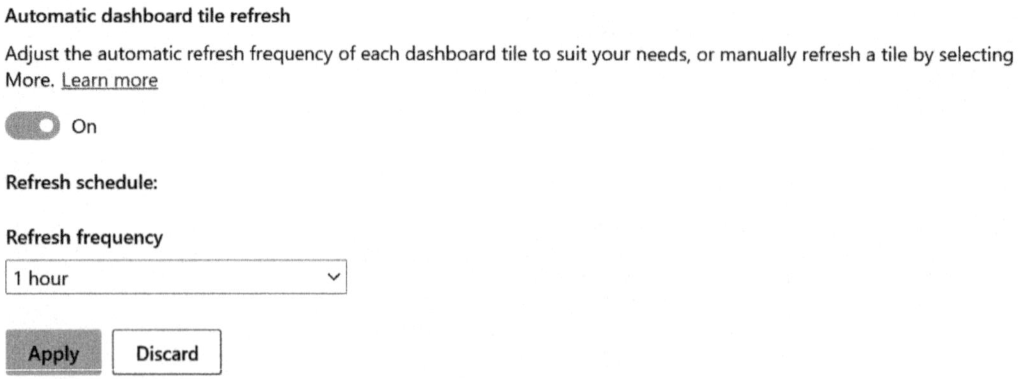

Automatic dashboard tile refresh

Adjust the automatic refresh frequency of each dashboard tile to suit your needs, or manually refresh a tile by selecting More. Learn more

On

Refresh schedule:

Refresh frequency

1 hour

Apply   Discard

Figure 10.12 – Automatic dashboard tile refresh settings

Once the automatic dashboard tile refresh is set, the service will handle updating the data cache used for dashboards, but users will still have the option to manually refresh if necessary. Remember that this will not impact report tiles, as data used for report tiles is always live, going back to the dataset of the report.

Optimized dashboards are a key ingredient to telling a story with data and make a Power BI solution useful from nearly any device at any location.

Summary

In this chapter, we learned about Power BI dashboards. Dashboards provide a way to bring attention to the most important information from multiple reports within a workspace.

We learned the differences between dashboards and reports, how they can be created, how visuals and reports can be pinned, and how users will use dashboards from the Power BI service on the web as well as from mobile devices anywhere. We learned the details of how pinning tiles works, dashboard layouts can be edited, tiles can be resized, and custom dashboard themes can be configured.

When it comes to optimizing dashboards, we learned that dashboards should be optimized for the screen size where they will be consumed, and the Power BI service provides a way to do this to optimize the flow of tiles on dashboards for smaller mobile device screens. We also learned how the performance inspector can help optimize dashboards to ensure the best performance.

In the next chapter, we'll explore ways of enhancing reports with capabilities such as navigation tooltips and buttons.

Questions

1. Dashboards can contain what type of content?

    A. Report visuals, web content, images, text, video, and streaming data

    B. Report visuals, report pages, images, text, video, and streaming data

    C. Report visuals, report pages, web content, images, text, and video

    D. Report visuals, report pages, web content, images, text, video, and streaming data

2. What is the shortest frequency for automatic dashboard tile refresh of cached data for pinned visuals?

    A. 30 minutes

    B. 15 minutes

    C. 5 minutes

    D. 1 hour

3. Dashboards can be optimized for viewing on what devices?

    A. Web and desktop
    B. Web only
    C. Web, iOS, Android, and Blackberry
    D. Web and mobile

11
Enhancing Reports

You already learned about the basic elements for creating a report in *Chapter 9, Creating Reports*. Now it's time to take the knowledge to the next level. After you've added your visuals, you can further enhance your report to allow you to tell your data-driven story the way you want to.

Using Power BI Desktop, you'll learn how to transform your report to provide your report consumers with reports that are better organized, with a more effective layout and interactions. You'll be able to provide your users with tools that allow them to explore the data more effectively or allow you, as the report writer, to tell your data story in the order you want it told.

In this chapter, we will cover the following:

- Using bookmarks
- Designing reports for mobile devices

Technical requirements

For this chapter, please make sure you have the following:

- Microsoft Power BI Desktop installed on a Microsoft Windows PC.
- We've also provided synthetic data that can be used, which is available in the GitHub repository for this book here: `https://github.com/PacktPublishing/Microsoft-Power-BI-Data-Analyst-Certification-Guide/tree/main/example-data`.

Using bookmarks

Power BI installs with many visuals you can use to tell your data story. These visuals allow you to highlight the data you want in order to explain insights you have discovered in your data that lead to actions your business can take. Bookmarks allow you to save the page as it is being viewed. By saving the page, potentially with cross-visual filtering, using bookmarks allows you to step through views of the report in a slide-like fashion to aid in telling a story with the data.

When you add a bookmark, you save the following:

- Current page
- Filters
- Slicers, including slicer type (for example, dropdown or list) and slicer state
- Cross-highlight filter state
- Sort order
- Drill-up/drill-down level
- Visibility of an object (by using the **Selection** pane)
- Focus
- Spotlight

The actual data on the report page is not saved, just the state of the visuals. This means that when the data is refreshed, the new data will be displayed, but with the same filters, slicers, visibility, and so forth.

To add a bookmark, first get the report page in the state you want to save it in, then select **Bookmarks** from the **View** tab. This will open the **Bookmarks** panel.

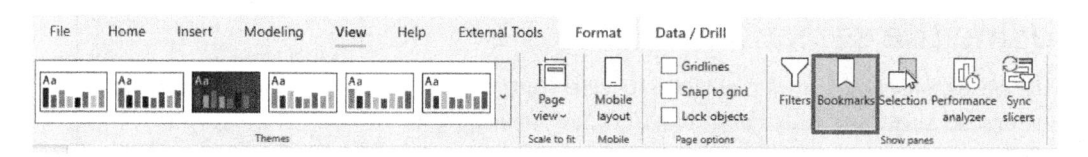

Figure 11.1 – The Bookmarks panel can be opened from the View ribbon

In the **Bookmarks** panel, you click on the **Add** button to save your current page in its current configuration. After adding the bookmark, you change the page's slicers, cross-filters, or cross-highlights and add a new bookmark to save those choices. You can switch pages and add bookmarks based on various configurations on that page.

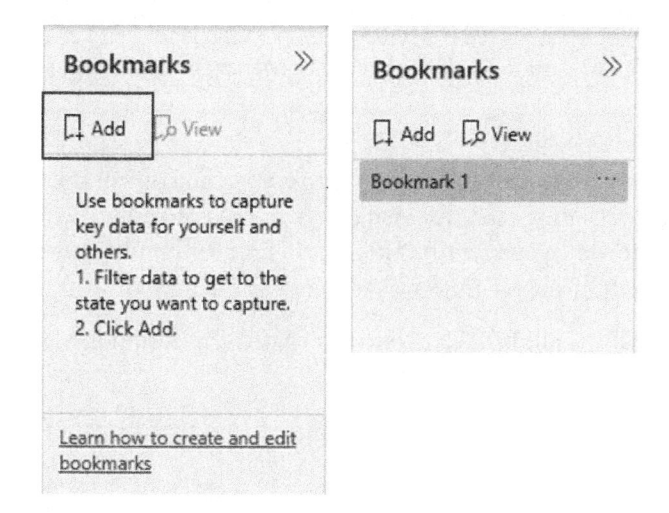

Figure 11.2 – Selecting the Add button saves the state of the report page to the Bookmarks panel

You can also rename your bookmarks, reorder them, and group them into sections.

Bookmarks can turn your report into a tool for repeatable presentations, allowing you to control the story, presenting your data in the order that you want it to be presented. Bookmarks will also allow you to freely go off script in your presentation. You can highlight other data points, change slicers, or even skip to a different page, all the while knowing that you can get right back to where you were with the click of a button.

You can also associate a bookmark with a button or an image. This will give your report a feeling of interactivity as your report consumers can click on buttons or images and get taken to a different page or the same page with different slicers and filters selected.

As we will see in the next section, you can use the Selection pane alongside bookmarks to take your report to whole new levels of interactivity.

Using the selection pane

The Selection pane allows you to do three things: control the layer order, control the tab order, and show and hide elements on the reporting page.

The **Select** pane can be toggled on and off from the **View** tab, the same as the **Bookmarks** panel.

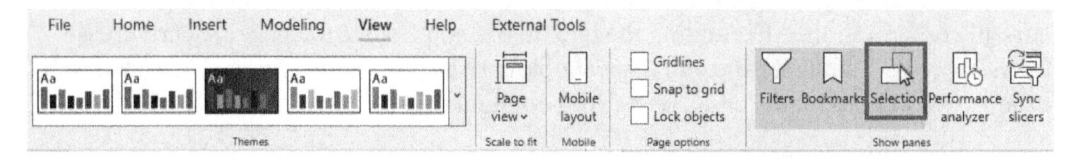

Figure 11.3 – The Selection panel can be opened from the View ribbon

Tab order

The first thing you need to know for the test is that you can control the tab order for your report page. This is very important for visually impaired consumers who might be using an adaptive device to view your report. This is also nice for hands-on-keyboard-type people who like to tab through things rather than use the mouse.

Tab order is just what it sounds like, it controls what visualization is next highlighted by hitting the *Tab* key.

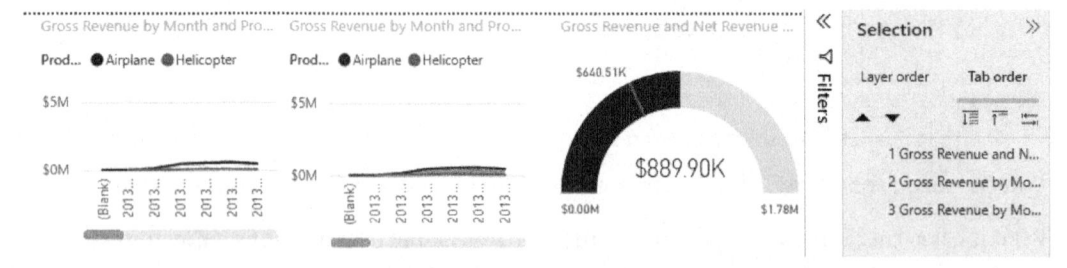

Figure 11.4 – Setting the tab order for our keyboard-first report users

Layer order

The **Layer order** tab controls the other two things in the Selection pane, the layer order and the visibility.

The layer order controls what visuals appear on top of other visuals. You can control this in two places: the **Selection** pane and the **Format** tab. The **Format** tab has the standard Microsoft Office **Bring forward** and **Send backward** choices. Using these buttons has the same effect as moving a visual upward or downward in the layer order.

Using bookmarks   227

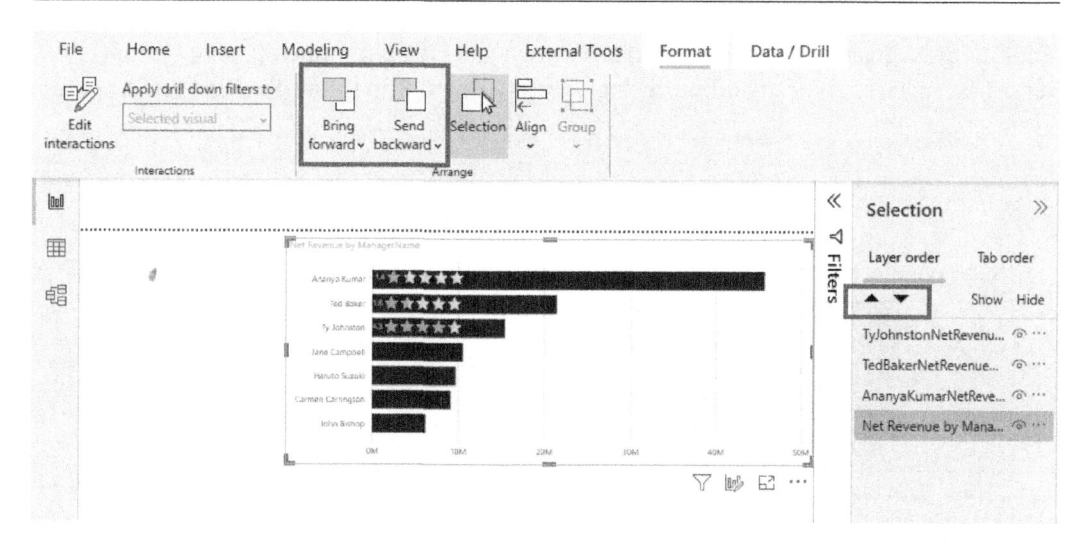

Figure 11.5 – Bring forward and Send backward work exactly the same as in other Microsoft products

The other key thing you can do in the **Layer order** pane is to hide and show visualizations. You can then bookmark the state of the page with the visuals shown or hidden.

Creating custom tooltips

Tooltips appear when you hover your mouse over a visualization. The tooltip will, by default, be a black box with gray text that displays information about the data point your mouse is over.

Figure 11.6 – By default, tooltips show the same data that's in the visualization

228　Enhancing Reports

Tooltips are a great way to add information to your report without cluttering up the reporting surface. You can add more data fields to the tooltip in the **Tooltips** region in the visuals pane.

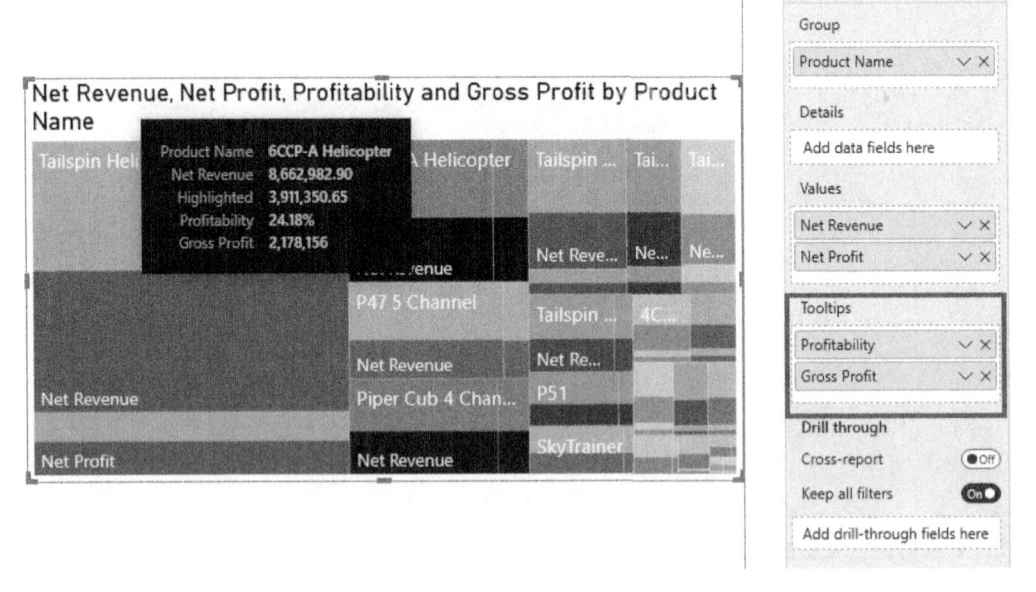

Figure 11.7 – Providing the end user with more information using tooltips

You are not limited to just the gray text on a black background. You can change the background color of the tooltip, the font of the text, and the color of both the label and the values.

This lets you customize the tooltip to fit in with the rest of the report, keeping fonts and colors consistent throughout the report.

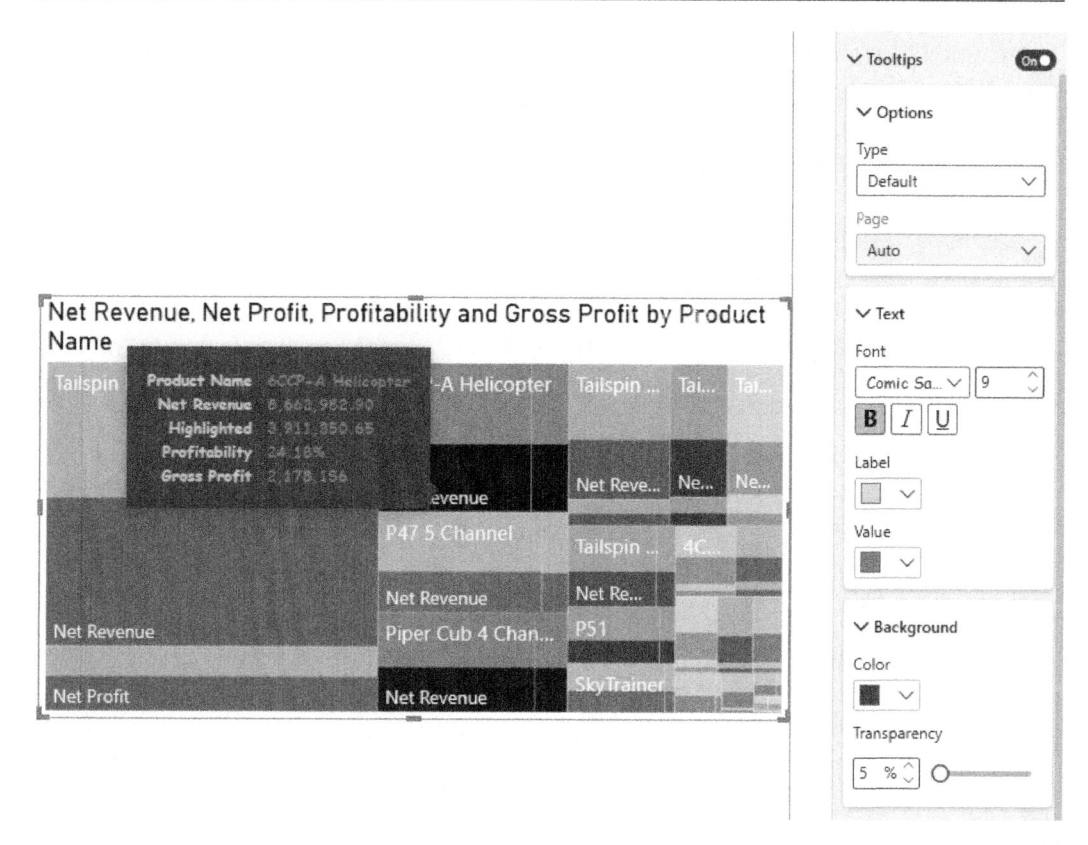

Figure 11.8 – You can change the colors and fonts for your tooltips. Just remember, with great power comes great responsibility

You can create an entire report page that will display as a tooltip. This allows you to place visualizations in a tooltip, adding yet another layer of information while keeping the report canvas less cluttered.

230　Enhancing Reports

To create a tooltip page, add a new page to the report. In the **Format** pane for the new page, click on the **Tooltips** slider. You may also want to resize the page to the default tooltip size, but that is not a requirement. Just remember, you want this page to appear over a portion of your report surface, not completely obliterate it.

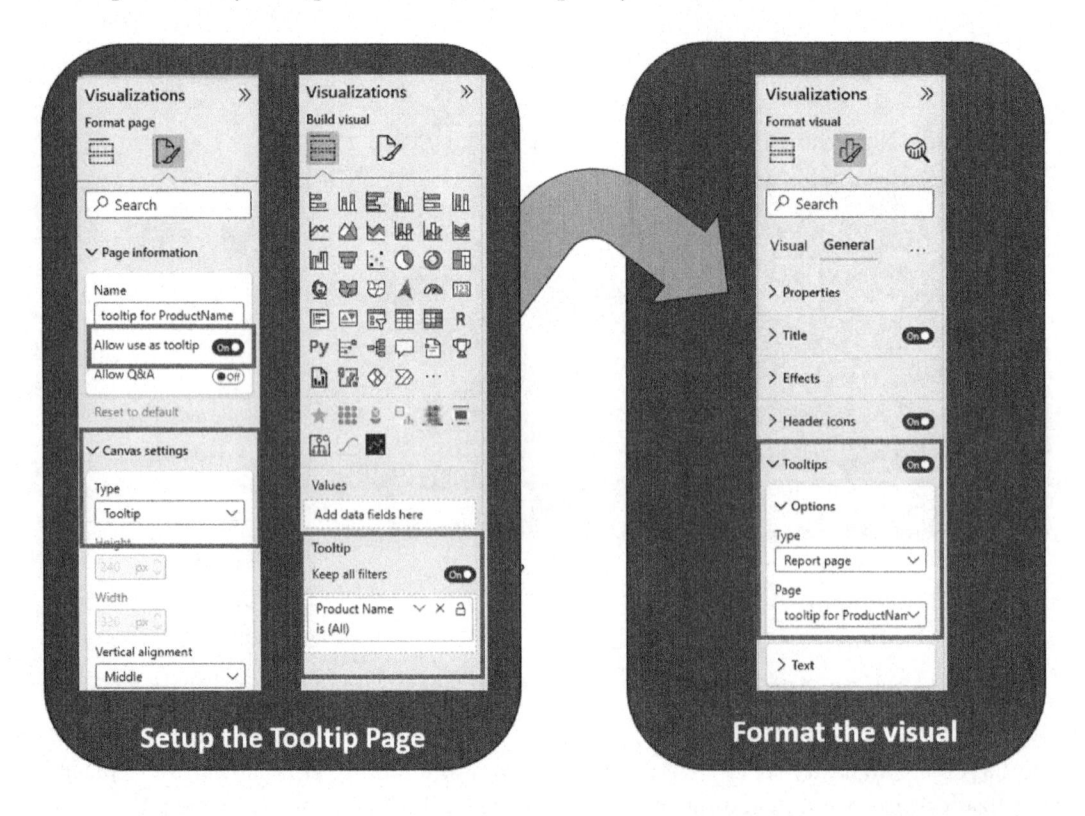

Figure 11.9 – Setting a page to be used for a tooltip

On the **Build** visual for the report page, add the fields you want to trigger the tooltip to the **Tooltip** area. You have the option of keeping all filters or not, much like a drillthrough page, which we will cover later in this chapter.

Once you have added the visuals that you want to your tooltip page, go back to the visual you want to use on the tooltip page.

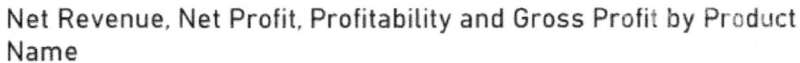

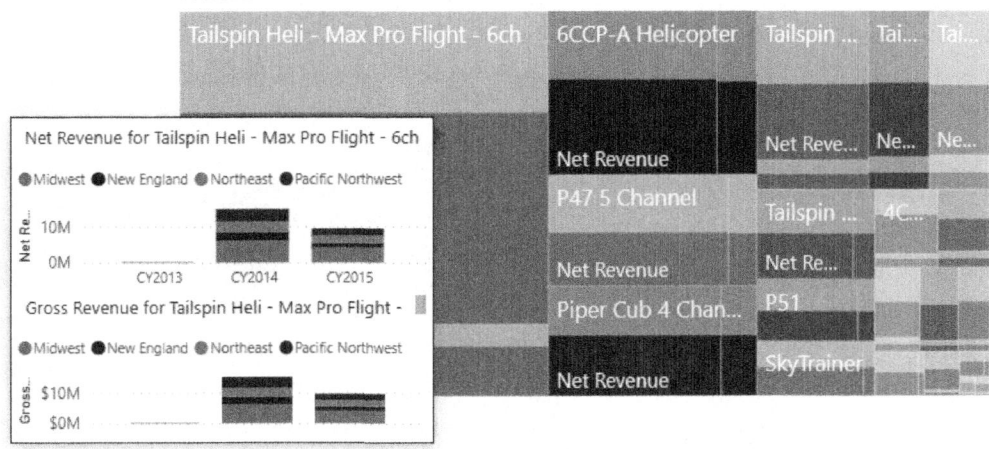

Figure 11.10 – Tooltip pages can really enhance your report, adding layers of data

Tooltip pages open new layers of reporting options.

Interactions between visuals

One of the key powers that Power BI has is its ability to cross-filter and cross-highlight visualizations. This power creates dynamic reports that allow users to interact with the data to explore the relationships between data points, creating new insights.

As the report creator, you can control how visuals interact with each other, or if visuals interact at all. Interactivity is great, but there may be times when you want a visual on your report page to remain static. You may want to display total sales in a corner of your page, even if a report consumer filters the rest of the visuals down to a region or sales segment.

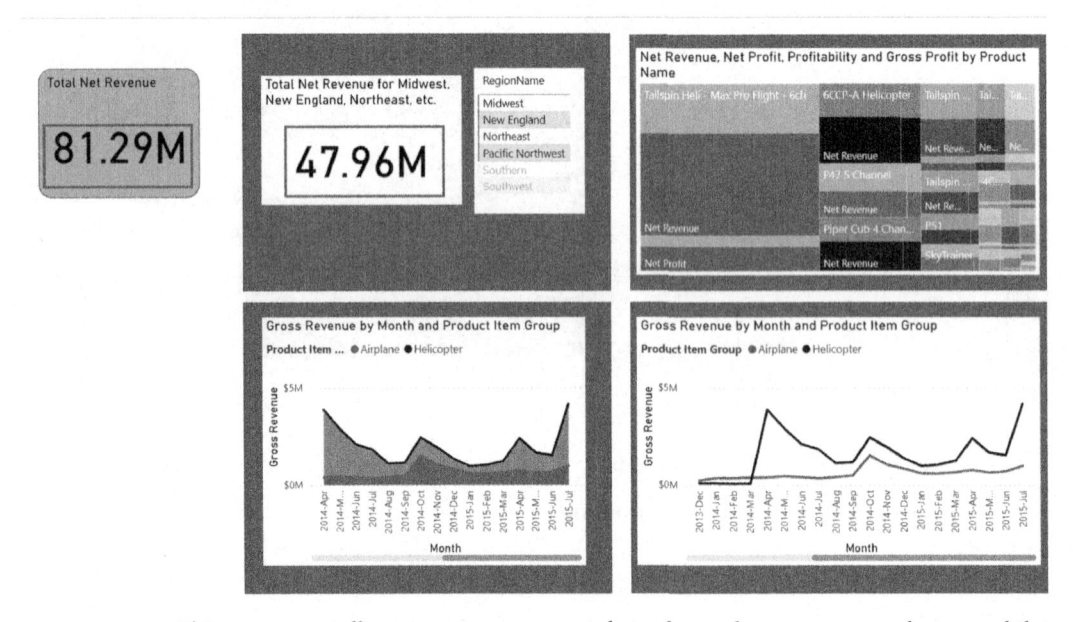

Figure 11.11 – This report page allows your report users to keep the total net revenue on the page while looking at the total net revenue for the regions

You can see in the figure that all the visuals on the blue rectangles are cross-filtered and cross-highlighted by the four region names. The card visualization in the gray box has the total for all the regions. This allows your report consumer to slice and dice the data any way they want and have a continual reference to the total number.

By default, Power BI will cross-highlight visuals when possible; it's not possible to cross-highlight a card or a line chart, they can only be filtered. It makes sense if you think about it. You can change this default behavior in the options for the report. This is not a general setting, so it will only affect the current report.

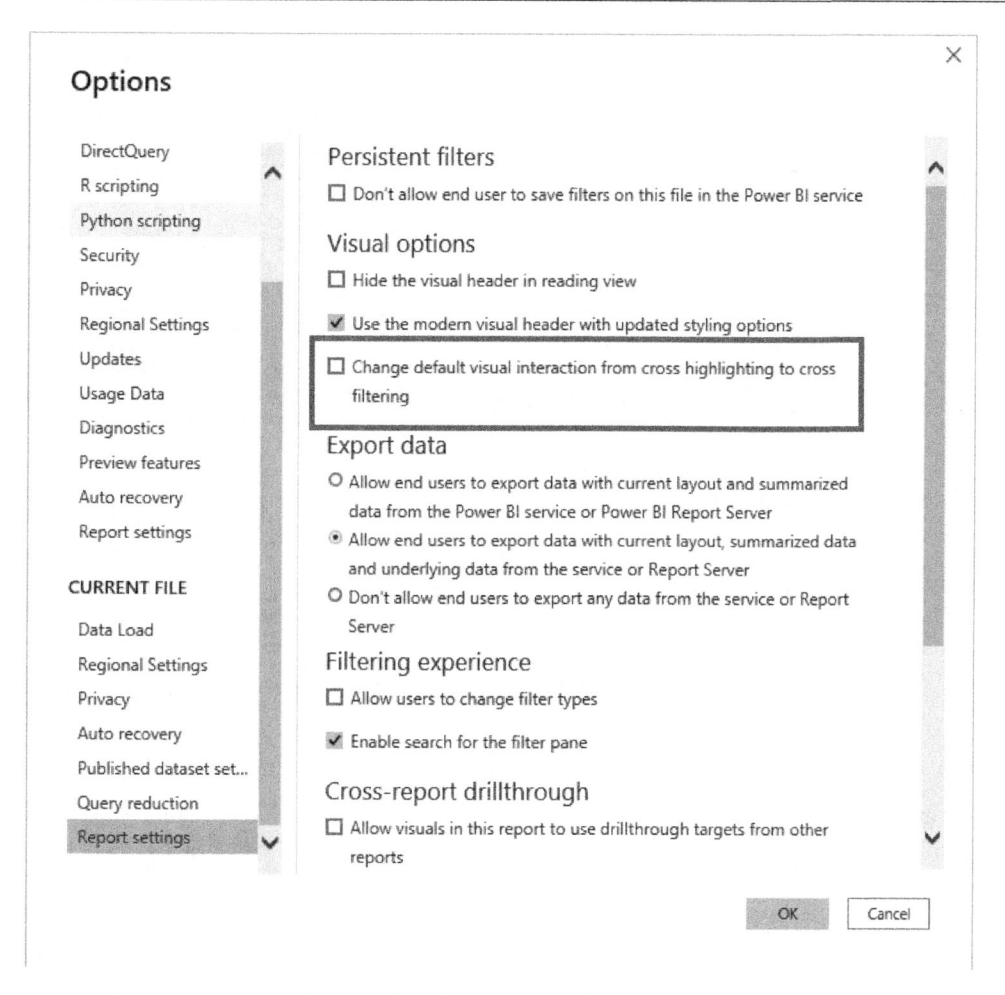

Figure 11.12 – Changing the default cross-highlighting behavior to cross-filtering

To change how individual visualizations interact, you must enable the **Edit interactions** option. To enable **Edit interactions**, select any visual on the report page to make the **Format** ribbon tab available. Select the **Format** ribbon tab and click the **Edit Interactions** button.

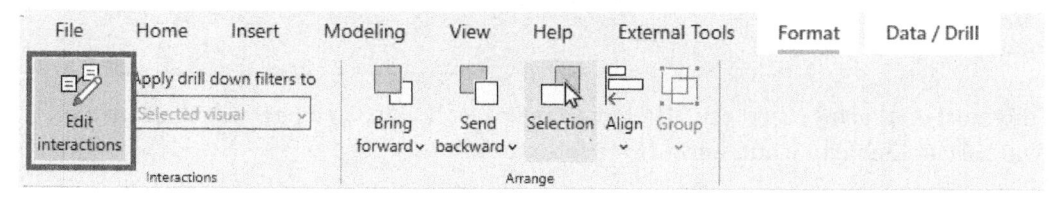

Figure 11.13 – Edit interactions is enabled from the Format ribbon tab

234   Enhancing Reports

This will now allow you to control how visuals interact with the highlighted visualization. The icons that now appear let you choose **Cross Filter** and, if available, **Cross Highlight**.

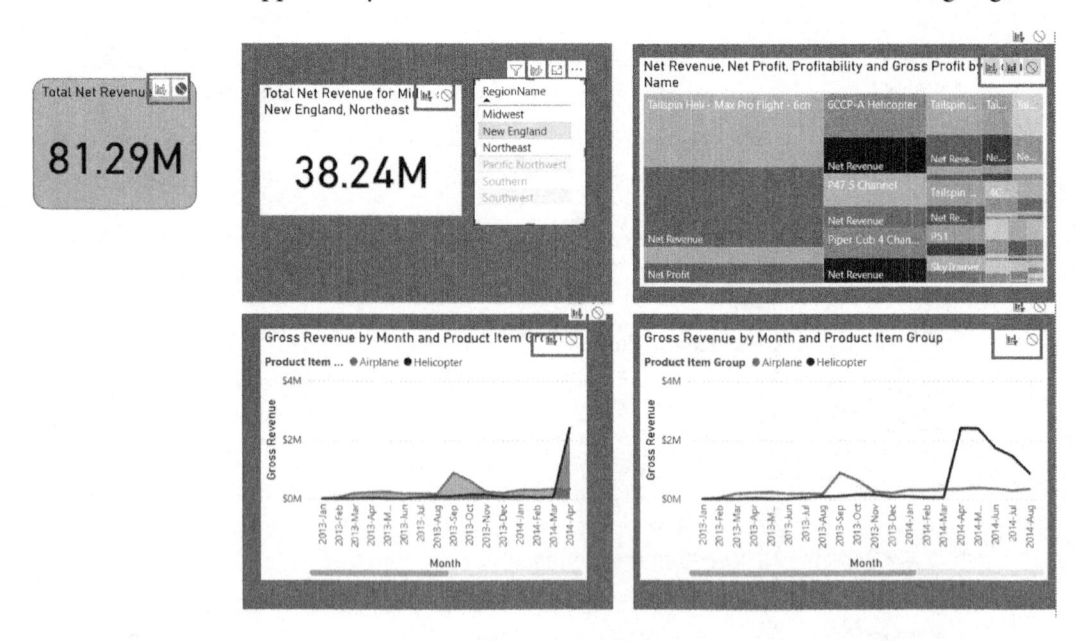

Figure 11.14 – Enabling Edit interactions adds buttons to every visualization

It is important to understand that this choice is for how the selected visualization interacts with all the other visualizations on the report page. For the **Total Net Revenue** card to *not* be cross-filtered, you must highlight each visual and select **None**.

Figure 11.15 – Selecting None means the highlighted visual won't interact with this one

You must do this for every visualization on the page. If you add a new visualization, you will have to highlight it and select **None** for interactions.

Configuring navigation for a report

Having a clear path to navigate your report goes together with the concept of using data to tell your story. Clear report navigation allows your report users to move from one page in your report to the next, move from one visual to another, and return to where they started. The design of your report navigation is important because if report consumers get confused navigating your reports, they will become frustrated and not use the report, so all your hard work will have been for nothing.

You have already seen one of the coolest ways to implement navigation: buttons linked to bookmarks!

Navigation buttons

To configure navigation within a report, it is recommended to use buttons. You will configure those buttons on either a dedicated page or a pane within your report. You can add a button to your report by selecting one of the buttons from the **Buttons** dropdown on the **Insert** tab of the ribbon. After selecting the button added to your report, you can enable an action for the button by clicking on it and then, under the **Format button** pane, toggling **Action**, and then selecting the kind of action you'd like the button to use, in this case a bookmark. Once the **Bookmark** type is selected, you then select which bookmark you'd like the button action to take.

Using an action associated with a bookmark can easily make it appear that a navigation pane opens and closes. All you need to do is create two bookmarks for the report page: one with the navigation pane hidden and one with it visible.

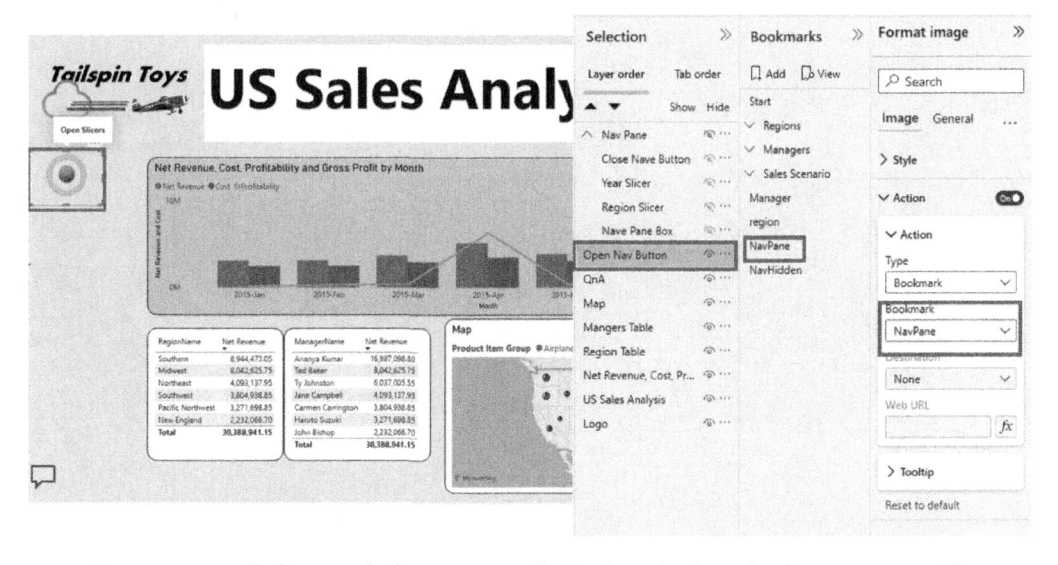

Figure 11.16 – Clicking on the button opens the bookmark where the slicer pane is visible

236　Enhancing Reports

Once the report consumer is done selecting the slicers, they can close it by clicking on another button that takes them to the page bookmarked with the slicer pane hidden.

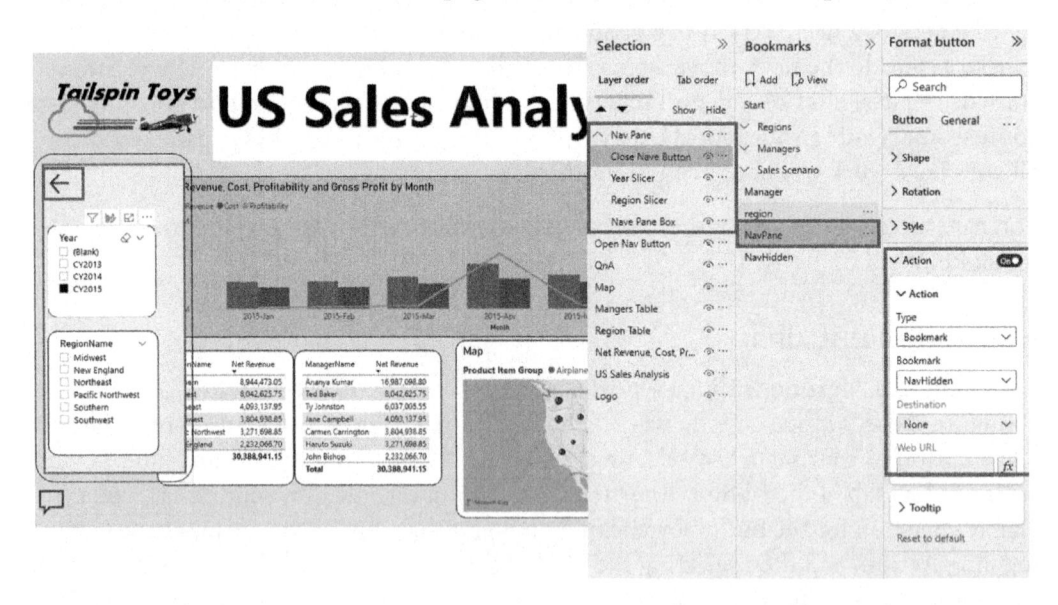

Figure 11.17 – Clicking on the arrow "closes" the slicer pane. We know it just takes us to the bookmark with the slicer pane hidden

This ability to use the selection pane, bookmarks, and actions on images and buttons can make your report more interactive and allow you to free up space for delivering information.

Applying sorting

By default, Power BI will sort data alphanumerically. Fortunately, this is case insensitive, but it still could be a limiting factor for using Power BI. After all, April is not the first month of the year.

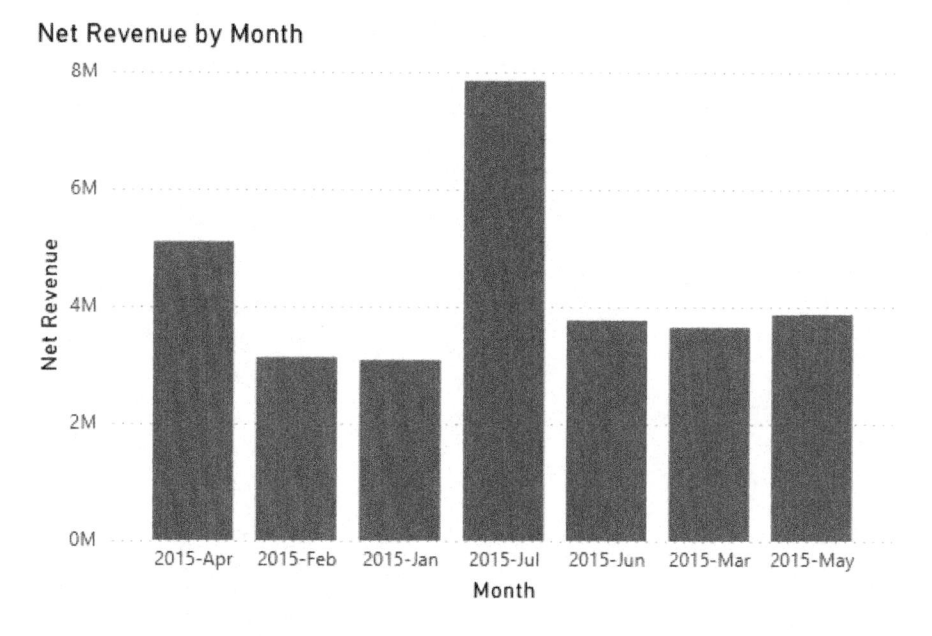

Figure 11.18 – This is not the order the months of the year should be in

We want our months to be sorted by month number, not by month name. In Power BI, we do this by choosing a different column to control the sorting. In the case of my `Month` column, I have a second column that is the year concatenated with the month number named `MonthKey`. I can choose this column as my sort column and it will force the `Month` column to sort numerically, not alphabetically.

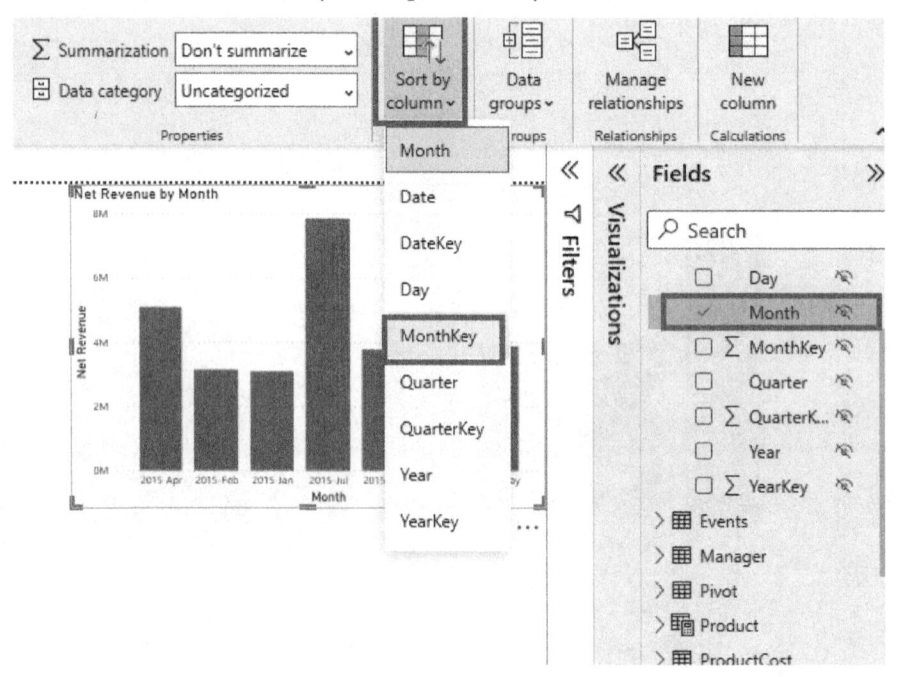

Figure 11.19 – Selecting a column that is sorted in the order you want

Now our visualization is sorted by a column that doesn't have to be displayed.

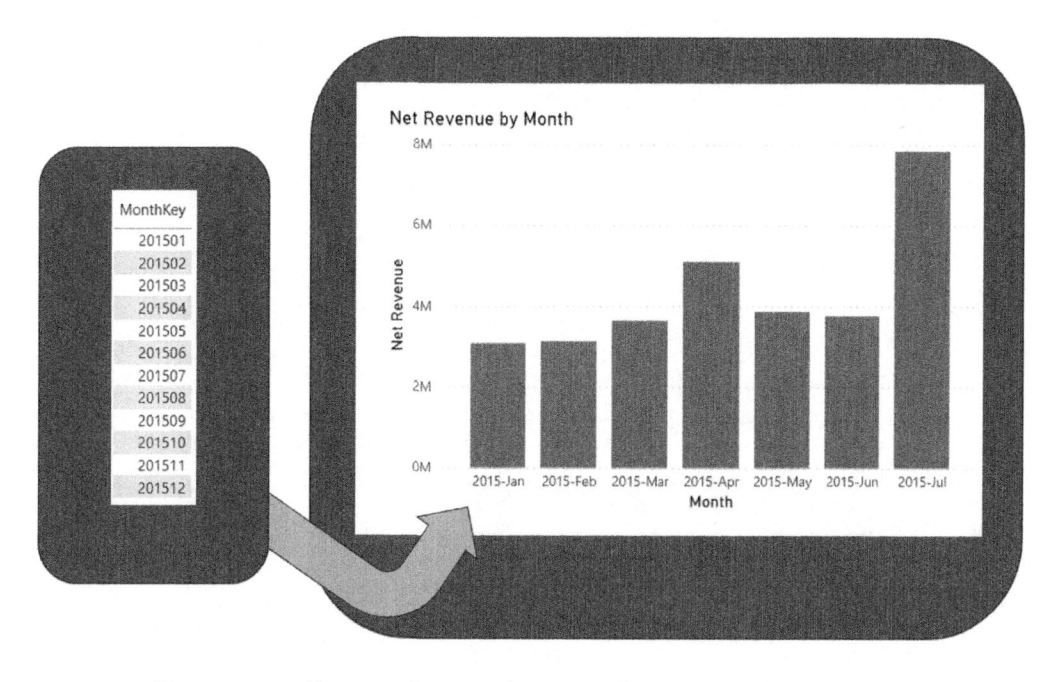

Figure 11.20 – Changing the sort column puts the months in the correct order

This is not just limited to date fields. If you have suborganizations that you always want to be sorted nonalphabetically, you can do the same thing to create a column to force the sorting the way you want it.

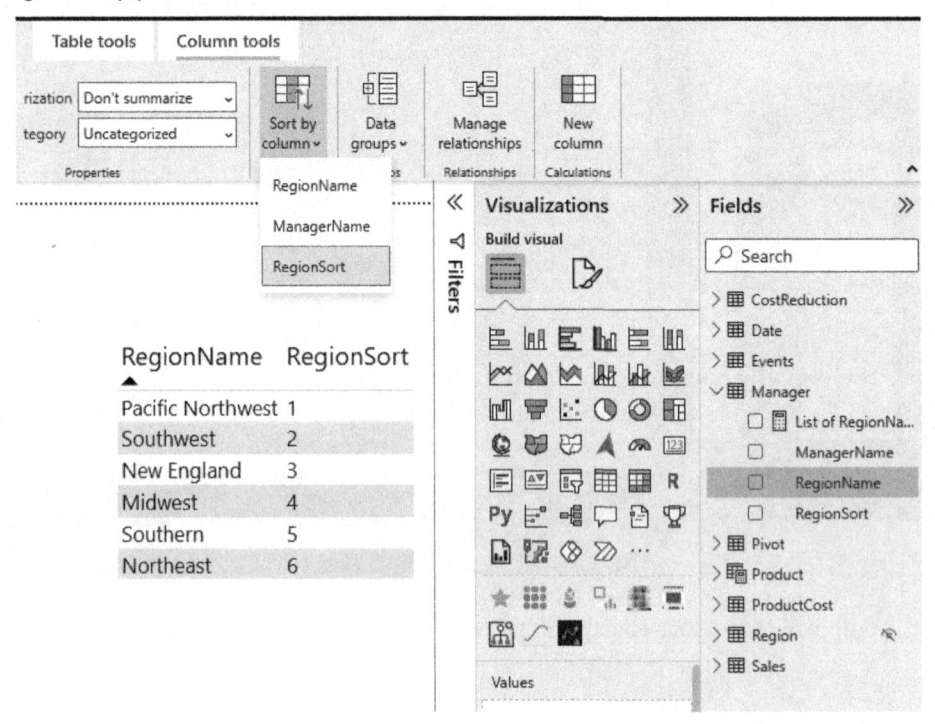

Figure 11.21 – Sort by is not just for dates. You can force other categorical values to sort in the order you need them to

This way, every time you create a visual sorted on this column, it will sort in the order you want.

It is important to know for the exam that you can choose to change the default sort order of a column by designating a sort by column. It is also noted that this does not just apply to date fields; you can use this for other types of columns too.

Sync slicers

You can control slicers and make a slicer on one page affect one or more other pages in the report. You do this by enabling the **Sync slicers** panel in the **View** ribbon.

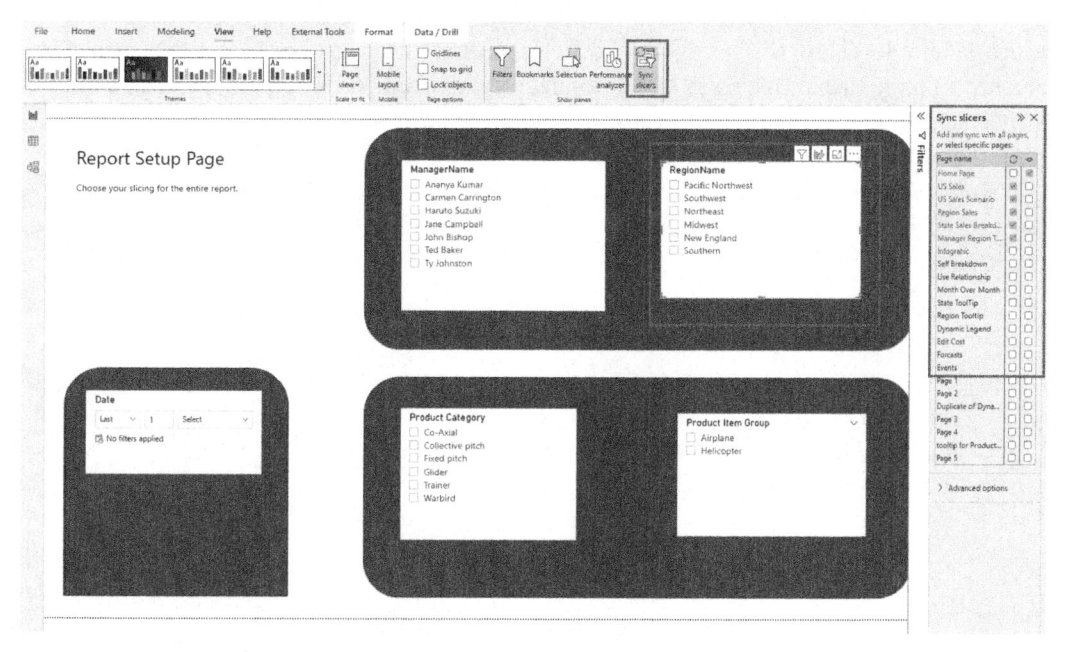

Figure 11.22 – A landing page of slicers

One of the nice things you can do is to set the start page of the report to have all of your slicers. This allows users to filter the rest of the report. This behavior more closely mimics the setting of parameters some of your report consumers may have experienced with SQL Server Reporting Services or paginated reports.

One thing to be aware of is that you can choose whether to have the slicer show up on the report page. Not displaying the slicer on a report page will give you more canvas to work on, at the expense of possibly confusing your report consumers on how the page has been sliced.

Using drillthrough and cross-filter

When creating reports, you may want to have a page of summary information and then pages with more detailed information for specific categories or subsets of data. In these cases, you can use the drillthrough feature to start viewing a report page at a wider and more general level and then drill into the detail on another page. For example, if you start at a report page that shows rolled-up sales data for all product categories, you can select a specific product or category of products and use drillthrough to navigate to a product page that is filtered to the selected product or category of products. Using this capability, you wouldn't need to design specific report pages for each product or product category, because each time, a potentially unique product filter would be applied per the selection of the user.

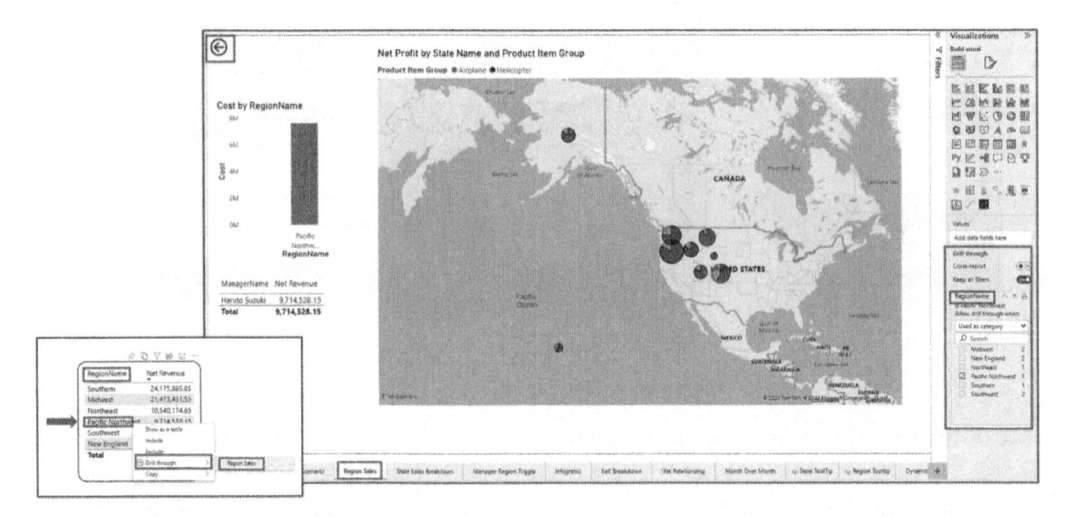

Figure 11.23 – Drillthrough allows you to navigate from one visual to another page

To create a drillthrough, you first create a report page. Then, from the **Values** section of the **Visualizations** pane, drag the field for which you want to enable drillthrough in the drillthrough filters as well.

You have the option of keeping all the filters from the source page, which is any slicer, filter, and cross-filter or cross-highlights selected, or only filtering the page on the selected category.

When a drillthrough is added to a report, Power BI will automatically add a back button to the report page. This is used for navigation but is fully editable by the report designer.

The cross-report drillthrough option is outside the scope of this exam, but you can use it to direct your report consumers to an entirely different report instead of just another page in the current report.

Drilling down into data using interactive visuals

Drilldown and drill up are totally unrelated to drillthrough. Drilldown relates to hierarchal visualizations, such as matrixes. If you have added a hierarchy to a matrix, you can go to the next level of the hierarchy or you can expand the entire level. You also have the option to have + and − signs to expand a single element while leaving the rest of the elements at their current level.

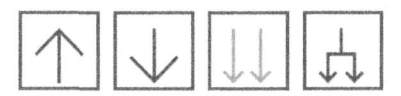

Figure 11.24 – The icons that let you navigate a hierarchy

Drill up and drilldown allow your report consumers to see summarized data and then the underlying data, if necessary.

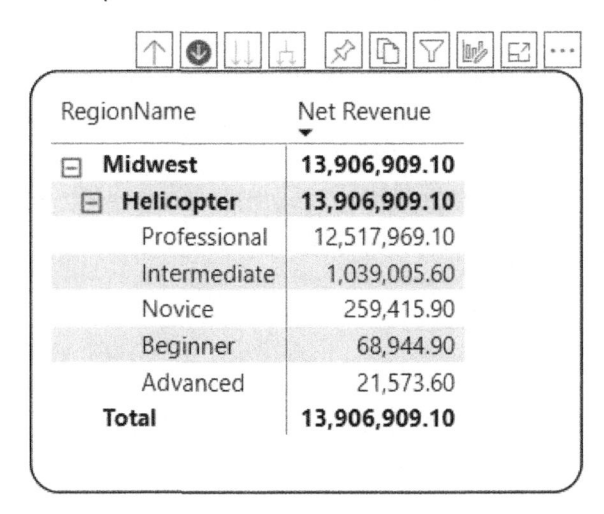

RegionName	Net Revenue
⊟ Midwest	13,906,909.10
⊟ Helicopter	13,906,909.10
Professional	12,517,969.10
Intermediate	1,039,005.60
Novice	259,415.90
Beginner	68,944.90
Advanced	21,573.60
Total	13,906,909.10

Figure 11.25 – Expanding a hierarchy with either the +/- or the drill up/drilldown buttons

You may be familiar with these behaviors from Excel.

Exporting report data

Although Power BI can be used to create awesome, interactive, digital-first reports, sometimes your report consumers might want to export the data from a visual. They may want this data for further analysis. They may want to use Power BI to filter a dataset down to the exact subset of data they need. They may just want to grab a historical record of the data.

244 Enhancing Reports

Some reports will use Microsoft Purview Information Protection and will prohibit the export of data. Some organizations will want to protect data in reports and not allow users to export where the data could be shared outside the organization or used for unintended purposes.

As the report creator, you can choose whether your report consumers can export data. This is a setting you set in Power BI Desktop. The default allows any end user to export summarized data only. If you want to change this, you must go to the **Report settings** page in the **Options** menu.

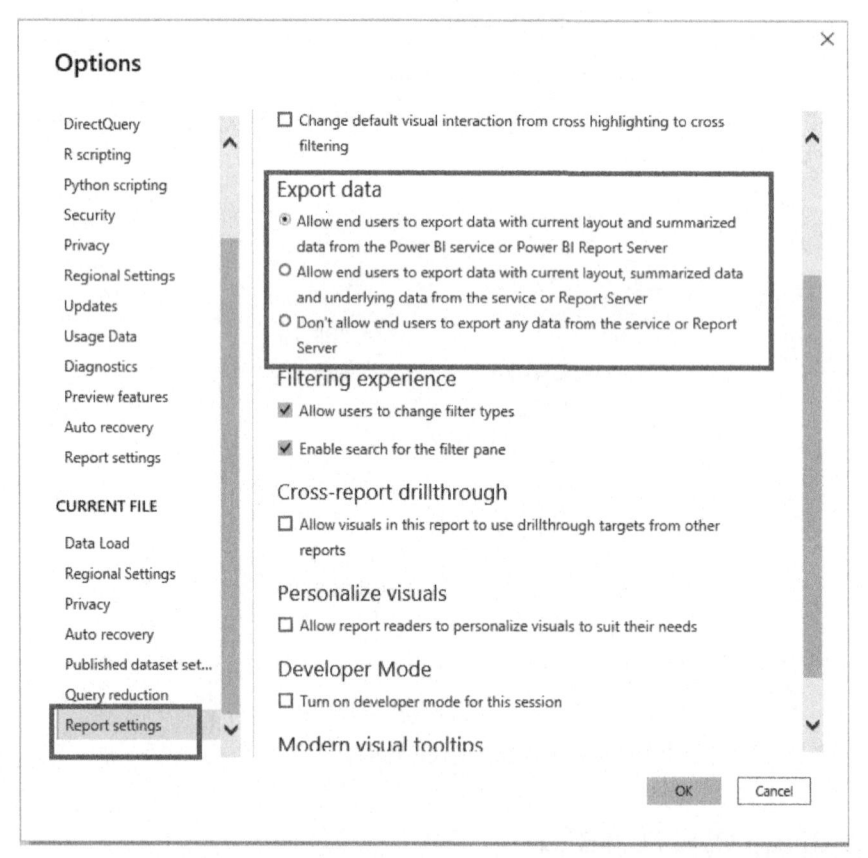

Figure 11.26 – Controlling how much, if any, data your report users can export

Your three choices are as follows:

- Allow end users to export summarized data.
- Allow end users to export summarized and underlying data.
- Don't allow export.

These three options can be set in your Power BI tenant. If they are, it's important to understand that the most restrictive option will be chosen. So, if your tenant allows the underlying data to be exported, but you choose, for your report, to not allow downloads, downloads will be disallowed.

> **Test Tip**
> Power BI enforces the most restrictive data export setting between the report and the tenant.

In this section, we learned about many ways we can enhance reports, including interactions between visuals, drillthrough, and securing data within a report, among other topics. Next, let's look at how we can design reports for mobile devices for use on the go.

Designing reports for mobile devices

Power BI embraces the mobile-first world that is quickly approaching, if it is not already here. Many report users will prefer interacting with reports on their mobile phones or tablets. Power BI works with all modern browsers, so this is not a problem. The problem is, especially for phones and smaller tablets, the default landscape orientation is not the way your end users usually use their phone. You can create an additional view that is optimized for mobile devices and displays in portrait orientation. Power BI has a mobile layout option that, alongside the Power BI app for those devices and the Power BI service, can detect when a device is in portrait mode and change to a more thumb-friendly vertical alignment.

To create a mobile-optimized version of your report, you can do the following:

- Design a mobile layout view, where you can drag and drop certain visuals onto a phone emulator canvas.
- Use visuals and slicers that are suitable for use on small mobile screens.

When you publish your report, the mobile version is published and enabled automatically.

To create a mobile-optimized view of your report, select the **Mobile layout** option on the **View** ribbon. This will open a scrollable canvas where you can add back the visuals that were on the report page. Drag the visuals you want from the **Page visuals** pane onto the reporting canvas. You can then resize and reposition them as you see fit.

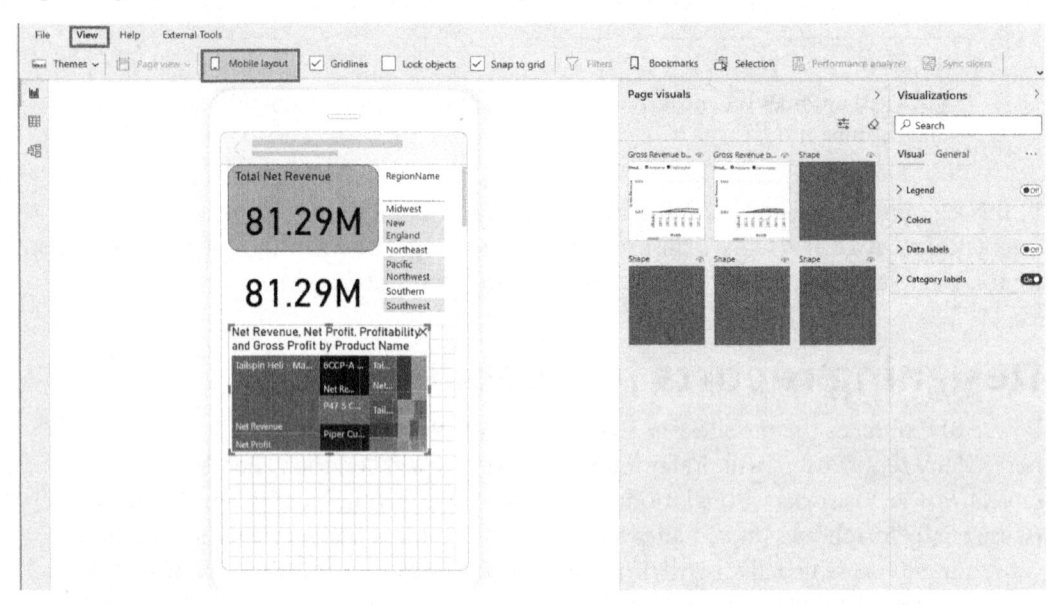

Figure 11.27 – Mobile report layout page

Visuals on the mobile page will continue to cross-filter and cross-highlight. Slicers will continue to work as before.

Sometimes you may want to change some of the options for your visualizations. Font sizes may need to be changed or background colors added or removed to make the report more readable. You make these changes by selecting the visualization and editing the options in the **Visualizations** panel. If you do make a change here, it will only affect the mobile layout. Power BI will also generate a small, visual marker on the section and the setting you changed.

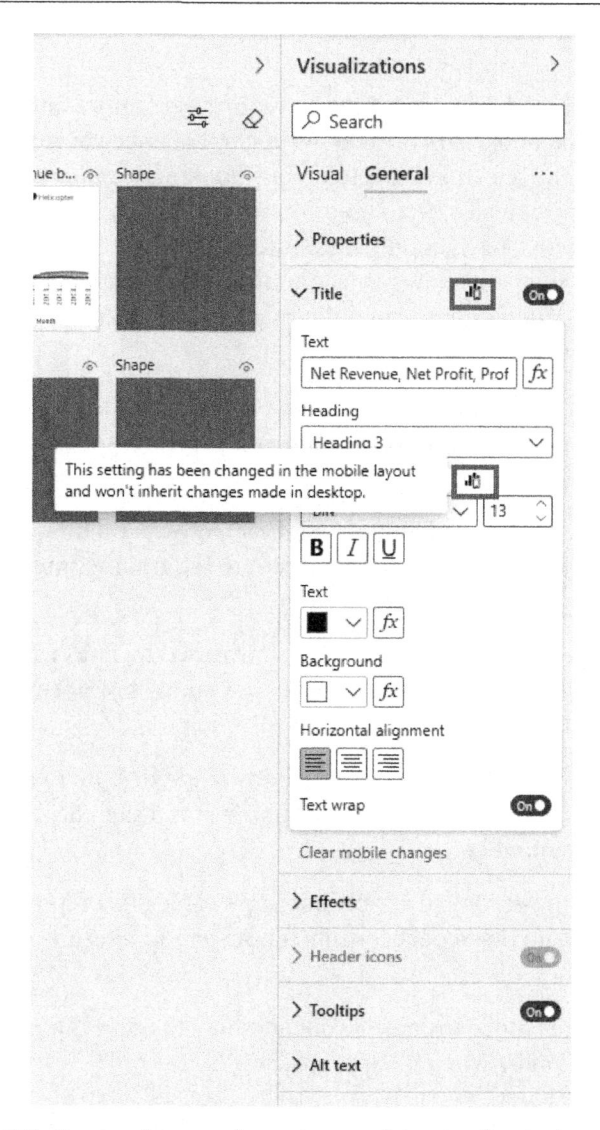

Figure 11.28 – Power BI indicating that you changed some of the visualization's properties in the mobile report view

Power BI fully embraces our mobile-first world and natively allows you to create mobile-friendly report layouts.

Summary

In this chapter, you learned how to make your reports even more interactive and user-friendly. We configured bookmarks that allow you to enhance your reports with a bit of storytelling. We used the selection pane to up our bookmark game, making our reports even more interactive. We also saw how we could use bookmarking and buttons to create our own highly interactive navigation panes. Alternatively, we can also affect navigation by using drillthrough filters to allow navigation from one visual to a whole page of visuals. Along these lines, we also set up synched slicers, allowing slicers on one page to filter visuals on one or more other pages.

You saw how custom tooltips allow you to create visually interesting mouse-overs, allowing you to keep your report pages cleaner and presenting data to your report consumers only when they want it.

We also looked at how visuals can interact with each other, and how and why we can prevent that interaction. Sometimes you want to filter, sometimes highlight, and sometimes you just want a visual to stand alone.

Speaking of sometimes not wanting the defaults provided by Power BI, we also explored the world of alternative sorting. The months of the year are not normally sorted alphabetically after all.

We used the power of hierarchies by using drilldown and drill up to navigate them. This lets report consumers initially see a summary number and then drill into the data to see an explanation for the number.

From a data standpoint, we looked at how our users can export report data from a visual. You can choose whether your report consumers can export all, summarized, or none of the data from a visual.

Finally, we looked at the mobile report layout and how to make our reports more mobile device- and thumb-friendly when it's appropriate.

We will explore exposing insights from our data in the next chapter.

Questions

1. Configuring a saved configuration of a report page with preset filtering and sorting is called what?

    A. Save points

    B. Favorites

    C. Bookmarks

    D. Saved view

2. Navigation can be configured in a report using what item from the Insert tab on the ribbon?

    A. New visual

    B. Paginated report

    C. New page

    D. Buttons

3. When designing a report for viewing on a mobile device, what view is used?

    A. Mobile layout

    B. App view

    C. Android viewer

    D. Web layout

Part 4 – Analyzing the Data

This section showcases how to use data for data analysis after it is properly modeled, and appropriate visuals are used to show the data and expose insights.

This section comprises the following chapters:

- *Chapter 12, Exposing Insights from Data*
- *Chapter 13, Performing Advanced Analysis*

12
Exposing Insights from Data

To get the most value out of your Power BI reports and dashboards, you'll want to make sure they answer the questions that are most valuable to your organization. Sometimes, that means you need to reduce the data that you're looking at, to best focus on specific elements of a dataset and best understand how those elements relate to others. Usually, this means that we're analyzing subsets of data or sets of records. For example, maybe our entire dataset includes sales from across the United States, but we want to understand the volume of sales for each state or only within one state. By doing this, we'll be able to draw insights from the data that are harder to find otherwise.

In this chapter, we'll look at the ways insights can be exposed from data in Power BI reports and dashboards. We will cover the following topics:

- Exploring slicers and filters
- The Analytics pane

Technical requirements

You will need the following tools for this chapter:

- Microsoft Power BI Desktop installed on a Microsoft Windows PC.
- A Power BI data model where we can apply the advanced features covered in this chapter.
- Examples in the text will use the Power BI data model and reports that you've created in previous chapters, but these are not required.

Exploring slicers and filters

Slicers allow Power BI users to apply filters dynamically to data shown in visuals. This is helpful when you have an entire dataset that can be divided or segmented to show different characteristics of the data. For example, our sales database contains both store sales and customer addresses and the associated relationship between the two. This means we can use the map and table visuals to see how many sales we have in each state of the United States, as shown in *Figure 12.1*:

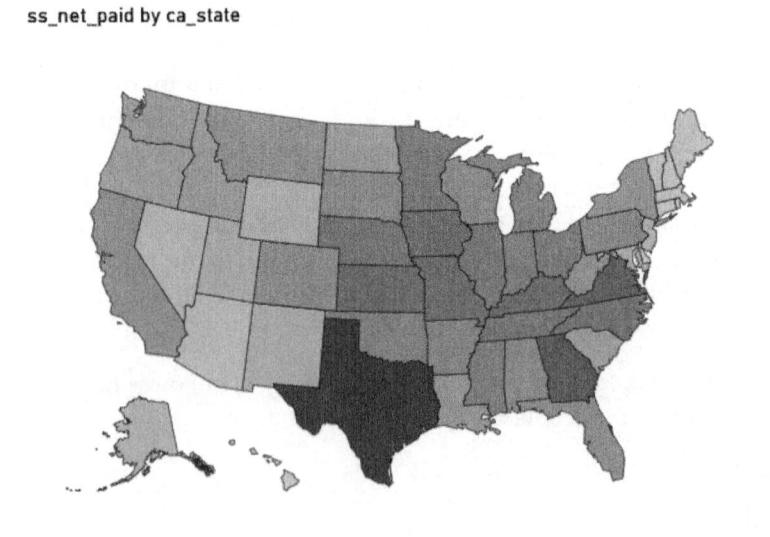

ss_net_paid by ca_state

ca_state	ss_net_paid
TX	63,536,214.96
GA	38,155,047.12
VA	34,405,515.49
KY	28,832,816.05
KS	27,773,547.53
MO	27,556,258.65
IA	27,334,634.10
NC	25,769,151.73
	24,672,651.99
TN	23,836,189.76
NE	23,795,672.15
IL	23,701,875.24
OH	22,875,863.66
MN	22,544,857.61
IN	21,208,129.74
MS	21,167,924.01
MI	20,040,631.08
	19,461,673.82
Total	**823,139,042.43**

Figure 12.1 – Map and table of net store sales

As we increase our understanding of this data, we will want to be able to better understand how the net store sales compare for each state. Some states seem to be very close in net store sales. To help us, we're going to use the slicer visual and add the `ca_state` column to the slicer visual. This means we can select just the states **Iowa** and **Missouri**. The table and map visuals will filter to only those states.

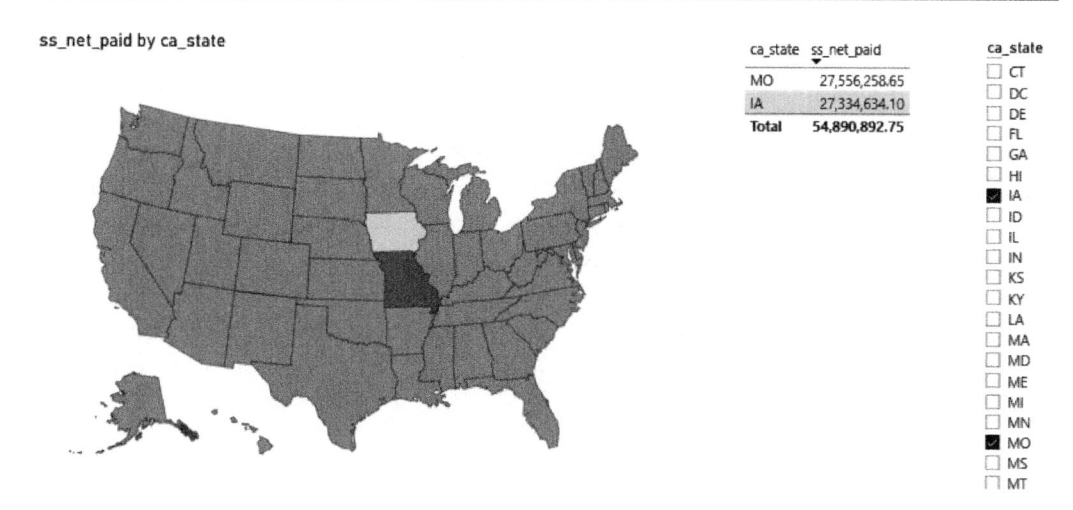

Figure 12.2 – Only Iowa and Missouri are selected with the slicer visual

By using the slicer, we filter the dataset to only contain records from the states **Iowa** and **Missouri**. When this filter has been applied, the map visual only highlights the two states and adjusts the colors accordingly. Now we can easily see that **Missouri** has higher net store sales than **Iowa**. We can also see the table being filtered to only show net store sales for the states of **Missouri** and **Iowa**.

Slicers have unique capabilities depending on the type of data being used to filter. For example, if filtering on numeric values such as net store sales, you'll be presented with a range slider that allows you to adjust a numeric range, as shown in *Figure 12.3*:

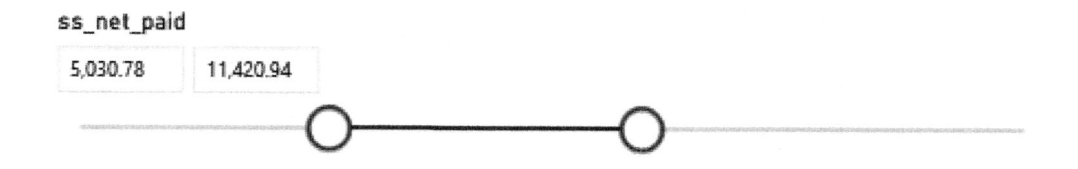

Figure 12.3 – Numeric slicer

By default, when a date field is added to a slicer, you will see a similar date range slider. However, since a date field was used, you can change the options on the slicer to filter data using **Between**, **Before**, **After**, **List**, **Dropdown**, **Relative Date**, or **Relative Time** operators. Each setting will be useful depending on the scenario. Relative date and relative time are useful for filtering based on the current date. For example, you can filter records for the last year, next year, or this year. You can set the numeric value and the time period (day, week, month, year), so it's also possible to use this relative date slicer to filter showing records for the last 6 months.

Figure 12.4 – Options for date slicers

Slicers can also be set to select a relative time if the column includes a time value. This will allow you to filter records by a relative time in the same way relative date works.

For slicers that show a selection list of values, it is also possible to make them responsive to the size of the visual on the report page. To do this, simply change to a horizontal orientation, as well as enabling the responsive option under the **General** heading on the format for visual. This means that instead of a vertical list of values, you have a horizontal list of buttons that can be selected. In horizontal and responsive configurations, the list of values changes the shape and positioning to best fit the size of the visual. Example positioning based on different sizes can be seen in *Figure 12.5* and *Figure 12.6*:

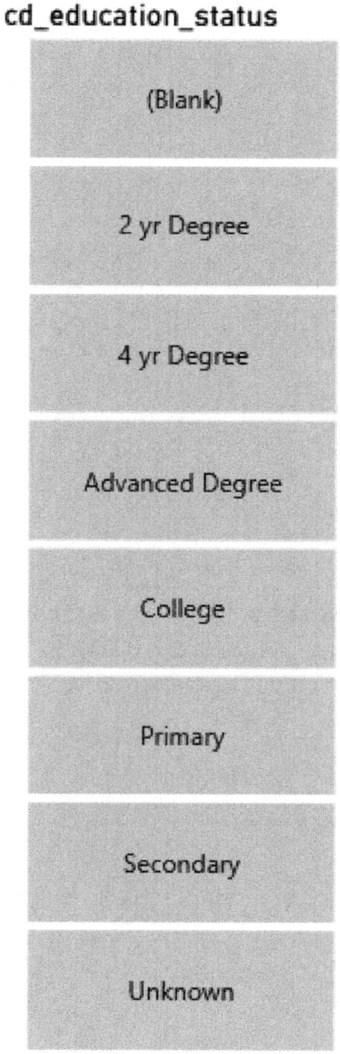

Figure 12.5 – Slicer with text values in vertical orientation

The same set of values in the slicer but shown in horizontal orientation will look something like *Figure 12.6*:

cd_education_status

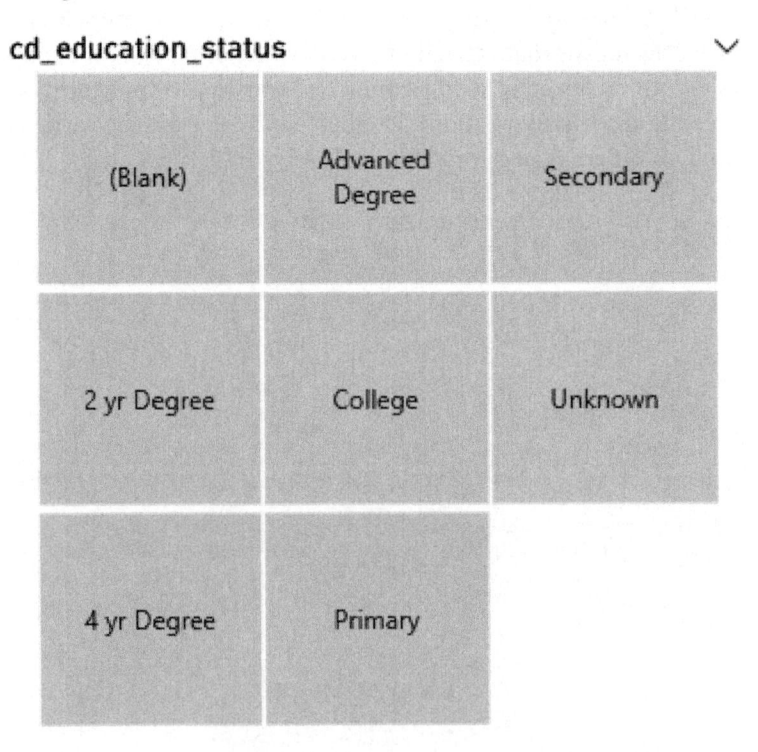

(Blank)	Advanced Degree	Secondary
2 yr Degree	College	Unknown
4 yr Degree	Primary	

Figure 12.6 – Slicer with text values in horizontal orientation

Lastly, when a field with a **hierarchy** is added to a slicer, it becomes possible to filter the data based on the hierarchical values of the column. For example, if you add a date hierarchy field to a slicer, then you will first filter on year, then quarter, then month, and finally, day.

Exploring slicers and filters 259

Year, Quarter, Month, Day

∨ ☐ 2021
∧ ■ 2022
　∧ ■ Qtr 1
　　∧ ■ January
　　　　■ 1
　　　　☐ 2
　　　　☐ 3
　　　　☐ 4

Figure 12.7 – Slicer configured with a hierarchical date field

Filtering data with slicers is a great way of making reports interactive, and additionally, it's possible to change how the slicers interact with each visual on the report page. With a slicer value selected, click **Edit interactions** under the **Format** tab on the Power BI Desktop ribbon to change into edit interactions mode, where each visual (except the one selected) now shows a selector to either filter the data or do nothing. Most visuals by default will have the interaction option set to **filter**. If you have a visual on the report page that you do not want to filter with the slicer, then you would need to ensure this option is set to **None**.

Figure 12.8 – Edit interactions

We've seen that a slicer is a visual that can be added to a report that filters other visuals. Additionally, both Power BI Desktop and the report view on Power BI online include a filtering pane. The filtering pane allows you to specify a data filter without having to use a visual. The **Filtering** pane is one of the primary three panes of the main Power BI Desktop window, along with **Visualizations** and **Fields**.

When the filtering pane is opened and nothing in the canvas is selected, you will see options to configure the scope of the filtering to be applied: filters on this page and filtering on all pages. When a visual has been selected, another option becomes available – filters on this visual. Filters work much the same as slicers here; you just need to drag the field you'd like to filter by into the proper location on the filtering pane to select a scope. For example, you might filter all pages in the entire report (PBIX file) by a desired fiscal year, while the filters on this page will only look at customers who own single-family homes, and within that page, you would have a filter on this visual set to only show records when that customer had a birthday in December. This kind of filtering allows you to be very granular for the data shown in your reports.

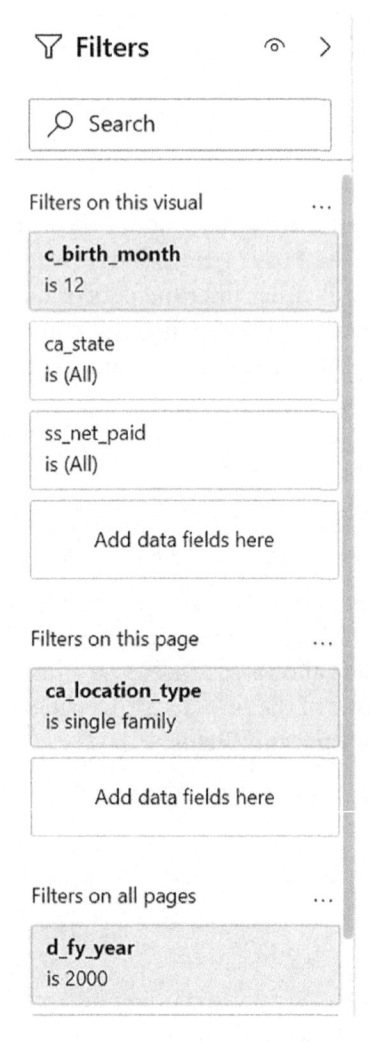

Figure 12.9 – Filtering pane showing filtering data by year, customer location type, and birth month

Power BI provides a wide range of options for filtering data and providing interaction between visuals.

Now, let's look at how we can use the Analytics pane to gain even more insights from our data.

The Analytics pane

Power BI Desktop includes the ability to add lines to a visual using the **Analytics** pane. Lines are useful to make it easier to see things such as trends, average, min, max, and other functions used in **statistical analysis**.

The type of lines that can be added depends on the visual used. Constant, trend, min, max, average, median, and percentile lines can be added to area, clustered bar, clustered column, line, and scatter chart visuals. X- and y-axis constant and symmetry shading can be added to scatter charts.

To add these lines to a visual, select the visual and then click the magnifying glass icon (*Figure 12.10*) to activate the Analytics pane portion of the Visualizations pane.

Figure 12.10 – Magnifying glass icon to activate the Analytics pane

In the Analytics pane, you can select which line you would like to add and select the options associated with each, such as the color, transparency, style, and configuration for combining the data series or highlighted values when the line gets rendered by Power BI.

262 Exposing Insights from Data

These analytics lines allow you to provide greater emphasis on things such as trends, min, or max while using visuals. For example, you might start with a visual as in *Figure 12.11* showing the count of sales by date:

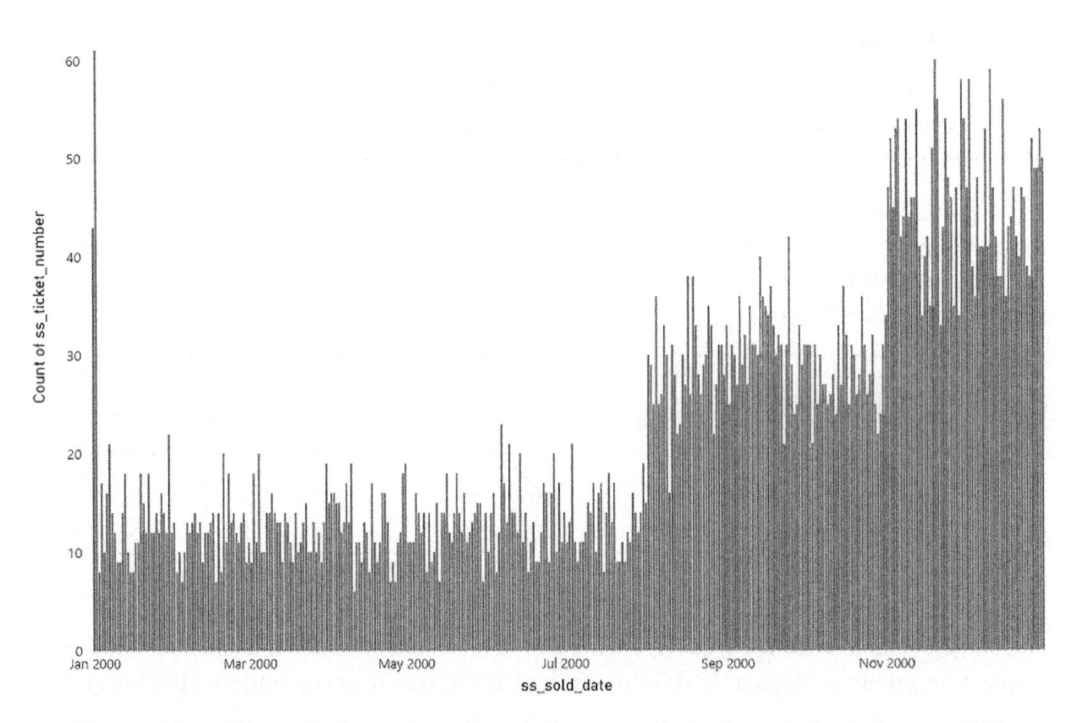

Figure 12.11 – Clustered column chart showing the count of sales for each day in the year 2000

To better emphasize how the count of sales has increased in the second half of the calendar year, we might add a trend line to this visual and we'll see the overall upward trend of the count of sales from `January 1, 2000`, through `December 31, 2000`, as shown in *Figure 12.12*:

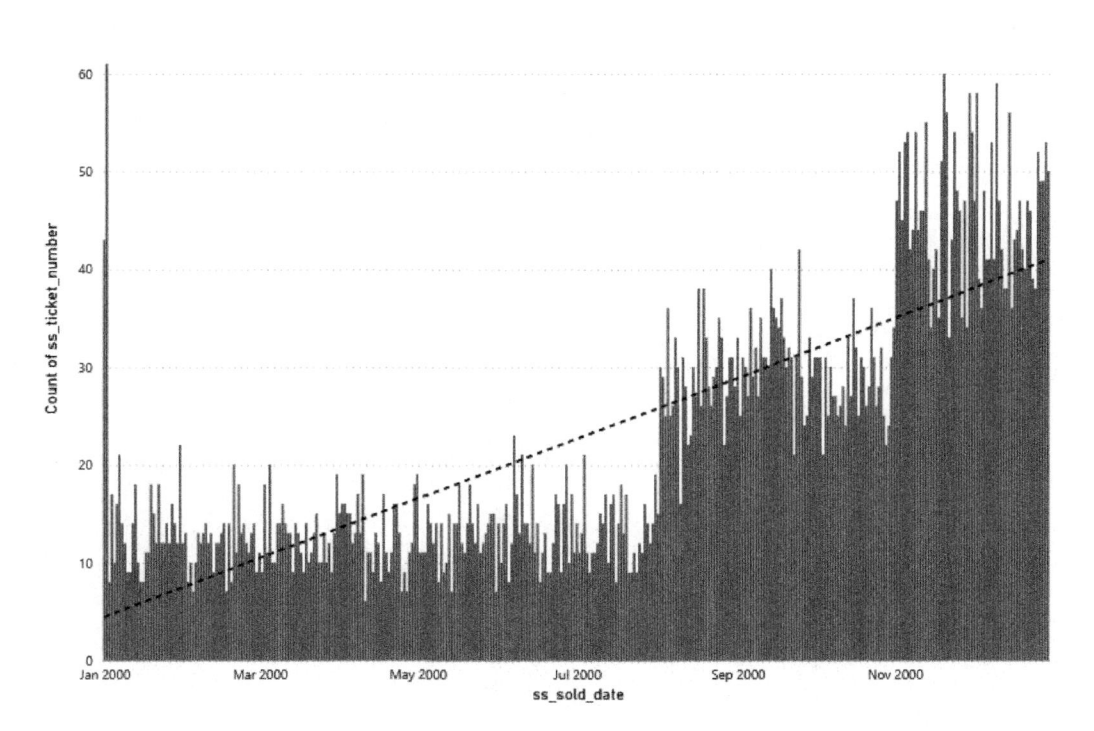

Figure 12.12 – Clustered column chart with a trend line showing the count of sales for each day in the year 2000

264   Exposing Insights from Data

The great thing is that these lines are dynamic based on the data presented in the visual. So, if we have a slicer that allows us to focus in on the first half of the year, we'll see that the trend in the first part of the year (`January 1 to June 30`) was going down slightly, as shown in *Figure 12.13*:

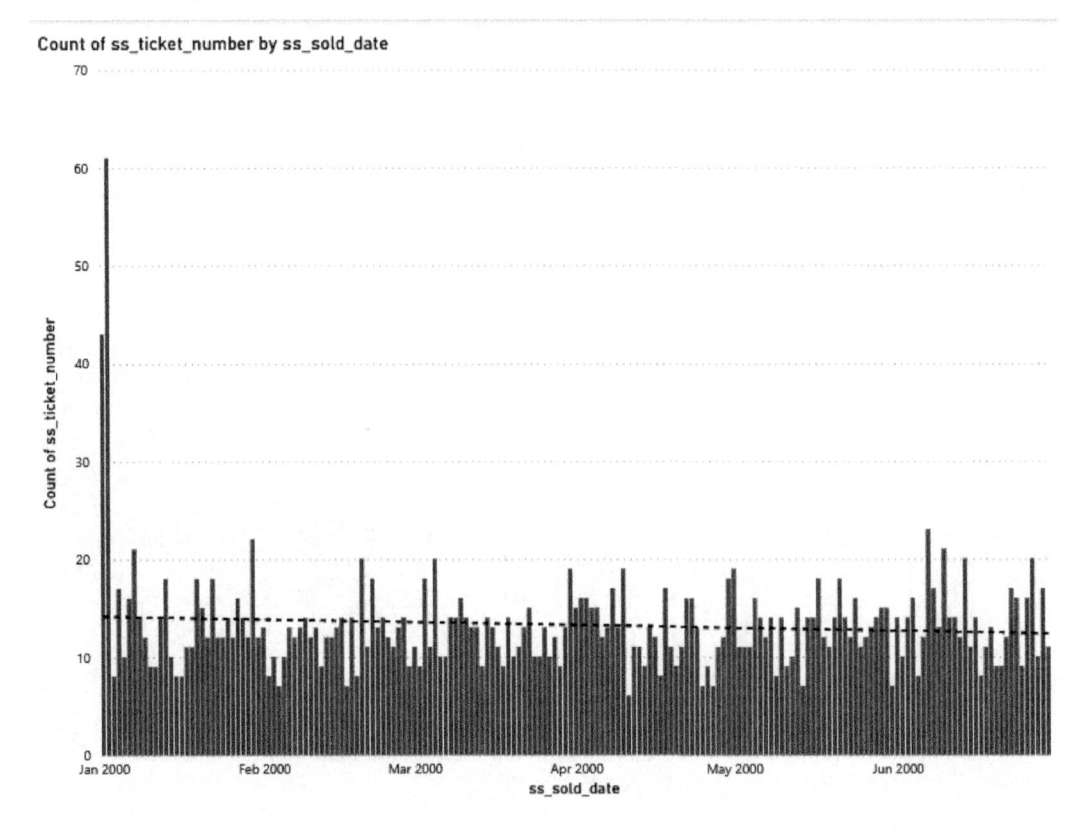

Figure 12.13 – Clustered column chart with a trend line showing the count of sales for each day from January 1 to June 30

We can see that creating analytic lines on visuals adds additional user-friendliness that makes getting value from visuals even easier for data consumers.

Summary

In this chapter, we learned about the ways we can expose more insights from our data using tools such as slicers, filters, and the Analytics pane of Power BI.

We learned how we can create **interactive visuals** for our users so they can filter data shown in report visuals in an intuitive way using slicers. We also learned how the built-in filters for reports provide a way of curating data for users by setting filters for all pages, the current page, or just specific visuals on a report.

We learned how the Analytics pane provides a way to enhance some visuals to show statistical lines such as min, max, average, and trend lines. These lines are generated dynamically based on the data shown in the visual, so paired with slicers and filters, this allows for enhanced insight generation from existing Power BI reports.

In the next chapter, we'll take a closer look at advanced analytics topics, such as time series analysis and binning.

Questions

1. The built-in report filters can be used to filter data where?

    A. Only on the current report page

    B. Only on the selected report visual

    C. On the current report page or the selected visual

    D. On the current report page, the selected visual, or all pages in the PBIX file

2. Responsive slicers must have which configuration property set?

    A. Responsive enabled and horizontal orientation

    B. Responsive enabled

    C. Responsive enabled and vertical orientation

    D. Responsive enabled and dynamic orientation

3. What type of lines can be added to a visual using the Analytics pane?

    A. Trend, median, min, max, average, and constant

    B. Trend, median, min, max, average, and standard deviation

    C. Trend, median, min, max, average, constant, and x- and/or y-axis constant

    D. Trend, median, min, max, average, constant, percentile, and x- and/or y-axis constant

4. Symmetry shading can be added to what kind of visual?

   A. Line
   B. Scatter chart
   C. Clustered bar
   D. Clustered column

13
Performing Advanced Analysis

We have already covered how, as a report author, you can use features to enhance your reports for analytical insights, such as Q&A and exporting. In this chapter, you will closely examine your data and Power BI reports and then extract value with deeper analysis. You will learn how to get a statistical summary for your data, analyze time series data, and group and bin your data. You will also apply and perform advanced analytics on the report for deeper and more meaningful data insights.

In this chapter, we will cover the following:

- Identifying outliers
- Using anomaly detection
- Conducting time series analysis
- Using grouping and binning
- Using the key influencers to explore dimensional variances
- Using the decomposition tree visual to break down a measure
- Applying AI insights

These are some of the more advanced features of Power BI. They allow you to become your own junior data scientist, granting you even more statistical insights into your data.

Technical requirements

For this chapter, please make sure you have the following:

- Microsoft Power BI Desktop installed on a Microsoft Windows PC.
- We've also provided synthetic data that can be used, which is available in the GitHub repository for this book here: `https://github.com/PacktPublishing/Microsoft-Power-BI-Data-Analyst-Certification-Guide/tree/main/example-data`.

Identifying outliers

An outlier is a data point in your dataset that is out of place or doesn't fit well with other data. For example, we might collect data about our daily revenue and see that each day we consistently have $1,000 in total sales. If we then have a day where our daily revenue is about $6,000, then that would be an outlier if the daily revenue then goes back down to $1,000. Outliers can be either positive or negative; in fact, they are just any deviation from a typical or expected result. It is important to identify and deal with outliers because they can cause problems when we try to make business decisions as they skew decisions; when outliers have been properly identified, they will help ensure the higher accuracy of insights gained from your data. You can define your calculations on what an outlier is. You can create measures to define what would be considered anomalous in your dataset.

> **Math**
>
> In mathematics, outliers are often defined as being more than 2 standard deviations away from the mean. As this is not a math course, I will not go into any more detail about it.

Calculated columns can be used to identify outliers; however, since we know calculated columns are only updated when data in the model is refreshed, the more dynamic approach would be using a visualization or DAX formula. After outliers have been identified, the most common next step would be to visualize them, likely using a scatter chart, as shown in *Figure 13.1*. Outliers can be highlighted or made easier to notice using filters or slicers:

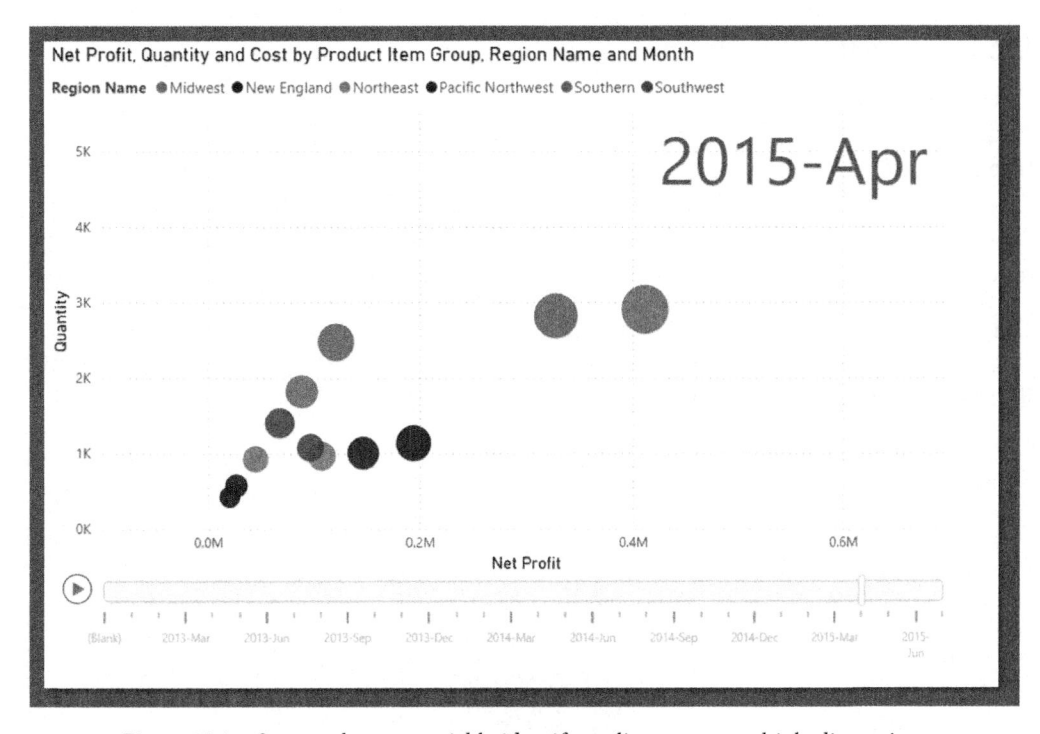

Figure 13.1 – Scatter plots can quickly identify outliers across multiple dimensions

By combining DAX measures and visualizations, you will be able to spot outliers and address them quickly. Just remember, not every outlier is a bad data point. Sometimes the real world conspires against our mathematical models. For example, as we previously discussed, you may have daily sales revenue data that is typically about $1,000 each day. On a day the daily sales are $6,000, it might have actually been the start of a huge new promotion, so just because it looks like an anomaly, doesn't immediately mean it's an outlier. We have to take other factors into consideration that might have caused that anomaly.

Now that we have learned all about the basics of finding outliers, we will explore a unique way to do so, using anomaly detection.

Using anomaly detection

One of the great ways to find outliers is using the built-in **Find anomalies** tool in the **Analysis** pane of a visualization in Power BI. This feature of Power BI uses **Artificial Intelligence (AI)** capabilities to identify which data points are most different from other values in your data. The purpose of this feature is to help with analyzing the data so that action can be taken either against the data before business decisions are made or to help report consumers better understand the data and make informed business decisions.

To use this capability, you need to be using a supported visual (such as a line or scatter chart) and only one field on the *y* axis or values. This feature is being improved; so, at the time of writing, this was the requirement.

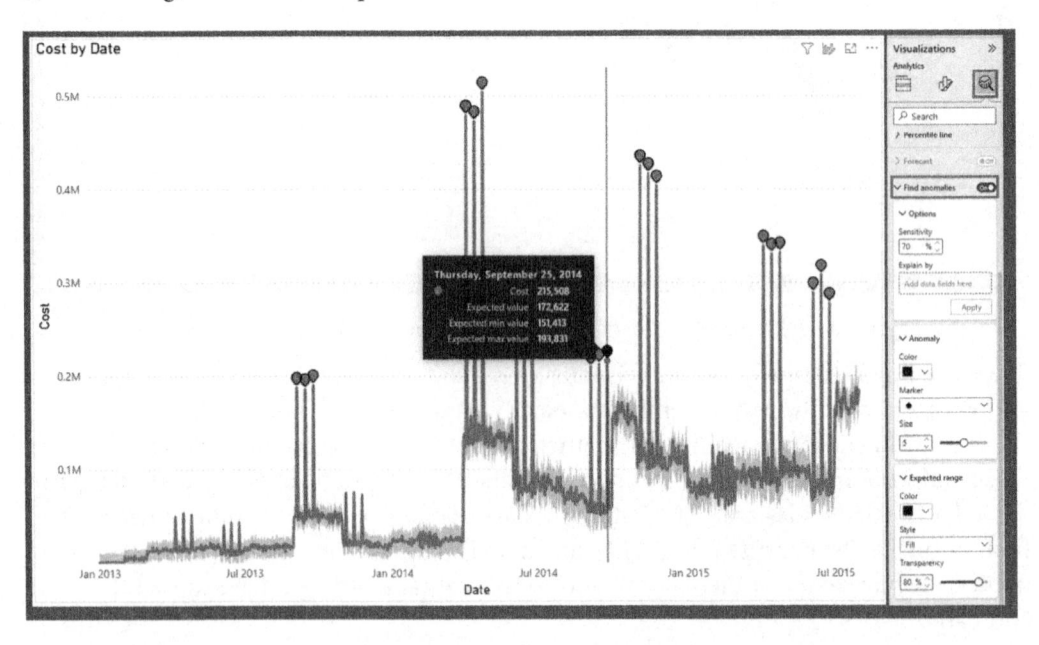

Figure 13.2 – Automated anomaly detection is built into some visualizations

Once this has been enabled, you can see the outliers identified with a gray dot. These are anomalies that have been identified. You can also set the sensitivity level, and even a categorical field to use as the basis for anomaly detection. With this capability, it is easy to quickly identify data values that are out of place or potentially outliers.

Now that we have an understanding of outliers, let's take a look at how we can analyze time series data in the next section.

Conducting time series analysis

Time series analysis involves extracting meaningful data and identifying trends by analyzing your data in time order. You can use this time-ordered data to make predictions about the future, forecasting future needs or desired actions.

Visuals such as line charts can be used alongside the forecasting pane to show how your time series data is predicted to change. Many times, time series analysis involves using plots such as Gantt charts, which can be helpful for scenarios such as project planning or monitoring stock market data. By looking at your data using these tools, you can best identify when events have influenced change in your business. Any events that impact your business should be represented in the data and thus be identifiable when looking at the time series data.

In *Figure 13.3*, we can see the phases of a project as it moves along the axis of time. Before **Feb 07**, we can see that the phase was **Scope**, while the **Analysis** phase started from **Feb 07** and has an end date before **Feb 14**. We can monitor the process of each phase as some will overlap and using this time series method, we can monitor the change over time and observe how events will impact the data.

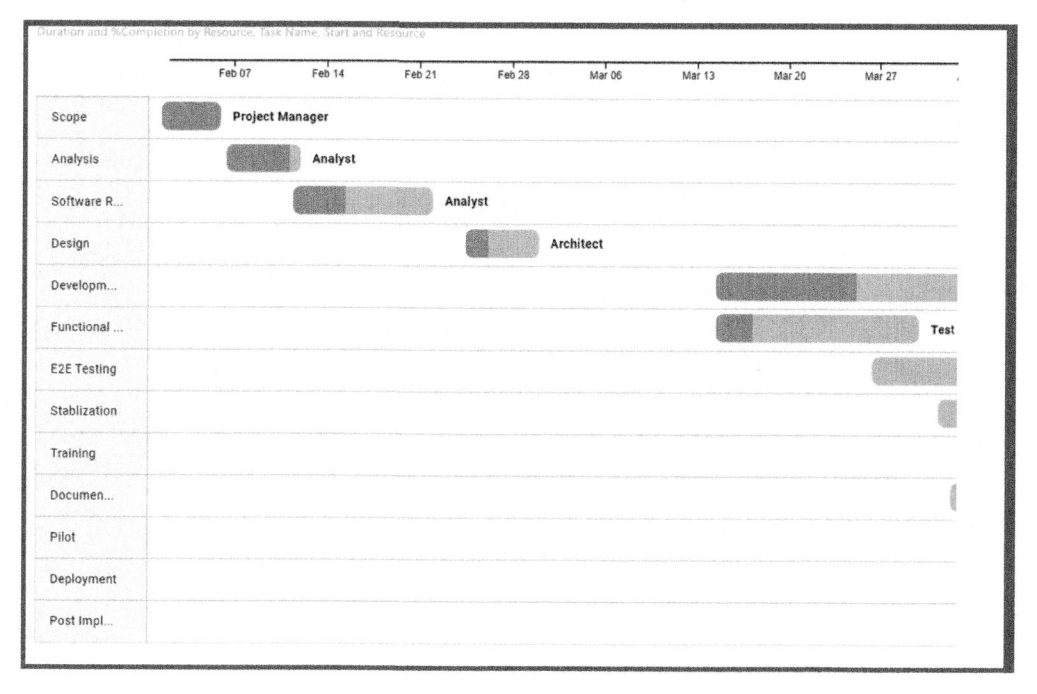

Figure 13.3 – Gantt charts are a staple of modern business, and a classic example of time series reporting

Another way to add time series information to your reports is by using **Play Axis**. The scatter chart in *Figure 13.1* has a play button in the lower left-hand corner. Clicking on it will have the chart "play" through the dates; you can watch your data change over time.

If you have a whole page of visuals you want to "play" over time, there is a custom visual called **Play Axis** that may help here, and it is available in Microsoft AppSource.

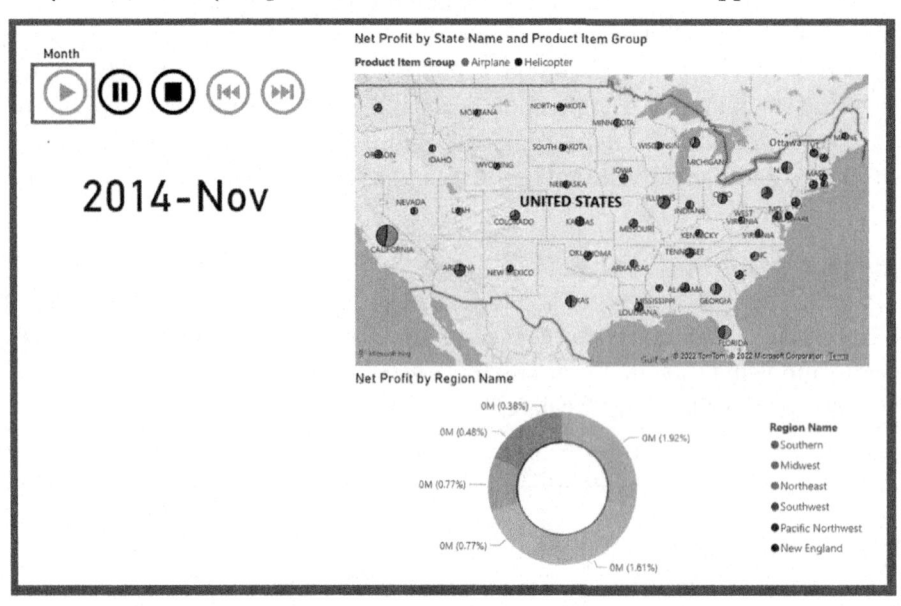

Figure 13.4 – Adding the Play Axis visualization to a report page

The **Play Axis** slicer can make a whole page of your report display your data ordered by date.

Grouping and binning

Grouping and binning are techniques used by analysts and statisticians to better understand data and draw insights from it. For example, you might sell products that have various sizes, such as extra small, small, medium, large, extra large, and 2X large. When you look at the sales data, the number of extra small, extra large, and 2X large sales might be much less than the other categories of products. So, in cases such as that, you might want to redefine the categories into small, medium, and large, grouping small and extra small together and large, extra large, and 2X large together to best understand your sales patterns by aggregating the data first. The same technique can be used for numeric or date types; however, in those cases, it's typically referred to as binning. For example, you may have sales data that is daily, but you want to understand long-term patterns, so you bin the data together by aggregating the daily data into weekly or monthly bins, so it becomes easier to analyze over longer periods of time. When you do this, you can also consider how you aggregate this date; sum, average, maximum, and count are all built-in aggregation functions that can be used in Power BI. Power BI will sometimes do grouping or binning automatically depending on the data, but you always have full control as the report designer to visualize your data to tell the story you want to tell.

Grouping

You can easily create a new group by either right-clicking on a field from the field well and selecting the **New group** option or using a visualization. If you right-click after multiselecting many categorical fields on a visualization, you will see the **Group data** option. Choosing this creates a new group based on the *x*-axis field.

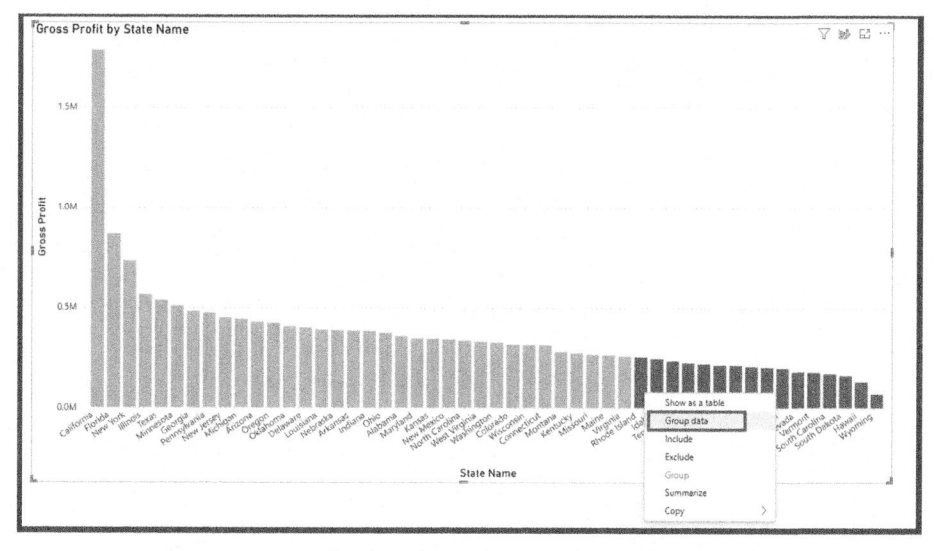

Figure 13.5 – Multiselecting a categorical field to create a group

274   Performing Advanced Analysis

When the group is created, notice that the visual updates show the new group. You may want to edit the visual to change the way the data is displayed. You may want to change the axis.

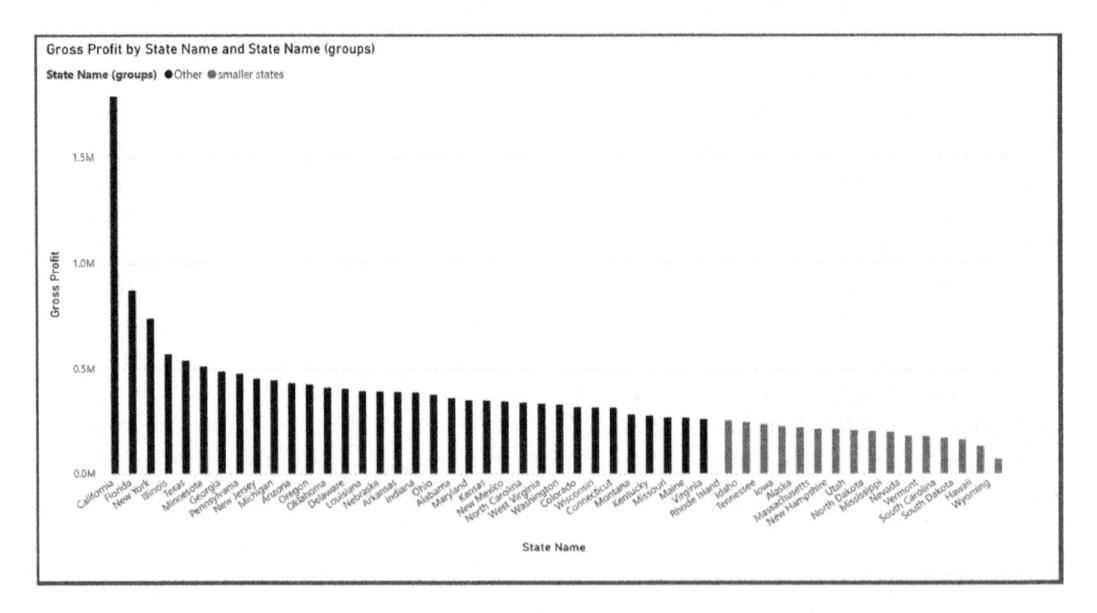

Figure 13.6 – Our visual is now showing our groups. The default group name has been edited to "smaller states"

After creating the group, you may want to edit it by renaming the group members, adding new subgroupings, or excluding the "other" grouping are all options. When you created the group, a new group type was added to the table that contains the values.

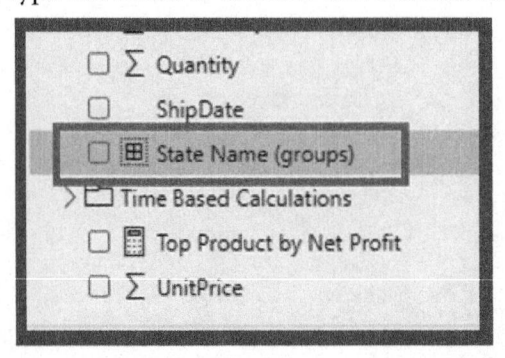

Figure 13.7 – Group type for state name. Notice the group type icon

If you right-click on the group, you will see the **Edit group** option.

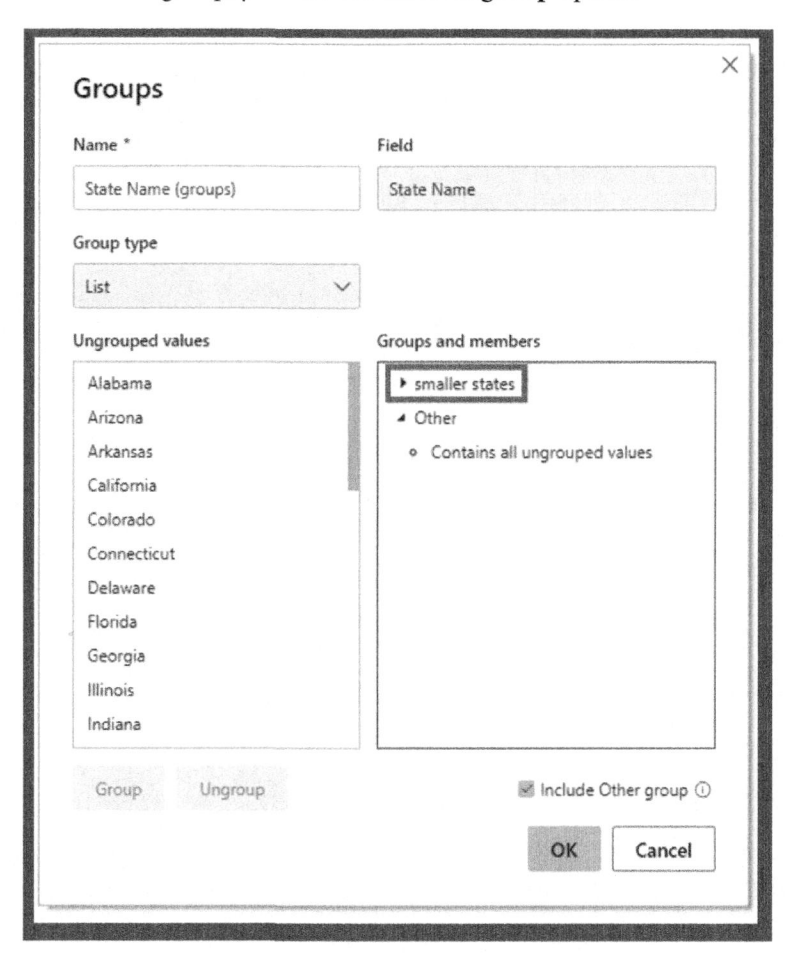

Figure 13.8 – Let's edit our group!

In the **Edit group** pane, you can add more subgroups, rename the group, and rename the subgroups. You also have the option to include or exclude ungrouped values from the column.

Binning

Binning is much like grouping except it's for numbers and dates. It's a way to turn continuous numbers into categorical fields. You create a bin by right-clicking on the numerical or date field you want to bin and selecting **New group**, just the same as for a categorical value.

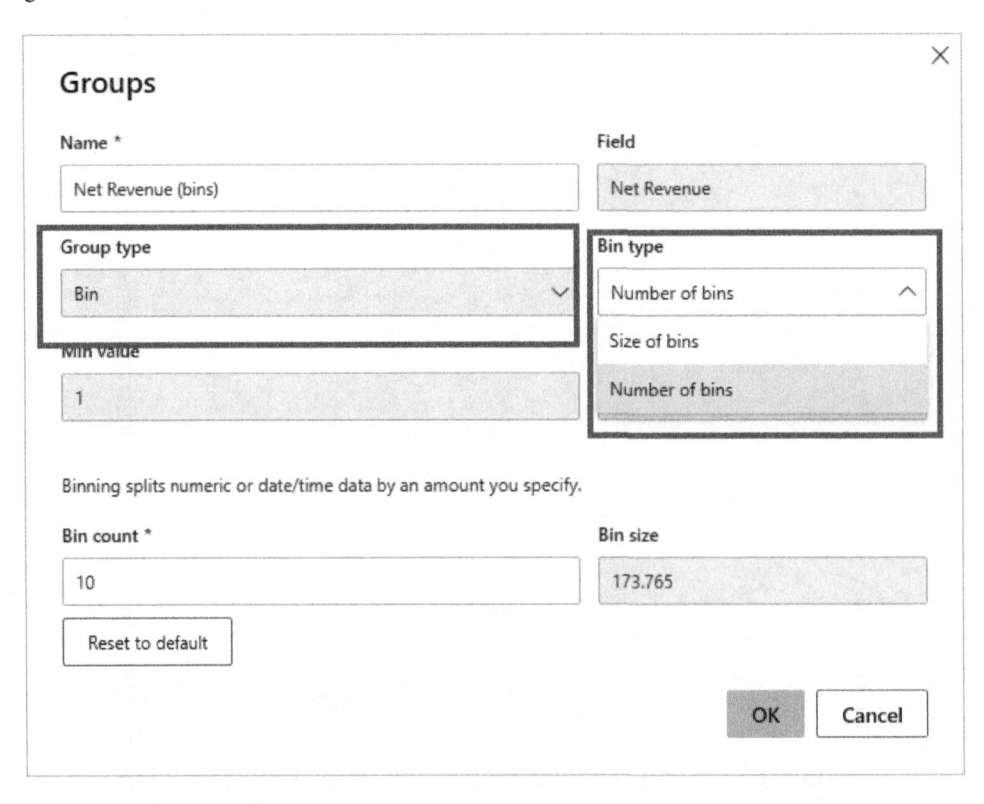

Figure 13.9 – Binning your numbers

Once the **Groups** dialog box opens, you will see a couple of changes. **Group type** will be **Bin**, not **List**, and you can choose your bin type. You can either force your numeric field into a fixed number of bins or you can choose how many elements go into each bin.

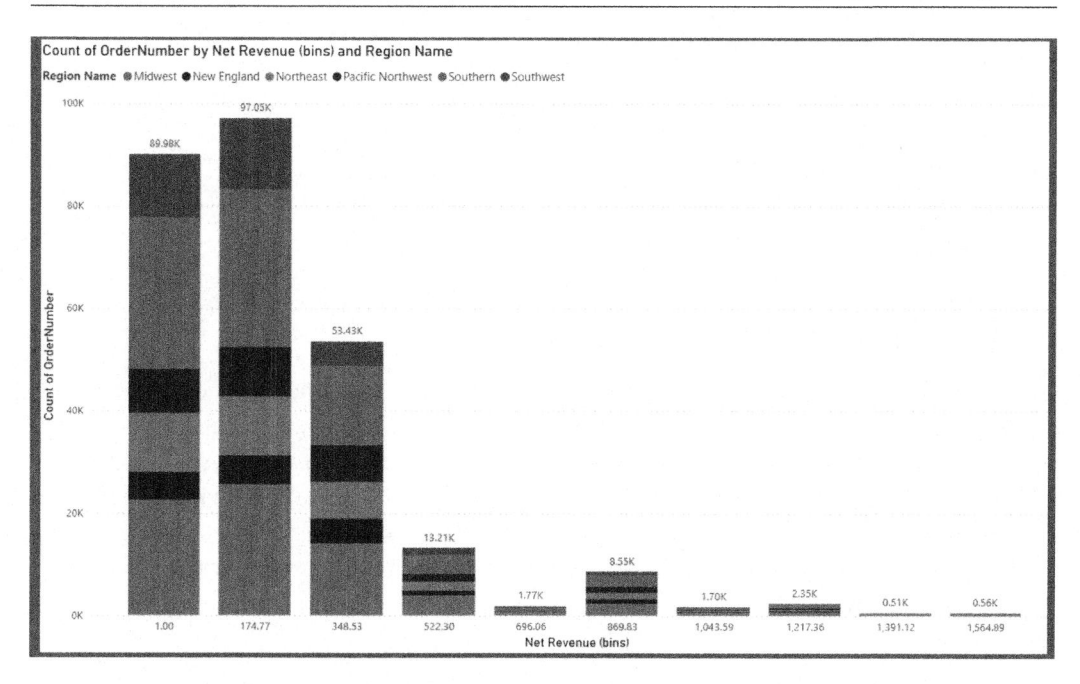

Figure 13.10 – Net revenue forced into 10 bins

Both binning and grouping let you create summarized data that is easier to digest.

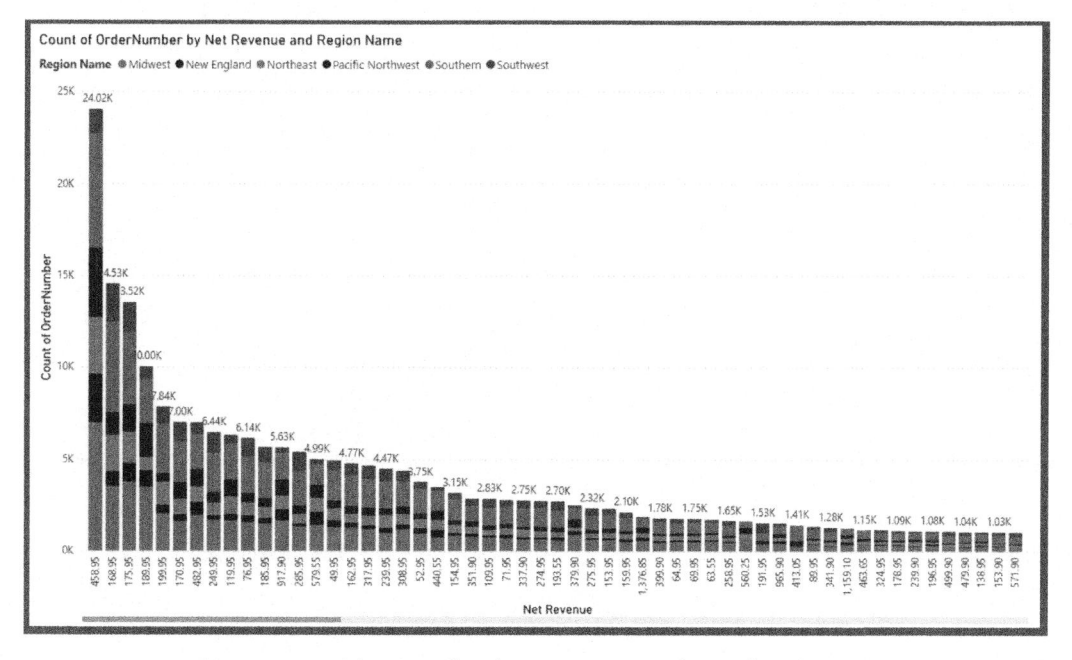

Figure 13.11 – The same data from Figure 13.10, but without binning

278　Performing Advanced Analysis

> **Tip**
> Be careful of smoothing out your data into too few bins. Too few bins and you may miss some peaks and valleys in your data.

Now that we have learned all about grouping and binning, let's move on to another key visual element that Power BI has, key influencers.

Key influencers

The key influencers visual is another helper visual that will help you analyze your data to determine which fields in your data influence others. For example, your sales data may also include customer demographics such as household income or employment status. Using the key influencers visual, you may come to find out that household income may be a factor that influences the total sales per customer. This visual performs statistical calculations in order to show the results and will typically require configuration to your data for best results.

The key influencers visualization can be found in the **Visualizations** pane. Once you have added it to the report, you start by selecting the field you want to analyze. You can then add one, or preferably more, fields to **Explain by**.

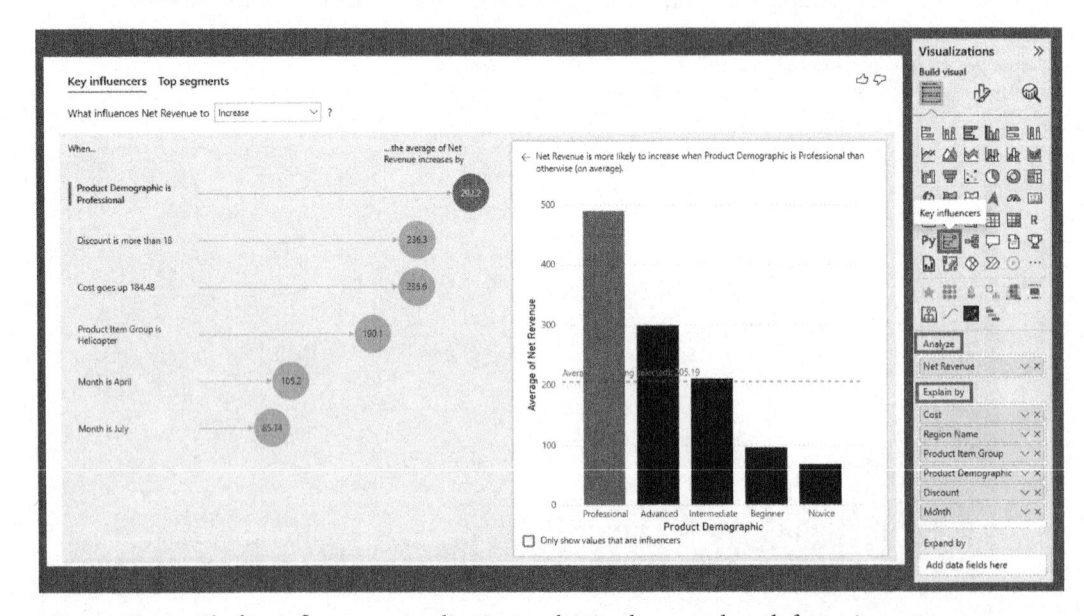

Figure 13.12 – The key influencers visualization explaining how much each factor impacts net revenue

Your report consumers can click on each category and get a breakdown of not only how much it impacts your chosen metric, but also what parts impact it. We'll now explore another visual similar to the key influencers one, that is, the decomposition tree visual.

Decomposition tree visual

Similar to the key influencers visualization, the decomposition tree visual also lets you see your data across multiple dimensions. You can use it for improvised exploration and conducting root cause analysis.

The decomposition tree visualization can be found in the **Visualizations** pane. Once you have added it to the report, you start by selecting the field you want to analyze. You can then add one, or preferably more, fields to **Explain by**. If this sounds familiar, it's because it's the exact same thing you did for the key influencers visual.

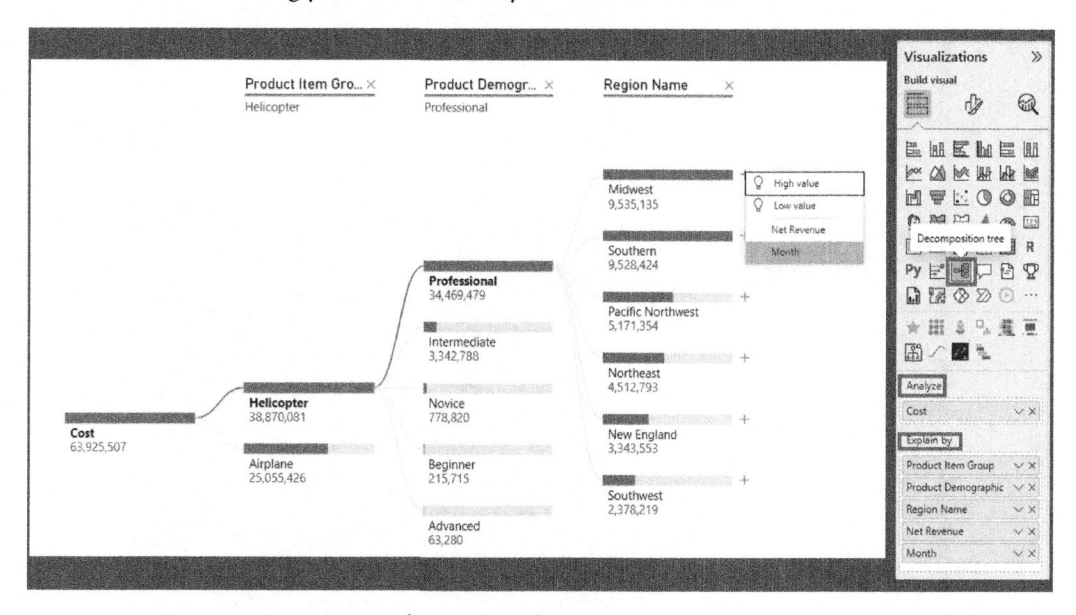

Figure 13.13 – You can choose the order you want to decompose your tree in

The decomposition tree visual will update as data fields are added to the **Explain by** configuration. When a new field is added to **Explain by**, the visual updates, with the + symbol being added to the visual. By clicking +, you can then select how you want the decomposition tree visual to generate the next level of understanding from the data. When the AI computation in the visual detects high values and low values in the data, this can also be selected and is referred to as an **AI split**. These are provided by the visual to help you better analyze the data using the decomposition tree visual.

Applying AI insights

When you have a dataset and don't know where to start, there is a feature that can help you. Quick insights is a machine learning-based capability built into Power BI that can automatically build visualizations and make some insights stand out. It is also useful to use on datasets that have been published but allows you to look for any insights that may have been missed. This capability can be used on some datasets that have been published to a Power BI workspace.

To use quick insights, click **Get quick insights** from the dataset menu for a dataset that has been published to the Power BI service. The service will then run statistical algorithms to automatically generate visualizations.

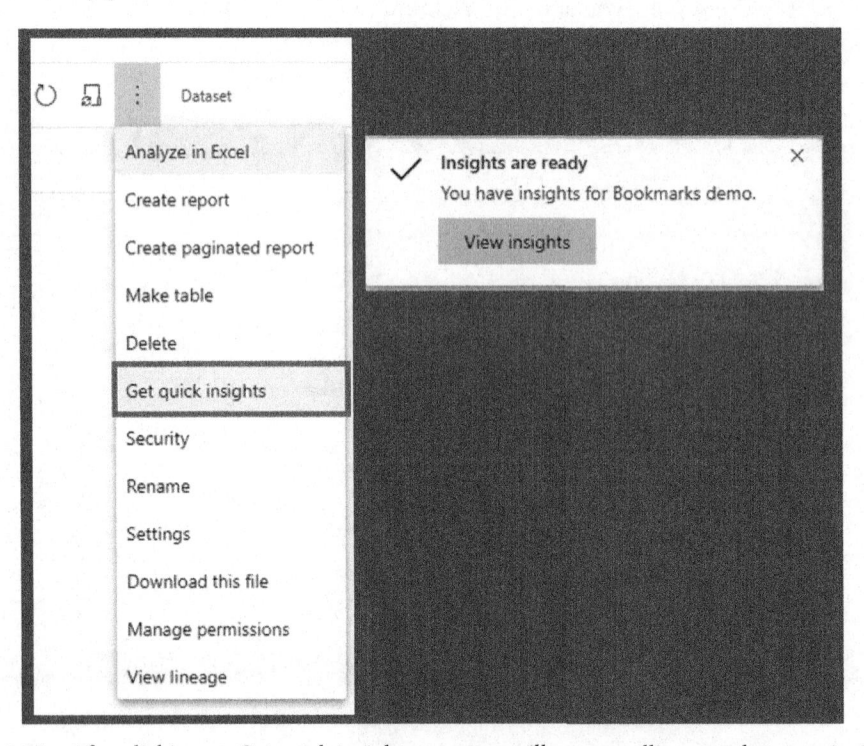

Figure 13.14 – After clicking on Get quick insights, a popup will appear telling you that your insights are ready

Once the process has completed, you need to click **View insights** to view the insights that have been generated by the service. When quick insights are generated, Power BI will create up to 32 different insight cards. Each card will have a visual and a short description. These visuals are the same as visuals you manually create. These visuals can be pinned to dashboards the same as visuals in reports.

Figure 13.15 – The output from quick insights. Power BI generated 37 visuals this time

Quick insights can give you a deeper understanding of your data and the potentially hidden relationships within. It's like having your dataset reviewed by a data scientist, but at a fraction of the cost!

Summary

What a fun chapter! These more advanced features of Power BI are phenomenal. They allow you to get a much deeper understanding of how data points in your dataset interact with, influence, and affect your business.

In this chapter, we covered how to identify outliers and anomalies in your data. You saw, ever so briefly, what makes an outlier, then quickly moved away from the math. Power BI can detect them for you, no math required.

Power BI is an awesome tool for analyzing your data over time. Some visualizations allow you to add a play axis that you can add a date field to; for the rest, you added the **Play Axis** slicer visualization to the page and made every visual change over time.

With grouping, we created our own subgroups within a column. You then used binning to change a continuous, numeric column into a categorical field. These two interrelated concepts allow you to simplify visuals or bin together smaller data points.

The key influencers chart allows you to explore dimensional variances and what makes up a number. You saw how different fields affect a data point and by how much. This visual allows your report consumers to really understand how different parts of your business interact.

The decomposition tree visual is like key influencers in that it breaks down a measure and explains how the number was arrived at. The decomposition tree allows your report consumers to choose AI splits and in what order they want to see them.

Finally, you applied AI insights to your dataset. You saw how this Power BI service feature can act as your very own data scientist looking for correlations and causations in your data.

In the next chapter, you will discover how to use workspaces in the Power BI service to share your reports and control permissions.

Questions

1. The key influencers visualization can be used to discover what about your data?

    A. Understand relationships between fields in your data model.

    B. Aggregate numeric data in your data model.

    C. Generate text summaries of insights.

    D. How many social media followers you have.

2. Which type of visual is often used with time series analysis?

    A. Gantt chart

    B. Pie chart

    C. Map visual

    D. Decomposition tree

3. When there are data values that don't fit well with other values, your data may contain what?

    A. Errors

    B. Bad records

    C. Outliers

    D. Empty records

Part 5 – Deploying and Maintaining Deliverables

This section teaches you how to create and secure workspaces so you can share your Power BI artifacts with users, configure datasets to refresh the data, and secure datasets using row-level security.

This section comprises the following chapters:

- *Chapter 14, Managing Workspaces*
- *Chapter 15, Managing Datasets*

14
Managing Workspaces

At the center of the Power BI value proposition is the ability to use it to create and communicate powerful and vivid stories about data. This enables the creation of information and value from raw data. As we have seen throughout the course of this book, Power BI Desktop on its own is a useful toolbox of capabilities for making sense of data and uncovering insights that can often get buried among many millions of rows and thousands of columns in typical enterprise data. However, when we combine Power BI Desktop with the services hosted on PowerBI.com, then we can unlock the potential for sharing information and using the dynamic and robust reporting and analytics capabilities of Power BI across large groups of users.

To share information created in Power BI with other users, Power BI has the concept of **publishing** content, and in this chapter, we will learn about **workspaces**, **apps**, how workspaces can be used for the **development life cycle**, and how we can monitor the **usage** and **performance** of our reports deployed to workspaces.

In this chapter, we are going to cover the following topics:

- Using workspaces
- Distributing reports and dashboards

- Using deployment pipelines
- Monitoring workspace usage

Technical requirements

We will need the following tools in this chapter:

- Microsoft Power BI Desktop installed on a Microsoft Windows PC
- A Power BI data model where we can apply the advanced features covered in this chapter
- At least the free tier of Power BI and logging into PowerBI.com with a work or school email address

Using workspaces

Power BI workspaces are places in the Power BI service where datasets, reports, and dashboards can be hosted or published for multiple users to use. Power BI Desktop is typically used to publish reports and datasets to workspaces; however, the service provides a REST API in which custom applications can interact with workspaces, including the management of assets on workspaces or even publishing. There are other workspace assets, such as dashboards and dataflows, that are created within a workspace using PowerBI.com but the primary authoring tool is Power BI Desktop.

Let's next explore the ways in which workspaces can be managed through roles and permissions.

Using workspace roles

Workspaces allow users to be given permission to objects stored in the workspace. Those permissions center around distinct **roles**, such as **Admin** (or administrator), **Member**, **Contributor**, and **Viewer**. These roles each have unique permissions inside the workspace. For example, the Admin role can delete content, add users, and change user roles, while Member roles cannot. *Figure 14.1* details the permissions attributed to each role. It's important to remember that products and services like Power BI change over time and it's best to look at the latest information available in the documentation here: `https://docs.microsoft.com/en-US/power-bi/collaborate-share/service-roles-new-workspaces#workspace-roles`.

Permission	Role			
	Admin	Member	Contributor	Viewer
View and interact with assets in a workspace	✓	✓	✓	✓
Read data from workspace dataflows	✓	✓	✓	✓
Modify connection settings in gateways [1]	✓	✓	✓	✗
Schedule data refreshes with on-premises gateway [1]	✓	✓	✓	✗
Create goals from workspace dataset [2]	✓	✓	✓	✗
Copy a report [2]	✓	✓	✓	✗
Create reports in another workspace using dataset in this workspace [2]	✓	✓	✓	✗
Publish reports to or delete content in this workspace	✓	✓	✓	✗
Update or delete content in this workspace	✓	✓	✓	✗
Change featured content on team member's home screen	✓	✓	✓	✗
Manage permissions on datasets [2]	✓	✓	✗	✗
Change featured apps on team member's home screen	✓	✓	✗	✗
Allow team members to reshare workspace assets [2]	✓	✓	✗	✗
Share workspace assets or an app [2]	✓	✓	✗	✗
Update an app	✓	✓	✗ [3]	✗
Publish, unpublish, or modify permissions for an app	✓	✓	✗	✗
Add others to the workspace (some roles limited)	✓	✓	✗	✗
Allow contributors to update an app	✓	✗	✗	✗
Add others to the workspace (with any role)	✓	✗	✗	✗
Modify or delete the workspace	✓	✗	✗	✗

Figure 14.1 – Workspace roles and permissions

1 Additional permissions will be needed on the gateway; the scope of this table is the permissions within the workspace.

2 Copying reports and using datasets across workspaces require build permission in the source workspace dataset. The simplest way to add this is via the Contributor role.

3 Admin users can allow contributors to update the app for a workspace. If this is enabled, contributors still cannot publish a new app or change who has permission to use it.

This table in *Figure 14.1* will help you when it comes to understanding the differences between the roles and how permissions within a workspace can be set up so that administrators have the permissions they need, while members or viewers have fewer permissions.

Next, we'll look at how workspace licensing works so we can understand some important differences between Power BI free, Pro, and Premium with respect to workspaces.

Workspace licensing

Workspaces store and host data for users and this takes server resources to achieve. So, for most organizations, this will involve **licensing** costs. Power BI does have a free tier, but it is limited when it comes to capabilities as many of the advanced features discussed in this chapter require either **Pro** or **Premium licensing**. Most organizations using Power BI will opt for paid licensing after seeing the value they can get from using the advanced capabilities of the Power BI service.

Workspaces are accessible via PowerBI.com; however, they can be hosted in a shared **Software-as-a-Service (SaaS)** environment, or they can be hosted in dedicated environments. Dedicated environments are called **Premium** and have various capacity sizes, or **SKUs**, as shown in *Figure 14.2*:

Premium Capacity SKU	vCores	RAM (GB)	Max Memory per Query (GB)
EM1	1	3	1
EM2	2	5	2
EM3	4	10	2
P1	8	25	6
P2	16	30	6
P3	32	100	10
P4	64	200	10
P5	128	400	10

Figure 14.2 – Power BI Premium capacity SKUs

The table in *Figure 14.2* has been adapted from the table in the Power BI documentation, available at this website: https://docs.microsoft.com/en-us/power-bi/admin/service-premium-what-is#capacity-nodes.

As you can see in *Figure 14.2*, each Premium capacity SKU has different **virtual cores**, or **vCores**, and memory characteristics that will be dedicated to hosting workspaces. *P*-type SKUs are for general enterprise reporting or embedding Power BI reports for your organization, while *EM* SKUs are for organizational report embedding. Some SKUs must be purchased through volume licensing, which we will not cover in this book. It's just important to understand that there are different types and sizes of Power BI Premium capacity SKUs.

Power BI **Premium Per User** (**PPU**) allows workspaces to be hosted in the shared SaaS environment but dedicated resources are given to the specific Power BI workspaces designated for that user. Between Premium capacity and PPU, there are multiple options to meet the needs of organizations, while at the same time unlocking advanced features and capabilities.

Premium relates to workspaces because workspaces will be hosted either on the shared environment or a Premium capacity or will be identified as having PPU. When this happens, there will be additional capabilities unlocked for the workspace, which will be covered in later sections, such as monitoring usage and performance.

Let's next look at how workspaces can help with distributing reports and dashboards.

Distributing reports and dashboards

Within a Power BI workspace, we have datasets, reports, dashboards, and other artifacts that make up a Power BI app. When reports and dashboards (or even datasets) get created and you want to enable other users within your organization to use them and get value from what has been created, you'll want to package these together as a Power BI app to make it easy to use by others in your organization. Workspaces that are published as an app can be placed on the user's **home screen**, given a logo and description, as well as be targeted to specific users or groups of users. For example, if there are multiple teams from finance and marketing that build datasets, reports, and dashboards for their respective teams, these sets of artifacts are also probably important to the CEO and CFO, who would like to consume a subset of the reports and dashboards from these workspaces in a very tailored way.

Let's explore how we'd create a Power BI app from an existing workspace so we can distribute the reports and dashboards in a specific way.

Creating a Power BI app

At a high level, the steps involved with creating a Power BI app are as follows:

1. Navigate to the workspace that contains the content you'd like to distribute as an app.
2. Click the **Create app** button in the upper right-hand corner of the page.
3. Provide the name and description of the app to be published.
4. Provide optional information, such as the app logo, theme color, contact information, and support URL.

290　Managing Workspaces

5. Configure navigation for the app by clicking the **Navigation** link at the top of the page.
6. Configure permissions for the app by clicking the **Permissions** link at the top of the page.
7. Click **Publish app** in the bottom right-hand corner of the page.

Next, we will look at each of the steps to publish a Power BI app in detail.

First, we'll need to start from an existing workspace that contains the reports and dashboard we'd like to distribute. This will be on the PowerBI.com service and will look something like *Figure 14.3*:

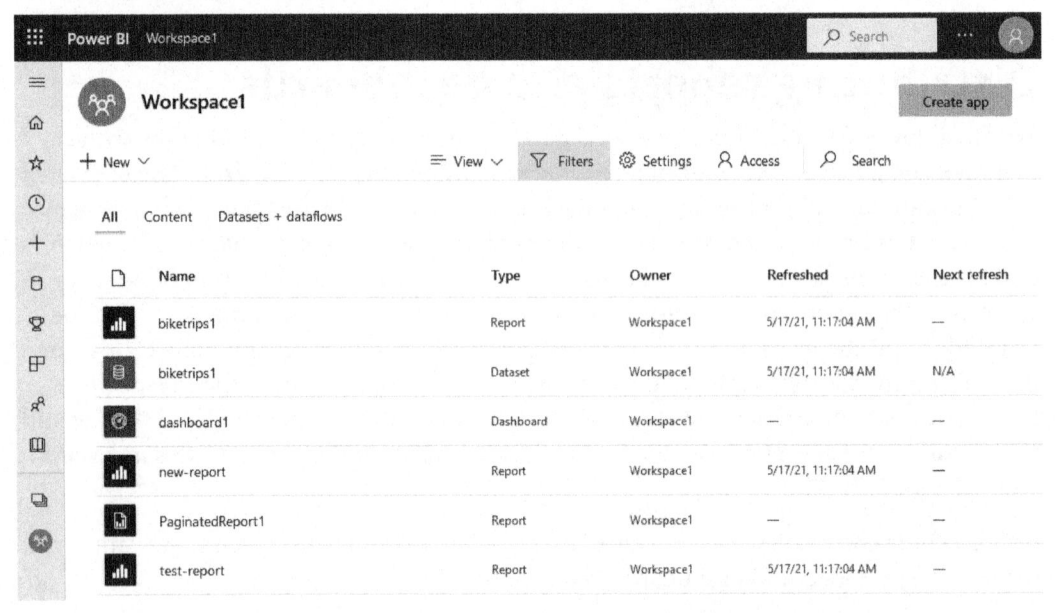

Figure 14.3 – A Power BI workspace with reports and dashboards

After clicking the **Create app** button, we'll see a wizard-like menu that will walk us through the creation of Power BI from the assets in this workspace.

Distributing reports and dashboards 291

The first things we need to provide to create the app are the name and description. After that, there are optional values, such as the URL to support, an app logo, the theme color, and contact information to go along with the app. These values are important because for any published data assets within an organization, it's important to know how to get support for that dataset as well as who is publishing the dataset (in this case, within the app), while the color and logo are important for building the brand of the app within the organization and to help users connect with the information presented in the app.

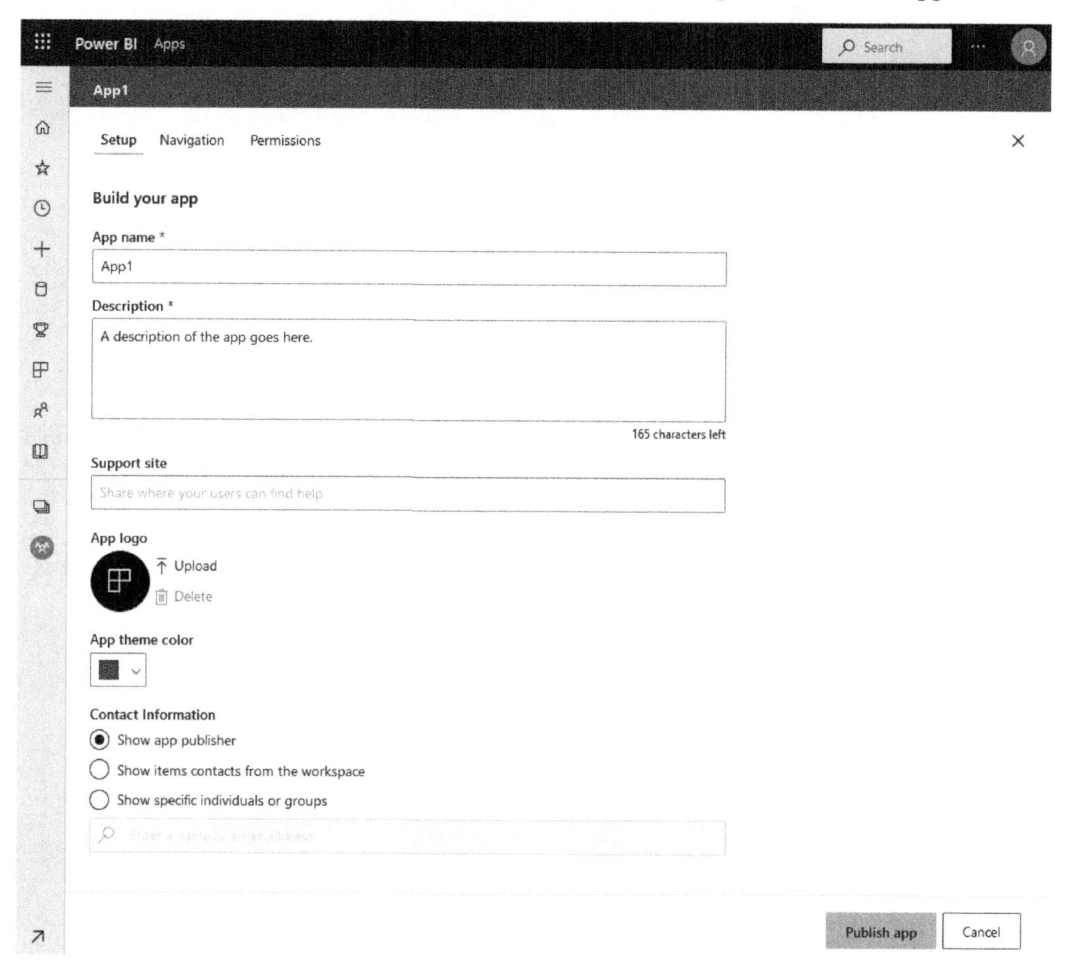

Figure 14.4 – Creating a Power BI app

The next configuration for the app includes the navigation. At the top of the configuration page, we can click the **Navigation** tab to set the preferences for navigating the content of the workspace.

Figure 14.5 shows the navigation configuration using the new navigation builder. The navigation screen is where we can change the order of the reports to be shown in the app, as well as hiding some reports or dashboards so they won't be included in the app:

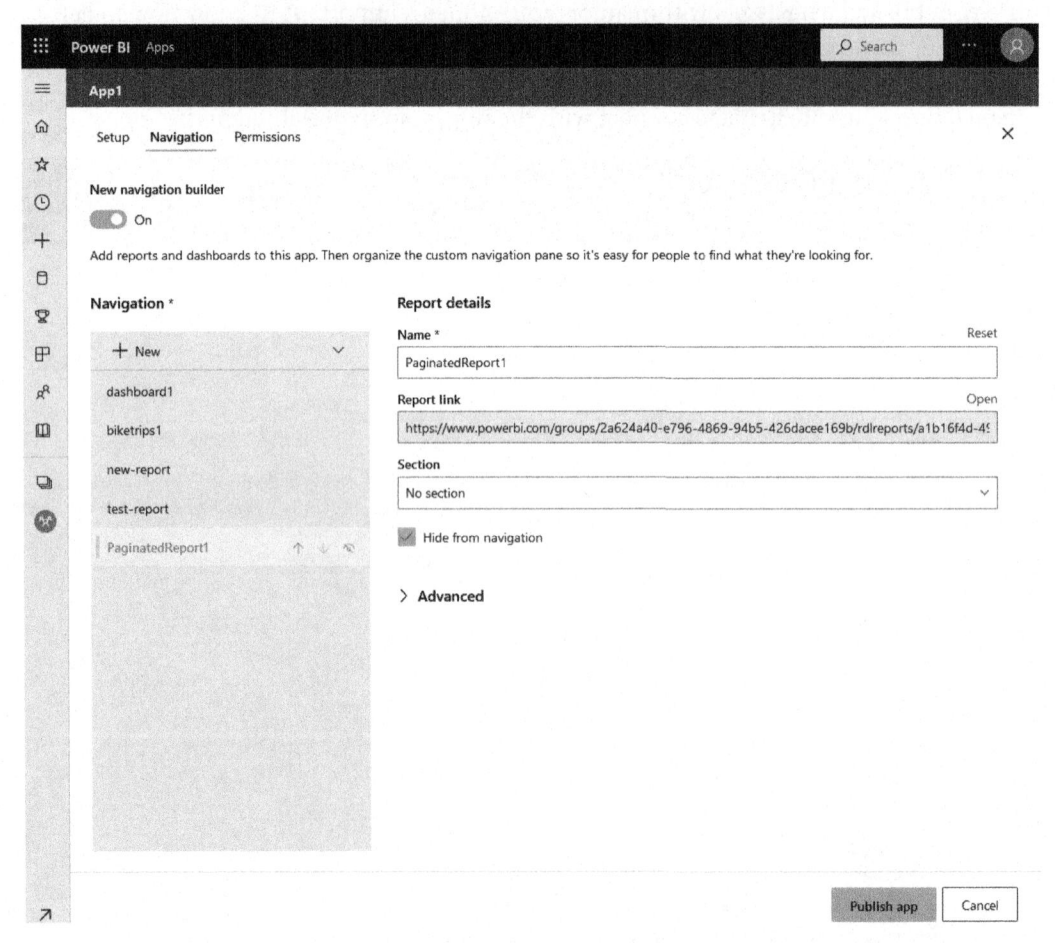

Figure 14.5 – Configuration of the app navigation

In our previous example, the finance team has been publishing reports and making dashboards in this workspace, but for the C-suite audience, maybe we don't need reports showing detailed financial information and instead only need to distribute the high-level information that the C-suite audience will need.

Hovering over each item on the left-hand side of the screen will show the up and down arrows as well as the eye icon, which can be used to hide that item. Using the **+ New** button, it's also possible to create sections that reports and dashboards can be grouped into as well as links to external content, as shown in *Figure 14.6*:

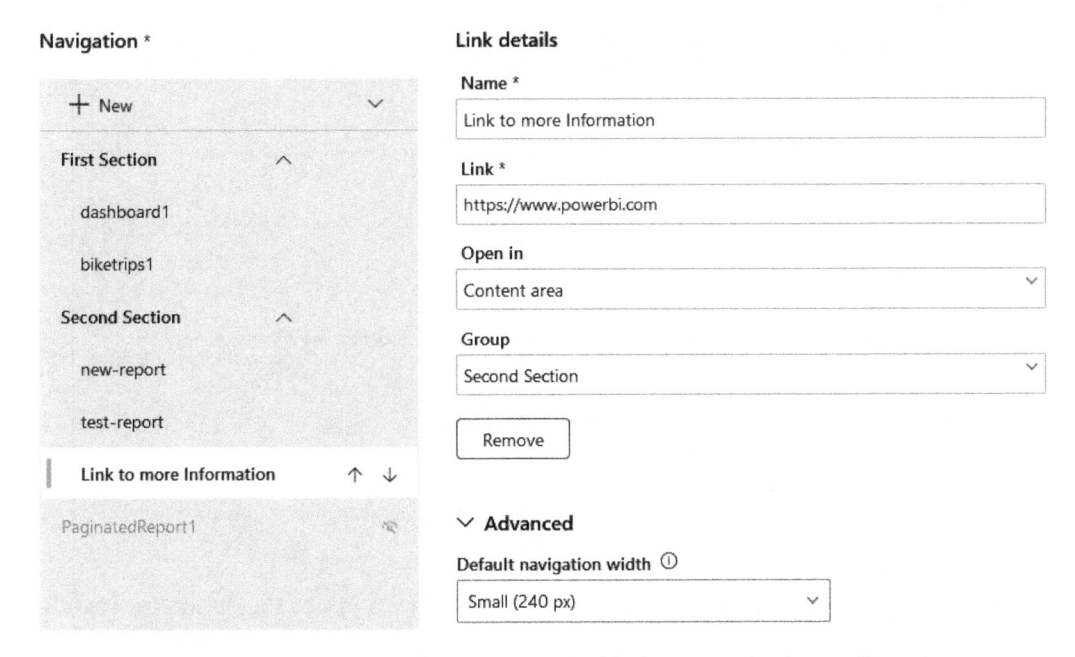

Figure 14.6 – Organizing workspace content inside the app navigation configuration

Lastly, you need to review the permissions that the app will have once it's published. Click the **Permissions** tab at the top of the screen to specify the users or groups that will have access to the app or that it will be available to all users in the organization.

294 Managing Workspaces

This is also where you specify downstream permissions that might need to change to the workspace and the containing assets, as well as giving (or revoking) permissions to copy reports in the app or allow sharing of the app and underlying assets.

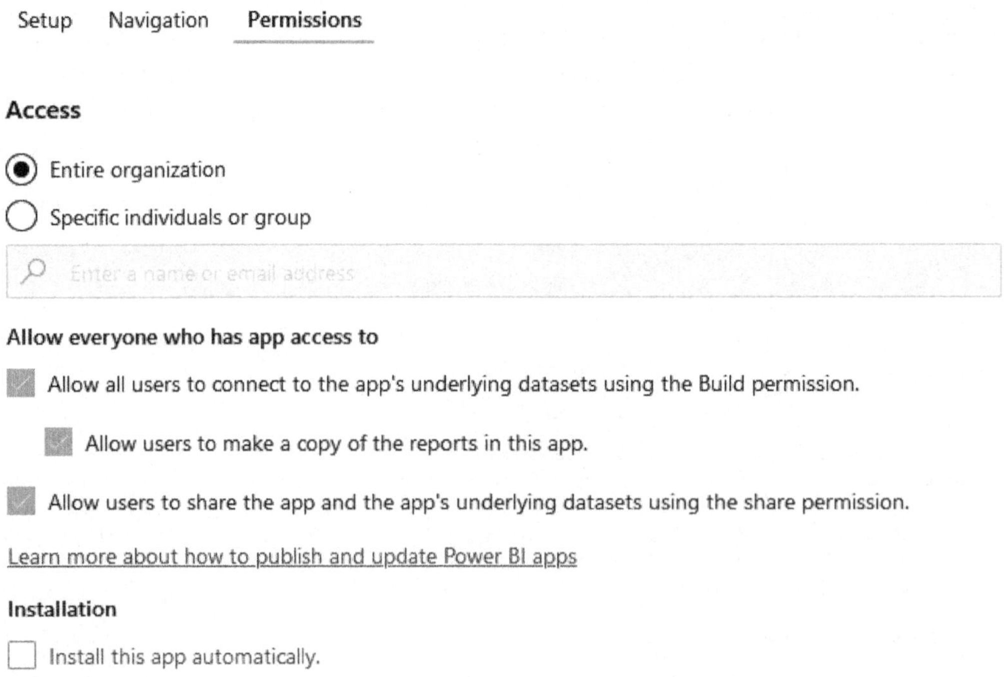

Setup   Navigation   **Permissions**

Access

◉ Entire organization

○ Specific individuals or group

🔍 Enter a name or email address

Allow everyone who has app access to

☑ Allow all users to connect to the app's underlying datasets using the Build permission.

☑ Allow users to make a copy of the reports in this app.

☑ Allow users to share the app and the app's underlying datasets using the share permission.

Learn more about how to publish and update Power BI apps

Installation

☐ Install this app automatically.

Figure 14.7 – Permissions configuration for a Power BI app

Figure 14.7 shows how permissions options can be set. You'll notice the option for **Install this app automatically.** is grayed out. This is disabled by default (as shown) but can be enabled in the Power BI admin portal by enabling it in **Tenant settings | Content pack and app settings | Push apps to end users**.

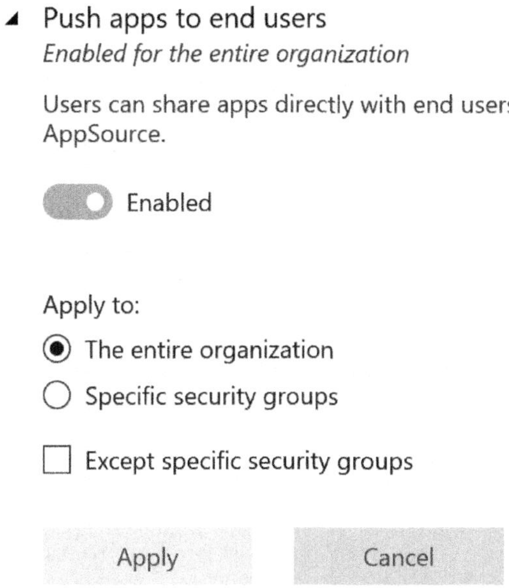

▲ Push apps to end users
Enabled for the entire organization

Users can share apps directly with end users without requiring installation from AppSource.

◖◗ Enabled

Apply to:
- ⦿ The entire organization
- ◯ Specific security groups

☐ Except specific security groups

[Apply] [Cancel]

Figure 14.8 – Enabling Push apps to end users in the Power BI admin portal

Once this default setting has been changed in the admin portal, as shown in *Figure 14.8*, then the option to install the app automatically for users will be available. Be aware that this option is only available if access to the app is for specific individuals or groups. In our example of publishing the app to the C-suite, we'd want to select a group that contains only the C-suite users and then install the app automatically so this published app is easily accessible to the end users.

Power BI apps are a useful way to help end users consume, find, and use reports and dashboards to answer important business questions. Apps provide content creators with a way to custom-tailor the content for the appropriate audience to increase impact.

In the next section, we'll see how workspaces are also helpful for the development life cycle.

Using deployment pipelines

In software development best practices, you never want to mix development work with work that has been completed, is of a known good quality, and is used for production. To do this, most organizations will have separate environments for development and production. Some organizations will have more environments in the middle, such as specific kinds of testing or preproduction. By securing who can access production environments, it will protect the code or artifacts deployed there from the introduction of software bugs or the running of code that has not been fully tested.

Most organizations will also use these multiple environments to set up specific teams of people who will be dedicated to the function of each environment. For example, only developers creating new artifacts or code will have access to the development environment, only testers will have access to the test environment, and only production operations teams will have access to the production environment. This is called **separation of duties**. By using separation of duties, the organization can help ensure that only properly developed and fully tested code or artifacts get used in production environments.

Power BI uses workspaces to help in the deployment process. Deployment pipelines allow you to set up a specific workspace for development, one for test and one for production. As we've already learned when workspaces are created, specific users or groups need to be added to them and a role defined for the users or groups. This provides the separation of duties capability that is required for proper development and deployment practices.

In addition to the workspace access capabilities, deployment pipelines in Power BI also provide a way to clone the content from one workspace to another. Connections within a workspace stay the same, which allows you to set up connections to development datasets (which tend to be smaller for the sake of storage and efficiency during development), while keeping testing and production datasets (which tend to be larger to serve production needs) intact in the testing and production workspaces.

By using deployment pipelines, Power BI developers can gain the benefits of software development best practices, such as testing out ideas in development environments before deploying to production, and organizations can gain peace of mind that production environments can be protected with separation of duties and putting proper testing in place before deploying to production.

Let's learn how we can use Power BI deployment pipelines in the next section.

Creating a deployment pipeline

To create a deployment pipeline for Power BI, log in to PowerBI.com with your work or school account. We need to be aware that deployment pipelines require the workspaces used to be deployed to either a Premium capacity or for PPU to be enabled in the workspace.

After logging into PowerBI.com, create or verify the workspaces that you'd like to use for each of the stages (development, test, and production). Be sure that these workspaces have been identified and click **Deployment pipelines** in the right-hand menu, as shown in *Figure 14.9*:

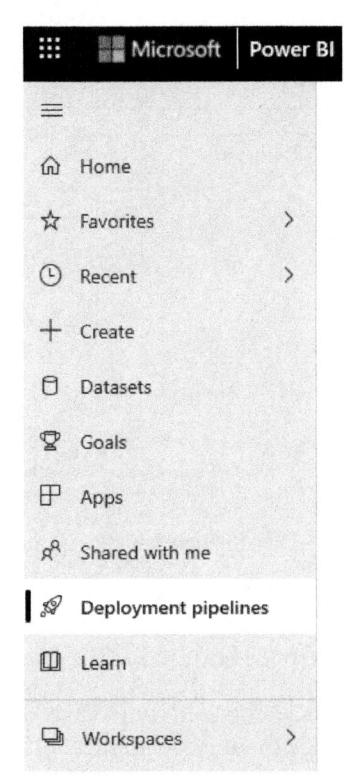

Figure 14.9 – Deployment pipelines in the Power BI menu

Deployment pipelines will not be available on the menu if you are not a Power BI Pro user and if your organization has not deployed Premium capacity or PPU. Deployment pipelines also require the new workspace (rather than the classic workspace) experience within Power BI.

On the **Deployment pipelines** screen, click the **Create pipeline** button. Provide a name and optional description for the pipeline and click **Create**.

298　Managing Workspaces

Next, you will see the main deployment pipelines configuration screen, as shown in *Figure 14.10*. This is where you will select which workspace is to be used for the development, testing, and production stages. To use a workspace for a deployment stage, you must be an admin of the workspace, it must not be assigned to another pipeline, and the workspace must reside on a Premium capacity or PPU license. Additionally, the workspace cannot contain Power BI samples (https://docs.microsoft.com/power-bi/create-reports/sample-datasets) and you must have the workspace members' permissions for adjacent stage workspaces.

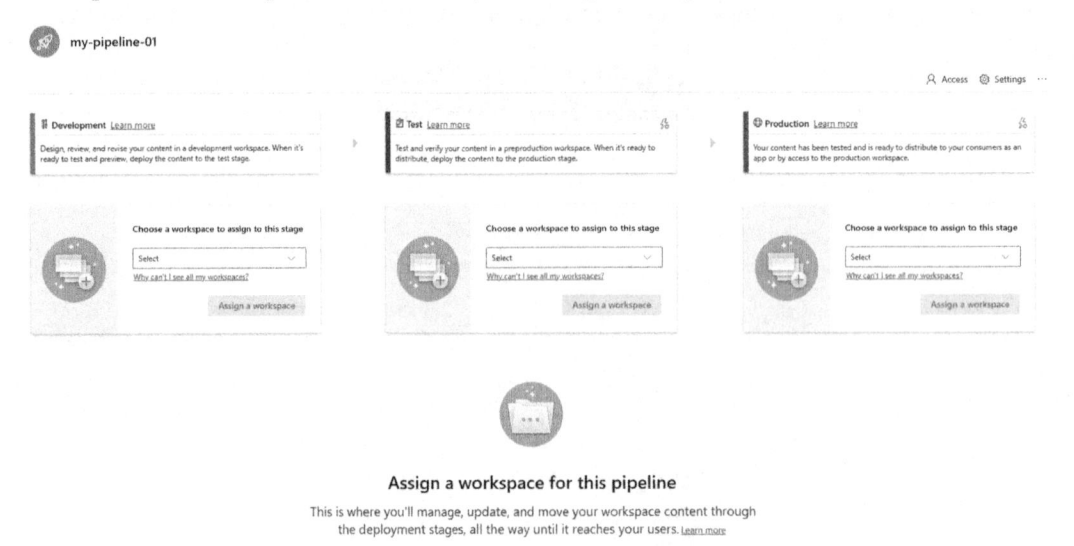

Figure 14.10 – Deployment pipelines configuration

On the deployment pipelines configuration page, you simply select the workspace to use for each stage from the drop-down list. Once the workspace is selected for a deployment stage, you click the **Assign a workspace** button and the workspace is assigned to the stage.

After this happens, the service checks the content of each stage workspace. If multiple stages are set up, then you'll also see the service identify differences between the stages. If both stages have the same content, then you'll see the symbol shown in *Figure 14.11* between the stages shown on the configuration page:

Figure 14.11 – Workspace stages are in sync

If there are differences between the stages, then you will see the symbol shown in *Figure 14.12* between the stages shown on the configuration page:

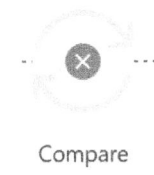

Compare

Figure 14.12 – Workspace stages are not in sync

When stages are not in sync and there are changes between them, the pipeline page makes it easy to see the differences by clicking **Compare**.

Compare will show the updates going from development to test or from test to production. This is helpful because there may be many reports, datasets, dataflows, or dashboards in a workspace and this tool will highlight the differences showing **New**, **Different**, and **Missing from**. It's helpful to have these highlights when verifying what needs to be reviewed between stages before deploying onward. In *Figure 14.13*, we can see that there are two new dashboards, one new report and a report and dataset, that are different from the test deployment stage. These are content items that you would need to review before moving from the development to the testing stages. The same process would happen between the testing and production stages:

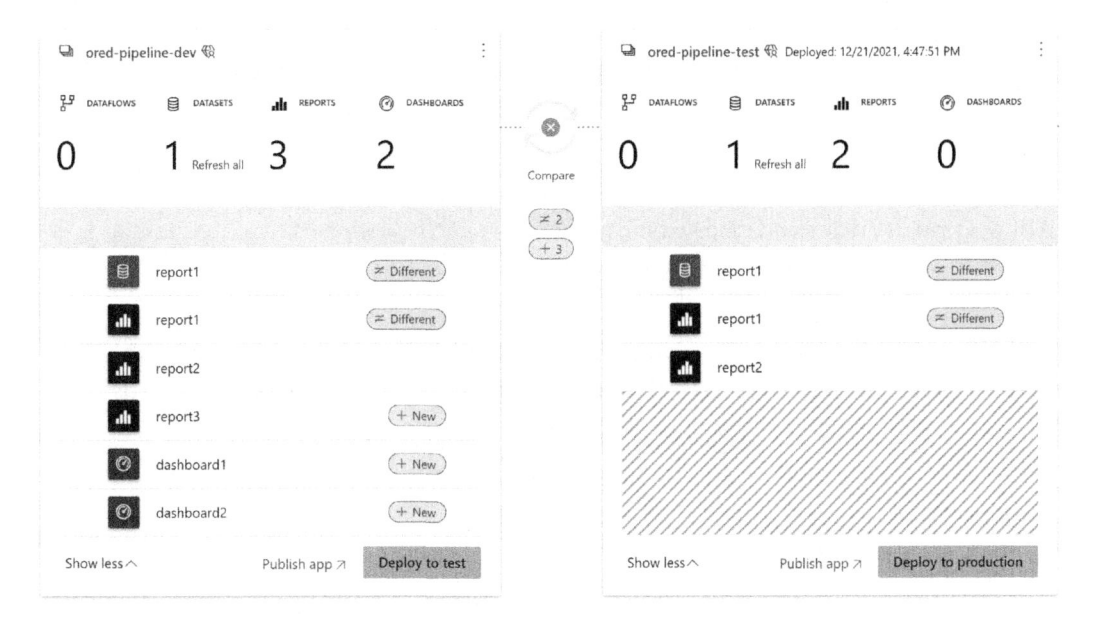

Figure 14.13 – Deployment pipeline showing changes between development and test

Once all content has been reviewed and established for your organization, you can move the content from development to testing by clicking the **Deploy to test** button. If there are items identified as **Different**, you will see a warning about replacing the content items in the next stage (testing, for example). When this has been confirmed by clicking **Continue**, then the process of cloning the content from the development stage workspace to the testing stage workspace will begin.

Unassigning a workspace to a deployment pipeline stage

It is possible to unassign a workspace from a deployment pipeline stage. To do this, click the menu for the stage and select **Unassign workspace**. The stage will need to be empty if you'd like to reassign the same workspace to this stage.

Automating deployment pipelines

Most software development teams utilize tools to automate processes and achieve continuous integration and continuous deployment. It's possible to use automation with Power BI deployment pipelines as well. There are multiple ways automation can be achieved with deployment pipelines.

For development teams that use Azure DevOps, there is either the open source extension for Power BI development pipelines (https://github.com/microsoft/powerbi-azure-pipelines-extensions) or the use of PowerShell to automate the process. You can find PowerShell examples in the Power BI developer samples GitHub repository (https://github.com/microsoft/PowerBI-Developer-Samples/).

It's also possible to automate deployment pipeline operations using the Power BI REST API (https://docs.microsoft.com/rest/api/power-bi/pipelines/). The REST API makes it possible to use many tools and processes, including custom applications, to facilitate the pipeline processes.

We will not go into depth on how to use these capabilities but for the purpose of the PL-300 exam, it is important to know these capabilities exist and how you would use them as an overall development process.

We will now look at how we can monitor the usage and performance of Power BI workspaces.

Monitoring workspace usage

Part of managing deployed workspaces includes understanding how the content they contain is used in the organization. Understanding how content such as reports and dashboards are used can help provide feedback on their improvement and the value the organization users get from them. For example, if a set of enterprise reports is created, tested, and deployed to production but never used or usage drops off, then it's possible something is missing; perhaps the analysis is correct but the way the information is presented in the report visuals make it less useful, so users stop using the reports. Knowing how users use reports that have been deployed is a key part of managing Power BI workspaces. **Usage metric reports** are the way the Power BI service provides insight into how end users interact with your workspace content.

Using usage reports

Usage for reports and dashboards are surfaced with the help of reports that are generated by the Power BI service. Usage metrics reports can be generated by selecting the **View usage metrics** report under the menu button for each report or dashboard, as shown in *Figure 14.14*:

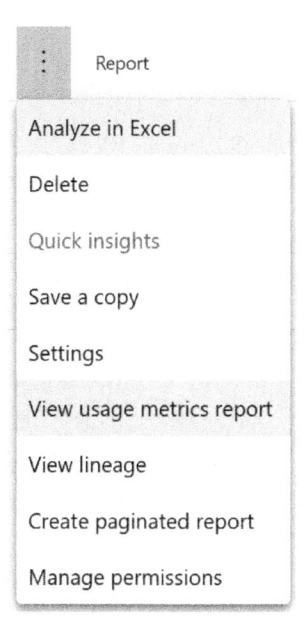

Figure 14.14 – Menu for a Power BI report

Usage metrics reports are generated by the Power BI service and at the time of writing contain data going back 30 days of usage history for new workspaces. When these reports are generated by the service, they create Power BI datasets and are accessible via the built-in reports as well as through the **Analyze with Excel** capability of Power BI. This allows for customization of reporting from the dataset.

Usage metrics reports include how many times reports are used or opened, unique viewers of reports, total report page views and by date, how end users arrived at the reports (via the workspace, shared from another user, or via an app), the time it takes for reports to open, the overall performance for the day and week, which web browsers are used, and many other metrics that are key to understanding the usability and value of the reports to the end users.

Usage metrics reporting requires Power BI Pro or PPU licensing to view. However, usage data is collected for all users of the reports. Additionally, Power BI administrators can enable or disable usage metrics for content creators, and per-user data also needs to be enabled in the admin portal.

Refining and improving your Power BI solutions requires a good understanding of how users are using the content available to them. Usage metrics reporting is an easy-to-use and helpful way of gathering these insights.

Summary

In this chapter, we learned about managing workspaces in Power BI.

We learned how user roles work in workspaces and how roles provide a way to manage users and groups within a workspace to ensure proper access and permissions are available to users as needed. We also learned how workspaces can have different kinds of licensing that will enable different advanced or enterprise capabilities. We learned that workspaces can be assigned different amounts of resources for hosting in a Premium capacity.

We learned how workspaces can be packaged as a Power BI app, which helps end users find and utilize the content created in reports and dashboards. Apps provide a way to curate content and distribute it among organizational users.

We also learned how software development best practices can be implemented using deployment pipelines. We learned that deployment pipelines use the basic unit of organization provided by workspaces.

Lastly, we discovered how important it is to understand and use the usage metric capabilities of the Power BI service to gain insights into how end users use the content being created in Power BI. Understanding how users use content is key to improving over time and providing the right value for the needs of the organization.

In the next chapter, we will look at how we can apply some best practices to managing Power BI datasets.

Questions

1. Advanced capabilities of Power BI may require a licensed version of Power BI. Licensed versions of Power BI include:

    A. Premium and Advanced

    B. Plus and Pro

    C. Power BI 2022

    D. Pro and Premium

2. Which workspace role has permissions to delete a workspace?

    A. Owner

    B. Admin

    C. Member

    D. Contributor

3. Which stages are used in Power BI deployment pipelines?

    A. Development and production

    B. Development, test, and production

    C. Development, test, preproduction, and production

    D. Development, integration testing, user acceptance testing, and production

4. How many days of history will usage metrics reporting show?

    A. 90

    B. 60

    C. 30

    D. Unlimited

15
Managing Datasets

Once you have published your Power BI report on the service, there are a few more things that need to be configured. When published, a Power BI report can create two artifacts in the Power BI service, the report itself and the report's dataset. The dataset is everything except the report pages; the tables, the columns, the relationships, and the measures all make up the dataset.

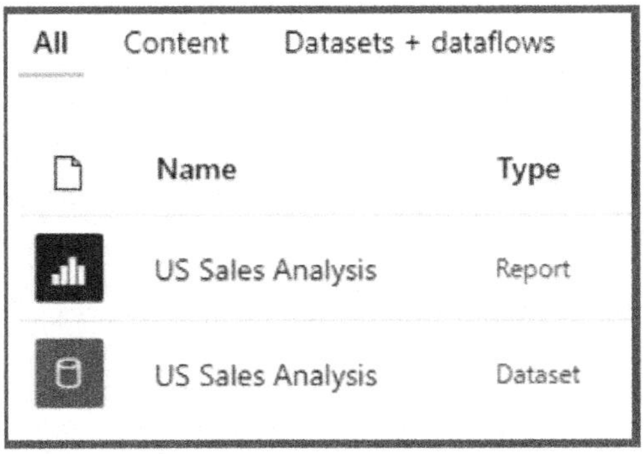

Figure 15.1 – One report in Power BI Desktop creates two artifacts in the Power BI service

In this chapter, we will cover how to administer the dataset, how to make sure the date data in the dataset is up to date, how to limit that data to only the people and groups who need it, and how to provide access to your dataset so other report creators can use it for their reports.

In this chapter, we will cover the following:

- Configuring a dataset scheduled refresh
- Identifying when a gateway is required
- Configuring row-level security group membership
- Providing access to datasets

This part of the exam is all about configuring your dataset after publishing. This is a very important step that if skipped could lead to out-of-date reports or report users accessing data that they should not.

Technical requirements

The following are the prerequisites in order to complete the work in this chapter:

- Microsoft Power BI Desktop installed on a Microsoft Windows PC.
- We've also provided synthetic data that can be used, which is available in the GitHub repository for this book here: `https://github.com/PacktPublishing/Microsoft-Power-BI-Data-Analyst-Certification-Guide/tree/main/example-data`.

Configuring a dataset scheduled refresh

It is very important to have not only accurate but also timely data for your reports. Looking at a sales forecast report for last year, or even last week's inventory report, may lead you to making the wrong business decisions. To keep your imported Power BI report data up to date, you will have to refresh the data by pulling data from the data source. You can manually refresh the data of a dataset, but this can be inconvenient, to say the least. An easier way is to have the Power BI service schedule the refresh for you.

To schedule a refresh, go to the workspace you published the report to and select the **Datasets + dataflows** option from the menu, then hover your mouse over the dataset name. When you do that, the refresh now and schedule refresh icons will appear; select the schedule refresh icon.

This will open the dataset settings page, where you can then set up scheduled refreshes.

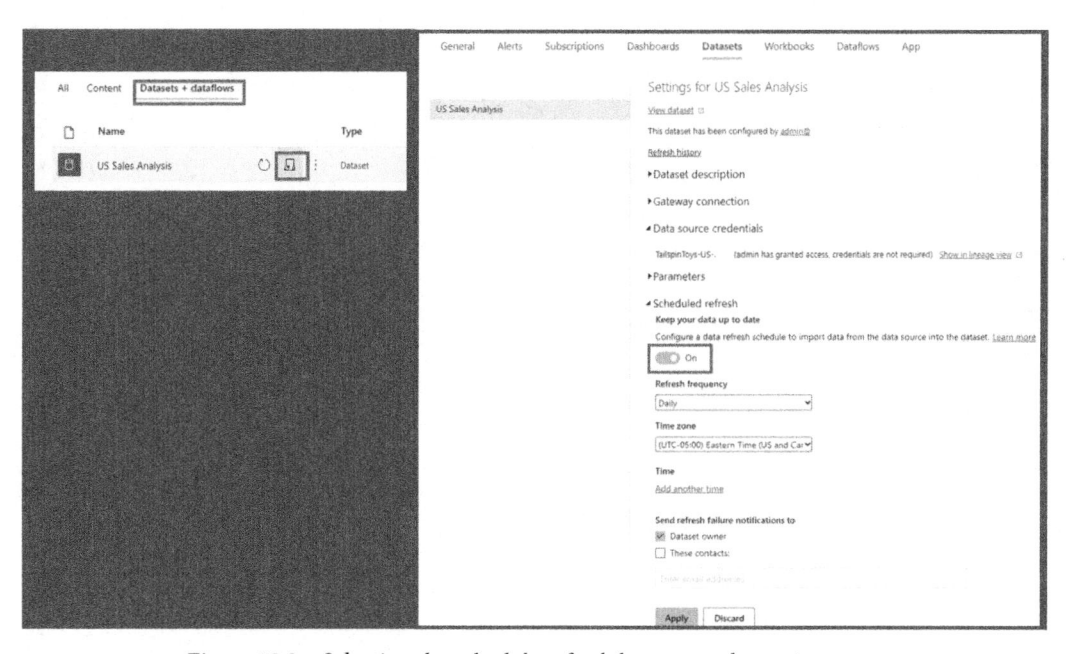

Figure 15.2 – Selecting the schedule refresh button on the settings page

Refreshes can be scheduled daily or weekly. You can schedule a dataset to be refreshed up to 48 times a day if the dataset is in a Premium workspace. If it is not, then you can only schedule up to eight refreshes daily.

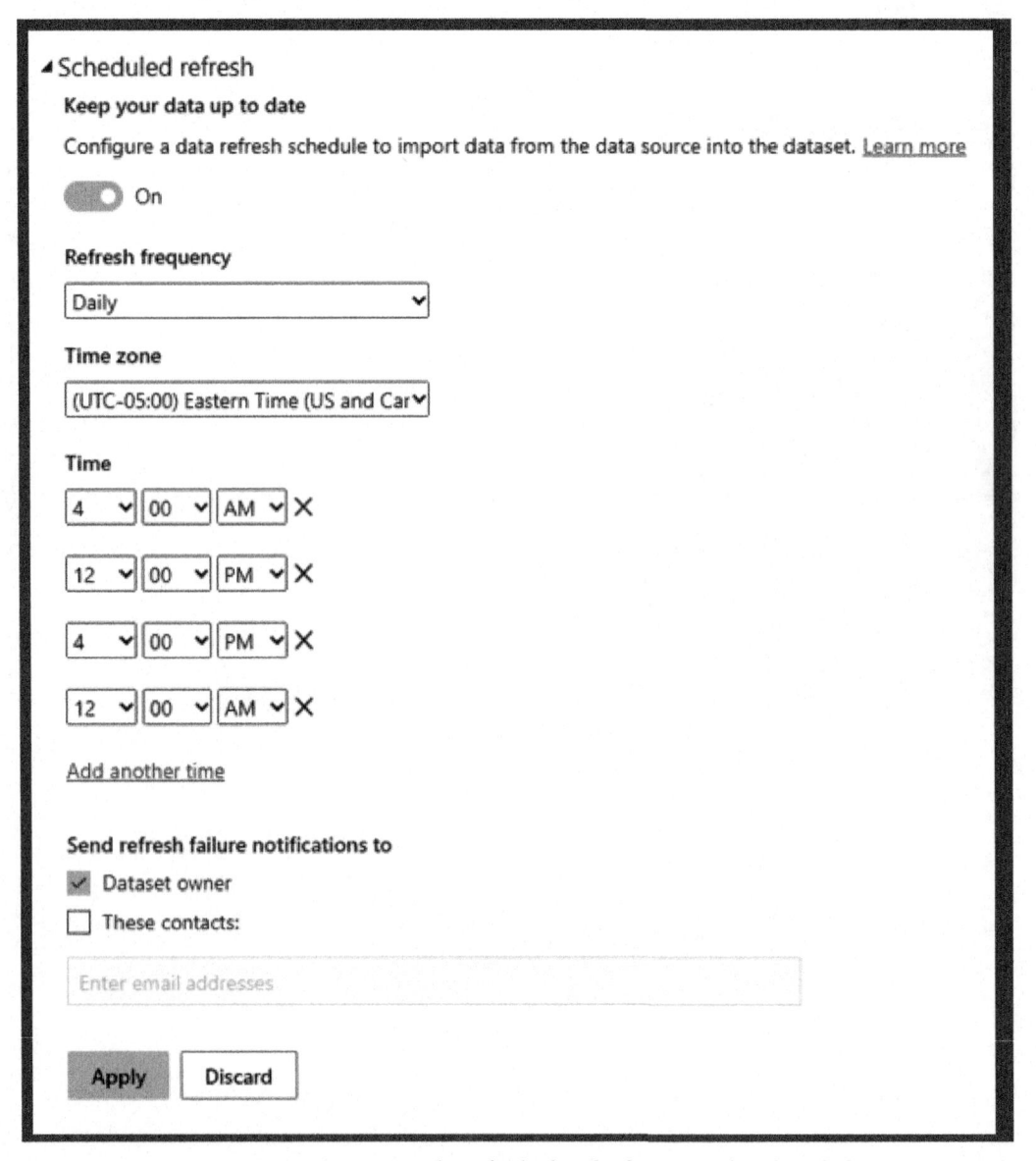

Figure 15.3 – Datasets can be refreshed multiple times a day if needed

You can also add people to be notified if a refresh fails.

Identifying when a gateway is required

Power BI can directly connect to most cloud-based data sources. If your data source is on-premises, you will need to install and configure an on-premises data gateway. You will not need to know how to install a gateway for the exam. But you *will* need to know when it is necessary.

The Power BI service will inform you if a gateway is necessary. There is a **Gateway connection** option on the dataset settings page. If your dataset requires a gateway, this section will inform you that you have not configured your dataset to use an on-premises data gateway.

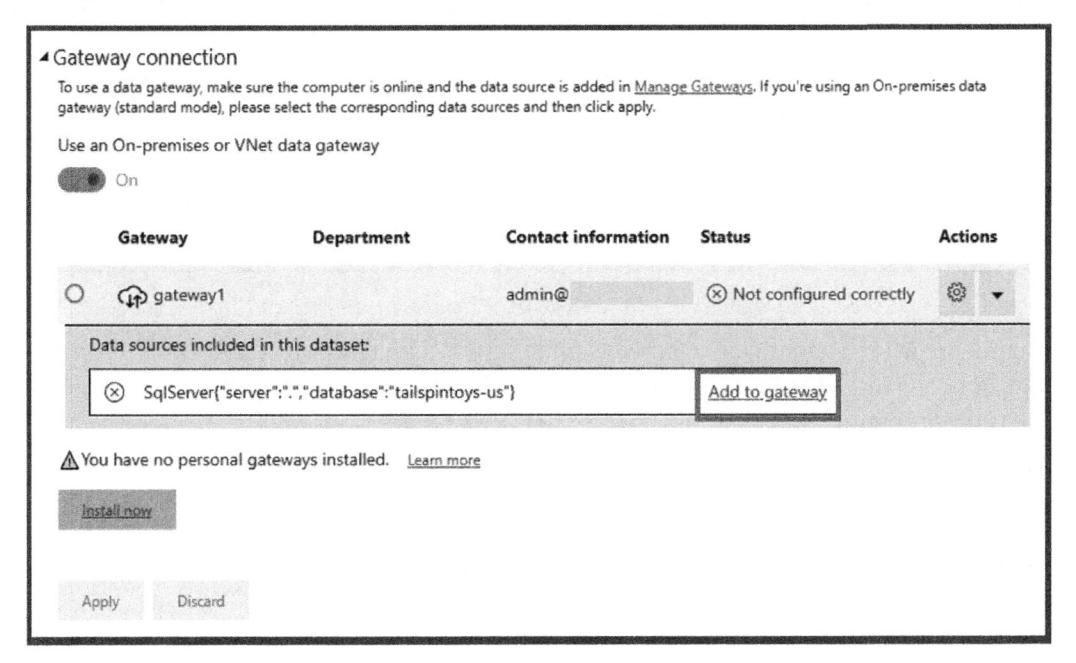

Figure 15.4 – If a gateway is needed, the Power BI service will inform you

Once you add your dataset's data source to the gateway, the error will go away and you can refresh the dataset as needed.

> **Test Tip**
>
> You will not be able to enable the slider to schedule a refresh if a gateway is required and not set up.

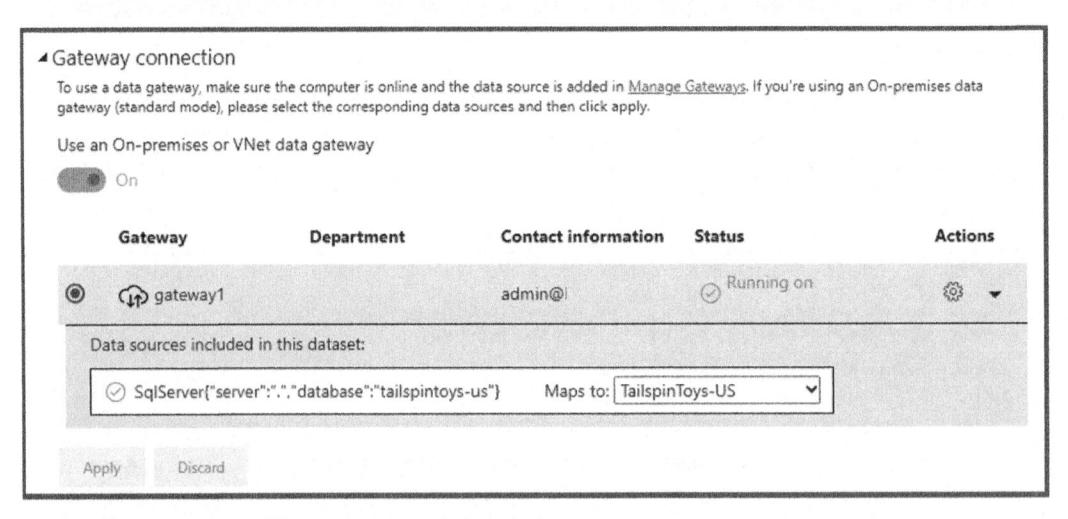

Figure 15.5 – A data source set to use a gateway

Identifying when a gateway is required is quite simple. The Power BI service will inform you, either by disabling the scheduled refresh or with a *not correctly configured* message in the **Gateway connection** area.

Configuring row-level security group membership

As you saw in *Chapter 5, Designing a Data Model*, you can use DAX to filter your reports for row-level security. Once you publish your dataset to the Power BI service, you can enforce row-level security by assigning users or groups to the roles you created.

Power BI uses **Azure Active Directory** (**AAD**) for security. You can add members or AAD security groups to the roles created in a report. Row-level security can use distribution groups, security groups, or mail-enabled security groups.

> **Test Tip**
>
> Row-level security cannot use Microsoft 365 groups.

Configuring row-level security group membership   311

It is important to note that row-level security only applies to users that have Viewer access to the workspace. If a user is directly assigned or a member of a group is assigned to a role with more elevated permissions, row-level security will not apply. That means that anyone who has been assigned the Contributor, Member, or Admin role in the workspace will see all the data, unfiltered by row-level security.

> **Test Tip**
>
> Row-level security does not apply to anyone with editing permissions to the workspace.

Assigning a user or group to a role starts with the dataset. Go to the **Datasets + dataflows** page from the menu, then hover your mouse over the dataset name and open the drop-down menu by clicking on the three vertical dots. Select the **Security** option from the menu.

Figure 15.6 – Row-level security is configured from the security page

This will open the row-level security page. If your dataset has roles defined, you will see them listed here.

Select the role you want to assign users or groups to and use the search box to find them in AAD. Once you have assigned the required members to the role, click **Save**.

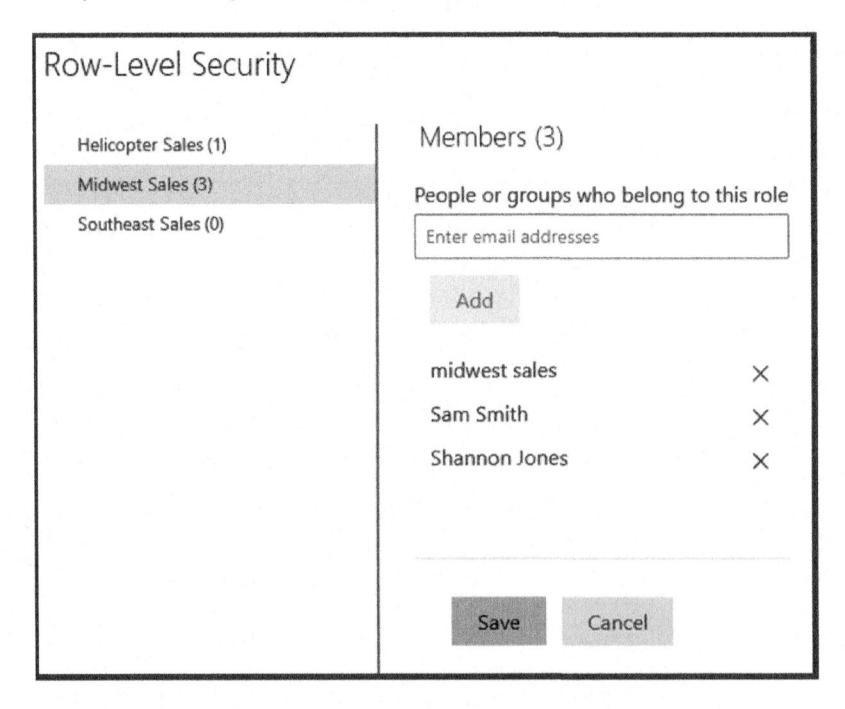

```
Row-Level Security

Helicopter Sales (1)          Members (3)
Midwest Sales (3)
Southeast Sales (0)           People or groups who belong to this role

                              [ Enter email addresses            ]

                                        Add

                              midwest sales                    ✕
                              Sam Smith                        ✕
                              Shannon Jones                    ✕



                                   Save      Cancel
```

Figure 15.7 – Adding users or groups to row-level security by searching AAD

Once you have populated all the row-level security roles, you are done.

Providing access to datasets

One of the great things about Power BI is that you can reuse datasets from other reports to create your own reports. This allows you to minimize the memory used by Power BI and keep all your reports consistent. If you have ever been to a meeting where everyone is arguing about the numbers and where they came from, then you know that having one, consistent source of data can be invaluable.

Another reason to use the same dataset is that you only have to refresh the data for one dataset instead of many. This leads to less strain on the source system.

You can automatically connect to any dataset in any workspace where you are a Contributor, Member, or Admin. You will need to be granted access to any other dataset, on a dataset-by-dataset basis.

To grant someone access, open the **Datasets + dataflows** page from the menu, then hover your mouse over the dataset name and open the drop-down menu by clicking on the three vertical dots. Select **Manage permissions** from the menu.

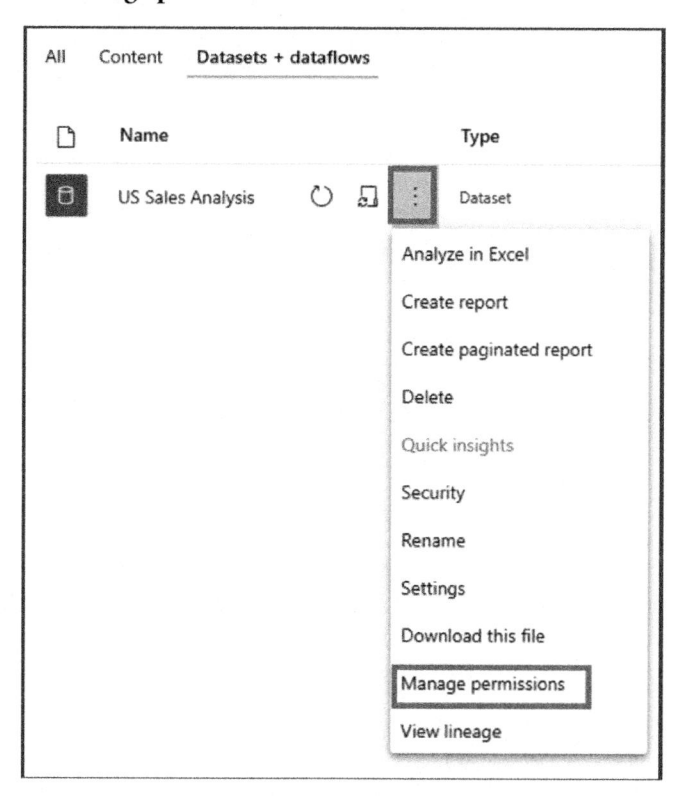

Figure 15.8 – Use Manage permissions to share your dataset

This will open the **Manage permissions** page. On this page, you can grant a user or group permission to use the dataset by clicking on the **+Add user** button. This will open a window that will let you grant access to users or groups.

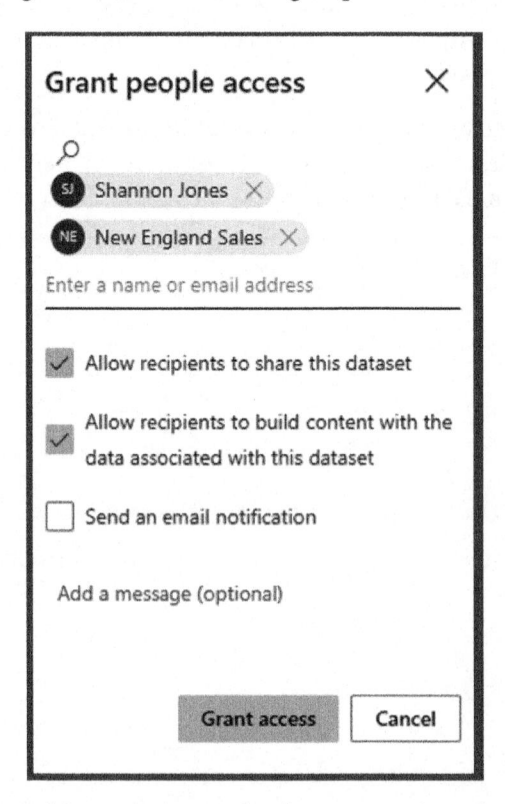

Figure 15.9 – Granting anything more than read-only access requires selecting one or more of the options

Granting access to the dataset grants the users read-only access to that dataset. This will allow them to see the dataset information page; it does not allow them to use the dataset to create new reports. For that, you have three additional permission choices:

- **Allow recipients to share this dataset**
- **Allow recipients to build content with the data associated with this dataset**
- **Send an email notification**

If you want a user or group to have permission to create new reports based on the dataset, make sure that the second choice is selected. If you want them to be able to share the dataset with others who may make reports, select the first. If you want to inform the users or groups that you have shared the dataset with them, check the **Send email** option.

You can create new reports using the datasets that you have published or that have been shared with you by selecting **Power BI datasets** under the **Get data** option or clicking on the Power BI dataset icon on the **Home** ribbon of Power BI Desktop.

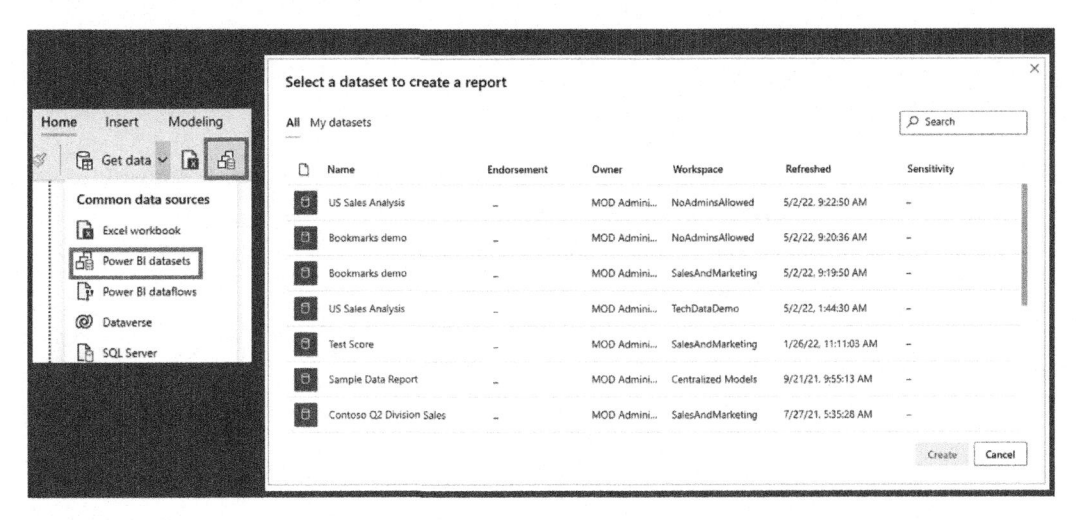

Figure 15.10 – Reusing datasets in Power BI Desktop

Once you have selected Power BI datasets as your source, all the datasets you have access to will be available for you to use.

Reusing Power BI datasets allows you to use the same, consistent data across multiple reports with a simplified refresh schedule.

Summary

In this chapter, you learned a lot about Power BI datasets, including the fact that when you publish a report to Power BI, the service splits the report into two artifacts, the report and the dataset.

Once you publish your report and dataset to the Power BI service, the data in the dataset should be kept up to date. Though you could just import the data into Power BI Desktop and republish it, you learned a much better way, which is scheduling a refresh. If your data is on-premises, you need to use an on-premises data gateway for that data refresh. The on-premises data gateway allows you to synchronize data between your on-premises data sources and your Power BI datasets.

You also learned about a very important topic, how to enforce the row-level security you built into your data model in Powe BI Desktop. Using AAD, row-level security allows you to assign DAX filters to users or groups so they only see the data that they are supposed to see.

Sharing datasets allows you and other report creators to use the same semantic model, with the same tables, columns, and measures. Sharing also means that you only have to refresh one dataset instead of many.

In the next chapter, you will look at how to manage Power BI workspaces in the Power BI service.

Questions

1. If I need to use an on-premises SQL Server as a source for my report that will use an import query of a dataset, what should I do?

    A. You must move all of your data to Azure.

    B. This is not possible.

    C. Use a self-hosted integration runtime.

    D. Use an on-premises data gateway.

2. How many times per day can a dataset refresh be scheduled in a Premium workspace?

    A. 24

    B. 48

    C. 96

    D. 12

3. Row-level security only applies to users who have workspace access at what level?

    A. Member

    B. Admin

    C. Viewer

    D. All of the above

Part 6 – Practice Exams

This section helps you get familiar with the exam format and also has sample questions that you can work on.

This section comprises the following chapter:

- *Chapter 16, Practice Exams*

16
Practice Exams

This chapter contains two practice tests that will help you better understand whether you are ready to take the exam. The sample exam questions and answers will give you the confidence you need to sit the exam. Please remember to pick the best answer for each question or statement.

This chapter comprises the following sections:

- Practice test 1
- Practice test 2
- Answer key for practice tests 1 and 2

Practice test 1

1. When a selected visual is shown over the entire canvas, what is this feature called?

    A. Enhanced mode
    B. Expanded mode
    C. Focus mode
    D. Fullscreen mode

2. If a report has slicers and a clustered column chart with a trend line, how often will the trend line update?

    A. When data is refreshed
    B. When a new visual is added
    C. When a slicer or filter changes or when data is refreshed
    D. When a filter is applied

3. To understand the top key influencers of a specific amount, such as for the order quantity to be exactly 5, which analysis type would you need to use in the key influencers visual?

    A. Numeric
    B. Statistical
    C. Categorical
    D. Continuous

4. Power BI is used by:

    A. Only enterprise organizations
    B. Only university students
    C. A variety of enterprise and citizen developers
    D. Only cutting-edge developers

5. To sort records by a whole number-type column from lowest to highest, what operation do you need to use?

    A. Sort low to high
    B. Sort ascending
    C. Sort descending
    D. Sort alphabetical

6. What are the required parameters of the RANKX function?

    A. Table, expression
    B. Table, expression, order
    C. Value, order
    D. Table, order

7. To use responsive slicers, the slicer must contain:

   A. A date range
   B. A time range
   C. Relative dates
   D. A selection list of values

8. What four possible cardinalities does Power BI have?

   A. Many-to-one, one-to-many, many-to-some, and one-to-one
   B. Many-to-one, one-to-many, many-to-many, and one-to-one
   C. Many-to-one, one-to-many, many-to-many, and one-to-two
   D. Many-to-two, one-to-many, many-to-many, and one-to-one

9. Which visual is the most similar representation of tabular data to a database table?

   A. Stacked bar chart
   B. Clustered column chart
   C. Table visual
   D. Pie chart

10. Which page do you set drillthrough up on?

    A. The starting page
    B. The target page
    C. The Power BI admin portal
    D. The workspace settings

11. To implement row-level security, what needs to be applied to the table?

    A. M query
    B. WHERE clause
    C. DAX expression
    D. SQL query

12. What are the three stages supported by deployment pipelines?

    A. Training, test, and production

    B. Training, integration testing, and production

    C. Development, test, and production

    D. Development, UAT, and production

13. Using Power BI will be familiar for users of which service?

    A. Microsoft Word

    B. Adobe Photoshop

    C. Microsoft Edge

    D. Microsoft Excel

14. To bring data together from multiple queries where the structure is different but there are matching columns from both tables, we use:

    A. A left outer join query

    B. A right outer join query

    C. An append query

    D. A merge query

15. The three types of geographical map visuals are:

    A. Map, filled map, and GIS map

    B. Map, filled map, and ArcGIS map

    C. Map, colored map, and GIS map

    D. Google Maps, Apple Maps, and Bing Maps

16. To change the data type of a column in the Power Query Editor, what do you need to use?

    A. Type selector under the Files tab

    B. Data type selector under the Queries tab

    C. Type selector under the Data tab

    D. Data type selector under the Transform tab

17. Which option is a way to reduce the data size?

    A. Multiplication
    B. Aggregation
    C. Duplication
    D. Miniaturization

18. Why is it important to cleanse and transform data?

    A. Date representations in datasets might be different.
    B. Data types of the matching columns might be different in datasets you need to merge.
    C. Datasets you need to merge might require creating columns.
    D. All of the above.

19. If your data contains demographic data about customers and you want to understand buying habits for certain age ranges, what technique would you use to analyze your data?

    A. Merging
    B. Ranging
    C. Aging
    D. Binning

20. Power BI uses two engines. What are the names of these two engines?

    A. Calculation and storage
    B. Formula and persistence
    C. Formula and storage
    D. V8 and diesel

21. The auto date/time option in the data load options will do what?

    A. Automatically save the current date and time to your report.
    B. Automatically add dates to all tables loaded.
    C. Create a hidden date hierarchy table.
    D. Create a hidden timetable.

22. Visuals from published reports can be added to a dashboard with a process called:

    A. Glueing
    B. Pinning
    C. Copy and paste
    D. Sharing

23. What does DAX stand for?

    A. DatabAses for eXcel
    B. Data Advanced Expressions
    C. Data Analysis for "X"
    D. Data Analysis eXpressions

24. To view descriptive statistical information about each column of your data, which tool do you need to use?

    A. Column information under the Data tab
    B. Column statistics under the View tab
    C. Column profile under the View tab
    D. Column profile under the Data tab

25. By default, the Power Query Editor uses how many rows of data?

    A. All of the data
    B. The first 100 rows
    C. The first 500 rows
    D. The first 1,000 rows

26. Power BI content and datasets are published to what?

    A. A database
    B. A workspace
    C. An environment
    D. A workbench

27. Which sets of methods are valid ways the Power Query Editor can add columns?

    A. Column from Example, Custom Column, and Key Column
    B. Column from Example, Custom Column, and Index Column
    C. Column from Example, Invoke Custom Function, and IF/THEN Column
    D. Column from Example, Custom Column, and Column from Join

28. What methods can be used with AI to generate data using the Power Query Editor?

    A. Language detection, language translation, sentiment analysis, and image tagging
    B. Language detection, key phrase extraction, mind reading, and image tagging
    C. Language detection, key phrase extraction, sentiment analysis, and image tagging
    D. Language detection, key phrase extraction, sentiment analysis, and text to speech

29. Scheduled data refreshes take place within a time window you set in the service. What is the length of the time window?

    A. 5 minutes
    B. 10 minutes
    C. 15 minutes
    D. 30 minutes

30. Which data sources can Power BI can connect to?

    A. Databases
    B. Filesystems
    C. Software-as-a-service providers
    D. All of the above

31. Power BI is designed to work with:

    A. Many data sources
    B. Only one data source
    C. Only two data sources
    D. One or two data sources

32. Which is an example of a non-additive measure?

    A. Percent increase
    B. Unit price
    C. Sales amount
    D. Purchase order total

33. Direct query performance optimization often includes:

    A. Reducing the size of data in the data model and indexing data in the data model
    B. Indexes on the source data, dimension-to-fact table key integrity, materializing data and dates, and distributed tables for MPP databases
    C. Only considering distributed tables for MPP databases
    D. Indexing the source files in a search engine

34. The usage metrics report capability in Power BI includes pre-built reports with what information?

    A. Premium Per User and Per Capacity usage, report usage, report performance, and report list
    B. Premium Per User capacity usage, report usage, report performance, and report list
    C. Report usage, report performance, and report list
    D. Report usage and report performance

35. Which mode needs to be installed for multiple users to access on-premises data sources?

    A. Personal mode on-premises data gateway
    B. Multi-user mode on-premises data gateway
    C. Standard mode on-premises data gateway
    D. Enterprise mode on-premises data gateway

36. To change the colors used on a visual, which section do you need to change?

    A. Change your visual.
    B. Edit your visual.
    C. Format your visual.
    D. Color your visual.

37. What is the recommended tool for optimizing measures?

    A. Microsoft Edge
    B. Visual Studio Code
    C. DAX Studio
    D. Power Query Editor

38. Power BI supports what kind of visuals?

    A. Only built-in
    B. Only custom
    C. Built-in and open source
    D. Built-in and custom

39. It is often hard for businesses to do what?

    A. Know how much they will pay for Power BI.
    B. Use Power BI to understand their data.
    C. Pay their employees what they are worth.
    D. See a complete picture of what is happening across the enterprise.

40. When using sensitivity labels in Power BI, when does downstream inheritance happen?

    A. When downstream data becomes unusable
    B. When downstream data is made available for everyone to use
    C. When the same sensitivity labels are applied to downstream data products
    D. When the same sensitivity labels are applied to all data products

41. The filtering pane allows filtering by:

    A. Visual and page
    B. Visual, page, and all pages
    C. Visual, page, all pages, and reports
    D. Visual, page, all pages, and dashboards

42. To update data in a Power BI dataset, what capability must you use?

   A. Data reload
   B. Update dataset
   C. Update model
   D. Data refresh

43. What is the default canvas type for a report?

   A. 4:3
   B. 3:2
   C. 10:5
   D. 16:9

44. What are two common types of encoding used by Power BI to compress data?

   A. Value and distinct
   B. Value and hash
   C. Value and Snappy
   D. Snappy and ZIP

45. For advanced natural-language queries using domain-specific words, you may need to use what?

   A. The built-in, general-purpose linguistic model
   B. A custom linguistic model
   C. A custom theme
   D. A custom data model

46. When enabling column quality in Power Query Editor, what values are shown for each column?

   A. Number of valid, duplicate, and empty
   B. Percent of valid, duplicate, and empty
   C. Percent of valid, error, and empty
   D. Number of valid, error, and empty

47. What feature of Power BI reports allows you to capture the current state of a report page?

    A. Snapshot
    B. Favorites
    C. Bookmarks
    D. Freeze page

48. What does being "data-driven" mean?

    A. Using autonomous automobiles
    B. Business process improvement
    C. Using data to make business decisions
    D. Using the latest technology

49. What is Power BI?

    A. Software you download
    B. Software and a service
    C. Only a service
    D. Only a mobile app

50. DAX functions must return how many values?

    A. Two
    B. One or more
    C. One
    D. Minimum of one

51. When you create a report that allows end users to jump to a target page in your report that focuses on a selected data value, what feature are you using?

    A. Drillthrough
    B. Bookmarks
    C. Hyperlinks
    D. Favorites

52. What configuration should be changed to use a measure in a drillthrough?

    A. Cross-filter direction set to both.
    B. Cross-filter direction set from starting page to target page.
    C. Allow drillthrough when summarized.
    D. Allow drillthrough when used as a category.

53. What are the three layout options for the bookmark navigator?

    A. Grid, upright, and level
    B. Grid, vertical, and level
    C. Grid, upright, and horizontal
    D. Grid, vertical, and horizontal

54. Which transformation replaces empty or null values in a column with the value from the adjacent row, defined as either up or down methods?

    A. Fill
    B. Replace
    C. Generate
    D. Create data

55. The formula engine interacts with data stored where?

    A. It doesn't interact with data.
    B. The storage engine and directly with data sources.
    C. Directly with data sources.
    D. The storage engine.

56. Slicers can be used to remove data from a report visual:

    A. Permanently from Power BI
    B. Temporarily until the next refresh
    C. Only while selected in the slicer
    D. Permanently from the source

57. What does the "BI" in Power BI stand for?

    A. Business intelligence
    B. Better intelligence
    C. Business interactive
    D. Business information

58. XMLA is the protocol used by:

    A. Extensible Markup Analytics
    B. Microsoft Analytics Cloud
    C. Power BI Analytics Services
    D. Microsoft SQL Server Analysis Services

59. What Azure service is used for **Bring Your Own Key (BYOK)** encryption in Power BI?

    A. Azure Power BI Embedded
    B. Azure Private Link
    C. Azure ExpressRoute
    D. Azure Key Vault

60. When a calculated column is added to a query with 100 rows, how many values are added to the storage of the query?

    A. 0
    B. 100
    C. 50
    D. 25

Practice Test 2

1. Why is it important to know about null and error rows in your data?

    A. Error rows always mean you need to reimport the data.
    B. Because null value rows make Power BI slower.
    C. So the rows can be fixed or removed.
    D. Because business value is always in the rows with null values.

2. Dashboards can be viewed from what kind of devices and software?

    A. Power BI Desktop
    B. Only mobile devices
    C. Desktop web browsers and mobile devices
    D. Only desktop web browsers

3. What feature allows you to use natural language to ask questions of a Power BI data model?

    A. Q&A
    B. Natural language processing
    C. Cortana
    D. Advanced questions

4. Which type of relationship is it recommended not to use?

    A. One-to-many
    B. Many-to-some
    C. One-to-one
    D. Many-to-many

5. What does Power BI Desktop run on?

    A. Windows and macOS operating systems
    B. Only Windows-based operating systems
    C. Windows, macOS, and Android operating systems
    D. Windows, macOS, and Linux

6. Custom visuals can be imported from a central service called what?

    A. Microsoft Store
    B. Office Store
    C. AppSource
    D. Power Platform Store

7. What is mobile layout used to configure?

    A. Mobile device management

    B. The layout of the dashboard for mobile devices

    C. The deployment of Power BI for mobile devices

    D. Which reports are viewable on mobile devices

8. What sort of information does the column profile in the Power Query Editor show?

    A. Count, min, max, and confidence interval

    B. Count, error, empty, min, max, average, and standard deviation

    C. Count, min, max, range, and standard deviation

    D. Min, max, average, empty, and variance

9. What is the default kind of slicer shown for a date column?

    A. Sharp slicer

    B. Checkbox slicer

    C. Range slicer

    D. Month slicer

10. For holistic data protection capabilities, sensitivity labels in Power BI integrate with what service?

    A. Cloud Information Analytics Services

    B. Microsoft Information Protection

    C. Microsoft Protect

    D. Power BI Data Protection Service

11. Which DAX function evaluates an expression in a modified filter context?

    A. CALCULATE

    B. SUM

    C. COMPUTE

    D. FILTERCALC

12. Which bin type options does Power BI support?

    A. Length of bins and number of bins

    B. Width of bins and number of bins

    C. Size of bins and number of bins

    D. Size of bins and count of bins

13. The concept of defining the smallest level of data used in our report is described as what?

    A. Rice

    B. Grain

    C. Detail level

    D. Magnification

14. What feature allows you to confirm whether row-level security has been set up correctly for another user?

    A. Impersonate user

    B. View as

    C. Performance Analyzer

    D. Security analyzer

15. What are the three Play Axis visual animation settings?

    A. Auto start, loop, and time

    B. Cycle mode, playback speed, and default animation

    C. Play/pause, stop, and next

    D. Cycle mode, loop, and time

16. Power BI dashboards are created using what tool?

    A. Power BI Desktop

    B. Power BI service

    C. Power BI Embedded

    D. SQL Server Reporting Services

17. What information does column distribution in the Power Query Editor show?

    A. Value distribution bar chart and number of distinct and unique values
    B. Value distribution bar chart and number of distinct and duplicate values
    C. Value distribution line chart and number of distinct and unique values
    D. Value distribution line chart and number of distinct and duplicate values

18. Power BI content is distributed using what?

    A. A collection
    B. A solution
    C. A Power BI app
    D. A Power app

19. Dashboards use data from where?

    A. Datasets in the same workspace
    B. Imported from many kinds of sources
    C. Datasets in any workspace
    D. Microsoft Excel

20. Which pane of the Power Query Editor window shows transformation steps that have been applied?

    A. Queries pane
    B. Transformation Steps under the Query Settings pane
    C. Applied Steps under the Query Settings pane
    D. Steps pane

21. To better understand the factors that contribute to an important metric in your data, what feature should you consider using?

    A. Scorecard visual
    B. Card visual
    C. Smart narrative visual
    D. Key influencers visual

22. Built-in roles for Power BI workspaces include which of the following?

    A. Admin, Associate, Contributor, and Viewer

    B. Admin, Member, Contributor, and Viewer

    C. Admin, Associate, Supplier, and Viewer

    D. Admin, Member, Contributor, and Observer

23. Which two types of queries does Power BI have?

    A. Direct and import

    B. Direct and indirect

    C. Direct and load

    D. Direct and internal

24. Which DAX function do you use to calculate the arithmetic mean?

    A. AVEDEV

    B. MEAN

    C. AVERAGE

    D. AVG

25. In which scenario does it make sense to use row-level security?

    A. When single-user data is stored in a Power BI data model

    B. When multi-user data is stored together but it's OK that each user sees all rows in the table or query

    C. When multi-user data is stored in separate tables or queries

    D. When multi-user data is stored together but you need to ensure each user only has access to their own data

26. To share only Power BI data connections (not reports), you should create what kind of file?

    A. PBIX

    B. PBID

    C. PBIDS

    D. PBIS

27. To change how slicers interact with visuals on the report page, what configuration needs to be used?

    A. Edit interactions
    B. Change slicer interactions
    C. Change filter interactions
    D. Edit slicer

28. To bring data together from multiple queries where the structure of the queries is the same, what do you use?

    A. A left outer join query
    B. A right outer join query
    C. An append query
    D. A merge query

29. To best understand the representative behavior of data, what feature would you add to a bar chart to show you whether the data was trending positive or negative?

    A. Trend line
    B. Behavior circle
    C. Line of duty
    D. Best fit square

30. Valid data types in the Power Query Editor include, but are not limited to, which of the following?

    A. Number, Text, Date/Time, and True/False
    B. Whole Number, Decimal Number, Text, and Date/Time
    C. Variable Character, Decimal Number, and Text
    D. Date/Time, Percentage, and String

31. Which data warehousing schema organizes your data into fact and dimension tables?

    A. Sun schema
    B. Star schema
    C. Moon schema
    D. Kimball schema

32. Viewing the data lineage for resources in a workspace is possible under which menu?

    A. File
    B. Edit
    C. View
    D. Data

33. To connect to local data sources, which software do you need to use?

    A. You can't connect to local data sources.
    B. Self-hosted integration runtime.
    C. On-premises data gateway.
    D. Power BI Report Builder.

34. When are measures calculated?

    A. When added to the data model
    B. In context including with filters
    C. In context including without filters
    D. When the calculator is opened

35. Slicers can have different behavior for visuals on the report page. Those interactions can be which of the following?

    A. Highlight or filter
    B. Highlight, filter, or none
    C. Filter or none
    D. Highlight or none

36. Which visual represents data as nested boxes?

    A. Filled map
    B. Treemap
    C. Pie
    D. Matrix

37. Buttons, text boxes, shapes, images, and smart narratives are added to report pages under which ribbon tab?

    A. Home
    B. Insert
    C. Modeling
    D. Information

38. Where can you find the Play Axis visual to use in Power BI reports?

    A. Microsoft Download Center
    B. Microsoft AppSource
    C. Built into Power BI
    D. Power BI extension downloads

39. Which option best describes quick measures in Power BI?

    A. Pre-built calculations that can be applied without DAX
    B. Measures that increase the performance of your data model
    C. The fastest way to measure something in Power BI
    D. Advanced measures that require using DAX

40. Dashboards display data stored where?

    A. Dashboard cache
    B. Formula engine
    C. Underlying data source
    D. OneDrive

41. What needs to be set up and configured for on-premises data sources to be used in reports or dashboards published to the Power BI service?

    A. On-premises data gateway
    B. Self-hosted integration runtime
    C. Power BI Report Builder
    D. DAX Studio

42. The performance of dashboards can be investigated using what tool?

    A. Dashboard speed gauge
    B. Dashboard inspector
    C. Performance Analyzer
    D. Performance inspector

43. To see differences highlighted between deployment pipeline stages, what feature should be used?

    A. Evaluate
    B. Contrast
    C. Match
    D. Compare

44. To visually identify outliers, which kind of visual would you use?

    A. Pie chart
    B. Scatter plot
    C. Card
    D. Treemap

45. What feature allows you to customize page navigation within a report?

    A. Navigation config
    B. Page navigator
    C. Page config
    D. Page format

46. The steps to optimize visuals on a report include, but are not limited to, which of the following?

    A. Limiting visuals to only those necessary
    B. Applying the most restrictive filtering
    C. Reducing the use of third-party visuals
    D. All of the above

47. To use sensitivity labels in Power BI, where must this be enabled?

    A. Azure portal
    B. Office 365 admin portal
    C. Power BI admin portal
    D. Options for Power BI Desktop

48. What setting do you use to change the background of a report page?

    A. Page settings
    B. Format background
    C. Canvas background
    D. Background color

49. Which is an example of a business rule that can be used for a measure?

    A. Revenue needs to increase each month.
    B. Revenue needs to increase or stay the same each month.
    C. Revenue needs to increase by 5% each month.
    D. We need to sell more products each month.

50. Value encoding compression can be used to reduce the size of what data type?

    A. Text
    B. Numeric
    C. True/false
    D. Binary

51. Which Power BI capability allows users to apply filters dynamically to visuals on a report?

    A. Dynamic filters
    B. Filter all
    C. Dicers
    D. Slicers

52. Which feature allows you to combine different data values together in a visual?

    A. Clubbing
    B. Combining
    C. Grouping
    D. Linking

53. What is the limit to the number of times Power BI Premium capacity can refresh data?

    A. 24 times per day
    B. 48 times per day
    C. 72 times per day
    D. 96 times per day

54. Power BI content can be pushed to end users. What does this setting apply to?

    A. Every Power BI user or your entire organization, with options except for specific security groups
    B. The entire organization or specific security groups
    C. The entire organization or specific users, with options except for specific security groups
    D. The entire organization or specific security groups, with options except for specific security groups

55. What are the multiple licensing options for Power BI?

    A. Free, Pro, Premium Per Capacity, Premium per User, and Embedded
    B. Free, Pro, Superior Per Capacity, Superior Per User, and Embedded
    C. Free, Expert, Premium Per Capacity, Premium Per User, and Embedded
    D. Free, Pro, Premium Per Capacity, Premium Per User, and For Business

56. What do you need to use to avoid a single point of failure with a connection to on-premises data sources?

    A. A Kubernetes cluster.
    B. A cluster of on-premises data gateways.
    C. High-availability Azure services.
    D. Pay your monthly Power BI Pro bill.

57. To modify relationships between tables, which tool do you use?

    A. Manage relationships
    B. Edit relationships
    C. Create relationships
    D. Modify relationships

58. What tool can be used to record the time taken by each visual to query and render in a report?

    A. Performance Analyzer
    B. Performance optimizer
    C. Query optimizer
    D. Speed analyzer

59. When reports and datasets are published, credentials to data sources are stored where?

    A. Saved offline.
    B. In the Power BI service.
    C. They are not stored and must be manually entered after publishing.
    D. In the dataset when published.

60. What does standard mode in an on-premises data gateway run as?

    A. A user-mode application
    B. A service
    C. A file configuration
    D. A principle application

Answer keys

This section contains the answer keys for both the practice tests.

Practice Test 1

1. C – Focus mode is when a visual is shown over the entire canvas.
2. C – Trend lines in visuals change when data changes.
3. C – Categorical analysis is required in this example.
4. C – Power BI is a popular BI tool with both enterprise and citizen developers.
5. B – Sort ascending will sort from lowest to highest.
6. B – The RANKX function requires table, expression, and order parameters.
7. D – Responsive slicers must contain a selection list of values.
8. B – Supported cardinalities are many-to-one, one-to-many, many-to-many, and one-to-one.
9. C – Table visual is the most similar to a database table.
10. B – Drillthrough is set up on the target page.
11. C – Row-level security requires a DAX expression.
12. C – Development pipelines support development, test, and production stages.
13. D – Using Power BI will be familiar for users of Microsoft Excel.
14. D – A merge query is used to bring data together where the structure is different.
15. B – Map, filled map, and ArcGIS map are the three types of map visuals.
16. D – The data type selector under the Transform tab is needed to change the data type of a column.
17. B – Aggregation is the only way to reduce data size from the choices provided.
18. D – Data types of matching columns should be the same when you need to merge queries.
19. D – Binning is the technique you would use to group customers together to understand buying habits.
20. C – Formula and storage engines are the two engines used by Power BI.
21. C – The auto date/time option will create a hidden date hierarchy table.
22. B – Visuals from reports use pinning to be added to a dashboard.
23. D – DAX stands for Data Analysis eXpressions.

Answer keys 345

24. C – Column profile under the View tab will show descriptive statistics about each column.
25. D – The Power Query Editor uses the first 1,000 rows by default.
26. B – Power BI content is published to a workspace.
27. B – Column from Example, Custom Column, and Index Column are the only valid ways to add columns from the options listed.
28. C – AI methods supported in Power Query Editor are language detection, key phrase extraction, sentiment analysis, and image tagging.
29. C – Scheduled refresh works with 15-minute time windows.
30. D – Power BI can connect to all of the listed data sources.
31. A – Power BI is designed to work with many data sources.
32. A – Percent increase is an example of a non-additive measure.
33. B – Indexes on the source data, dimension to fact table key integrity, materializing data and dates, and distributed tables for MPP databases are often direct query performance optimization techniques.
34. C – Usage metric reports include report usage, report performance, and report list information.
35. C – Enterprise mode needs to be used in the on-premises data gateway for multiple users to be able to use the gateway.
36. C – You need to format your visual in order to change the color.
37. C – Of the tools listed, DAX Studio is the recommended tool for optimizing measures.
38. D – Power BI supports both built-in and custom visuals.
39. D – It is often hard for businesses to see a complete picture of what is happening across the enterprise.
40. C – Downstream inheritance is when the same sensitivity labels are applied to downstream data products.
41. B – The filtering pane can filter by visual, page, or all pages.
42. D – Data refresh is the capability used to update data in a Power BI dataset.
43. D – The default canvas for a report is 16:9.
44. B – To compress data, Power BI can use value and hash encoding.
45. B – A custom linguistic model makes it possible to use domain-specific words in natural-language queries.

346　Practice Exams

46. C – Column quality shows percent of valid, error, and empty values.
47. C – Bookmarks allow you to capture the current state of a report page.
48. C – Being data-driven means using data to make business decisions.
49. B – Power BI is software and a service.
50. C – DAX functions must return one value.
51. A – Drillthrough is when users can jump to a target page in your report that focuses on a selected data value.
52. C – Allow drillthrough when summarized is the configuration that should be changed.
53. D – Bookmark navigator can use the grid, vertical, and horizontal options.
54. A – Fill transformation replaces empty or null values in a column with values from the adjacent row using the up or down method.
55. D – The formula engine interacts with data stored in the storage engine.
56. C – Slicers will only remove data when the slicer is being used or selected.
57. A – The "BI" stands for business intelligence.
58. D – XMLA protocol is used by Microsoft SQL Server Analysis Services.
59. D – Azure Key Vault is the Azure service used for bringing and storing encryption keys.
60. B – There will be 100 values stored in the query when using a calculated column on a query of 100 rows.

Practice Test 2

1. C – Null or error rows will need to be fixed or removed from a table.
2. C – Desktop web browsers and mobile devices can view dashboards.
3. A – The Q&A feature allows you to use natural language to ask questions of a Power BI data model.
4. D – It is recommended not to use many-to-many.
5. B – Power BI Desktop only runs on Windows-based operating systems.
6. C – Custom visuals can be imported from AppSource.
7. B – The layout of the dashboard for mobile devices can be configured with the mobile layout capability.
8. B – Count, error, empty, min, max, average, and standard deviation are shown in the column profile.

9. C – Range slicer is the default used for date columns.
10. B – Power BI integrates with Microsoft Information Protection for holistic data protection capabilities.
11. A – The CALCULATE function evaluates an expression in a modified filter context.
12. C – The Power BI options for bin types include the size and number of bins.
13. B – Grain, or granularity, is the concept of defining the smallest level of data used in a report.
14. B – View as is the feature that allows you to confirm whether row-level security and been set up correctly for another user.
15. A – Animation settings for the Play Axis visual include auto start, loop, and time.
16. B – Power BI dashboards are created on the Power BI service.
17. A – A value distribution bar chart and the number of distinct and unique values are shown in column distribution in the Power Query Editor.
18. C – Content is distributed using a Power BI app.
19. A – Dashboards can use data from datasets in the same workspace.
20. C – Transformation steps are shown in Applied Steps under the Query Settings pane.
21. D – The key influencers visual allows you to understand the factors that contribute to important metrics in your data.
22. B – Admin, Member, Contributor, and Viewer are the built-in roles for Power BI workspaces.
23. A – Direct and Import are the two types of Power BI queries.
24. C – The AVERAGE function is used to calculate the arithmetic mean.
25. D – Row-level security can be used when multi-user data is stored together but you need to ensure each user only has access to their own data.
26. C – A PBIDS file stores the data connections from Power BI.
27. A – Edit interactions is used to change how slicers interact with visuals on the report page.
28. C – An append query is used to bring data together where the structure of the queries is the same.
29. A – A trend line can be used to better understand the behavior of data trends.
30. B – Data types in the Power Query Editor include Whole Number, Decimal Number, Text, and Date/Time.

348   Practice Exams

31. B – Star schema organizes data into fact and dimension tables.
32. C – You can view data lineage for resources in a workspace under the View menu.
33. C – The on-premises data gateway software allows you to connect to local data sources.
34. B – Measures are calculated in the context, including with filters.
35. B – Slicers can highlight, filter, or have no similar behavior to other visuals on the report page.
36. B – The treemap visual represents data in nested boxes.
37. B – Buttons, text boxes, shapes, images, and smart narratives are under the Insert tab.
38. B – The Play Axis visual can be found in Microsoft AppSource.
39. A – Quick measures are best described as pre-built calculations that can be applied without writing DAX.
40. A – Dashboards display data stored in the dashboard cache.
41. A – The on-premises data gateway needs to be set up so on-premises data sources can be used.
42. D – Performance inspector is the tool to use when investigating the performance of dashboards.
43. D – Compare should be used to see differences between deployment pipeline stages.
44. B – Of the visuals mentioned, the scatter plot would be best suited to identify outliers.
45. B – Page navigator is the feature that allows you to customize page navigation within a report.
46. D – All of the options presented will help optimize visuals on a report page.
47. C – Sensitivity labels can be enabled in the Power BI admin portal.
48. C – The report page background setting is set under the canvas background setting.
49. C – Of the options presented, only revenue needs to increase by 5% each month is an example of a business rule that can be used with a measure.
50. B – Value encoding compression can be used to reduce the size of numeric data.
51. D – Slicers allow users to apply filters dynamically.
52. C – Grouping is the feature that allows you to combine different data values together.

Answer keys

53. B – Power BI Premium capacity can refresh data 48 times per day.
54. D – The pushing data to users setting applies to the entire organization or specific security groups, with options except for specific security groups.
55. A – Power BI can be free, Pro, Premium Per Capacity, Premium Per User, or Embedded.
56. B – To avoid a single point of failure with an on-premises data gateway, you need to configure a cluster.
57. A – The manage relationships capability is used to modify relationships between tables.
58. A – Performance Analyzer is the tool used for visuals to query and render in a report.
59. C – Data source credentials are not saved or stored at publish time but must be entered after publishing.
60. B – On-premises data gateway Standard mode runs as a service.

Appendix: Practice Question Answers

Here, you can find the answers to all of the practice questions found at the end of each chapter.

- *Chapter 1, Overview of Power BI and the PL-300 Exam*
- *Chapter 2, Connecting to Data Sources*
- *Chapter 3, Profiling the Data*
- *Chapter 4, Cleansing, Transforming, and Shaping Data*
- *Chapter 5, Designing a Data Model*
- *Chapter 6, Using Data Model Advanced Features*
- *Chapter 7, Creating Measures Using DAX*
- *Chapter 8, Optimizing Model Performance*
- *Chapter 9, Creating Reports*
- *Chapter 10, Creating Dashboards*
- *Chapter 11, Enhancing Reports*
- *Chapter 12, Exposing Insights from Data*
- *Chapter 13, Performing Advanced Analytics*
- *Chapter 14, Managing Workspaces*
- *Chapter 15, Managing Datasets*

Chapter 1, Overview of Power BI and the PL-300 Exam

1. What does the "BI" in Power BI stands for what?

    A. Business information

    B. Bidirectional information

    C. **Business intelligence**

    D. Big industry

2. The Power BI service allows you to:

    A. Download software allowing you to explore data and create reports.

    B. Create spreadsheets that calculate values based on formulas.

    C. Author presentations using the slideshow concept.

    D. **Share reports dashboards and apps with other users.**

3. How often must Microsoft exams be renewed?

    A. Never, they last forever.

    B. Every 6 months.

    C. **Every 2 years.**

    D. Every 4 years.

Chapter 2, Connecting to Data Sources

1. Which data sources can Power BI connect to?

    A. Only local, on-premises data sources

    B. **On-premises, cloud, and SaaS sources**

    C. Only SaaS sources

    D. On-premises and cloud sources

2. What are some ways to tune the performance of Power BI queries?

   A. Running a shrink on the data model
   B. **Importing only the required data**
   C. Zipping the PBIX file
   D. Removing all queries

3. XMLA is the protocol used for which software or service?

   A. **Microsoft Analysis Services**
   B. Microsoft Excel
   C. Azure Synapse Analytics
   D. Microsoft SQL Server Management Studio

Chapter 3, Profiling the Data

1. Which tool is used to transform data?

   A. Power Edit
   B. Transform Data
   C. Query Tool
   D. **Power Query**

2. By default, the Power Query Editor will use how many rows of data?

   A. 100 rows
   B. **1,000 rows**
   C. 2,000 rows
   D. Entire dataset

3. Column distribution view can be enabled by selecting the checkbox under which tab on the ribbon?

   A. Tools
   B. Statistics
   C. **View**
   D. Home

Chapter 4, Cleansing, Transforming, and Shaping Data

1. If you need to transform a column by adding a prefix to every record, which transform would you use?

   A. Format

   B. Pivot

   C. **Replace Values**

   D. Parse

2. What is used to combine data from multiple queries or tables?

   A. **Merge query**

   B. Join query

   C. Append query

   D. Left Outer query

3. What are some of the ways Power BI can be used to enrich data using AI?

   A. Linear regression, language detection, key phrase extraction, and sentiment analysis

   B. Language detection, key phrase extraction, and sentiment analysis

   C. Language detection and key phrase extraction

   D. **Image tagging, key phrase extraction, language detection, and sentiment analysis**

Chapter 5, Designing a Data Model

1. Which type of table relationship describes a scenario where each unique value in one table occurs only once in another table?

   A. Many-to-many

   B. **One-to-one**

   C. One-to-many

   D. Unique relationship

2. What is the DAX formula needed to build a quick measure to calculate the weighted average per category?

   A. AVG(CATEGORY).

   B. AVGW(CATEGORY).

   C. AVERAGE([QUERY] . [CATEGORY]).

   D. **DAX isn't needed for a quick measure.**

3. If your data has sales by store by day, are you able to find sales by hour?

   A. No.

   B. Yes.

   C. **Sort of, it will be averaged by store by day.**

   D. Sort of, it will be averaged by store by hour.

Chapter 6, Using Data Model Advanced Features

1. Which of the following does Power BI use as the default sensitivity labels?

   A. Top secret, secret, official, public

   B. Confidential, official, public

   C. Confidential, general, public

   D. **Whatever your organization uses for MIP sensitivity labels**

2. If the data model for sales data includes columns for Country, State, and Postal code, what are some potential ways we can implement row-level security to filter data?

   A. Use a DAX expression to filter by Country, State, or Postal code.

   B. Use a DAX expression to filter by State or Postal code.

   C. Use a DAX expression to filter by Country or State.

   D. **Use a security filter by Country.**

356   Appendix: Practice Question Answers

3. What kind of model (or YAML file) is used for domain-specific language natural-language querying in Power BI?

   A. Data model
   B. Super model
   C. **Linguistic model**
   D. Dimensional model

Chapter 7, Creating Measures Using DAX

1. What are quick measures?

   A. Measures that move around the screen quickly
   B. **Calculated fields that can be added without coding**
   C. Measures that can quickly be added by writing DAX code
   D. Custom visuals added from Microsoft AppSource

2. What is used to evaluate an expression in the context of a modified filter?

   A. COMPUTE
   B. APPRAISE
   C. SUM
   D. **CALCULATE**

3. If you only have the `Sales Amount` and `Total Product Cost` fields, which function would be best to use to calculate the sum of margin?

   A. **SUMX**
   B. MARGIN
   C. DISTINCTCOUNT
   D. FILTER

Chapter 8, Optimizing Model Performance

1. Which technique will increase the performance of data models?

    A. Adding more memory to Power BI Desktop

    B. Changing the data source to Microsoft Excel

    C. Publishing reports to Power BI Premium

    D. **Removing unnecessary data from the data model**

2. Aggregating data will do what?

    A. **Reduce the number of columns and rows.**

    B. Reduce the number of columns only.

    C. Increase the number of rows only.

    D. Both b and c

3. Filtering in a Power BI report can be applied to what?

    A. **All pages in a report file, a single page, only a visual.**

    B. Filtering can only be applied to visuals.

    C. A single page or a visual.

    D. A dashboard, a page, or a visual.

4. Which tool or capability should be used to determine how much of a query duration uses the formula engine or the storage engine?

    A. Query diagnostics

    B. Query analytics

    C. **DAX Studio**

    D. Tabular Editor

5. When using query diagnostics, which kind of diagnostics should be used to analyze multiple steps in a query?

    A. Multiple-step diagnostics

    B. Session diagnostics

    C. **Step diagnostics**

    D. Model diagnostics

Chapter 9, Creating Reports

1. Power BI reports can use custom visuals added from what resource?

    A. **Microsoft AppSource**

    B. Microsoft Store

    C. Power BI VisualStore

    D. Office 365 templates

2. Which visual makes the most sense to use for geographical information?

    A. Clustered bar chart

    B. Stacked bar chart

    C. Scatter chart

    D. **Map**

3. If you want to make the color of data change based on its value, what feature will you use?

    A. The Edit tab

    B. **Conditional formatting**

    C. Bold formatting

    D. Conditional settings

Chapter 10, Creating Dashboards

1. Dashboards can contain what type of content?

    A. Report visuals, web content, images, text, video, and streaming data

    B. Report visuals, report pages, images, text, video, and streaming data

    C. Report visuals, report pages, web content, images, text, and video

    D. **Report visuals, report pages, web content, images, text, video, and streaming data**

2. What is the shortest frequency for automatic dashboard tile refresh of cached data for pinned visuals?

    A. 30 minutes

    B. 15 minutes

    C. 5 minutes

    D. **1 hour**

3. Dashboards can be optimized for viewing on what devices?

    A. Web and desktop

    B. Web only

    C. Web, iOS, Android, and Blackberry

    D. **Web and mobile**

Chapter 11, Enhancing Reports

1. Configuring a saved configuration of a report page with preset filtering and sorting is called what?

    A. Save points

    B. Favorites

    C. **Bookmarks**

    D. Saved view

2. Navigation can be configured in a report using what item from the Insert tab on the ribbon?

    A. New visual
    B. Paginated report
    C. New page
    D. **Buttons**

3. When designing a report for viewing on a mobile device, what view is used?

    A. **Mobile layout**
    B. App view
    C. Android viewer
    D. Web layout

Chapter 12, Exposing Insights from Data

1. The built-in report filters can be used to filter data where?

    A. Only on the current report page
    B. Only on the selected report visual
    C. On the current report page or the selected visual
    D. **On the current report page, the selected visual, or all pages in the PBIX file**

2. Responsive slicers must have which configuration property set?

    A. Responsive enabled and horizontal orientation
    B. **Responsive enabled**
    C. Responsive enabled and vertical orientation
    D. Responsive enabled and dynamic orientation

3. What type of lines can be added to a visual using the Analytics pane?

    A. Trend, median, min, max, average, and constant
    B. Trend, median, min, max, average, and standard deviation
    C. Trend, median, min, max, average, constant, and x- and/or y-axis constant
    D. **Trend, median, min, max, average, constant, percentile, and x- and/or y-axis constant**

4. Symmetry shading can be added to what kind of visual?

   A. Line

   B. **Scatter chart**

   C. Clustered bar

   D. Clustered column

Chapter 13, Performing Advanced Analytics

1. The key influencers visualization can be used to discover what about your data?

   A. **Understand relationships between fields in your data model.**

   B. Aggregate numeric data in your data model.

   C. Generate text summaries of insights.

   D. How many social media followers you have.

2. Which type of visual is often used with time series analysis?

   A. **Gantt chart**

   B. Pie chart

   C. Map visual

   D. Decomposition tree

3. When there are data values that don't fit well with other values, your data may contain what?

   A. Errors

   B. Bad records

   C. **Outliers**

   D. Empty records

Chapter 14, Managing Workspaces

1. Advanced capabilities of Power BI may require a licensed version of Power BI. Licensed versions of Power BI include:

   A. Premium and Advanced

   B. Plus and Pro

   C. Power BI 2022

   D. **Pro and Premium**

2. Which workspace role has permissions to delete a workspace?

   A. Owner

   B. **Admin**

   C. Member

   D. Contributor

3. Which stages are used in Power BI deployment pipelines?

   A. Development and production

   B. **Development, test, and production**

   C. Development, test, preproduction, and production

   D. Development, integration testing, user acceptance testing, and production

4. How many days of history will usage metrics reporting show?

   A. 90

   B. 60

   C. **30**

   D. Unlimited

Chapter 15, Managing Datasets

1. If I need to use an on-premises SQL Server as a source for my report that will use an import query of a dataset, what should I do?

    A. You must move all of your data to Azure.

    B. This is not possible.

    C. Use a self-hosted integration runtime.

    D. **Use an on-premises data gateway.**

2. How many times per day can a dataset refresh be scheduled in a Premium workspace?

    A. 24

    B. **48**

    C. 96

    D. 12

3. Row-level security only applies to users who have workspace access at what level?

    A. Member

    B. Admin

    C. **Viewer**

    D. All of the above

Index

Symbols

*.yaml (YAML) file 102

A

accessibility
  configuring 198, 199
  designing 198, 199
additive measures 133
adjective phrasings 105
Advanced Editor
  about 63
  using 63, 64
advanced section 84
aggregations
  data model, optimizing with 148, 149
AI Insights
  applying 280, 281
  options 59
AI services
  used, for enhancing data 59
AI split 279
ALL function 116, 118
Analytics pane 261, 263, 264
anomaly detection
  using 270
append queries 58
ArcGIS service 180
area chart 170
Artificial Intelligence (AI) 270
attribute phrasings 105
automatic page refresh
  configuring 200, 201
Azure Active Directory (AAD) 310
Azure Analysis Services 17
Azure Information Protection (AIP) 96
Azure Logic Apps 17
Azure Maps 180
Azure ML 63
Azure Service Bus 16
Azure Synapse Analytics SQL
    dedicated pool 19

B

bar chart 168
basic statistical functions
  using, to enhance data 123
binning 273, 276-278

Index

bookmarks
  selection pane, using 226
  using 224, 225
business intelligence (BI)
  about 4
  reference link 4

C

calculated columns
  usage scenario 122
  versus measures 112
CALCULATE function
  using, to manipulate filters 114
cardinality
  about 78
  many-to-many relationship 78
  many-to-one relationship 78
  one-to-many relationship 78
  one-to-one relationship 78
card visualization 175
Chief Financial Officer (CFP) 209
Cloud App Security 97
cloud data sources 15
Cognitive Services 59, 63
column chart 168
column properties
  configuring 81
columns
  adding 54, 55
  managing 51
column transformations
  columns, adding 54, 55
  data type columns, transforming 52
  date and time columns, transforming 54
  number columns, transforming 53

  text columns, transforming 53
  using 51, 52
combination chart 174
combine files 58, 59
complex measures
  building, with DAX 110, 111
composite models
  aggregations 25
  optimizing 24
  table storage 25
conditional formatting
  configuring 187-189
context 113, 114
cross-filter
  using 242
cross-filter direction
  about 79
  both directions 79
  single direction 79
custom tooltips
  creating 227-229, 231
custom visual
  importing 185, 186

D

dashboards
  distributing 289
  visuals, optimizing 147
data
  drilldown, with interactive visuals 243
  enhancing, with basic statistical functions 123
Data Analysis Expressions (DAX)
  about 110
  complex measures, building 110, 111
  used, for implementing time intelligence 118

Index

data anomalies
  column properties, interrogating 38, 39
  data structures, examining 39, 40
  identifying 36-38
data combining
  about 56
  append queries 58
  combine files 58, 59
  merge queries, using 56, 57
data enhance, with AI services
  about 59
  Azure ML 63
  image tagging 61, 62
  key phrase extraction 60
  language detection 60
  sentiment analysis 60, 61
data exfiltration 97
data gateway
  download link 17
  identifying 309, 310
data granularity
  level, defining 91, 92
data labels 185
data model
  about 137
  designing, to meet performance requirements 92
  numeric and text column data, splitting 140, 141
  optimizing 137, 138
  optimizing, with aggregations 148, 149
  Q&A capability, optimizing 106
  unnecessary columns, removing 138, 139
  unnecessary rows, removing 138, 140
data science 65
dataset access
  providing 312, 314, 315

dataset scheduled refresh
  configuring 306, 308
data size
  reducing 22, 23
data sources
  connecting to 16
data sources options
  cloud data source 15
  databases 15
  files 15
  local data sources 15
  SaaS data source 15
data statistics
  column distribution 41, 42
  column profile 42-45
  interrogating 41
data type columns
  transforming 52
data types 39
data visualization 65
data warehouse design 56
data warehouse environments 56
date and time columns
  transforming 54
date math 90
date table
  about 118, 119
  creating 87
  role playing with 91
  using 89, 90
DAX expression 97
DAX Studio
  about 142
  URL 142
decomposition tree visual 279
default summarization
  about 113
  modifying 124

deployment pipelines
  automating 300
  creating 297-300
  reference link 300
  using 296
  workspace, unassigning 300
dimensional modeling
  reference link 56
dimension-to-fact table key integrity 23
DirectQuery
  about 18
  data sources, optimizing 23, 24
distributed tables 24
distribution groups 99
donut chart 171
downstream inheritance 96
drillthrough
  using 242
dynamic variable 99

E

Enterprise Data Warehouse (EDW) 138
Enterprise Resource Planning (ERP) 6
entities section 104
Excel PivotTables
  Power BI datasets, using 204, 205

F

F#
  URL 63
FILTER function 115, 116
filtering 49, 50

filters
  about 190, 192
  customizing 192
  exploring 254, 255, 257-260
  manipulating, with CALCULATE function 114
focus mode 213
formatting section
  about 82
  date formatting options 83
  numeric formatting options 82
Formula Engine (FE) 141
funnel visualization 176
fuzzy matching
  about 57
  settings 57

G

gauge chart 177, 178
general section 81, 82
grouping 273-275

H

histograms
  binning 125-128
  grouping 125-128

I

image tagging 61, 62
Import Query 18, 19
indexes 23
interactive visuals
  used, for drilling down into data 243

K

key influencers visual 278
key phrase extraction 60
key phrases 60
keywords 60

L

language detection 60
line chart 170
linguistic model
  about 103
  entities section 104
  relationships section 104
linguistic schema 102

M

Machine Learning (ML) 62
mail-enabled groups 99
many-to-many relationships
  resolving 86, 87
many-to-one relationship 106
map visuals 179
Massively Parallel Processing (MPP) 24
matplotlib
  URL 66
matrix visualizations 167
measures
  creating 112
  numeric calculated columns,
    replacing with 120
  optimizing 141-146
  usage scenario 122
  versus calculated columns 112
merge queries
  using 56, 57

merge queries, join types
  Full Outer 57
  Inner 57
  Left Anti 57
  Left Outer 57
  Right Anti 57
  Right Outer 57
Microsoft Azure 59
Microsoft Information
    Protection (MIP) 96
Microsoft Power BI
  using, in PL-300 Data Analyze 8
ML applications 65
mobile devices
  reports, designing 245, 246
model size 90
multiple visualization
  configuring 190

N

name phrasings 105
NaN (not a number) 42
natural-language query 103
navigation
  configuring, for report 235
Navigation buttons 235, 236
Node.js 186
non-additive measures 134
noun phrasings 105
number columns
  transforming 53
numeric calculated columns
  replacing, with measures 120

O

Office 365 groups 99
on-premises data gateway 16, 17
outliers
  identifying 268, 269

P

paginated report
  creating 202-204
  visuals, optimizing 147
pandas
  URL 66
parent-child hierarchy
  about 72
  cardinality 78
  cross-filter direction 79
  relationships 76
  star schema 73
performance inspector 219
personal mode 17
phrasings 104
phrasings, types
  adjective phrasings 105
  name phrasings 105
  noun phrasings 105
  preposition phrasings 105
  verb phrasings 105
pie chart 171
PL-300 Data Analyze
  knowledge 9
  Microsoft tests 8
  question types 8, 9
  strategies 10
  timelines 10
  with Microsoft Power BI 8
Power Apps 17

Power Automate 17
Power BI
  accessibility features 199
  built-in features 199
  capabilities 159-161
  certification 7
  challenges, reporting 5, 6
  for business intelligence (BI) 4, 5
  overview 4
  Power Query, accessing 48
  visualization items, adding
    to reports 161-164
Power BI admin portal 96
Power BI app
  creating 289-291, 293-295
Power BI dashboards
  about 208-210
  creating 210, 211
  optimizing 217
  performance, optimizing 219, 220
  theme, setting 212, 213
  tiles, pinning 214-216
  URL 208
  using 213
  views, configuring 217, 218
Power BI dataflows 17, 20, 21
Power BI datasets
  about 20
  using, in Excel PivotTables 204, 205
Power BI Data Source (PBIDS) files
  about 29, 31
  reference link 15
Power BI date hierarchy tables 88
Power BI Desktop
  about 6
  reference link 10
Power BI Desktop file (PBIX) 29
Power BI Premium 59

Index   371

Power BI service 7
Power BI workspace
  licensing 288, 289
  reference link 286
  roles and permissions 286, 287
  usage metric reports, using 301, 302
  usage, monitoring 301
  using 286
Power BI workspaces
  licensing 288
Power Query
  about 48
  accessing, in Power BI 48
Power Query advanced operations
  Advanced Editor, using 63, 64
  Python scripts 65, 66
  Query Dependencies tool, using 65
  R scripts 65, 66
  using 63
Power Query M formula functions
  reference link 54
Power Query parameters
  about 28
  Any Value 28
  List of Values 28
  query 29
Premium capacity 21
Premium licensing 288
Premium Per User (PPU) 21, 289
preposition phrasings 105
Pro licensing 288
properties pane
  advanced section 84
  formatting section 82
  general section 81, 82

Python
  URL 65
Python scripts 65
  using 66
Python visual
  adding 193

Q

Q&A capability
  linguistic model 103
  natural language, applying 99
  optimizing, in data model 106
  using, in dashboards 100-102
  using, in reports 100-102
Q&A visualization
  about 180
  core characteristics 181
Query Dependencies tool
  using 65
query diagnostics
  about 149, 151
  session diagnostics 149, 150
  step diagnostics 149, 151
  tables 150
query performance tuning
  about 22
  composite models, optimizing 24
  data size, reducing 22, 23
  DirectQuery data sources,
    optimizing 23, 24
query types
  DirectQuery 18
  exploring 18
  Import Query 18, 19
quick measures 84, 86, 111

R

ranking function 128, 129
reader role 63
relationships
  about 76
  Edit relationship 77, 78
  Manage relationships 76, 77
  optimizing 146
  test tips 79
relationships section 104
report
  navigation, configuring 235
report accessibility checklist
  about 200
  reference link 200
report data
  exporting 243-245
report page
  configuring 196, 198
reports
  designing, for mobile devices 245, 246
  distributing 289
  visuals, optimizing 147
role-playing dimensions
  about 80, 119, 120
  date table 80
row-level security
  about 97
  group membership, configuring 310-312
  implementing 97
  managing 99
  setting up 97, 98
row transformations
  using 55
R project
  URL 65

R scripts
  about 65
  using 66
R visual
  adding 193

S

SaaS data sources 15
scatter chart 178
security groups 99
selection pane
  layer order 226, 227
  tab order 226
  using 226
semi-additive measures
  creating 133, 134
sensitivity labels
  requisites 96
  using 96
sentiment analysis 60, 61
separation of duties 296
session diagnostics 149, 150
simple filtering 115
slicers
  about 190-192
  cases 191
  exploring 254, 255, 257-260
  options 192
smart narrative visual
  adding 193-196
Software-as-a-Service (SaaS) 217, 288
Software Development Kit (SDK) 186
sorting
  about 49, 50
  applying 237-240
splitting columns 141
SQL Server Data Tools (SSDT) 31

Index 373

SQL Server Management
    Studio (SSMS) 31
standard mode 17
star schema
    about 73
    complicated model 74
    simpler model 75
statistical analysis 261
step diagnostics 149, 151
Storage Engine (SE) 138, 141
Sync slicers panel 241
synonyms 82
syntactic sugar 118

T

table properties
    configuring 81
tables 72
table storage modes
    DirectQuery 25
    Dual 25
    Import 25
table visualizations 166
text columns
    transforming 53
text-processing algorithm 60
Third Normal Form (3NF) 106
tiles
    pinning 214-216
time intelligence
    implementing, with DAX 118
time series analysis
    conducting 271, 272
top N analysis
    implementing 128
top N filter 130, 131
top N function 129, 131, 133

top N list 130
treemap visual 171, 173

U

usage metric reports
    about 301
    using, in Power BI workspace 301, 302

V

value encoding 140
verb phrasings 105
VertiPaq 18, 138
virtual cores (vCores) 288
visual formatting 185
visualization
    configuring 181, 182
    formatting 181
visualization, formatting options
    about 182
    general formatting 182-185
    visual formatting 185
visualization type
    about 164, 165
    area chart 170
    bar and column charts 168, 169
    card visualization 175
    combination chart 174
    donut chart 171
    funnel visualization 176
    gauge chart 177, 178
    line chart 170
    map visuals 179
    pie chart 171
    Q&A visualization 180
    scatter chart 178
    table and matrix visualizations 165

treemap visual 171
waterfall chart 178
visuals
　interactions between 232-234
　optimizing 146
　optimizing, in dashboards 147
　optimizing, in paginated reports 147
　optimizing, in reports 147

W

waterfall chart 178
what-if parameters 26, 27

X

X functions 121
XMLA endpoint 31
XML for Analysis (XMLA) 26
xmSQL 142

Packt>

Packt.com

Subscribe to our online digital library for full access to over 7,000 books and videos, as well as industry leading tools to help you plan your personal development and advance your career. For more information, please visit our website.

Why subscribe?

- Spend less time learning and more time coding with practical eBooks and Videos from over 4,000 industry professionals
- Improve your learning with Skill Plans built especially for you
- Get a free eBook or video every month
- Fully searchable for easy access to vital information
- Copy and paste, print, and bookmark content

Did you know that Packt offers eBook versions of every book published, with PDF and ePub files available? You can upgrade to the eBook version at packt.com and as a print book customer, you are entitled to a discount on the eBook copy. Get in touch with us at customercare@packtpub.com for more details.

At www.packt.com, you can also read a collection of free technical articles, sign up for a range of free newsletters, and receive exclusive discounts and offers on Packt books and eBooks.

Other Books You May Enjoy

If you enjoyed this book, you may be interested in these other books by Packt:

Learn Power BI - Second Edition

Greg Deckler

ISBN: 9781801811958

- Get up and running quickly with Power BI
- Understand and plan your business intelligence projects
- Connect to and transform data using Power Query
- Create data models optimized for analysis and reporting
- Perform simple and complex DAX calculations to enhance analysis
- Discover business insights and create professional reports
- Collaborate via Power BI dashboards, apps, goals, and scorecards
- Deploy and govern Power BI, including using deployment pipelines

Artificial Intelligence with Power BI

Mary-Jo Diepeveen

ISBN: 9781801814638

- Apply techniques to mitigate bias and handle outliers in your data
- Prepare time series data for forecasting in Power BI
- Prepare and shape your data for anomaly detection
- Use text analytics in Power Query Editor
- Integrate QnA Maker with PowerApps and create an app
- Train your own models and identify the best one with AutoML
- Integrate an Azure ML workspace with Power BI and use endpoints to generate predictions

Packt is searching for authors like you

If you're interested in becoming an author for Packt, please visit `authors.packtpub.com` and apply today. We have worked with thousands of developers and tech professionals, just like you, to help them share their insight with the global tech community. You can make a general application, apply for a specific hot topic that we are recruiting an author for, or submit your own idea.

Share Your Thoughts

Now you've finished *Microsoft Power BI Data Analyst Certification Guide*, we'd love to hear your thoughts! Scan the QR code below to go straight to the Amazon review page for this book and share your feedback or leave a review on the site that you purchased it from.

`https://packt.link/r/1-803-23856-9`

Your review is important to us and the tech community and will help us make sure we're delivering excellent quality content.

Printed in Great Britain
by Amazon